Peacebuilding, Power, and Politics in Africa

CAMBRIDGE CENTRE OF AFRICAN STUDIES SERIES

Series editors: Derek R. Peterson, Harri Englund, and Christopher Warnes

The University of Cambridge is home to one of the world's leading centers of African studies. It organizes conferences, runs a weekly seminar series, hosts a specialist library, coordinates advanced graduate studies, and facilitates research by Cambridge- and Africa-based academics. The Cambridge Centre of African Studies Series publishes work that emanates from this rich intellectual life. The series fosters dialogue across a broad range of disciplines in African studies and between scholars based in Africa and elsewhere.

Derek R. Peterson, ed.
Abolitionism and Imperialism in Britain, Africa, and the Atlantic

Harri Englund, ed.
Christianity and Public Culture in Africa

Devon Curtis and Gwinyayi A. Dzinesa, eds.
Peacebuilding, Power, and Politics in Africa

Peacebuilding, Power, and Politics in Africa

Edited by Devon Curtis and Gwinyayi A. Dzinesa

Foreword by Adekeye Adebajo

Ohio University Press • *Athens*

Ohio University Press, Athens, Ohio 45701
ohioswallow.com
© 2012 by Ohio University Press
All rights reserved

Printed in the United States of America
Ohio University Press books are printed on acid-free paper ⊚ ™

20 19 18 17 16 15 14 13 12   5 4 3 2 1

Library of Congress Cataloging-in-Publication Data
Peacebuilding, power, and politics in Africa / edited by Devon Curtis and Gwinyayi
A. Dzinesa ; foreword by Adekeye Adebajo.
    p. cm. — (Cambridge Centre of African Studies series)
Includes bibliographical references and index.
ISBN 978-0-8214-2013-3 (pb : alk. paper) — ISBN 978-0-8214-4432-0 (electronic)
1. Peace-building—Africa. 2. Peace-building—Africa—International cooperation.
3. Africa—Politics and government—1960– I. Curtis, Devon. II. Dzinesa, Gwinyayi
Albert. III. Series: Cambridge Centre of African Studies series.
JZ5584.A35P44 2012
327.1'72096—dc23
                                        2012019442

Contents

Contents

Foreword

ADEKEYE ADEBAJO

Executive Director, Centre for Conflict Resolution, Cape Town, South Africa

It was fortuitous that, after five years, I was able to take time out from my position as the executive director of the Centre for Conflict Resolution (CCR), in Cape Town, South Africa, in 2008/9 to spend a five-month sabbatical in the wonderful surroundings of the Centre of African Studies (CAS) at Cambridge University in England. In pursuit of its pan-African vision, the overall theme of CCR's Africa program in 2008–12 was "Peacebuilding in Africa," with a book planned specifically to assess the continent's peacebuilding challenges. Under the dynamic supervision of Devon Curtis, CAS was itself preparing a book project on the same topic. This volume is the result of the fruitful marriage of both projects between an African institution and a European institution, involving scholars from Africa, Europe, and North America, as well as an Indian-Australian scholar. Several of the authors have practical experience of peacebuilding in Africa. Thematic debates involving issues of mediation, governance, the security sector, disarmament, and demobilization are combined here with assessments of African and global institutions, bolstered by rich case studies spanning the Great Lakes region, Southern Africa, West Africa, and the Horn of Africa. This is truly a unique volume, which we hope scholars, civil society activists, and practitioners around the world working on peacebuilding issues in Africa will find useful.

A seminar at the University of Cambridge in March 2009 helped shape the conceptual and empirical contents of this project. Five months later, CCR organized and largely funded a policy seminar in Gaborone, in cooperation with the universities of Botswana and Cambridge, attended by about forty scholars and practitioners. My colleagues at the Centre for Conflict Resolution deserve particular praise for the flawless organization of this logistically challenging meeting. Commissioned papers were presented at the seminar over three days, and authors received feedback to revise their chapters in a rigorous editing process. A few more chapters were commissioned based on gaps identified at the Gaborone seminar. We thank all the authors for cooperating so efficiently with this arduous process. I particularly acknowledge the contributions of Devon Curtis, who did the most to shape and edit the book (including spending a few weeks in Cape Town in 2010 completing this project). I also thank the director of CAS, Megan Vaughan, for supporting this collaboration. Devon Curtis's co-editor and former CCR colleague, Gwinyayi Dzinesa, also deserves recognition for his contributions. I take this opportunity to pay tribute to Glenn Cowley, former publisher of the University of KwaZulu-Natal Press, with whom CCR published seven important books on Africa's post–Cold War international relations. At the Gaborone seminar in August 2009, he skillfully chaired a session on how to turn the papers into a coherent edited volume. Glenn unfortunately died in May 2011, and his great warmth, experience, and insights will be sorely missed.

CCR, one of the very few centers of excellence on the UN's role in Africa, has established its expertise in this important area, organizing important policy seminars since 2004 on critical peacebuilding challenges in Southern, West, Eastern, and Central Africa that involved key actors from the African Union (AU), Africa's regional organizations, civil society, the UN, and external donor representatives. The center has also published three books on UN peacebuilding issues, as well as three other volumes covering issues of transitional justice in Africa, Africa's human rights architecture, and the African Union and its institutions.

Peacebuilding was popularized in the 1992 publication, *An Agenda for Peace,* by the first African United Nations secretary-general, Egypt's Boutros Boutros-Ghali. Africa has since become the world's most important peacebuilding laboratory, making this book particularly timely in assessing two decades of post–Cold War peacebuilding experiences on the continent. The concept of peacebuilding is often associated with the "second generation" of post–Cold War UN missions in countries such as Namibia, Angola, Mozambique, and Somalia, where efforts were made to adopt a holistic approach to peace. More recent cases, also covered in this book, have involved the Democratic Republic of the Congo (DRC), Burundi, Rwanda, Sierra Leone, Liberia, Nigeria's Niger Delta, and Sudan. Not only are diplomatic and military tools employed in building peace; today's peacebuilders also focus on the political, social, and economic causes of conflicts, as well as the need to promote socio-economic justice.

The peacebuilding office established by the UN in Liberia in 1997 was the first ever such office. Others were subsequently established in Sierra Leone, Central African Republic (CAR), Guinea-Bissau, Angola, and Burundi. There are also UN peacebuilding offices for west Africa, central Africa, and the Great Lakes region. Both the UN High-Level Panel report of 2004 and the 2005 report *In Larger Freedom*, by the second African UN secretary-general, Ghana's Kofi Annan, called for the establishment of a Peacebuilding Commission, as well as a Peacebuilding Support Office within the UN secretariat. Both were approved by the UN General Assembly in December 2005 and established in 2006. The Peacebuilding Commission aims to improve UN postconflict planning, focusing particularly on establishing viable institutions, ensuring financing in the period between the end of hostilities and the convening of donor conferences, and improving the coordination of UN bodies and other key regional and global actors. This commission is mandated to interact both with the UN Security Council and its Economic and Social Council (ECOSOC), and involves the participation of international financial institutions such as the World Bank and the African Development Bank (AfDB).

The UN Peacebuilding Commission is composed of thirty-one members from the Security Council, ECOSOC, and the most significant contributors of financial support and peacekeeping troops to the UN. The first chair of the commission in 2006 was Angola's respected permanent representative to the UN, Ismael Gaspar Martins, and the first two countries to be reviewed were Burundi and Sierra Leone. The commission has also been involved in Guinea-Bissau, Central African Republic, and Liberia, and Africa remains its main theater of work. A multiyear standing fund was established with voluntary contributions. However, based on UN experiences in Rwanda, Sierra Leone, Liberia, and Central African Republic, many Africans feel that this commission may represent yet another effort at political alchemy that does not do enough to mobilize the resources required for effective postconflict reconstruction efforts in Africa. The first six years of the commission's existence have proved disappointing and have so far failed to match the great expectations at its birth that it would promote improved peacebuilding in Africa and improve UN coordination in the field.

Africa, however, remains the continent most in need of effective peacebuilding to ensure that countries emerging from conflict do not relapse into war because of a lack of strong institutions and adequate resources to ensure that fighters bid a final farewell to arms. African regional bodies are also seeking a role in peacebuilding efforts on the continent, though they often lack the resources. A proper division of labor must therefore be established between African security and financial institutions, external donors, the UN, and the World Bank—another important topic tackled in this book.

Last but certainly not least, I wish to thank the main funders of CCR's Africa program—the governments of Denmark, the Netherlands, and Sweden—who provided the support for holding the Botswana seminar in 2009, commissioning chapters, and disseminating this book, as well as the report and policy brief from the project. We hope that this unique study will contribute to efforts to shape a more effective peacebuilding architecture on the continent in pursuit of Pax Africana.

Acknowledgments

The book arises out of a partnership between the Centre of African Studies (CAS) at the University of Cambridge, and the Centre for Conflict Resolution (CCR) in Cape Town. It reflects a truly collaborative effort, cutting across disciplines, perspectives, and experiences to analyze the local and global dimensions of the peacebuilding project in Africa. We thank all the chapter authors, who grappled with these difficult themes and from whom we have learned a great deal.

A large number of people have been involved in the seminars, workshops, and conferences leading to this book. We thank, in particular, Adekeye Adebajo, who was an unwavering source of inspiration, enthusiasm, and support from the project's inception. We are also grateful to colleagues at CCR, including Dawn Nagar and Fatima Maal, who brilliantly organized a seminar with scholars and practitioners in Gaborone in August 2009. The conference in Gaborone also benefited from the organizational support and intellectual contributions from faculty and researchers at the University of Gaborone, particularly Mpho Molomo and Gabriel Malebang.

The Centre of African Studies provided a convivial setting for discussions and debates leading to this volume. We are grateful to Megan Vaughan and to CAS for ensuring such an enjoyable and intellectually stimulating environment. Assistance from Dorian Addison and Judith Weik was invaluable in organizing a seminar series and also a workshop in Cambridge in March 2009, and we thank them along with all presenters and participants.

It is impossible to thank all those who have helped shape our ideas about peacebuilding. We owe special thanks, however, to Margaret Angucia, Karen Ballentine, Tarak Barkawi, Adam Branch, Sheila Bunwaree, Catherine Gegout, Barry Gilder, James Mayall, Mireille Affa'a Mindzie, David Moore, Mwelwa Musambachime, Musifiky Mwanasali, and Gérard Prunier. We benefited enormously from their stimulating ideas, contributions, and criticisms, and this book was shaped by all of them. Martha Cheo, one of the Visiting Fellows at the Centre of African Studies at Cambridge, strengthened our arguments and ideas and constantly reminded us of the need to think about the contributions of women to peacebuilding in Africa. Martha passed away suddenly in Nigeria in March 2012. Her lively intellect, her warmth, and her collegiality will be sorely missed.

The comments from the series editors and two anonymous reviewers greatly strengthened the volume. Jason Cook did a tremendous job in helping with copyediting. It has been a great pleasure to work with Derek Peterson, Harri Englund, and Chris Warnes, the series editors, as well as Gillian Berchowitz, the editor at Ohio University Press.

We were very lucky to have had the support of the British Academy UK–Africa Partnership Fund and the Leverhulme Trust, in addition to CCR's donors. We are grateful for their interest and generosity.

Finally, special thanks to our families, friends, and students. Our students at the University of Cambridge and at Witwatersrand University have been some of our most engaging interlocutors, asking critical questions and forcing us to rethink our own assumptions and ideas. We hope that the ideas in this book will inspire and provoke students, scholars, and practitioners in Africa and beyond.

Devon Curtis and Gwinyayi A. Dzinesa

Abbreviations

AAPAM	African Association for Public Administration and Management
AfDB	African Development Bank
AFDL	Alliance of Democratic Forces for the Liberation of Congo-Zaire
AFL	Armed Forces of Liberia
AFRC	Armed Forces Revolutionary Council (Sierra Leone)
AMIB	African Union Mission in Burundi
AMIS	African Union Mission in Sudan
AMU	Arab Maghreb Union
ANC	African National Congress (South Africa)
ANPP	All Nigeria People's Party
APC	All People's Congress (Sierra Leone)
APRM	African Peer Review Mechanism
APSC	Africa Public Service Charter
ASSN	African Security Sector Network
AU	African Union
BINUB	United Nations Integrated Office in Burundi
CAR	Central African Republic
CCR	Centre for Conflict Resolution (South Africa)
CDC	Congress for Democratic Change (Liberia)
CIDA	Canadian International Development Agency
CNDP	National Congress for the Defense of the People (DRC)
COTOL	Coalition for the Transformation of Liberia
CPA	Comprehensive Peace Agreement
CPIA	Country Policy and Institutional Assessment (World Bank)
CPRU	Conflict Prevention and Reconstruction Unit (World Bank)
DDR	Disarmament, demobilization, and reintegration
DDRR	Disarmament, demobilization, rehabilitation, and reconstruction
DFID	(UK) Department for International Development
DPA	Department of Political Affairs (UN)
DPKO	Department of Peacekeeping Operations (UN)
DRC	Democratic Republic of the Congo
EC	European Commission
ECCAS	Economic Community of Central African States
ECOMOG	Economic Community of West African States Monitoring Group
ECOSOC	Economic and Social Council (UN)
ECOWAS	Economic Community of West African States

ELCIN	Evangelical Lutheran Church in Namibia
ERSG	Executive Representative of the Secretary-General (UN)
EU	European Union
FAR	Armed Forces of Rwanda
FDLR	Democratic Liberation Forces of Rwanda
FIW	Federation of Ijaw Women
FRELIMO	Liberation Front of Mozambique
GDP	Gross domestic product
GEMAP	Governance and Economic Management Assistance Program (Liberia)
GPA	General Peace Agreement
HIPC	Highly indebted poor country
HRW	Human Rights Watch
IBRD	International Bank for Reconstruction and Development
ICC	International Criminal Court
ICG	International Crisis Group
ICISS	International Commission on Intervention and State Sovereignty
ICJ	International Court of Justice
ICTJ	International Center for Transitional Justice
IDA	International Development Association
IDDRS	Integrated DDR standards
IDPs	Internally displaced persons
IFIs	International financial institutions
INGOs	International nongovernmental organizations
IGAD	Intergovernmental Authority on Development
IMATT	International Military Assistance Training Team (Sierra Leone)
IMF	International Monetary Fund
IRC	International Rescue Committee
JEM	Justice and Equality Movement
JTF	Joint Task Force (Niger Delta)
KLA	Kosovo Liberation Army
LDF	Lofa Defense Force
LICUS	Low-income countries under stress
LPC	Liberia Peace Council
LRA	Lord's Resistance Army
LURD	Liberians United for Reconciliation and Democracy
MEND	Movement for the Emancipation of the Niger Delta
MDRP	Multi-Country Demobilization and Reintegration Programme (World Bank)
MODEL	Movement for Democracy in Liberia
MONUA	United Nations Observer Mission in Angola
MONUC	United Nations Organization Mission in the Democratic Republic of the Congo

MONUSCO	United Nations Organization Stabilization Mission in the Democratic Republic of the Congo
MOU	Memorandum of understanding
MPLA	Movement for the Liberation of Angola
MSF	Médecins sans Frontières
NATO	North Atlantic Treaty Organization
NDA	National Democratic Alliance (Sudan)
NDDC	Niger Delta Development Commission
NDF	Namibian Defense Force
NDLF	Niger Delta Liberation Force
NDPVF	Niger Delta People's Volunteer Force
NDV	Niger Delta Vigilante
NEPAD	New Partnership for Africa's Development
NGO	Nongovernmental organization
NIF/NCP	National Islamic Front/National Congress Party (Sudan)
NNPC	Nigerian National Petroleum Company
NPA	National Peace Accord (South Africa)
NRA	National Resistance Army (Uganda)
OAU	Organisation of African Unity
OCHA	Office for Coordination of Humanitarian Affairs (United Nations)
OECD	Organisation for Economic Cooperation and Development
OMPADEC	Oil Mineral Producing Areas Development Commission (Nigeria)
ONUB	United Nations Operation in Burundi
ONUC	United Nations Operation in the Congo
OTP	Office of the Prosecutor (ICC)
PBC	Peacebuilding Commission (UN)
PBF	Peacebuilding Fund
PBSO	Peacebuilding Support Office (UN)
PCIA	Peace and conflict impact assessment
PCRD	Postconflict reconstruction and development
PCU	Post Conflict Unit (World Bank)
PDP	People's Democratic Party (Nigeria)
PLAN	People's Liberation Army of Namibia
PRE	Economic Rehabilitation Programme (Mozambique)
PRES	Economic and Social Rehabilitation Programme (Mozambique)
PRSP	Poverty Reduction Strategy Paper
R2P	Responsibility to protect
RCD	Rally for Congolese Democracy
RCD-ML	RCD–Movement for Liberation
RECs	Regional economic communities
RENAMO	Mozambican National Resistance
RPA	Rwandan Patriotic Army

RPF	Rwandan Patriotic Front
RUF	Revolutionary United Front
SADC	Southern African Development Community
SADF	South African Defense Force
SAP	Structural adjustment program
SIDA	Swedish International Development Cooperation Agency
SLAF	Sierra Leone Armed Forces
SLM	Sudan Liberation Movement
SLPP	Sierra Leone People's Party
SPF	State and Peacebuilding Fund (World Bank)
SPLA	Sudan People's Liberation Army
SPLM	Sudan People's Liberation Movement
SRSG	Special Representative of the Secretary–General (UN)
SSG	Security sector governance
SSR	Security sector reform
STD	Sexually transmitted disease
SWAPO	South West Africa People's Organisation (Namibia)
SWAPOL	South West African Police
SWATF	South West Africa Territorial Force
TWP	True Whig Party (Liberia)
UDF	United Democratic Front (South Africa)
UIC	Union of Islamic Courts (Somalia)
UK	United Kingdom
ULIMO	United Liberation Movement for Democracy in Liberia
UN	United Nations
UNAMSIL	United Nations Mission in Sierra Leone
UNAVEM	United Nations Angola Verification Mission
UNDP	United Nations Development Programme
UNIOSIL	United Nations Integrated Office in Sierra Leone
UNITA	National Union for the Total Liberation of Angola
UNMIL	United Nations Mission in Liberia
UNOMOZ	United Nations Operation in Mozambique
UNTAG	United Nations Transition Assistance Group (Namibia)
UP	Unity Party (Liberia)
UPC	Union of Congolese Patriots (DRC)
UPDF	Uganda People's Defence Forces
US	United States
USAID	United States Agency for International Development

The Contested Politics of
Peacebuilding in Africa

DEVON CURTIS

THE AFRICAN UNION (AU) DECLARED 2010 TO BE THE "AFRICAN YEAR of Peace and Security," with the campaign slogan urging people to "Make Peace Happen." At a meeting in Tripoli in August 2009, African leaders committed themselves to dealing with conflict and violence, saying: "We as leaders simply cannot bequeath the burden of conflict to the next generation of Africans."[1] The chairperson of the African Union Commission, Jean Ping, said that "of the many challenges facing the AU and Africa, the quest for peace and security is the most pressing" and reaffirmed the AU's commitment to peacebuilding efforts, in partnership with the international community.[2]

Indeed, Africa has been the site of a large number of international and continental projects to promote peace. In 2011, Africa hosted seven of the sixteen United Nations (UN) peacekeeping missions in the world. The first five countries on the agenda of the United Nations Peacebuilding Commission, established in December 2005, are all African: Sierra Leone, Burundi, the Central African Republic (CAR), Guinea-Bissau, and Liberia. The first four cases before the International Criminal Court (ICC) are also all African: Uganda, the Democratic Republic of the Congo (DRC), Sudan, and the CAR.[3]

The AU's 2010 declaration therefore appears to be backed by a range of institutions, mechanisms, and programs to help build peace on the continent. Furthermore, the increased attention to peacebuilding in

Africa has occurred alongside an overall decrease in violent conflict on the continent. The 2007 Human Security Brief published by the Human Security Centre shows that between 1999 and 2006, the number of state-based and non-state-based armed conflicts in sub-Saharan Africa declined significantly.[4] The number of battle deaths also declined, with the fatality toll dropping by two-thirds in sub-Saharan Africa between 2002 and 2006.[5] The 2006 Human Security Brief said that the greatest decline in armed conflict was in sub-Saharan Africa, with the result that it was no longer the world's most conflict-affected region.[6] Both briefs suggested that this decline was related to the major increase in international efforts to end wars and prevent them from restarting, including peacebuilding missions.[7]

This volume is a critical reflection on peacebuilding efforts in Africa. In light of new global and African institutions, initiatives, and activities set up in support of peacebuilding efforts, the time is ripe for a reassessment of peacebuilding concepts, practices, and implications in Africa. The contributors to the volume interrogate whether the optimism reflected in policy reports is merited, and question how and why certain peacebuilding ideas and initiatives are adopted over other ones in Africa.

The volume grows out of a collaborative project between the Centre of African Studies at the University of Cambridge in the United Kingdom, and the Centre for Conflict Resolution (CCR), based in Cape Town, South Africa, involving Africa-based as well as Western-based scholars with diverse perspectives on peacebuilding in Africa. The volume represents a small selection of the work presented by scholars from a weekly Cambridge seminar series in 2008–9, at the March 2009 Cambridge workshop "Rethinking Peacebuilding in Africa," and at a large international conference of scholars and peacebuilding practitioners organized by CCR in Gaborone, Botswana, in August 2009, in collaboration with the University of Botswana and the Cambridge Centre of African Studies. Although not all of this work is included here, the contributions of all participants have helped inform the ideas and arguments in this volume.

Taken together, the contributions in this volume show that there is no consensus about the role, aims, and effects of continental and international peacebuilding programs and initiatives in Africa. The contributors highlight that although the local, regional, and global spaces for peace in Africa have been altered through discourses and practices of peacebuilding, these practices play out differently in different locales.

Peacebuilding ideas and initiatives are at various times reinforced, questioned, subverted, or reappropriated and redesigned by different African actors. Thus, the trajectories of peacebuilding programs and initiatives tend to be messy and multifaceted. Procedures and practices established in one venue or by one institution are subjected to a thorough reworking as they play out in another venue, such as Somalia, Sierra Leone, or the DRC.

The volume includes contributions from policy scholars and scholars involved in on-the-ground case studies. The contributors adopt a variety of approaches, but they share a conviction that peacebuilding in Africa is not a script that is authored solely in Western capitals and in the corridors of the UN. Rather, the writers in this volume focus on the interaction between local and global ideas and practices in the reconstitution of authority and livelihoods after conflict, showcasing the tensions that occur within and between the multitude of actors involved in the peacebuilding industry, as well as their intended beneficiaries.

Highlighting the diverse expressions and contexts of peacebuilding helps us understand the intended and unintended consequences and limitations of peacebuilding programs in Africa. Contrary to the insular character of much of the peacebuilding discourse and some of the peacebuilding scholarship, the authors in this volume show how peacebuilding cannot be positioned above politics and history.

This introductory chapter briefly traces the evolution of peacebuilding ideas and practices, as well as the growing body of scholarship that has accompanied the rise of the peacebuilding industry. It pays particular attention to the dominant ways of thinking about peacebuilding, including what is often called "liberal peacebuilding," and the range of critiques that have emerged in the scholarly literature. The chapter then goes on to show why existing frameworks for understanding peacebuilding are largely insufficient. Rather than interpreting peacebuilding as a fixed set of procedures and practices leading to some universally defined end called "peace," the introduction and the chapters that follow suggest that peacebuilding may be best thought of as a set of multiple ideas, relationships, and experiences that are embedded within hierarchies of power and knowledge. Hierarchies exist within and between peacebuilding institutions, within knowledge about peacebuilding, and within funding for peacebuilding, but the chapters show that these hierarchies are not fixed or immutable.

The Concept of Peacebuilding and its Trajectory in Africa

The idea and the practices of peacebuilding are not new. Conflict is a generative force that alters social norms and institutions in Africa as elsewhere. The experience of conflict typically brings issues of political authority, security, society, and economy to the fore, albeit in different ways in different places. Questions of how to reestablish political authority and security after violence, what to do about ex-combatants, how to renegotiate and manage the changed social relations, mistrust, and destruction that accompanies violence, and what to do about changed patterns of production or livelihoods as a result of conflict have been addressed in a myriad of different ways in different African locales over time. For instance, under the Oyo Empire in Nigeria, the victorious Oyo granted substantial political autonomy to the vassal colonies following wars in the seventeenth and eighteenth centuries, as long as the colonies reaffirmed their loyalty to Oyo. Agents from Oyo resided in the colonies to monitor local politics.[8] In western Côte d'Ivoire, Mike McGovern describes the historic highly structured social relations between "strangers" and "hosts" that emerged partly as a response to precolonial labor requirements in areas of low population density. Yet if the autochthone "hosts" were conquered by "strangers," the autochthones often adapted and assimilated and the relationships were recalibrated. Thus, the host-stranger relationship was "an elastic social idiom that facilitated the process of making do and getting on with life, even in the face of endemic violence and insecurity."[9] In the early nineteenth century, Shaka, the Zulu chief and state-builder, consolidated a number of military innovations. By the mid-1820s, he had a large standing army of over 40,000 people. Shaka did not allow members of military regiments to marry until after they finished their military service, often in their late thirties for men and late twenties for women. After marriage, men and women left the regiments and set up their homesteads, so the issue of a transition from a fighter to a "civilian" was resolved through the social institution of marriage.[10] Thus, examples of "peacebuilding" strategies in Africa are as old (and as diverse) as conflict. Drawing on Derry Yakubu's research, Tim Murithi argues that conflict resolution and peacebuilding mechanisms in precolonial Africa had a "significant degree of success in maintaining order and ensuring the peaceful coexistence of groups."[11] Murithi describes various institutions in their historic and contemporary incarnations, such as the *jir* mediation forum of the Tiv in Nigeria and the *Mato Oput* reconciliation mechanism among the Acholi in northern Uganda, to highlight that peacebuilding is not a new preoccupation in Africa.

International actors also have a long history of attempting to shape war-affected communities and politics. Colonial rulers developed a wide variety of coercive and noncoercive strategies to deal with the effects of war. And external actors continued to influence politics in postcolonial Africa, with the wide-ranging UN operation in the Congo from 1960 to 1964 often described as the precursor to the peacebuilding operations of the 1990s.[12] Yet as a distinctive area of international policy interventions, peacebuilding rose to prominence at the end of the Cold War at the time of the UN operation in Namibia in 1989–90. The end of the Cold War led to a renewed emphasis on the possibilities of international engagement in support of peacebuilding. *An Agenda for Peace*, published in 1992 by the then UN secretary-general, Boutros Boutros-Ghali, provided a coherent conceptualization of peacebuilding for a post–Cold War era. This important report defined peacebuilding as the medium- to long-term process of rebuilding war-affected communities through identifying and supporting "structures which will tend to strengthen and solidify peace in order to avoid a relapse into conflict."[13] Essentially, *An Agenda for Peace* saw peacebuilding as a worthy and distinct area of international attention, and conceived of it as the promotion of activities and structures that reduce the likelihood of violent conflict.

At the time of the publication of *An Agenda for Peace*, the number of UN peacekeeping operations was rapidly expanding, and many of these operations took place in Africa. Peacebuilding came to be an important component of these missions. Yet since the *Agenda for Peace* was published in 1992, three changes with respect to peacebuilding are notable: an expansion of peacebuilding activities, a proliferation of institutions tasked with peacebuilding, and an increase in peacebuilding scholarship.

First, the number and kinds of activities that are considered under the rubric of peacebuilding programs have grown, and peacebuilding has become more intrusive. Whereas the *Agenda for Peace* emphasized state sovereignty, later reports, such as the 2004 United Nations High-Level Panel report *A More Secure World*, focused on the rights of the individual as well as state sovereignty.[14] Peacebuilding therefore expanded to include not only the cessation of hostilities and the rebuilding of infrastructure, but also the protection of human rights, the reconstitution of individual identities and the reforging of individual and community relationships.

This expansion in activities reflected a willingness to conceptualize peace not only as negative peace (the absence of direct physical violence), but also as positive peace (the absence of structural violence). According to proponents of positive peace, focusing only on negative peace is insufficient, as it ignores the multiple ways that people suffer.[15] A narrow focus on negative peace meant that great efforts and resources went into helping to reach cease-fires between belligerent groups, and to guarantee these agreements through peacekeeping missions, but other forms of insecurity, inequalities, and vulnerabilities were left unaddressed. For instance, negative peace does not address the unequal status of women or domestic sexual violence.[16] In 2000, the United Nations Brahimi Report on Peacekeeping Reform explained that peacebuilding consisted of activities to "provide the tools for building on those foundations something that is more than just the absence of war."[17] Some authors have claimed that peacebuilding entails moving from a condition of negative peace to one of positive peace.[18] The areas of concern to peacebuilders have therefore broadened to include issues and activities that were formerly considered to be outside its scope.

The concept of human security further expanded the types of peacebuilding measures on the agenda of international institutions. Although positive peace is not the same as human security, the two ideas are closely connected. Human security focuses on the security of the individual rather than the security of the state. The concept was first elaborated by the United Nations Development Programme (UNDP) in 1994 and has since been widely accepted at the United Nations.[19] Nonetheless, there are large disagreements over the scope of the concept. The UNDP uses definitions that are closer to notions of positive peace, and says that human security includes "safety from such chronic threats as hunger, disease and repression,"[20] whereas the Human Security Centre uses a definition that focuses on "violent threats to individuals."[21] The UN Secretary-General's High-Level Panel on Threats, Challenges, and Change in 2004 identified poverty, infectious disease, and environmental degradation as major threats to security, along with armed conflict, terrorism, organized crime, and weapons of mass destruction.[22] Alongside the rise in human security, peacebuilding has therefore deepened to target not only the state and its institutions, but also individuals and their local communities. Social transformation has become an object of peacebuilding concern and intervention, including initiatives to improve individual psychosocial well-being.

These expanded activities and initiatives to address and prevent violent armed conflict could occur at different phases of conflict cycles. Previously, peacebuilding was usually conceptualized as part of a linear progression, starting with humanitarian relief and conflict management, then settlement, then peacebuilding and reconstruction, then development. Increasingly however, it was acknowledged that transitions from conflict rarely follow such a linear path. Activities to strengthen "peace" can take place before, during, or after conflict. Likewise, "peace" and "war" may exist simultaneously in different parts of the same country. For instance, in Sudan the conflict in Darfur escalated even after the Comprehensive Peace Agreement formally ended the conflict between the North and the South in 2005 (see Srinivasan, this volume). Uganda is typically viewed as a "peaceful" country since the National Resistance Army won the war and brought President Yoweri Museveni to power in 1986. However, this obscures the ongoing conflict involving the Lord's Resistance Army in the northern part of Uganda and across its borders (see Omach, this volume).

Thus, in the two decades since *An Agenda for Peace,* the concept of peacebuilding has broadened, deepened and been applied to different points in the conflict cycle. A second important change since the publication of *An Agenda for Peace* is the proliferation of institutions, units, and programs tasked with peacebuilding in Africa. These include institutions at the global level, the continental, regional, and national levels, as well as local programs led by community and nongovernmental organizations (NGOs). Several international agencies created special units to deal with postconflict reconstruction in the middle to late 1990s. For instance, in 1997, the Organisation for Economic Cooperation and Development (OECD) created the Conflict Prevention and Post-Conflict Reconstruction Network to help better coordinate aid agencies' peacebuilding activities. That same year, the World Bank adopted a framework for World Bank involvement in postconflict reconstruction, and established the Post-Conflict Fund to make fast loans and grants to conflict-affected countries (see Harrison, this volume).[23] In 2001, the UNDP created the Bureau for Crisis Prevention and Recovery to "provide a bridge between the humanitarian agencies that handle immediate needs and the long-term development phase following recovery." In 2005, the United Nations Peacebuilding Commission was established, with the aim of bringing together relevant actors and proposing integrated strategies for postconflict peacebuilding in specific countries (see Olonisakin and Ikpe, this volume).[24]

The AU and subregional organizations in Africa have also developed peacebuilding units, programs, and initiatives at an accelerated pace. Earlier, the Organization of African Unity (OAU) created the Mechanism for Conflict Prevention, Management, and Resolution in 1993, and the Economic Community of West African States (ECOWAS) established the Mechanism for Conflict Prevention, Resolution, and Peacekeeping in 1999. More recently, the AU Peace and Security Council was established in 2004 and the AU Panel of the Wise was established in 2007. The New Partnership for Africa's Development (NEPAD) and the AU separately developed postconflict reconstruction frameworks in June 2005 and July 2006 respectively (see Khadiagala, this volume).[25] In 2008, ECOWAS adopted a Conflict Prevention Framework, to strengthen efforts to "prevent violent conflicts within and between States, and to support peace-building in post-conflict environments."[26] The Southern African Development Community (SADC) Council of Non-Governmental Organisations has a program for Governance, Peace and Security in accordance with its organizational strategy for 2009–13. In 2002, the Intergovernmental Authority on Development (IGAD) established the Conflict Early Warning and Response Mechanism, with a particular focus on pastoral and related conflicts. These new continental and regional structures and programs underline a commitment to peacebuilding, alongside their increasing involvement in peace operations. To date for instance, the African Union and African regional organizations have mounted peacekeeping operations in countries such as Burundi, Comoros, Côte d'Ivoire, Guinea-Bissau, Liberia, Sierra Leone, Somalia, and Sudan. These new institutions and programs in Africa have grown along with calls for "local ownership" in peacebuilding programming.

The third notable development since the publication of *An Agenda for Peace* is the expansion of peacebuilding scholarship, which has accompanied the broadening and deepening of peacebuilding activities, as well as the proliferation of peacebuilding institutions. A growing but disparate body of academic work has attempted to make sense of peacebuilding efforts and their consequences.[27] A number of specialized scholarly journals focusing on peace and conflict themes have been established since the early 1990s, such as *International Peacekeeping* (1994), *Global Governance* (1995), *The International Journal of Peace Studies* (1996), *Civil Wars* (1998), *African Journal on Conflict Resolution* (1999), *Conflict, Security and Development* (2001), *Peace, Conflict and*

Development: An Interdisciplinary Journal (2002), *Journal of Peacebuilding and Development* (2002), and *Journal of Intervention and Statebuilding* (2007).[28] Some of this scholarship concentrates on African peace and conflict issues. Indeed, many African universities now offer course programs in peace and conflict studies.[29] Think tanks and policy institutes have followed suit, offering peace research and peace training, often with a vast array of recommendations on how to improve international and continental peacebuilding practice. And yet, as explained below, much of this scholarship fails to fully capture the multifaceted nature of peace and the contested local and global politics of peacebuilding. It treats peace as an uncontroversial, ahistoric "end," and peacebuilding as the means to get there.

Peacebuilding Frameworks and Debates

There are at least three main frameworks for understanding peacebuilding that are prevalent in the literature. Although there are important areas of overlap between these positions, they rest on different conceptions of power and politics in Africa. Each of these views contains important normative assumptions about the nature of peace and about the identity and motivations of peacebuilders. They lead to different conclusions about the role of the state in peacebuilding, the type of economic policies best suited to recovery, the appropriate ways to encourage societal reconciliation, and how best to ensure security.

Liberal Peacebuilding

The dominant framework for understanding peacebuilding is a liberal framework. A significant amount of peacebuilding scholarship positions itself either within this liberal tradition or against it. According to this view, peacebuilding is understood to be part of a global project of liberal governance, promoted by international and regional institutions and other actors. Certainly, the goal and promise of a liberal peace is found within the pages of many donor documents and institutional reports. *An Agenda for Peace* described political and economic liberalization as key elements in the transformation of war-torn societies. Paragraph 9 sees new opportunities for peace now that "many States are seeking more open forms of economic policy"; paragraph 56 talks of social and economic development; and paragraph 59 recommends the strengthening of new democratic institutions, the rule of law, and good governance.[30]

The perceived success of (liberal) war-to-peace transitions in Namibia and Mozambique reinforced these ideas. Indeed, the idea of a "liberal peace," with its roots in European Enlightenment thinking of the seventeenth and eighteenth centuries, has guided much of the peacebuilding programming at the UN and elsewhere. Multiparty electoral democracy and a market economy are seen as inherently peaceful and desirable, and it is thought that all "good things" go together. Peacebuilding therefore consists of activities and initiatives to help bring about and facilitate this desired liberal end. More recently, the 2005 UN report *In Larger Freedom*, produced under the leadership of the then UN secretary-general, Kofi Annan, echoed this view: "Humanity will not enjoy security without development, it will not enjoy development without security, and will not enjoy either without respect for human rights."[31] The chairperson of the AU commission, Jean Ping, said that "Africa's attention to peacebuilding reflects the continent's recognition that peace is the foundation of prosperity."[32]

Liberal peacebuilding is thus both a normative agenda, as well as a framework for understanding the diverse activities and initiatives to promote peace on the continent. Even with the expansion of peacebuilding activities and the move toward conceptions of positive peace and human security, the privileged focus on liberal peacebuilding has largely remained intact within the dominant global peacebuilding community. Liberal peacebuilding is assumed to have universal relevance, therefore techniques and lessons can be learned from different parts of the world. A standardized approach that includes multiparty elections and institution-building, constitutional and legal reform, and economic pro-market reform can be applied in such diverse settings as Mozambique, El Salvador, Cambodia, Sierra Leone, and Timor-Leste, with only limited adaptations to suit the "local" context.

The problem, as some scholarship has pointed out, is that the experiences of many countries emerging from conflict do not correspond to these liberal predictions. Already by the end of the 1990s, the achievements of liberal peacebuilding in Africa and elsewhere were being questioned. Even countries that are often judged as peacebuilding successes, such as Namibia and Mozambique, have experienced high rates of inequality and persistent insecurity among some communities. Furthermore, these qualified "successes" were overshadowed by horrendous failures such as Angola in 1992, Rwanda in 1993–94, Sierra Leone in 1999, Sudan in 2005, and Côte d'Ivoire in 2010.

For advocates of liberal peacebuilding, these failures do not represent the limits of liberal peace, but rather, the flawed implementation of liberal ideas. For them, peacebuilding failures had more to do with improper sequencing or a lack of coordination or insufficient commitment by outsiders, not problems with the liberal idea itself. For instance, in a widely cited argument, Roland Paris notes that rapid political and economic liberalization in postconflict countries can trigger a renewal of conflict instead of a reinforcement of structures of peace.[33] Paris does not criticize economic and political liberalization per se; he simply argues that it cannot be done too quickly in the immediate aftermath of violent conflict. Rapid political liberalization can exacerbate tensions, since elites may use violence to gain electoral support, and rapid economic liberalization can generate tensions through increased unemployment and economic uncertainties. Instead, Paris argues in favor of "institutionalization before liberalization," meaning building state institutional capacity first, in order to enable liberal values and practices to take hold over time.

This argument and others like it do not fundamentally question the content of liberal postconflict peacebuilding but suggest ways that the international peacebuilding community may improve practices to get to their desired outcomes. Unsurprisingly, many policy practitioners through lessons-learned units and evaluations divisions have adopted similar conclusions about peacebuilding failures. The UN High-Level Panel on Threats, Challenges and Change, for instance, made a case for greater policy coherence and donor coordination and more careful attention to sequencing.[34]

This approach therefore assumes that peacebuilding is a liberal script authored primarily by outsiders, perhaps with the assistance and input of enlightened locals. Advocates believe that this can lead to optimal peaceful results if the program is properly implemented. All actors in conflict-affected countries are identified vis-à-vis their position on liberal peace, and those who violently disagree with liberal peace are labeled "spoilers" who must be socialized or marginalized.[35] The liberal peacebuilding scholarship tends to be prescriptive, offering advice on how to better deal with these "spoilers." Peace, development, and governance go hand in hand and reinforce one another in this liberal framework.

Peacebuilding as Stabilization

A second position on peacebuilding shares the liberal concern with order, but rather than focusing its attention on order within states, it sees peacebuilding as being primarily concerned with maintaining the international status quo. The view has become increasingly important since the 9/11 attack on the United States (US), and the subsequent global "war on terror." Although this view acknowledges the multitude of activities conducted under the peacebuilding umbrella, the rationale for these activities is to maintain global security and stability.

The recent conflation of antiterrorism measures with peacebuilding is an indication that this way of thinking about peacebuilding may be gaining currency.[36] The language of peacebuilding is indicative. In the United Kingdom, the Post Conflict Reconstruction Unit was renamed the Stabilisation Unit in late 2007, jointly owned by the Department for International Development, the Foreign and Commonwealth Office, and the Ministry of Defence. Within the US Department of State, the Office of the Coordinator for Reconstruction and Stabilization was created in 2004–5 to "promote the security of the United States through improved coordination, planning, and implementation for reconstruction and stabilization assistance for foreign states and regions at risk of, in, or in transition from conflict or civil strife."[37] The UN peace operation in the DRC changed its mission and its name from MONUC (United Nations Organization Mission in the Democratic Republic of the Congo) to MONUSCO (United Nations Organization Stabilization Mission in the Democratic Republic of the Congo) in 2010. A central part of MONUSCO's mandate is to assist the Congolese government in strengthening its military capacity, and to support the Congolese government in consolidating state authority (Lemarchand, this volume). With China's increasing involvement in Africa, including China's participation in UN peace operations, one can expect that peacebuilding as stabilization will continue to rise in importance, given China's preoccupation with order and state authority rather than "good governance," democratization, or civil society.[38]

According to this view, the emphasis for peacebuilders is the creation of stable, secure states with well-policed borders. Although it shares many of the same preoccupations of the peacebuilding as liberal governance view, the stabilization view holds less faith in the possibilities of transformation and socialization. For example, if part of the problem in Africa is perceived as Africans' stubborn attachment to parochial identities, peacebuilding as stabilization controls the expression of those identities, without seeking to transform them. Low-intensity conflict and localized violence or repression may be acceptable (or perhaps inevitable) under this view, so long as it does not affect international order and stability. Paradoxically then, increased militarization comes to be seen as peacebuilding.

As with the liberal peacebuilding literature, some of the stabilization scholarship is normatively driven and prescriptive, offering guidelines and suggestions to policymakers on how to stabilize first (and sometimes liberalize later, depending on whether internal conditions are "conducive").[39] Other scholars are much more critical of these types of peacebuilding practices, seeing peacebuilding as reminiscent of previous forms of external domination in Africa, or as disguised imperialism.[40] For them, peacebuilding is a cover for the political and economic interests of the West, mirroring the role of imperial power in the construction and order of colonial states.[41] This view asks "whose peace" is served by peacebuilding programs and activities. In contrast to advocates of peacebuilding as liberal governance who believe in the shared benefits of liberalism, a peacebuilding as stabilization framework implicitly acknowledges that the benefits of peacebuilding may be unequal and selective. Although much of the peacebuilding as liberal governance literature focuses on African elites and their identities and interests as being the main objects to reshape through peacebuilding, the stabilization literature takes account of the interests of external peacebuilders themselves. It shows that global powers and institutions are not disinterested actors or neutral vessels (see Harrison, Olonisakin and Ikpe, and Nouwen, this volume), and that their peacebuilding programs are not divorced from other political interests (see Lemarchand, Ero, and Clapham, this volume).

Peacebuilding as Social Justice

Like the previous two views, peacebuilding as social justice is both a normative position and a descriptive framework for understanding peacebuilding activities. This position tends to be put forward by people who believe that the previous two views place undue focus on maintaining order. They see peacebuilding as stabilization and/or liberal governance as part of a strategy to maintain the global status quo, with its inequalities and selective privileges intact. In the case of liberal peacebuilding, these intentions may be obscured by the universalist language of human security, peacebuilding, the "responsibility to protect," and development, whereas in the case of peacebuilding as stabilization the intentions to impose order is clear. For both however, the aim is to subvert radical challenges to the global and national distribution of power and resources and to stabilize the international system. Hegemony and domination are maintained through discursive and material means.[42]

Although stabilization relies more heavily on coercion and on building the coercive apparatus of the state, and liberal governance relies more extensively on building institutions and markets, both share a preoccupation with stability.

In contrast, some authors believe that peacebuilding can and should be based on social justice, rather than liberal governance or stabilization. Structural violence is the problem to be addressed through peacebuilding, and peacebuilding therefore involves programs to encourage inclusive access to resources and institutions, to empower marginalized groups, to end discrimination against women and other disadvantaged groups, and to redistribute income and land ownership.[43] In other words, peacebuilding becomes focused on reaching the condition of "positive peace."

Peacebuilding as social justice addresses international inequalities as well as inequalities within countries. According to this view, peacebuilding cannot be divorced from a discussion of global capitalism and the distribution of the world's resources. Liberal peacebuilding tends to focus on how to restructure economies internally so that countries can attract foreign investment and be better integrated into the global economy, but the networked economies in the DRC, Sierra Leone, Nigeria, Angola, and Sudan show that both violent conflict and violent peace are compatible with markets that are well integrated internationally, albeit unevenly. An emphasis on social justice involves raising questions about international economic inequality. Seeing uneven global capitalist structures as the indisputable and inevitable context for peacebuilding severely limits possibilities.

In calling for a redistribution of resources both within countries and internationally, peacebuilding as social justice echoes earlier claims made by dependency theorists such as Samir Amin.[44] But, as Mahmood Mamdani points out, it also involves the deracialization of power, the redressing of systemic group disadvantage, and the formation of an inclusive redefined political community.[45]

Within this perspective, however, there are disagreements about the agents of peacebuilding. Although some African governments and African institutions may seek to draw attention to international inequalities, it is debatable whether governments and regional institutions are effective vehicles for the promotion of social justice. Some authors highlight the developmental potential of African-level institutions (Landsberg, this volume), but a key question is whether African-level institutions reflect kinds of knowledge similar to Western-based ones, or whether they capture different kinds of experiences in their research and programming. The early experiences of the AU, NEPAD, and the African Development Bank (AfDB) suggest that these institutions adopt peacebuilding logics that are similar to those of their international counterparts (Khadiagala, this volume), relying on liberal governance packages. The African Union policy framework provides an overall strategy from which individual country programs can develop their own context-specific plans, but it is unclear that this represents an alternative peacebuilding template. Devolving responsibility to African governments will not necessarily achieve social justice or satisfy the transformative aspirations of other local groups. Elites tend to revert to strategies that reproduce their positions of power, and there is nothing to indicate that there is more of a consensus on issues of social justice among inhabitants within Africa countries.

The Local and Global Practices of Peacebuilding

The three frameworks for understanding peacebuilding are not necessarily mutually exclusive, and indeed institutions such as the United Nations and the African Union use the language of all three. It is possible for the same actor or agency to hold a normative commitment toward social justice, but to encourage stabilization and/or liberal governance. Indeed, despite their stated common goals, different agencies prioritize different activities. Notwithstanding the common use of the term peacebuilding, different institutions show important variation. In a survey of twenty-four governmental and intergovernmental bodies active in peacebuilding, Barnett et al. show that there are great divisions among these bodies regarding the specific approaches to achieve peace, often depending on prevailing organizational mandates and interests.[46]

Much of the peacebuilding scholarship, however, presumes to know what constitutes peace and sees peacebuilding as a series of activities, initiatives, and policies to help reach predetermined goals, whether those goals are defined as liberal governance, stabilization, and/or social justice. The scholarship tends to be prescriptive, based on the author's knowledge of peace.[47] Even the concepts of social justice and positive peace tend to be defined from the perspective of powerful societies.[48] Thus, whether it is understood as liberal governance, stabilization, or social justice, peacebuilding programming is often driven by external ideas and by the disciplining power of external norms rather than by the meanings and values from within African countries and locales.

Academic research is not separate from these systems of power. Perhaps scholars are so concerned with their research being policy-relevant that they tend to focus on operational and technical aspects of peacebuilding.[49] In other words, perhaps peacebuilding practitioners search for knowledge that reinforces their own practices and experiences.[50]

Is it possible to reject these frameworks for peacebuilding, and rely instead on African ideas and alternatives? Claude Ake observed that the problem is not so much that development has failed in Africa as that it has never really been tried in the first place.[51] Ake's complaint was that development practices were based on earlier European experiences and ignored the specificities of African experiences, and one could argue that African peacebuilding faces a similar constraint. Isaac Albert describes several African conceptions of peace and argues that whereas Western conceptions of peace place heavy emphasis on prosperity and order, African conceptions are based on morality and order.[52] The underpinnings of peace in Africa, according to Albert, can be located in the commitment to cultural values, beliefs, and norms as well as in societal role expectations.[53]

Other authors have discussed the possibility of uncovering peacebuilding alternatives in local societies.[54] Mark Hoffman points out that the emphasis on individual rights, accountability, and transplantation of Western institutions may not sit easily with cultures that emphasize community and family over the individual.[55] Oliver Richmond argues that the pursuit of liberal peace "may be socially atomizing, hegemonic and lead to the valorization of predatory state elites who gain easy access to an international economic and political cartography."[56] Instead, Richmond proposes "localized everyday peaces," or unscripted conversations between local actors.[57] Alternative practices of peace may be found within the informal economy (see Oyefusi, this volume), within religious groups (see Clapham, this volume), within community groups (see Hutchful, and Omach, this volume), with representatives of ethnic communities and others who may fall outside the parameters of the liberal peace.

This literature on "local peace" has usefully uncovered a range of different ideas about peace and peacebuilding. Nonetheless, it is impossible to separate the "local" from the "international" in Africa, even if one intends to privilege local understandings of peace. It is notoriously difficult to discern who is the "local." Sometimes, local is used to mean the national country in which a peacebuilding intervention takes place. Yet a national actor from the capital city may be an outsider when entering into another local community.[58] Furthermore, although power relations are present, the local, regional, and global are mutually constitutive. Politics in Africa is not simply the product of hegemonic external forces, and it is not a failed or incomplete example of something else. This denies Africans of their agency and connections with the rest of the world.[59] Jean-François Bayart argues that through a strategy of extraversion, African states were not passive recipients of structural adjustment.[60] Similarly, African states have adjusted and shaped international peacebuilding strategies. John Heathershaw shows that when peacebuilding takes the form of a rational design or technique to do something to an "other" in order to elicit behavioral change, local actors may subvert its techniques and reappropriate resources to further their own authority.[61]

The ideas and resources of international and regional actors are therefore contingent (see Olonisakin and Ikpe, Nouwen, and Khadiagala, this volume), and are shaped, adapted, subverted, and reappropriated by different local elites (see Srinivasan, Lemarchand, Ero, Oyefusi, Dzinesa, and Clapham this volume). Yet these actors are intimately connected, and an authentic "local" does not exist separately from the regional and transnational networks within which it resides.[62]

The Volume

Peacebuilding is therefore not a script authored by outsiders, nor is it a script solely authored by Africans. Instead, peacebuilding is a set of ideas and practices, mediated by the interaction between local communities and international, national, and regional actors. The contest over peacebuilding is not only a contest for funds but also a contest over meanings and interpretation.

In different ways, the chapters in this volume explore the multiple, shifting, and interacting meanings, discourses, and agendas underlying peacebuilding efforts in Africa. The authors do not share a common understanding of the ultimate objective of peacebuilding, and indeed they disagree on whether finding such an objective is productive or possible. They use different approaches and methods, but they all analyze the tensions and debates between various peacebuilding ideas and programs. They agree that peacebuilding is a site of political and social contestation and interaction, which raises questions about power and hierarchy. Given the trade-offs, shifting identities, and multiple meanings of peace and peacebuilding, the chapters in this volume ask which ideas take hold and to what effect. Because hierarchies in the production of knowledge may mean that certain voices have been privileged in peacebuilding debates and discussions, the authors paid close attention to a range of voices. The authors themselves come from diverse geographic, disciplinary, and intellectual backgrounds and traditions.

Thus, the volume cannot resolve peacebuilding tensions, but it highlights what happens when various peacebuilding logics come into contact with realities on the ground. The contributors analyze key areas typically associated with peacebuilding (political authority, security, economy, society) and the institutions involved in peacebuilding, to illustrate the contested politics of peacebuilding, and to describe how peacebuilding is reinterpreted and reshaped by Africans.

For instance, the very logic of a negotiated peace agreement can be different for outside actors and for local political competitors (see Keen, and Srinivasan, this volume). Peace agreements themselves are replete with tensions. Outside actors may view a peace agreement as a binding commitment between different belligerents that sets out a common vision for a postconflict future, whereas the parties themselves may see it in instrumental and contextual terms. This has happened, for instance, in the DRC and Sudan, where political elites continually adjusted their strategies to a changed context (see Lemarchand and Srinivasan, this volume). Elites that were included or excluded in the peace agreements maintained the use or the threat of violence as a parallel tool in what Alex de Waal calls the political marketplace, where social affinities and patronage networks take precedence over state institutions.[63] Peace agreements may institutionalize violence by giving a share of governance to former military or rebel leaders who have committed human rights abuses or who maintain links to regional and global war economies (see Keen, this volume). Yet excluding these groups, if they retain the capacity for violence, may be equally dangerous. Throughout the peacebuilding process, state elites and former rebels may seek international recognition in order to bolster their own agendas. International actors make intrusive interventions, and local actors engage in their own transnational practices in order to gain political, material, and discursive support from outside parties and networks.[64]

Unlike some of the other literature on peacebuilding, the volume raises doubts about whether the question of political authority can be resolved through the sequencing of peacebuilding activities. Some of the authors of this volume do point to problems in peacebuilding sequencing and coordination (see Omach, Ero, and Dzinesa), but argue that better coordination and sequencing alone cannot resolve the tensions and contradictions of peacebuilding in Africa. A focus on sequencing ignores the fact that there may be strong political reasons for a lack of coordination, and competing visions and ideas of what peacebuilding is meant to achieve.

Statebuilding is another practice fraught with contradictions and trade-offs. By the early 2000s, most multilateral peacebuilding institutions had agreed that durable peace depended on the construction or strengthening of state institutions. As Khadiagala, Landsberg, and Olonisakin and Ikpe show in this volume, this meant that for many institutions, statebuilding came to be seen as an important aspect of peacebuilding.[65] Peacebuilding therefore involves setting priorities and establishing legitimate institutional hierarchies at the level of the state. The goal is to ensure a regime that is accountable to international norms, that is legitimate, and that has earned its sovereignty.[66] Yet as Dominik Zaum points out in this volume, there are contradictions between vertical legitimacy and horizontal legitimacy in the statebuilding project that may not be possible to reconcile. Zaum shows that identifying relevant societal groups to empower may require a very large external peacebuilding footprint, raising other accountability issues. Similarly, Comfort Ero describes in this volume how in Liberia people who wanted change were allied with international actors against a status quo coalition. Ero highlights a tension between the transformative aspirations underlying the statebuilding enterprise and the idea of local ownership.

Christopher Clapham suggests that international actors have taken for granted that the international system is composed of states, and therefore have no conception of how peace can exist without one. And yet Clapham shows the futility of a peacebuilding through statebuilding approach in Somalia. He argues that the engagement of external actors in Somalia has intensified conflict rather than moderating it, in part because attempts to build peace have assumed the existence of a state in Somalia or the possibility of creating one. Externally driven attempts to negotiate peace led to further factionalism in Somalia, as Somali leaders sought to present themselves as independent operators in order to gain external recognition and a seat at the table. Clapham shows that one of the keys to Somaliland's peacebuilding success was its insulation from external engagements, whereas the focus on statebuilding in Somalia led to the marginalization of local mediators and elders. More generally, a focus on the state and on the formal institutions of politics may overlook the local dimensions of authority and conflict (see Lemarchand, this volume).[67] Furthermore, if institutionalized statehood is the assumed goal, local voices that do not use or aspire to that language are disempowered.[68]

Like the reconstitution of political authority after conflict, the reestablishment of security is not uncontroversial. Peacebuilding occurs when security is, at best, unevenly distributed, but there is no consensus that peacebuilding strategies and programs succeed in reducing insecurity for all. Eboe Hutchful shows how security lies in the eyes of the beholder. The question of whether one's security increases or decreases as a result of peacebuilding programs and initiatives depends on one's position vis-à-vis the conflict (see Keen, this volume). Security governance that emphasizes ownership as well as formal and informal measures to enhance security may be helpful (see Hutchful, this volume), but the ability to shape the interpretations of peace and conflict is also often a very powerful tool in the struggle.

Disarmament, demobilization, and reintegration (DDR) programs are indicative of some of the contradictions of peacebuilding. Gwinyayi A. Dzinesa shows how DDR programs in Namibia, Angola, and Mozambique were supposed to contribute to creating sustainable, secure, peaceful transitions. But these programs were affected by a number of different factors, including the synchrony between global, regional, and local actors, and the political context. In Angola in the 1990s for instance, DDR foundered owing in part to the collusion between different actors who sought to undermine the potential of DDR. Paul Omach in this volume points to a disconnect between international DDR programs and local realities, even when local actors do not seek to undermine DDR. For instance, Omach says that the way in which DDR programs define "ex-combatants" does not always reflect the flexible and variable roles played by people involved in conflict.

Peacebuilding strategies to revitalize the economy are also the site of tensions and contradictions, and privilege some interests over others. International peacebuilding programs tend to focus on the formal economic sector, whereas many livelihoods in Africa are based on informal economic activities and exchange. Women in particular may be disadvantaged when peacebuilding programs fail to acknowledge informal economies.

As discussed previously, reinvigorating the market has been a core component of peacebuilding in Africa. In the 1980s and 1990s, key institutions, including the Bretton Woods institutions—the International Monetary Fund (IMF) and World Bank—blamed the failure of African development on bloated bureaucracies and corrupt leaders. Rather than looking historically at why such leaders emerged and locating the failure of development in the international system, the prescriptions given by the Bretton Woods institutions were rooted in efforts to create more effective markets and to downsize the state, arguably limiting the capacity of these "corrupt" leaders to do damage. The resulting structural adjustment programs often included drastic cuts in public services, liberalization, privatization, and the elimination of subsidies (see Harrison, this volume).[69]

Market approaches to peacebuilding have since been widely criticized for their detrimental consequences on security and well-being, but they are often still promoted in African contexts, albeit sometimes with a longer-term time frame and different sequencing.[70] These efforts, however, often have unintended consequences. In Sierra Leone, for instance, privatization resulted in the transfer of state assets to a small oligarchy, reinforcing interests that were opposed to political transformation (see Ero, this volume).[71]

During hostilities and afterward, the political economy of an area is reshaped, with some beneficiaries and some losers. In conflict, there are profits to be made for the large number of individuals and companies connected to the arms trade as well as for natural resource traders who benefit from weak laws and regulations. As René Lemarchand outlines in this volume, conflict in the Great Lakes region of Africa is sustained through trading and multiple webs of economic networks and interests involving state and nonstate actors. Aderoju Oyefusi in this volume explains how peacebuilding has been stunted in Nigeria's Niger Delta, due to the continued economic incentives in that region. Thus the effects of peacebuilding cannot be separated from the global and local political economies of war. In some cases, the large amounts of foreign aid that accompany peacebuilding has been used by the holders of state power as an additional rent that can be used for decidedly nonpeaceful purposes.[72]

Last, although authors recognize that conflict affects the social fabric of societies in terms of population dislocation, mistrust, shifting identities, and the erosion and creation of new social bonds, there is no consensus about whether—or how—peacebuilders should address this. Omach, for instance, believes that peacebuilding can be a further way for powerful states and interests to monitor, intervene, and regulate the peoples of the South.[73] Vanessa Pupavac has shown that peacebuilding programs focusing on healing psychosocial trauma problematically apply models developed in the West to very different local contexts.[74] Furthermore, there may be opportunities for progressive social change arising out of conflict (Hutchful, this volume). Gendered approaches to peacebuilding have usefully highlighted the ways in which women sometimes continue to be marginalized within peacebuilding programs and peacebuilding knowledge, but also how the processes of conflict and peace can sometimes bring new opportunities for women.[75]

Even programs in support of justice or reconciliation may be fragmented, contradictory, and contested. For instance, in 2001 the Rwandan government instituted the *gacaca* jurisdictions to hear and judge the cases of genocide suspects. Supporters saw this as a homegrown, historically rooted way of achieving postconflict reconciliation and justice in Rwanda. Critics saw it as the reinvention of tradition with the aim of further extending the power of a repressive Rwandan state. In Uganda, *mato oput* ceremonies have been discussed as a locally appropriate way to address community reconciliation in northern Uganda. Yet critics say that the emphasis on *mato oput* serves the interests of some foreign aid organizations and older male Acholi who want to reinforce their diminishing power, rather than being something that is universally accepted among the Acholi.[76]

The promotion and protection of human rights in the context of postconflict countries may lead to consequences that do not achieve the goals of their advocates.[77] Tensions between different conceptions of rights complicate peacebuilding. Like the other peacebuilding elements discussed in this volume, rights do not reside "out there," waiting to be discovered. Rather, they represent areas of contestation and multiple interpretations. The disagreements over the role of the ICC in Uganda and Sudan raise important questions about whose interests are served by emphasizing certain forms of justice over others (see Nouwen, this volume).

Structure of the Volume

The volume is not an exhaustive account of all peacebuilding efforts and initiatives in Africa, but the various chapters provide examples of how global, regional, and local interests, practices, and ideas interact in peacebuilding programming on the continent.

The volume is divided into three parts. Part 1 deals with peacebuilding themes and debates, exposing the tensions and contradictions in different clusters of peacebuilding activities. Each chapter explores the myriad of international and local ideas and practices, the challenges and trade-offs that have been encountered, and the alternatives that have been proposed in specific areas of peacebuilding, including peace negotiations, statebuilding, security sector governance, and DDR. The chapters show how and why the consequences of peacebuilding initiatives have not always been as anticipated in Africa.

Part 2 addresses the institutional framework for peacebuilding in Africa and the ideological underpinnings of key institutions, including the African Union, NEPAD, the African Development Bank, the Pan-African Ministers Conference for Public and Civil Service, the UN Peacebuilding Commission, the World Bank, and the International Criminal Court. The chapters in this section address the extent to which these institutions have been successful in achieving their mandates and visions, and the conceptions of peace and peacebuilding on which these mandates rest.

Finally, Part 3 examines how the themes and institutions analyzed in Parts 1–2 have operated in particular African contexts. These six case-study chapters allow for detailed analyses of local constraints to, and opportunities for, peacebuilding in different African locales, highlighting how peacebuilding procedures and activities are reshaped by different actors. Some of the case-study chapters deal with single-country cases, and other chapters adopt a regional approach; some case chapters deal with a single peacebuilding activity whereas others analyze the range of peacebuilding efforts in a specific area. The chapters address the conflicting ideas of peace in the negotiations in Sudan; overlapping networks of conflict and peace in the Great Lakes region; statebuilding in Sierra Leone and Liberia; the political economy of peace and conflict in the Niger Delta; DDR in Namibia, Angola, and Mozambique; and the failure of peacebuilding in Somalia. The case studies highlight the interplay among the local, regional, continental, and global levels, and the ways in which spaces for peace are constantly being rearticulated and renegotiated through particular programs in particular spaces.

One Peace or Many?

There is no denying that violent conflict has horrific costs in Africa, in terms of lives lost, dreams shattered, and livelihoods destroyed. The horrors of violence urge us toward an imagined shared alternative named "peace," where hope can be reclaimed and livelihoods restored.

When international peacebuilding programs prove insufficient or inadequate, we look toward African institutions and African agency. Yet African agency, like any other agency, contains worthy elements as well as lamentable ones, and cannot be separated from the world in which it is a part.

Peacebuilding is a political contest involving questions of authority, legitimacy, equality, and knowledge. The chapters in this volume treat peace not as something to be discovered or imposed, but as a number of different and continually contested practices. The political meanings of peace and peacebuilding are subject to negotiation between international, regional, and local actors. Masking the subjective nature of peace disguises ideology and power and may obscure the various ways that peace is understood and experienced in different contexts. Being cognizant of the wide range of interests and views involved in peacebuilding leads to questions about whether peacebuilding should continue to be described primarily in nonideological terms as a force for good.

Thus a single, all-encompassing definition of peacebuilding is elusive. The chapters in this volume show that different organizations, institutions, and actors may have different notions of the foundations for peace, leading to tensions in peacebuilding programming and unintended consequences on the ground. When international or regional peacebuilding projects have failed to achieve their objectives, this is usually blamed on poor implementation or lack of commitment, rather than on the contradictory logic of peacebuilding itself.

When competing conceptions of peace are incompatible, there is no independent perspective that can adjudicate between them. This is not to say, however, that there is no power or hierarchy in peacebuilding. To the contrary, the chapters in this volume show that some conceptions of peace are privileged in Africa, and some activities are emphasized over others. Yet all actors with a stake in peacebuilding bring their own ideas, norms, and practices to a situation that is highly political and that may alter the local landscape in unexpected ways. Likewise, the local context may be refracted back to regional and international institutions. Sometimes this may provide an opportunity for learning and change, but in other instances the consequences may be more problematic. In order for scholars, students, and practitioners to propose peacebuilding change, they must have an awareness of the forces that constrain, obstruct, or give meaning to different peacebuilding practices.

Notes

I thank Adekeye Adebajo, Adam Branch, David Keen, Derek Peterson, and Sharath Srinivasan for their helpful comments on this introduction.

1. *Tripoli Declaration,* Heads of State and Government of the African Union, special session, "Consideration and Resolution of Conflicts in Africa," August 31, 2009.

2. Ping, "Take a Stand for Africa's Peace," 15.

3. In March 2010 the ICC prosecutor was authorized to open an investigation into the situation in Kenya. In March 2011, the ICC prosecutor announced his decision to open an investigation into the situation in Libya.

4. The brief shows that between 1999 and 2006 there was a 56 percent decline in state-based armed conflict (from sixteen to seven incidents), and that between 2002 and 2006 there was a 46 percent decline in non-state-based armed conflict (conflicts without the involvement of a government). Human Security Centre, *Human Security Brief 2007,* 22–25.

5. Ibid., 24.

6. In terms of both the number of state-based conflicts being waged on its soil, as well as the number of battle-deaths. See Human Security Centre, *Human Security Brief 2006.*

7. Human Security Centre, *Human Security Brief 2007,* 26–31.

8. Falola, "Past in the Yoruba Present," 155.

9. McGovern, *Making War in Côte d'Ivoire,* 74.

10. Many thanks to Derek Peterson for pointing out this example.

11. Murithi, "African Indigenous and Endogenous Approaches to Peace and Conflict Resolution," 18–19. However, examples of failed peacebuilding also have a long history. To mention but one example, the king of Rwanda in the late nineteenth century, Mwami Kigeri Rwabugiri, was a skilled military tactician, and through military means he extended Rwandan control to several areas, including Ijwi island in Lake Kivu. Rwandan chiefs were placed on the island and the king himself spent time there. Yet Rwandan rule was superficial; there was no attempt at assimilation or any kind of integration (or peacebuilding), and when Rwabugiri died, the Rwandan chiefs left the island, leaving very little in the way of a legacy despite twenty years of domination. See Newbury, *Land beyond the Mists,* chaps. 5, 6.

12. The mixed success of that earlier UN operation foreshadowed some of the limitations of later peacebuilding efforts (see Lemarchand in this volume). See also Abi-Saab, *United Nations Operation in the Congo, 1960–1964;* Urquhart, *Hammarskjold;* Dobbins et al., *UN's Role in Nation-Building;* Nzongola-Ntalaja, *Congo from Leopold to Kabila.*

13. Boutros-Ghali, *Agenda for Peace,* para. 21.

14. United Nations, *More Secure World.*

15. For a discussion of positive and negative peace, see Galtung, "Violence, Peace, and Peace Research," 167–91.

16. See, for instance, Martha Cheo, "Women and Peacebuilding in Sierra Leone: Initiatives and Limitations."

17. United Nations, *Report of the Panel on United Nations Peace Operations* (Brahimi Report).

18. Ali and Matthews, introduction to *Durable Peace,* 7.

19. United Nations Development Programme (UNDP), *Human Development Report 1994.*

20. Ibid., 23.

21. Human Security Centre, *Human Security Report 2005.* For discussions on human security definitions and debates, see Owen, "Human Security," 373; Paris, "Human Security."

22. United Nations, *More Secure World.*

23. See also World Bank, *Role of the World Bank in Conflict and Development;* Van Houten, "World Bank's (Post-)Conflict Agenda."

24. See also Bellamy, "Institutionalisation of Peacebuilding."

25. New Partnership for Africa's Development (NEPAD), *African Post-Conflict Reconstruction Policy Framework;* African Union, *Policy Framework on Post-Conflict Reconstruction and Development in Africa.*

26. Economic Community of West African States, "ECOWAS Conflict Prevention Framework," sec. 2, para. 5.

27. See, for instance, Ali and Matthews, eds., *Durable Peace;* Call, *Building States to Build Peace;* David Francis, ed., *Peace and Conflict in Africa;* Jeong, *Peacebuilding in Post-conflict Societies;* Pugh, Cooper, and Turner, eds., *Whose Peace?;* Richmond, ed., *Palgrave Advances in Peacebuilding;* Darby and Mac Ginty, eds., *Contemporary Peacemaking.*

28. This rapid proliferation of journals that focus on peace and conflict themes has not been seen since the late 1950s to the early 1970s, when the field of peace research was established with its dedicated institutions and journals, such as *Journal of Conflict Resolution* (1957), *Journal of Peace Research* (1964), *Peace and Change: A Journal of Peace Research* (1972).

29. David Francis, "Introduction," 13. These programs exist outside Africa as well. In 1995, the Consortium on Peace Education, Research and Development Directory listed 136 colleges and universities in the United States with peace studies programs. Quoted in Harris, Fisk, and Rank, "Portrait of University Peace Studies."

30. Boutros-Ghali, *Agenda for Peace.*

31. United Nations, *In Larger Freedom,* 1.

32. Ping, "Take a Stand for Africa's Peace," 15.

33. Paris, *At War's End.*

34. United Nations, *More Secure World.*

35. For a discussion of spoilers, see Stedman, "Spoiler Problems in Peace Processes." See also Heathershaw and Lambach, "Introduction: Post-Conflict Spaces and Approaches to Statebuilding," 285.

36. See Stepanova, *Anti-Terrorism and Peace-Building.*

37. United States National Security Presidential Directive/ NSPD-44, Washington, 7 December 2005. In September 2008, US Congress passed the Reconstruction and Stabilization Civilian Management Act, which codified the existence and functions of the Office of the Coordinator for Reconstruction and Stabilization (S. 3001, P.L. 110–417). The first United States State Department Quadrennial Diplomacy and Development Review recommended the creation of a Bureau for Crisis and Stabilization Operations ("Leading through Power," chap. 4).

38. Ampiah and Naidu, eds., *Crouching Tiger, Hidden Dragon?*

39. See also the idea of "interim stabilization" in Colletta et al., *Interim Stabilization.*

40. See, for instance, Schellhaas and Seegers, "Peacebuilding: Imperialism's New Disguise?"; Chandler, *Empire in Denial;* Albert, "Understanding Peace in Africa."

41. For a discussion of colonial order, see Mamdani, *Citizen and Subject.*

42. See Duffield, "Social Reconstruction and the Radicalization of Development Aid."

43. See, for instance, Diana Francis, *People, Peace, and Power;* Anderlini, *Women Building Peace;* Daley, *Gender and Genocide in Burundi.*

44. See for instance Amin, *Imperialism and Unequal Development.*

45. Mamdani, "From Justice to Reconciliation."

46. Barnett, Kim, O'Donnell, and Sitea, "Peacebuilding: What Is in a Name?"

47. For instance, Daniel Serwer and Patricia Thomson developed a "standardized framework" for fragile states and societies emerging from conflict that assumes common "ultimate goals." According to Serwer and Thomson: "While particular circumstances vary dramatically, there is remarkable consensus in the post–Cold War period on the end-states desired, even though there may be a good deal of debate on how best to achieve them." Serwer and Thomson, "Framework for Success," 372. It is notable, however, that this was developed using exclusively US sources, including the Center for Strategic and International Studies, the RAND Corporation, and the US State Department's Office of the Coordinator for Reconstruction and Stabilization.

48. Albert, "Understanding Peace in Africa," 34.

49. Schellhaas and Seegers, "Peacebuilding," 10.

50. This leads to important questions about the role of African scholars and think tanks in defining the peacebuilding agenda. Is there a risk that African researchers become data collectors for the West, finding evidence to reinforce and justify the prevailing preferred peacebuilding approaches? If so, how can this be addressed?

51. Ake, *Democracy and Development in Africa.*

52. Albert, "Understanding Peace in Africa," 36.

53. For instance, Albert says that the Yoruba word for peace, Alafia, "is not only referring to order but also the physical well-being of the individual and his larger community." Albert, "Understanding Peace in Africa," 40.

54. See, for instance, Pugh, Cooper, and Turner, *Whose Peace?;* Lidén, Mac Ginty, and Richmond, eds., "Liberal Peacebuilding Reconstructed."

55. Hoffman, "What Is Left of the Liberal Peace?" 10–11.

56. Richmond, "Becoming Liberal, Unbecoming Liberalism," 326.

57. Ibid., 328–29.

58. Pouligny, "Local Ownership," 175.

59. For a discussion, see Mbembe and Nuttall, "Writing the World from an African Metropolis," 347–72.

60. Bayart, "Africa in the World."

61. Heathershaw, "Seeing Like the International Community," 331.

62. For a discussion of the global-local interactions, see Callaghy, Kassimir, and Latham, eds., *Intervention and Transnationalism in Africa.*

63. De Waal, "Mission without End?"

64. See Heathershaw and Lambach, "Introduction: Post-Conflict Spaces."

65. See also Paris and Sisk, "Introduction: Understanding the Contradictions of Postwar Statebuilding"

66. See Deng et al., *Sovereignty as Responsibility.*

67. See also Autesserre, "DR Congo."

68. Richmond, "Becoming Liberal, Unbecoming Liberalism," 331.

69. For criticisms of these programs, see Mkandawire, "Thinking about Development States in Africa"

70. For criticisms of a market approach to peacebuilding, see Mwanasali, "The View from Below"; Woodward, "Economic Priorities for Successful Peace Implementation"; Duffield, "Social Reconstruction."

71. See Keen, *Conflict and Collusion in Sierra Leone.*

72. Pierre Englebert and Denis M. Tull, "Postconflict Reconstruction in Africa," 123; David Keen, *Complex Emergencies.*

73. See also Duffield, *Development, Security, and Unending War.*

74. Pupavac, "Therapeutic Governance." See also Pupavac, "Refugee Advocacy."

75. See Willett, "Introduction: Security Council Resolution 1325"; Cheo, "Women and Peacebuilding in Sierra Leone."

76. Allen, "The International Criminal Court and the Invention of Traditional Justice in Northern Uganda."

77. Putnam, "Human Rights and Sustainable Peace."

PART ONE

Peacebuilding: Themes and Debates

ONE

Peace as an Incentive for War

DAVID KEEN

THIS CHAPTER LOOKS AT THE INCENTIVES FOR FURTHER VIOLENCE that may be established by peace agreements. It does not aim for a comprehensive discussion but rather seeks to highlight a key element of building peace that has been somewhat neglected both at the policy level and in academic discussions. This is risk of "incentivizing" further violence through the very act of peacemaking.

The question of how "inclusive" or "exclusive" a peace agreement should be is a difficult and critical one. A considerable measure of inclusion of the main armed groups—both at the negotiating table and in government—would appear to be necessary. Why else would they agree to lay down their arms? The case of Liberia is instructive here. In the four years prior to the 1996 Abuja II peace agreement, as Adekeye Adebajo has shown,[1] the Economic Community of West African States (ECOWAS), through its Cease-Fire Monitoring Group (ECOMOG), made a serious attempt to marginalize Liberian warlords and support a civilian government in Monrovia. Yet peace agreements in this period simply did not stick, as powerful warlords refused to disarm and clung to their profitable economic activities. By 1996, subregional mediators exhibited a new determination to bring warlords into political power in Monrovia. Distasteful as this "warlords' peace" was, it had the significant advantage that the agreement could actually be implemented; in this new climate, both demobilization and elections became possible.[2]

The constraints imposed by warring parties may be severe; but going too far in the direction of including and appeasing war leaders may damage equity, deepen impunity, and store up trouble for the future. There are grave dangers in excluding civil society and politicians not linked to armed groups. A key problem is the signal sent out: in particular, it may sometimes be difficult to discern the exact difference between rewarding people for giving up violence and rewarding people for taking it up.

Armed groups have proliferated in many conflicts, and there may be many political interests who might potentially turn to arms if their grievances are not met. To what extent should a peace process embrace a proliferation of armed groups? Is it possible that a peace process could itself encourage such proliferation?

Incentive-based approaches to peacemaking tend to focus on the violent (who constitute the immediate problem) while often ignoring those who have not (or not yet) been drawn into participation in violent processes. By contrast, those emphasizing a need for justice and an "end to impunity"—including human rights organizations—tend to focus on the importance of signals, notably to those who might one day contemplate violence. However, the advocates of both positions often "talk past" each other.

Incentivizing Violence: Three Mechanisms

There are three key incentive problems when it comes to peacemaking. The first key danger is that a peace process may exclude major armed groups taking part in a war, who will therefore have little incentive to abide by the peace. An extreme example was the 1997 Khartoum Peace Agreement in Sudan, an agreement that actually excluded the main rebel organization, the Sudan People's Liberation Army (SPLA), and predictably did not bring the war to an end. Also in Sudan, the May 2006 Darfur Peace Agreement was not accepted by two of the three rebel factions, and the Khartoum government then set about attacking and intimidating the nonsignatories, in alliance with the one faction (under Minni Minawi) that had signed the agreement. The exclusion of the Arab militias—often referred to as Janjaweed—from the Darfur peace process has also caused significant risks.

A second problem is that even when the main armed groups *are* represented, the underlying causes of violence are likely to remain unaddressed. In particular, where large sections of civil society are excluded, this will tend to prolong or even exacerbate the grievances of ordinary citizens. What forms of corruption are being institutionalized in a particular peace process? Economic initiatives may help cement a peace agreement between armed factions, perhaps by providing the right mix of incentives and disincentives, but a key danger is that deep fissures in the society may simply be "papered over." In practice, armed actors who have been able to use violence to secure control of production, trade, and emergency aid in wartime may be able to carve out for themselves a degree of control over production, trade, and development and reconstruction aid after a peace settlement.[3] By consolidating exploitation and corruption, an exclusive peace agreement may store up problems for the future.[4] When civilians fall victim to an exclusionary peace agreement that institutionalizes corruption, this may sometimes be an extension of collaborative warfare that targeted and exploited civilians.[5]

The dangers of consolidating corruption and exploitation were illustrated in the case of Liberia. What looks to some people like realism and pragmatism may look to others like appeasement. After the 1995–96 Abuja II peace process had brought a number of warlords (most notably Charles Taylor) into the political settlement, Taylor, who was subsequently elected president in 1997, proved unwilling to engage in substantial reform of the security services while promoting widespread corrupt practices and harassing civil society and the press.[6] In Sierra Leone, the controversial appointment of Revolutionary United Front (RUF) leader Foday Sankoh as vice president and head of a new mineral resources commission (under the 1999 Lomé Peace Agreement) was profoundly offensive to many Sierra Leoneans: it looked even more distasteful when the RUF returned to war in 2000.[7] The 2003 peace agreement in the Democratic Republic of the Congo (DRC), while in many ways a step forward, was also seen by many as a kind of "warlords' peace" that entrenched the exploitation of economic resources by various military commanders, often with foreign backing, who were given a degree of power within the state apparatus and a degree of political legitimacy.[8]

An earlier and revealing example of a political fix that "papered over" important societal grievances came at the end of Sudan's first civil war. The 1972 Addis Ababa Peace Agreement, which ended Sudan's first civil war, included important concessions to the southern rebels, such as incorporation into the national army, but it did not produce the kind of accountable political system that was capable of remedying the extreme underdevelopment of the south or the marginalization of significant groups within the north. In effect, a military government entered into alliance with former rebels at the expense of rival political forces within the north. When President Jaafar Nimeiri and his successors courted some of the discontented elements in the north (especially the western part of northern Sudan) during the 1980s, the south was left without protection. In these circumstances, the limited economic rehabilitation in the south after the first civil war served merely to regenerate resources, notably cattle, that could be raided by disgruntled northern pastoralists allied to the government.

Twenty-three years after the Addis Ababa agreement, Sudan's 2005 Comprehensive Peace Agreement (CPA), which ended Sudan's second civil war, also carried the seeds of major problems in relation to opposition groups in the north. The agreement excluded the opposition National Democratic Alliance, and the CPA allocated only 14 percent of positions in the national and state executive and legislative branches to the northern opposition, compared to 52 percent to the National Congress Party and 28 percent to the Sudan People's Liberation Movement (SPLM).[9] As in 1972, peace meant an alliance with the southern rebels but also an exclusion of many elements of northern, and even southern, civil society. Opponents of the current regime have included those Muslims who hoped, wrongly as it turned out, that common religion could be a basis for common citizenship; with southern secession, many in the north also fear that they will now have no option but to become part of an Islamic state.[10] Key grievances in the north have included, first, years of neglect by the government and, second, the loss of access to land by both smallholders and pastoralists as a result of the expansion of Sudan's large semimechanized farms.[11] Leben Moro has presented the north-south peace in Sudan as a rather exclusive business, even in terms of the south. This is manifest, for example, in the difficulty that many displaced people have experienced in returning to oil-rich areas that the government in Khartoum, which came to include the SPLM/A, was interested in exploiting.[12]

Away from Africa, many similar concerns have attached themselves to peace agreements. In Cambodia in the 1990s, the institutionalization of corruption in a peace process helped deprive the treasury of revenue, and this was subsequently a source of some instability.[13] In Tajikistan following the 1992–97 civil war, a considerable degree of stability has been brought about by a peace process that effectively "bought off" a range of warring factions, not least with the benefits of a privatization program. However, the entrenchment of corruption and of oligopolistic markets has raised concerns about the long-term sustainability of this peace.[14] In the former Yugoslavia, the 1995 Dayton Peace Agreement can be seen as rewarding local elites who had already rewarded themselves through violent accumulation in wartime.[15]

In Afghanistan, as Antonio Giustozzi has highlighted, warlords have tried to use peace agreements to become "respectable" and to consolidate their ill-gotten gains; indeed, this impulse may even help to explain why elements of peace became possible.[16] Some analysts suggest that during negotiations over the composition of an interim government starting in November 2001 in Bonn, the United States, in concert with senior United Nations (UN) officials, actually strengthened the morale of, and support for, Afghan warlords (some of them described as "paper tigers") at a moment when they could have been weakened.[17] It appears that concerns beyond "human security" were influential, including the need to "incentivize" and then reward allies in the Northern Alliance in the context of the "war on terror" and the US-led war against the Taliban. One of the longer-term problems that resulted was that powerful warlords were able to withhold a great deal of customs revenue from the center, making reconstruction and restoring some kind of central authority more difficult. As Ahmed Rashid wrote in 2007: "The lack of developmental activities in the south [of Afghanistan] has resulted in part from [President Hamid] Karzai's failure to purge corrupt or drug-trafficking officials from powerful positions. This has fuelled disillusionment among Pashtuns, the dominant ethnic group in southern and eastern Afghanistan, many of whom are now offering to fight or at least offer sanctuary to the Taliban."[18]

A third problem is that peace agreements may actually reward violent behavior, sending potentially damaging signals perhaps internationally as well as nationally about the utility of violence. These signals may be acted upon by a variety of (excluded) groups within a country that is undergoing a peace process and perhaps in the wider region too. Yet being more "inclusive" during a peace process (for example by bringing in smaller military factions) does not necessarily solve the problem. In fact, it may even make matters worse, since it is possible that this will send a signal to an ever-widening group of people that they too need to resort to violence if they are to find a stake in the peace.

In Liberia, civilian organizations have often opposed recognition of armed faction leaders in peace negotiations, arguing that this rewards their violence and boosts their prestige and their ability to attract a following.[19] The early 1990s in Liberia saw a rapid proliferation of factions, and this seems to have been driven in part by the desire of various military leaders to claim a place at the negotiating table through seizing territory.[20] Adekeye Adebajo has noted:

> ULIMO [United Liberation Movement for Democracy in Liberia], the LPC [Liberia Peace Council], and the LDF [Lofa Defense Force] hoped to obtain a share of political power in a future government through the conquest of territory, which would then provide them with some leverage during negotiations. ULIMO's presence at the Cotonou talks in 1993, after its exclusion from Yamoussoukro in 1991, was a clear sign to other factions that gaining territory was the most viable way of winning a place at the negotiating table. New factions had much to lose and nothing to gain from the successful implementation of Cotonou. It was in their interest that the agreement failed, as it had been in ULIMO's interest that Yamoussoukro failed in 1991.[21]

It is worth setting this account alongside an analysis of the peace process in the DRC by Denis Tull and Andreas Mehler. Referring to the 1999 Lusaka Peace Agreement, they note:

> While insurgencies may be prone to defections, it is no coincidence that as soon as the political terms of Lusaka (power-sharing, transitional government) had been established, the defections from the RCD [Rally for Congolese Democracy] and the proliferation of smaller insurgencies started in earnest, including the RCD-National and the RCD-ML [RCD–Movement for Liberation] which progressively fragmented even further into factions led by Wamba, Tibasima, Nyamwisi and Lubanga, striving to become rebel leaders in their own right. Given the underlying logic of power-sharing agreements according to which all armed insurgents are to be included in negotiations, these personalities understandably expected to be treated accordingly by the mediators; indeed, this was the very reason the new groups were created.[22]

This damaging dynamic has persisted. In a 2009 article, Koen Vlassenroot and Timothy Raeymaekers highlight important negative effects of the strategy of luring DRC warmongers to the negotiating table: "The message sent out to Congolese rebel groups is that violence pays. A recurrent pattern since the 1999 Lusaka ceasefire agreement is that every negotiated peace deal in the DRC has been followed by the pro- liferation and fragmentation of armed groups that each want a portion of existing power agreements."[23]

In Sudan, as noted, a near-exclusive international focus on Khartoum and the rebel SPLA, in line with a binary understanding of a north-south or even a Muslim-Christian divide, has tended to encourage a neglect of the interests of those northerners who oppose the government of Omar al-Bashir. Some of these northerners, notably in Darfur, turned to violence in an attempt to win the international recognition and the place at the negotiating table that had been accorded to the SPLA, for whom violent resistance seemed at last to have paid dividends.[24]

Darfur's rebel Sudan Liberation Movement (SLM), headed by Minni Minawi, noted in 2003: "The government is negotiating with the south because of pressure from the international community and military pressure in the south, in the west and in the east."[25] In some sense, violence was seen to have "worked."

The problem of incentivizing violence through peace subsequently re- curred *within* Darfur. Clea Kahn and Elena Lucchi, two aid workers who were based in Darfur with the Office for Coordination of Humanitarian Affairs (OCHA) and Médecins sans Frontières (MSF), observed:

> For rebel groups or armed insurgents, when humanitarians
> negotiate with them for access to people living in their areas of
> control, this interaction can be used to demonstrate that they
> are legitimate, or "recognised." In eastern Chad and Darfur, this
> has been turned on its head: in both areas, power and legitimacy
> are derived not from fostering positive relationships with the
> humanitarian community, but through demonstrations of brute
> force. The result is a "Toyota war," in which the seizure of vehicles
> by force from humanitarian organisations confers legitimacy.
> In Darfur this pattern is particularly clear, as the parties that
> are invited to the negotiating table are generally those with the
> greatest military strength, and asset targeting peaks just prior to
> peace talks. Theft increases as rebel groups with ever-decreasing
> accountability to the people they claim to represent aim for a seat
> at the table.[26]

The danger of "incentivizing" violence is present well beyond these African examples. In Cambodia, the peace deal with elements of the Khmer Rouge under Ieng Sary in the mid-1990s was often seen as sending out potentially damaging signals on the acceptability of violence and corruption. For example, Amnesty International complained that the deal contributed to a climate of impunity. Also in the mid-1990s, the peace process in the former Yugoslavia demonstrates some of the dangers of incentivizing violence. Consider this measured assessment by Alexandros Yannis:

> The Dayton Peace Accords, which in 1995 settled the conflict in Bosnia-Herzegovina, had a major destabilizing effect on Kosovo. On the one hand, the Dayton Accords left the question of Kosovo's political future unresolved, thereby exacerbating the simmering frustrations of Kosovo Albanians. On the other hand, the accords acted as a major disincentive for the continued pursuit of peaceful political solutions; the Kosovo Albanians could not fail to observe that the underlying logic of the peace accords was largely the ratification on paper of the ethnoterritorial gains made on the ground by the use of force. Consequently, the Dayton Accords strengthened the political commitment of radical Albanians to the use of force. Popular support for the militant program of the Kosovo Liberation Army (KLA) increased at the expense of the moderate strategy of Ibrahim Rugova.[27]

Rugova's ability to rein in extremists in the Albanian community was premised on the belief that Kosovo would be included when the conflict in Bosnia was finally settled. So it was logical that his position would be dramatically undermined by the exclusion of Kosovo from Dayton. Meanwhile, the message that violence had paid dividends, in particular for the Bosnian Serbs, appears not to have been lost on either the KLA or the Serbs in Kosovo. Peter Russell argues that, even though the deteriorating situation in Kosovo was fairly well understood internationally, there was some justification for excluding the issue of Kosovo at Dayton, since inclusion could have jeopardized the immediate and pressing goal of ending the conflict in Bosnia, which had until that point been a much more destructive conflict than the conflict in Kosovo.[28] In particular, Slobodan Milosevic was a pivotal figure at Dayton, particularly given his influence over the Bosnian Serbs, and his willingness to enter into the agreement might have been compromised by pushing for major concessions on Kosovo, especially as championing the Serbs in Kosovo had formed the platform for Milosevic's original rise to power in the late 1980s and the issue was still the most reliable way for him to rally Serb support. In contrast with Russell's argument, Alex Bellamy describes the lifting of international sanctions as an "overriding concern" for Milosevic, and suggests that this presented an opportunity for pushing for concessions on Kosovo.[29] It is difficult to know for sure just how far Milosevic could have been pushed. Although sanctions, which were renewed as violence in Kosovo escalated, did eventually contribute to Milosevic's downfall, the many advantages—both political and economic—that the Milosevic cabal derived from these sanctions[30] suggest that removing them may not have been an absolute priority for him in 1995.

In Sierra Leone, many local people saw the 1999 Lomé Peace Agreement, which brought the RUF inside the government, as an unfortunate necessity given the preceding attack on Freetown and the grave weakness of international protection. Mediators in Sierra Leone also used educational scholarships as an incentive for peace. But if necessity is the mother of concession, what kind of message does this send? An analysis of the various coups and renewed rebellions in Sierra Leone from the 1992 coup onward suggests that a variety of groups have tried to use violence to force their way inside the existing system of rewards and benefits.[31] A young man working on the demobilization scheme told me in 2001: "If you pay much attention to perpetrators without recognising the civilians or helping them like the ex-combatants, you are sending another signal. There might be another uprising. . . . Civilians will get up and say the people who caused this havoc, they are now living big."

In addition to incentivizing rebellion through this kind of "demonstration effect," peace agreements may dangerously free up military resources for new targets and they may encourage those who are accustomed to living off a war economy to look for "fresh pastures." Albanian fears of escalating Serb oppression in Kosovo were heightened when notorious Serb paramilitary leader Zeljiko "Arkan" Raznatovic announced that he was moving his headquarters to the Kosovo capital of Pristina. Many Albanians believed that warmongers among the Serbs would transfer their attention to Kosovo once the conflict in Bosnia had been resolved, a prediction that proved disturbingly accurate.[32] Sudan's 2002 cease-fire agreement, the precursor to the 2005 Comprehensive Peace Agreement, seems to have released some military resources for war-making in Darfur, which became the new justification for high military spending and maintaining a sense of national emergency.[33] These cases underline the need, at the very least, for outsiders to anticipate that peace in one region may encourage war in another.

Ways Forward

It is one thing to raise a problem but quite another to suggest a sensible solution. In an interesting contribution, Tull and Mehler, after noting that violence may be incentivized by peace agreements, mention "two rather bold solutions" to this problem: "first, let conflicts run their course; second, always provide support (diplomatically, militarily) to incumbent regimes attacked by insurgents."[34] Tull and Mehler go on to note that letting wars run their course—in line with Edward Luttwak's injunction to "give war a chance"[35]—is hardly a very humanitarian option, adding, first, that it ignores the role of external actors in fueling wars over long period and, second, that the victory of a rebel group may not even bring a war to an end. These are powerful objections with which one can readily agree. As for providing support to incumbents, Tull and Mehler note that this means bolstering authoritarian regimes and stifling any political change. Arguing that civil wars happen when they are physically *feasible,* and moving away from a focus on *motivation,* Paul Collier has stated: "If the feasibility hypothesis is right it has a powerful implication: violent conflict cannot be prevented by addressing the problems that are likely to motivate it; it can only be prevented by making it more difficult. Whether rebellion is easy or difficult basically comes down to whether rebels have access to guns and money, and whether the state is effective in opposing them."[36]

Yet this line of analysis, like the earlier "greed discourse," seems to delegitimize all rebellion and to throw the weight of "reason" behind all counterinsurgency.[37] A major worry here is that many wars have revealed a tendency for abuses to flourish within a counterinsurgency while international attention and condemnation are focused on the insurgency:[38] giving "carte blanche" to counterinsurgency will only make this worse.

Here I highlight three more constructive ways forward. The first, emphasized by Tull and Mehler, is through ensuring some rather demanding criteria for inclusion in a peace process. As Tull and Mehler suggest:

> External brokers need to raise the threshold which grants
> insurgents a place at the negotiating table. As such, it is

imperative to think beyond violence as the primary measure of political inclusion. Armed groups preying on local communities and committing serious human rights abuses should be disqualified as negotiating partners. By contrast, some rebels provide some measure of order or even collective goods such as security, and they should therefore receive a political premium in negotiations, for they come at least close to carrying out functions that a government is supposed to fulfil.[39]

There may be some very severe practical constraints, but in many ways this makes good sense. It is important to recognize that armed groups have many political, economic, and ideological reasons for *not* abusing civilians, as well as many reasons for abusing them.[40] As much as possible, these relatively benevolent tendencies can be encouraged by including some of the better actors: it is not usually necessary or helpful to dismiss everyone as a greedy warlord. There are precedents for discouraging some of the more abusive behavior, moreover. In Liberia, nongovernmental organizations (NGOs) implemented a joint operation policy in 1996 after massive looting of relief resources in Monrovia. NGOs made it clear that they were not prepared to put up with repeated looting. They limited activities to essential life-saving tasks, and they tried to ensure that they were not played off against each other by local warlords. Philippa Atkinson and Nicholas Leader argue that cooperation between humanitarian agencies at this time helped put civilian protection on the agenda, feeding into a peace process in combination with a range of more diplomatic and legal pressures.[41]

However, Tull and Mehler's emphasis on disqualifying abusers does raise difficult questions. In particular, what is to be done about those who have been preying on civilians? There are likely to be many such groups. One option is to wage war on them, but this puts civilian lives further at risk and raises the question of whether the peace process really deserves that name. Waging war may also solidify an abusive rebel leadership's control over reluctant recruits.[42] Some degree of incorporation of these groups may be necessary, particularly as an apparently "implacable" spoiler may change, in new circumstances, into a less violent entity.[43]

A second way forward is through the provision of other incentives, perhaps alongside a formal peace agreement that can discourage violence in various ways. One of these might be criminal prosecutions, for example by the International Criminal Court (ICC), though here the advantages of reducing impunity have to be weighed against the possibility that armed actors will prolong conflict rather than risk prosecution in conditions of peace.[44] A good disarmament, demobilization, and reintegration (DDR) program can lure soldiers away from loyalty to leaders, who often have a particularly strong vested interest in continuing conflict and in avoiding the accountability and punishment that peace might bring.[45] Loss of faith in a greedy leadership can be an advantage here, and this was one element that helped facilitate the disarmament of rebels in Sierra Leone.[46] Weak chains of command in modern wars, as well as creating difficulties in enforcing peace agreements, can play a positive role in encouraging belligerents to negotiate.[47] Another way of providing incentives beyond a formal peace process is through focusing on the instruments of counterinsurgency. Improved conditions for government soldiers proved extremely important in reining in the decade-long civil war in Sierra Leone, where the understandable demonization of rebels had long diverted attention from the substantial role of government soldiers and other government actors in fueling the conflict.

In the DRC, governmental "spoilers" have often been damagingly absent from international radar screens.[48] The embezzling of soldiers' pay by senior military officials encouraged looting of civilians. Poor or nonexistent pay also reportedly encouraged government army soldiers to take bribes from the Democratic Liberation Forces of Rwanda (FDLR), who are linked to the former Rwandan génocidaires, encouraging the government soldiers to tolerate the presence of FDLR soldiers and even to assist the FDLR in taxing and looting civilians.[49] In an important 2006 report, the International Crisis Group (ICG) noted:

> While donors have supported MONUC [United Nations Organization Mission in the Democratic Republic of the Congo] at an operational rate of approximately $1 billion a year to improve the situation in the East, they have balked at the concept of providing basic equipment to the integrated brigades, let alone decent living conditions. . . . The integration centres at Mushaki, Nyaleke and Luberizi were largely unsuitable for human habitation, let alone training, forcing some soldiers to live in straw huts amid outbreaks of disease such as cholera and tuberculosis.[50]

A third way forward is to treat peace as an ongoing process in which a peace agreement or cease-fire is only a beginning. Given the right internal and external pressures over an extended period, a greater degree of inclusion and accountability may become possible over time, even where short-term pragmatism has put warlords or faction leaders into positions of power at the expense of civil society.[51] What is clear is the urgency of addressing the concerns of those elements, whether of civil society or armed groups that are considered potentially cooperative, even once a peace agreement has been reached.

If a society is to move from a situation of extreme violence and exploitation to a more peaceful and accountable system, then some kind of process of democratization will clearly be necessary and desirable. But there are also grave dangers here. Work by Edward Mansfield and Jack Snyder in particular has shown just how difficult it is to ensure compliance from elites for a project of democratization.[52] Another worry is the possibility that a peace agreement only becomes possible as a result of the assumption that it will not be implemented.

It is striking, however, that the process of democratization has often been handled in a crude and precipitous manner, not least in the tragic case of Rwanda.[53] Combining rapid democratization with rapid economic liberalization would appear to be particularly dangerous.[54] In Liberia, the resources that Charles Taylor was able to acquire in wartime, along with the threat of resumed war, helped him to win the presidential election in 1997.[55] Commenting on Bosnia-Herzegovina in a 2004 article, Peter Andreas observed: "Leading actors in the covert acquisition and distribution of supplies during the war have emerged as a new elite with close ties to the government and nationalist political parties."[56]

The case of Sudan after the 2005 peace agreement also suggests that rather excessive faith has been placed, not least by international donors, in elections as something that will in themselves sort out the conflict in that country. In some ways, almost magical powers have been attributed to the democratic process. The withdrawal from the 2010 elections by Sadiq al-Mahdi and of the SPLM's Yasir Arman effectively handed victory to Omar al-Bashir, even without the resort to census manipulation and vote-rigging.[57] Al-Bashir was also able to use the very considerable patronage of the (increasingly oil-rich) Sudanese state to cement his political constituency. Meanwhile, Khartoum largely escaped criticism for its purchase of enhanced weapons systems and its domestic weapons production, with much of the weaponry being deployed in or near the oil regions in the north-south border area.[58] The decision of southern Sudanese to secede has been followed by widespread human rights abuses by the Sudanese army in the Abyei area and by the movement of large numbers of the seminomadic Messiriya Arab population into the region, apparently as part of an attempt to stake a claim to this contested and oil-rich area.[59]

A large measure of realism is important in peace negotiations: peace is unlikely to be possible without "buying off" the major armed actors. However, the dangers with this process also need highlighting—and counteracting. This requires a conscious—and prolonged effort—to extend the benefits of peace beyond these armed groups. In particular, where nonviolent, or even relatively nonviolent, actors feel they are receiving a significant "peace dividend," the incentive to join the ranks of armed groups who may have benefited more directly from a peace settlement will be reduced. The analysis here also suggests a need to accommodate genuine grievances, notably those of civilians, and to reward armed groups whose behavior is at least relatively favorable toward civilians. Peace is usually a "dirtier" business than we like to think; but if this is taken too far, the perverse incentives for further violence are not to be underestimated. If peace is accompanied by a process of democratization, the economic context is likely to be crucial and a sustained reconstruction effort can provide a relatively promising environment, helping to extend benefits beyond the main armed groups.

Notes

1. See Adebajo, *Liberia's Civil War.*

2. Adebajo, "Liberia: A Warlord's Peace."

3. Keen, "War and Peace." See also Keen, *Complex Emergencies;* Menkhaus and Prendergast, *Political Economy of Post-Intervention Somalia;* Berdal, *Building Peace after War.*

4. On postconflict corruption, see, for example, work by the London- and Jerusalem-based NGO Tiri (http://www.tiri.org).

5. Keen, "War and Peace."

6. Adebajo, "Liberia."

7. International Crisis Group (ICG), *Liberia and Sierra Leone.*

8. See, for example, Vlassenroot and Raeymaekers, "Politics of Rebellion and Intervention in Ituri"; Raeymaekers, "Sharing the Spoils"; Autesserre, "DR Congo."

9. See, for example, ICG, *Khartoum-SPLA Agreement.*

10. Johnson, *Root Causes of Sudan's Civil Wars.*

11. Ibid. See also Keen, *Benefits of Famine;* Coalition for International Justice, *Soil and Oil.* On grievances in eastern Sudan, see Pantuliano, "Comprehensive Peace?"

12. Moro, "Oil, Conflict, and Displacement in Sudan."

13. Le Billon, "Political Ecology of Transition in Cambodia, 1989–1999." See also Malone and Nitzschke. "Economic Agendas in Civil Wars."

14. Torjesen and MacFarlane, "R before D."

15. Yannis, "Kosovo."

16. Giustozzi, *Respectable Warlords?*

17. Hoffman, "Pragmatist"; Chayes, "Dangerous Liaisons."

18. Rashid, "Letter from Afghanistan," 19.

19. See, for example, Armon and Carl, eds., *Accord*, no. 1: *The Liberian Peace Process, 1990–1996.* Similar concerns have been expressed by civilian organizations in Somalia. See also Menkhaus and Prendergast, *Political Economy of Post-Intervention Somalia.*

20. Adebajo, "Liberia."

21. Ibid., 612.

22. Tull and Mehler, "Hidden Costs of Power-Sharing," 393.

23. Vlassenroot and Raeymaekers, "Kivu's Intractable Security Conundrum," 476.

24. ICG, *Darfur Rising.*

25. Ibid., 19.

26. Kahn and Lucchi, "Are Humanitarians Fuelling Conflicts?"

27. Yannis, "Kosovo," 171.

28. Russell, "Exclusion of Kosovo from the Dayton Negotiations."

29. Bellamy, *Kosovo and International Society.* Although many studies have noted the problem in retrospect, few outsiders highlighted the problems that Dayton was likely to cause in Kosovo.

30. See, for example, Keen, *Complex Emergencies.*

31. Keen, *Conflict and Collusion in Sierra Leone.*

32. Russell, "Exclusion of Kosovo from the Dayton Negotiations."

33. See, for example, Keen, *Complex Emergencies.*

34. Tull and Mehler, "Hidden Costs of Power-Sharing," 394.

35. Luttwak, "Give War a Chance."

36. Collier, *War, Guns, and Votes,* 139.

37. On the danger of delegitimizing rebellion and even protest in general, see Duffield, *Global Governance and the New Wars.*

38. Keen, *Conflict and Collusion in Sierra Leone;* Keen, *Complex Emergencies;* Dolan, *Social Torture.*

39. Tull and Mehler, "Hidden Costs of Power-Sharing," 395.

40. Slim, *Killing Civilians,* 121–79; Keen and Lee, "Civilian Status and the New Security Agendas."

41. Atkinson and Leader, "Joint Policy of Operation." On the diplomatic front, see Adebajo, *Liberia's Civil War;* Adebajo, "Liberia."

42. See, particularly, University Teachers for Human Rights-Jaffna (UTHR-J), *Let Them Speak.*

43. Greenhill and Major, "Perils of Profiling." See also Stedman, "Spoiler Problems in Peace Processes."

44. See, for example, Allen, *Trial Justice;* Tull and Mehler, "Hidden Cost of Power-Sharing." See also Nouwen in this volume.

45. See Omach in this volume.

46. Keen, *Conflict and Collusion in Sierra Leone.*

47. King, *Ending Civil Wars.*

48. Vlassenroot and Raeymaekers, "Kivu's Intractable Security Conundrum."

49. Autesserre, "DR Congo."

50. ICG, *Security Sector Reform in the Congo,* 25–26.

51. For an example of where such hopes have been expressed (but remain largely unrealized), see Pantuliano, "Comprehensive Peace?"

52. Mansfield and Snyder. *Electing to Fight.*

53. See, for example, African Rights, *Death, Despair, and Defiance;* Paris, *At War's End.*

54. Paris, *At War's End.*

55. Adebajo, "Liberia."

56. Andreas, "Criminalized Legacies of War," 5.

57. Malik, "Sudan Election Didn't Need Fraud."

58. Ibid. See also Prendergast and Jensen, "Sudan."

59. See, for example, Human Rights Watch, *Sudan.*

Statebuilding and Governance

The Conundrums of Legitimacy and Local Ownership

DOMINIK ZAUM

SINCE THE END OF THE COLD WAR, STATEBUILDING HAS INCREASINGLY come to be seen as a central strategy for establishing sustainable peace after civil conflicts.[1] Following the eruption of conflicts in many developing countries, where already weak state structures often crumbled under the double blow of the sudden termination of superpower patronage and the pressures of globalization, the need to strengthen the capacity of states to provide basic services such as security to the population, and to establish institutions that enjoy relatively broad popular consent, became critical. As Kofi Annan suggested in 2001, during his tenure as secretary-general of the United Nations (UN), "The natural conflicts of society can be resolved through the exercise of state sovereignty and, generally, participatory governance."[2] The attacks of September 11, 2001, further enhanced the focus on so-called weak and failing states as sources of insecurity not only for their own populations but also for the West, because of the former's potential association with international terrorism and organized crime. This reinforced the association between statebuilding and peacebuilding.

Despite the inherent link between the two concepts, and the fact that they have often been used interchangeably by donors and analysts alike, peacebuilding and statebuilding are conceptually different. Boutros Boutros-Ghali's *Agenda for Peace* defines peacebuilding as "action to identify and support structures which will tend to strengthen and solidify peace in order to avoid a relapse into conflict."[3] Statebuilding, in contrast, encompasses efforts to build or strengthen political and administrative institutions with the aim of establishing a legitimate local political order in the eyes of relevant societal groups.[4] Whereas the former focuses on preventing renewed outbreaks of violence after conflict, the latter is concerned with the character of the relationship between state and society,[5] and the legitimacy of state institutions, a concern that has important implications for peacebuilding but also broader implications for development and governance that are distinct from dealing with the consequences of conflict.

As Charles Call has argued, there are a range of tensions between the practices and priorities of peacebuilding and statebuilding.[6] One common peacebuilding practice, for example, is the formation of power-sharing agreements,[7] which are used to engage potential spoilers and give them a stake in a successful peace process. Such power-sharing agreements have been particularly common in African peacebuilding processes, for example in Côte d'Ivoire, the Democratic Republic of the Congo (DRC), Sudan, and Zimbabwe.[8] However, while such arrangements have often been successful in containing spoilers and preventing the renewed outbreak of conflict, they have in some cases undermined the development of state capacity and the transformation of state-society relations. This has occurred in particular where leaders of different factions use their access to the state for private gain rather than developing effective institutions to provide public goods, or when they instrumentalize the political process to block the strengthening of state institutions at the expense of parallel institutions they control. Although peacebuilding tends to emphasize the impartiality of outsiders to engage all relevant parties in a peace process, statebuilding often requires international actors to take sides and to make deeply political decisions about access to power and control of resources that are incompatible with impartiality. The strengthening of state institutions can fuel the resistance of those groups that stand to lose most from a state effectively exercising the monopoly of violence, or encourage them to use violence to capture the state—a dilemma that has characterized the failed attempts at statebuilding in Somalia, as Christopher Clapham and Ken Menkhaus have argued.[9]

Although such tensions do not suggest that statebuilding cannot make a critical contribution to building sustainable peace, they do underline the need to examine the impact of statebuilding on peace in the political, economic, and social contexts of each case. As argued in this chapter, many of these tensions are actually inherent in statebuilding, as they reflect different aspects of the complex social construct that is the state. Although most international statebuilding efforts have focused predominantly on the strengthening of formal political and administrative institutions (the state's vertical legitimacy), the state is also an institutional arrangement that enshrines power balances in a society[10] (reflecting its horizontal legitimacy), and the requirements for these two aspects of statehood can easily conflict in weak, postconflict states.

Two decades of postconflict statebuilding have resulted in practices that are too complex to be described as a single approach. Statebuilding has involved a wide range of different international actors with different priorities and perspectives on the role of the state,[11] and some of these actors have arguably learned lessons from their involvement and changed their statebuilding practices. At times they have drawn on specific local traditions, for example in Afghanistan, where the Loya Jirga mechanism was used to legitimate the political settlement of the 2001 Bonn conference following the military intervention of the United States and its defeat of the Taliban. There is also a growing recognition that in many developing countries, particularly in Africa, the state has never resembled the Weberian model that has informed international statebuilding efforts, which raises questions about the effectiveness of the existing approaches.[12] However, one can argue that over the past two decades, the most important statebuilding actors, such as the UN, the international financial institutions, and Western donors, have generally adopted top-down approaches focusing on the creation and strengthening of formal-legal state institutions rather than indigenous political practices.[13] This chapter focuses predominantly on these actors and their practices. Their statebuilding efforts have been driven by the objective of creating what Roland Paris has called "liberal market democracies," which are characterized by democratic government, the rule of law and promotion of human rights, market liberalization, and reasonably effective public administration.[14]

In this chapter, I argue that the central contribution to peacebuilding made by international statebuilding efforts is the legitimation of the state. Legitimacy, though, is a complex social phenomenon, and the structures, practices, and processes that can generate and sustain the legitimacy of the state vis-à-vis its population are shaped by societal-specific norms. Although the Western donor states and the international organizations most deeply involved in statebuilding (such as the

UN, the World Bank, the European Union [EU], and the Organisation for Economic Cooperation and Development [OECD]) have arguably recognized this, the key mechanism through which they attempt to reconcile their own normative commitments and interests with those of local actors—the concept of local ownership—can in practice have problematic implications for both statebuilding and peacebuilding.

This chapter presents the case for the centrality of legitimacy and the problem of local ownership as a legitimation strategy in three steps. First, it explores the concept of legitimacy and why it matters for successful postconflict statebuilding. Second, it surveys how international statebuilding efforts have tried to strengthen the legitimacy of postconflict states, and examines some of the legitimacy challenges they have faced, in particular the failure of internationally imposed institutions to reflect local norms, and the conflicts between new formal state institutions and existing (informal) local structures that developed or transformed during conflict to compensate for the absence or predatory nature of formal state institutions. I argue that these tensions are inherent in the multifaceted character of the state, which puts competing demands on statebuilding efforts. Third, the chapter examines in more detail the practices of local ownership in statebuilding, one of the key strategies for reconciling the normative commitments and strategic objectives of international statebuilders with the values and needs of local communities. I argue that meaningful local ownership that allows for substantive local participation in all aspects of statebuilding is likely (though counterintuitively) to involve extensive international involvement. Some states, especially those that are suspicious about activities that might compromise their sovereignty—a category that includes most African states—will find this difficult to accept.

The Importance of Legitimacy

The importance of legitimacy for a stable political order has long been recognized, and has become increasingly prominent in discussions of statebuilding among both scholars and practitioners.[15] A state is legitimate if its power is justified in terms of normative beliefs shared by both those who exercise power and those over whom power is exercised— beliefs about the ends toward which a state exercises power, but also about the way in which power should be exercised, and in which those who exercise power should be chosen.[16] According to Rodney Barker, "Legitimacy is precisely the belief in the rightfulness of a state, in its authority to issue commands, so that these commands are obeyed not simply out of fear or self-interest, but because they are believed in some sense to have moral authority because subjects believe they ought to obey."[17] Thus legitimacy is primarily a social phenomenon and is attributed on the basis of judgments about the congruence of the state and its institutions with the beliefs, values, and expectations that provide a justification for its power.

Legitimacy is an important objective of state- and peacebuilding for several reasons. First, if the legitimacy of a state is weak in the eyes of its population or among particular societal groups, they are more likely to refuse to comply with the state's laws and decisions, and more likely to support actors who violently challenge the state. The failure of the state to fulfill the expectations of certain social groups because of corruption or its inability or unwillingness to provide public goods undermines its legitimacy and can lead to rebellions against it. In the case of Sierra Leone, for example, the corruption of the government, the collapse of the education system, and the lack of economic opportunities for young people fueled support for the Revolutionary United Front (RUF) among a marginalized young population at the beginning of the 1991 war.[18] In Côte d'Ivoire, the legitimacy of the state was not only undermined by poor governance but also by the consequence of systematic discrimination against Ivorians of mixed parentage and "foreigners" after 1993, whose grievances then fueled an armed rebellion in 2002.[19]

Second, legitimate state institutions are more likely to be effective in the provision of public services. As Michael Carnahan and Clare Lockhart argue, legitimate states find it easier to collect revenue—a fundamental condition for sustaining the capacity of the state to provide social services and public infrastructure.[20] As the ability of the state to provide such services helps strengthen its legitimacy, Carnahan and Lockhart identify a mutually reinforcing relationship between a state's legitimacy and its effectiveness.

Finally, legitimacy is central to the sustainability of state institutions. Weak legitimacy was at the root of many of the "failed states" in Africa that descended into conflict at the end of the Cold War when their rulers, deprived of financial or military support from the United States or Soviet Union, could no longer contain resistance to their rule through patronage or coercion.[21] This development has been highlighted most dramatically by the cases of Somalia and the DRC. Similarly, if the state institutions that are established or strengthened by international efforts are not considered legitimate by society, they are unlikely to outlast the international presence that sustains them with money (and if necessary, force) for long. To be long-lasting, institutions need to be embedded in the wider normative structures of a society, in order to ensure the local support necessary for their sustainability beyond the international presence.

The legitimacy of a state can be based on different sources. A state's legitimacy vis-à-vis its population depends on the extent to which its core principles reflect the normative beliefs and expectations of this particular community. The normative criteria against which local communities judge the legitimacy claims of a state might differ substantially from those applied by international statebuilders, and in pluralist and divided societies also between different local groups, which in itself can become a source of conflict. Legitimacy can result in a state's ability to promote shared social goals, such as its effectiveness in providing security, economic development, public infrastructure, or social services.[22] It can be procedural, arising from the way in which the state is governed—for example, whether institutions are accountable and relatively transparent, or whether they involve all relevant societal groups in their decision making. Finally, legitimacy can be structural, meaning that the state is legitimate and "becomes a repository of public confidence because it is 'the right organization for the job.'"[23] It is perceived as particularly suited to address particular challenges like guaranteeing security or delivering economic prosperity. The different sources of legitimacy of a particular state depend on contextual factors such as the state's history and sociopolitical structures.

There is therefore no template for what constitutes a legitimate state, and hence no template for building legitimate states. Nonetheless, most statebuilding efforts by international organizations and Western donors have been driven by liberal understandings of state legitimacy.

Statebuilding and Legitimacy

International statebuilding efforts have aimed at building the legitimacy of postconflict states in a range of different ways, but three aspects of statebuilding in particular have been directed toward this end. First, attempts to strengthen the capacity of state institutions to provide public services, and in particular to establish the monopoly of legitimate violence across the state, have aimed at improving the performance of the state to enable it to deliver on its responsibilities under the social contract. Second, the focus on the rule of law, which has become one of the key priorities of postconflict statebuilding, and the related international efforts to address postconflict corruption, have been directed at making the state effective but also more accountable to its citizens, thus strengthening both the output and the procedural legitimacy of the state. Third, statebuilding operations have prioritized the legitimation of the new institutional framework through democratic elections. These legitimation efforts reflect a fundamentally liberal conception of the state, where political authority is based on popular consent, and on an implicit social contract, central to which is the provision of security and public services to society. This understanding of the content of statehood is epitomized by the emerging yet still contested norm that states have a "responsibility to protect" (R2P) their citizens, expressed most clearly by the International Commission on Intervention and State Sovereignty (ICISS) in its report on the R2P concept.[24]

International statebuilding efforts have thus mostly addressed what Kalevi Holsti has called the vertical dimension of legitimacy.[25] Vertical legitimacy establishes the conditions for the right to rule[26]—the social contract between society and the state. It outlines the responsibilities the state takes on in return for its power, and defines the ends toward which it can legitimately use that power. This emphasis on capacity (such as the ability of the state to provide public services) and accountability (for example through democratic institutions) focuses attention on the character of this social contract, on the state's ability to deliver its part of the bargain, and on society's ability to democratically control this stronger state.

This can be contrasted with the horizontal dimension of legitimacy, which emphasizes "the attitudes and practices of individuals and groups within the state toward each other and ultimately to the state that encompasses them."[27] It is thus concerned with the ways in which different groups within society relate to each other, and how these relationships are mediated through the state. International statebuilding efforts have tried to enhance the horizontal legitimacy of the state in different ways. They have used power-sharing institutions to encourage the participation of a wider range of different groups, and to co-opt potential spoilers into state institutions, as in the transitional governments in Burundi, Côte d'Ivoire, the DRC, and Liberia. They have promoted the integration of rebels into the armed forces or state-run militias, in order to extend the reach of the state into social groups and territories it previously did not control. This form of legitimacy involves a complex web of social relations, and horizontal legitimacy claims need to address different audiences with distinct interests. These claims need to be recognized not only by various societal groups but also by the distinct elites leading these groups, who during the conflict might have provided a degree of protection and governance when state institutions were either absent or predatory, and who as a result might make claims on legitimacy that compete with those of the state. However, these efforts to enhance the inclusiveness of a political settlement and of new state institutions have been mostly limited to elites and have neglected civil society and its transformed relationship to the state following conflict.[28] This might be informed by the high priority that statebuilding operations have accorded to stability, as renewed conflict would not only set back any humanitarian and statebuilding gains achieved but also undermine the legitimacy of the international presence.

The practices used to extend the horizontal legitimacy of the state can conflict with the requirements for greater vertical legitimacy. Co-opting different elites into power-sharing institutions, for example, at times involves the tacit acceptance of corruption as the price to pay for their participation in the state structures, thus undermining the capacity of the state to deliver public services in a transparent and effective manner and thus undermining its legitimacy.[29] Efforts to enhance horizontal legitimacy thus tend to create a different kind of state—not a strong, centralized state exercising a monopoly of violence, but a weak state where political authority and control over state resources is parceled out among different parties. Such a fragmented state is undoubtedly less able to promote economic development and establish a monopoly of legitimate violence.

However, the attachment to a state with strong capacity and vertical legitimacy is premised on the assumption that in all countries a society's political life is most effectively organized by formal institutions and that such institutions universally enjoy structural legitimacy. It suggests an understanding of international order where political authority around the world rests on a substantive shared (liberal) normative framework that legitimizes the institutions of both international and domestic order. Whereas in the aftermath of World War II the formal principle of organizing international society—sovereign statehood—was universalized through the decolonization process, statebuilding in the aftermath of the Cold War has promoted the universalization of the substantive elements of the Western conception of liberal statehood, promoting a particular model of organizing political authority domestically. From this perspective, such statebuilding efforts are seen as necessary for the completion of a liberal order.

Without succumbing to moral relativism, such a strong normative consensus remains elusive, challenging the viability of statebuilding efforts that focus solely on the construction of Weberian states. Post-conflict countries are characterized by alternative conceptions of authority and by informal power structures that, having emerged in the context of conflict, interact with formal state structures in complex ways.[30] With regard to African countries, Alex de Waal argues that the prevalence of patrimonial sociocultural rules in many African states suggests that political life should better be understood as a "patrimonial marketplace" where a stable political order is the consequence of the most inclusive "buy-in" of relevant elites,[31] rather than the capacity of formal state structures. When the state is not seen as a neutral arbiter and provider of public goods, interventions geared to strengthen its institutional capacity are perceived as partial and as influencing power balances in favor of those groups who control state institutions, thus "upsetting" the marketplace and making less likely a reasonably stable order that minimizes violence. One of the consequences of the top-down character of liberal statebuilding is therefore that some groups may feel marginalized in the developing political order, and use violence to oppose it in order to maintain their previous social and political positions and privileges.[32]

Reconciling the Tensions in Statebuilding: The Promise of Local Ownership

To reconcile the top-down character of postconflict statebuilding with local needs and conditions, and to resolve some of the tensions between vertical and horizontal legitimation efforts, many commentators have emphasized the importance of local ownership, arguing that, in the words of Jarat Chopra, local ownership constitutes "a minimum standard and a moral imperative."[33] The perceived lack of local ownership has been central to most criticisms of "liberal statebuilding" and its emphasis on the Weberian state and the institutionalization of Western liberal norms, highlighting the limited local involvement in deciding on the character of the new political and social institutions.[34]

Calls for more local ownership have also come from leading statebuilding practitioners, who have attributed the poor record of postconflict statebuilding, in terms of both development and return to conflict, to a lack of local ownership, which they argue would make statebuilding efforts both more effective and sustainable.[35] These arguments are based on three core claims. First, institutions need to reflect relevant social norms to be able to command compliance and to be sustainable. If not, they will be brittle and weak, and unlikely to play a meaningful role in the absence of constant outside support. Local involvement in the design and establishment of institutions is thus said to help with their sustainability and effectiveness.

Second, and related, local ownership allows international statebuilding efforts to draw on local "practical" knowledge, or *metis* in the words of James Scott, to complement the abstract, technical knowledge *(techne)* of outsiders.[36] This makes it more likely that the envisaged political order will reflect the sociocultural rules of a society and provide a better match between the scope of the envisaged state institutions and the available local resources. As Sarah Cliffe and Nick Manning argue, postconflict environments are no *terra nullis* onto which statebuilders can project their institutional visions, and local knowledge can help identify both institutions and practices that are well adapted to local conditions and resources, and structures that are obstacles to reform.[37]

Third, local ownership is thought to help in the building and maintenance of local capacity. As Ashraf Ghani and Clare Lockhart argue, one of the consequences of the structure of the international aid complex is the development of parallel bureaucracies in postconflict countries to implement statebuilding projects.[38] Rather than building capacity, such parallel structures contribute to the "sucking out" of local capacity, in the memorable words of Michael Ignatieff,[39] depriving the state both of financial resources, which are instead channeled through the parallel bureaucracy, and of its most qualified public servants, who instead work for international actors able to pay substantially larger salaries. Although some donors, most notably Britain's Department for International Development (DFID),[40] have recognized this and have increasingly channeled their aid through the budget and state institutions, many major donors continue to direct most of their aid at projects implemented by nonstate actors, replicating the institutions they want to strengthen.

The UN also identifies local ownership as central to the success of its peacebuilding and statebuilding efforts. As stated in the secretary-general's report on peacebuilding:

International support in such complex and rapidly evolving situations is therefore a fundamentally political and often high-risk undertaking. Efforts that bolster the power of unrepresentative leaders, or empower one group at the expense of another, can exacerbate the causes of conflict or create new sources of tension. International actors need to be mindful of these considerations. Local and traditional authorities as well as civil society actors, including marginalized groups, have a critical role to play in bringing multiple voices to the table for early priority-setting and to broaden the sense of ownership around a common vision for the country's future. The full participation of women in these processes is essential, both as victims of the conflict and as important drivers of recovery and development.[41]

Local ownership is thus seen as transformative of key statebuilding relationships, not only of the relationship between local and international actors, but, equally important, of the relationship between communities and local elites, empowering otherwise marginalized groups, giving them voice in the reconstruction process, and involving them in its implementation. As a consequence, local ownership is vested with expectations of emancipation and empowerment—expectations that the concept is inherently unable to fulfill.

Invocations of local ownership of statebuilding processes raise two important questions. First, how is local ownership operationalized in postconflict statebuilding operations? One of the main pathways for local ownership has involved compact mechanisms, such as the UN's integrated peacebuilding strategies and strategic peacebuilding frameworks, or the World Bank's poverty reduction strategy papers, that are based on joint planning and locally led monitoring of program implementation. The aim of these strategies, in the words of Yukio Takasu, former chair of the UN Peacebuilding Commission, is the establishment of "mutual accountability" of local and international actors.[42] Although these mechanisms might involve local actors in decision making and implementation of statebuilding policies, they fall short of establishing meaningful mutual accountability. Ultimately, the international part of the bargain—the financial and institutional support offered by international actors in the context of these frameworks—is not enforceable. Whereas donors can decide to withhold aid if they think that local partners are not fulfilling their responsibilities under such a compact, no such sanctioning mechanism is available to local actors, short of evicting donors from the country. So although there might be accountability, it is neither mutual nor local.

The second question that the concept raises concerns who should exercise ownership. Which local actors should be involved in the design and implementation of statebuilding policies? Postconflict societies are normally very heterogeneous, encompassing groups with diverging interests and capacities to participate in statebuilding. The groups relate to each other, to the state, and to international actors in a wide range of different ways. If substate groups are given ownership of the allocation and distribution of aid, the process bypasses the central state and arguably weakens it further. Does local ownership mean "government ownership," or the extensive involvement of civil society? Should it be limited to formal institutions, or also involve traditional or customary institutions?

In practice, the way in which local ownership has been operationalized in statebuilding operations has often entrenched wartime power structures and inequalities. Key statebuilding policies that aim at increasing local ownership can contribute to empowering particular elites over others rather than contribute to substantive local ownership. Efforts at consultation and co-option into state structures, in particular in the context of transitional institutions that form part of a peace settlement and incorporate the major conflict parties, tend to focus on traditional authorities or wartime leaders who are seen as speaking for particular communities. Substantial development aid in the aftermath of conflicts has tended to empower governing elites at the center, who can use aid to sustain support from key constituencies, and traditional elites locally, who act as gatekeepers controlling the local access to aid.[43] In the absence of functioning state institutions, reconstruction aid is channeled through parallel donor networks and directly to local communities. Often, traditional authorities become involved in the administration and disbursement of this aid, and can use it for patronage, and to enhance their authority vis-à-vis the local population, often exacerbating existing inequalities and marginalizing and alienating other societal groups.[44] In Sierra Leone, for example, humanitarian and development aid was channeled through the Paramount Chiefs, whose rule was reinstated with help of donors despite the grievances with regard to the role the chieftaincy played in causing the civil war. As Monica Das Gupta and her collaborators highlight, local communities are often characterized by substantial inequalities and power imbalances, which complicate collective decision making for the common good and can lead to the capture of aid and development programs by local elites who monopolize their benefits.[45] These policies selectively endow particular elites with outside recognition and legitimacy, as well as access to resources.

For local ownership to have the emancipatory effect identified in the previously cited UN secretary-general's report on peacebuilding, and envisaged by authors such as Chopra, it must go beyond "government ownership" and the co-option of self-appointed local elites. Instead it must involve the participation of a wide and inclusive range of societal groups. This, however, requires not only identification of relevant groups but also establishment of new mechanisms for consultation and participation, beyond existing state institutions and customary local authority structures, which need to be linked to the existing structures of the state and the international presence. In Sierra Leone, the international community pressed hard for decentralization and the establishment of local governance structures to that end, but although these structures have been established at the district and local levels, their competences overlap with the traditional authority of the Paramount Chiefs, with whom they compete in regard to both function and control over resources. As Béatrice Pouligny has argued, many attempts of donors and international organizations to involve "civil society" have ignored the great diversity of local civil society actors and the fact that "some sectors of society are just as discredited as the state,"[46] and have underestimated the importance of the "state-society relationship" for "rebuilding a state apparatus and re-creating a new society out of the ashes of conflict."[47]

Enabling such emancipatory ownership requires that international actors not only make fundamentally political judgments about existing local structures and the character of political and social relationships in postconflict countries but also that they intervene deeply in the internal affairs of postconflict societies. It requires of international statebuilders a role that is fundamentally at odds with general understandings of local ownership that focus on self-determination and the "light footprint" of such interventions that should result from the greater role of local actors in the statebuilding process. Local ownership thus fails to resolve the inherent tensions of postconflict statebuilding, and arguably even adds to them. The intrusive involvement necessary to obtain emancipatory ownership is unlikely to find much support among governments who are concerned about shoring up their own position in a postwar order, and who are supported in their resistance by a restrictive interpretation of sovereignty and nonintervention shared by most developing countries. Indeed, local elites have used references to local ownership to argue for a more limited and less intrusive role for international statebuilding actors,[48] both to accelerate the transition toward local rule and to strengthen their own power domestically. Thus in Burundi in 2006, the newly elected government called for less foreign interference in its affairs and asked the UN to close its peacekeeping operation in the country (ONUB) and limit its involvement to economic development activities. At the same time, it tried to strengthen its position through patronage and by clamping down on the press.[49] The choices by international actors that emancipatory ownership requires are likely to challenge the legitimacy of the statebuilding efforts and of the ownership arrangements.[50]

Legitimacy contributes to the sustainability and effectiveness of the state. I have argued in this chapter that central to contemporary statebuilding practices is the legitimation of new state institutions, both vertically (by enhancing the capacity and accountability of institutions) and horizontally (through their inclusiveness). From such a perspective, it becomes clear that many of the apparent tensions between peacebuilding and statebuilding are actually inherent in contemporary statebuilding practices. They are particularly pronounced in countries where the state has traditionally been shallow, has coexisted and competed with alternative substate authority structures, and has played only a limited role in organizing social relations. Many postconflict countries in Africa fall into this category.

I have further argued that a greater emphasis on local ownership, which has become so central to the rhetoric of the UN, major donors, and recipient countries that it constitutes part of the new orthodoxy of statebuilding, fails to resolve these tensions. Instead, the actual donor practices associated with pursuing local ownership have often focused on government ownership, strengthened and entrenched wartime elites, and done little to change state-society relations in ways that create the conditions for sustainable peace and development.

Underlying these tensions are inherently political and moral questions about self-determination, the substantive content of sovereignty, and the nature of the state. These are questions that cannot be resolved by tinkering with the processes of state- and peacebuilding, by increasing the available resources, or by enhancing coordination among international actors. This, however, has been the focus of recent institutional innovations in postconflict statebuilding, for example through the UN Peacebuilding Commission or the "Whole of Government" approaches by different donors.[51] The presence of such inherent contradictions does not mean that statebuilding should be abandoned as a part of peacebuilding strategies. Instead, greater awareness of such tensions and contradictions, and of the specific character in particular peacebuilding contexts, can help actors to better understand the impact of particular statebuilding policies on the political and economic structures and relationships that shape the possibilities for peace and development in postconflict countries, and can inform the prioritizing of particular statebuilding objectives and activities.

Notes

1. See, for example, Call with Wyeth, eds., *Building States to Build Peace;* Fukuyama, *State-Building;* Ghani and Lockhart, *Fixing Failed States;* Paris, *At War's End.*

2. United Nations, *No Exit without Strategy*, 2.

3. Boutros-Ghali, *Agenda for Peace.*

4. For a similar definition, see Organisation for Economic Cooperation and Development (OECD), *Concepts and Dilemmas of Statebuilding in Fragile Situations*, 14.

5. For a detailed discussion of this issue, see Zaum, *Sovereignty Paradox.*

6. Call, "Building States to Build Peace?"

7. Hartzell and Hoddie, *Crafting Peace.*

8. See, for example, Curtis, "South African Approach to Peacebuilding in the Great Lakes Region of Africa."

9. See Clapham in this volume, and Menkhaus, "Governance without Government in Somalia."

10. Papagianni, "Participation and State Legitimation," 51.

11. See, for example, Roger Mac Ginty's discussion about the differences between "Western" and "Islamic" statebuilding in "Reconstructing Post-War Lebanon."

12. See, for example, De Waal, "Mission without End?"

13. There has been recognition of this problem as reflected in an OECD Expert Statebuilding Panel Policy Guidance Note for Western Donors to support endogenous statebuilding processes in 2009. See OECD, *Supporting Statebuilding in Situations of Conflict and Fragility, Policy Guidance.*

14. Paris, *At War's End;* Zaum, *Sovereignty Paradox.*

15. See, for example, Call with Wyeth, *Building States to Build Peace;* Ghani and Lockhart, *Fixing Failed States;* Del Castillo, *Rebuilding War-Torn States;* Zaum, *Sovereignty Paradox.* Sergio Vieira de Mello emphasized the importance of legitimacy for the success of UN state- and peacebuilding operations in his unpublished review of his experience as Special Representative of the Secretary-General (SRSG) in Kosovo and East Timor, "How Not to Run a Country: Lessons for the UN from Kosovo and East Timor" (on file with the author of this chapter).

16. This definition follows Beetham, *Legitimation of Power*, 11.

17. Barker, *Political Legitimacy and the State*, 11.

18. Olonisakin, *Peacekeeping in Sierra Leone*, 12–13. See also Keen, *Conflict and Collusion in Sierra Leone*.

19. Adebajo, "Security Council and Three Wars in West Africa," 470.

20. Carnahan and Lockhart, "Peacebuilding and Public Finance."

21. Herbst, "Responding to State Failure in Africa."

22. This is also known as "output legitimacy." See Scharpf, *Governing Europe;* Thakur, "Developing Countries and the Intervention-Sovereignty Debate."

23. Suchman, "Managing Legitimacy," 581.

24. International Commission on Intervention and State Sovereignty, *Responsibility to Protect*. See also United Nations, *Implementing the Responsibility to Protect*.

25. Holsti, *State, War, and the State of War*. See also Englebert, *State Legitimacy and Development in Africa*.

26. Holsti, *State, War, and the State of War*, 97.

27. Ibid., 87.

28. See Pouligny, "Civil Society and Post-Conflict Peacebuilding."

29. See, for example, Cheng and Zaum, eds., *Corruption and Post-Conflict Peacebuilding*. See also Keen in this volume.

30. See, for example, Cramer, *Civil War Is Not a Stupid Thing*.

31. De Waal, "Mission without End?"

32. Reno, "Bottom-Up Statebuilding?" 144.

33. Chopra, "Building State Failure in East Timor," 999.

34. See, for example, Chandler, *Empire in Denial;* Chopra, "UN's Kingdom in East Timor"; Jahn, "Tragedy of Liberal Diplomacy." pts. 1–2.

35. Ghani and Lockhart, *Fixing Failed States;* Del Castillo, *Rebuilding War-Torn States*.

36. Scott, *Seeing Like a State*.

37. Cliffe and Manning, "Practical Approaches to Building State Institutions," 165.

38. Ghani and Lockhart, *Fixing Failed States*.

39. Cited in Fukuyama, *State-Building*, 139.

40. Department for International Development (DFID), *Providing Budget Support to Developing Countries*.

41. United Nations, *Report of the Secretary-General on Peacebuilding in the Immediate Aftermath of Conflict*, June 11, 2009.

42. Takasu, "Note for Effective Joint Endeavours for Peacebuilding."

43. Kahler, "Aid and State Building"; Nakaya, *Aid in Post Conflict (Non) State Building*.

44. Jackson, "Chiefs, Money, and Politicians."

45. Das Gupta, Grandvoinnet, and Romani, *Fostering Community-Driven Development*.

46. Pouligny, "Civil Society and Post-Conflict Peacebuilding," 500.

47. Ibid., 496.

48. For a discussion of such a strategic use of self-determination norms and local ownership discourses, see Zaum, "Norms and Politics of Exit."

49. International Crisis Group, *Burundi*.

50. Paris and Sisk, "Conclusion: Confronting the Contradictions," 305.

51. See Patrick and Brown, *Greater Than the Sum of Its Parts?*

THREE

Security Sector Governance and Peacebuilding

EBOE HUTCHFUL

SECURITY SECTOR GOVERNANCE (SSG) IS ACCEPTED AS A CRITICAL
element in state- and peacebuilding.[1] This focus is justified, not least, by
the intimate link between breakdowns of SSG and the genesis of conflict. Repression and abuses by security institutions have often laid the
foundation or provided the trigger for broad-based, even catastrophic,
conflict. There have, however, been few postconflict contexts in Africa
where building institutions of security governance, as opposed to stabilizing and normalizing the security situation, has been a priority. South
Africa, and to a much more limited extent Sierra Leone, are exceptions. Engagement with justice reform and rule of law issues, essential
underpinnings of democratic SSG, has also been weak in postconflict
contexts. Nevertheless, conflict can have, and has had, transformational
effects on SSG, offering incentives to take reform of security practices
and governance more seriously. Conflict produces a proliferation of structures of force that render effective security governance imperative, but
challenging, in a context of widespread institutional weakness. Security
sector governance will need to be recast in a more inclusive direction if
it is to capture the diversity of institutions, such as private, nonformal,
and community-based, involved in delivery of security and justice on
the ground.

The chapter provides an analysis of three case studies of security sector reform in the context of postconflict reconstruction—Liberia, Sierra
Leone, and South Africa—and asks why SSG has been a lower priority
in Liberia and Sierra Leone compared to South Africa. Various factors

may explain this apparent paradox, the central argument being that ownership was present in the case of South Africa, but largely absent in the other two. Ownership becomes important in light of the complex and sometimes competing objectives that characterize contemporary peacebuilding under international auspices.

SSG in the African Context

Reconstructing SSG in the aftermath of conflict can be a particularly daunting task, but it is nevertheless important to locate the issue in broader context. There has been prioritization of building "effective" security and state systems rather than *accountable* security and state systems founded on due process and rule of law—in other words, security sector reform (SSR) rather than security sector governance. Security governance in Africa as a whole has remained largely resistant to democratization. Military coups continue to be part of the political dynamic in a number of countries, such as Mauritania, Madagascar, Guinea, and Guinea-Bissau. There are also more insidious forms of "securitization" that transcend even the most "democratic" regimes in Africa, mainly related to weak rule of law environments. In sum, even where "coups" are not obviously on the agenda, security services have remained the mainstay of "softer," civilianized autocracies masquerading under the guise of electoral democracy. The AU dream of a community of democratic states with accountable and democratically governed security forces remains, at best, some way in the future.[2]

Dynamics and Challenges of Force in Postconflict Contexts

Conflict and postconflict situations give rise to particularly complex landscapes of force, arising from the need to prosecute multilayered, crosscutting conflicts. These encompass international forces; governmental military, paramilitary, and other security elements; warlords, rebel forces, and various militia with equally variable loyalties; community, traditional, and local security organs; and private (commercial) security. "Asymmetric" or "composite" forces are a recognized feature of counterinsurgency and civil wars,[3] with both states and nonstate actors driven by various and incongruent calculations and motivations.[4] Although not necessarily generating or controlling private security companies, states both strong and weak have sought to tap into private commercial as well as noncommercial circuits of violence for their own interests.[5] Due to this multitiered and often intertwined landscape of force, it is necessary to reframe security governance in countries emerging from conflict. SSG should be recast in a more inclusive direction, to capture the diversity of institutions—formal, private, nonformal, and community-based—involved in the actual delivery of security and justice on the ground. The "security sector" itself will have to be defined more broadly. Given that "security" is a critical variable that has to be in place for postconflict reconstruction to proceed, effective security governance is all the more imperative.

The concept of "inclusive security governance" involves full participation by all four dimensions of the "civil"—executive (policy), legislative (oversight), judicial (rule of law), and civil society and media (oversight and critical input).[6] It incorporates local, communal, and customary organs of security and justice, and ensures adequate representation along the lines of gender, race, and ethnicity. It also bases security on justice and rule of law (rights or rule-based security) in both the formal and the informal or nonformal (customary) spheres, and thus connects SSR with justice reform.

Potential Transformational Impact of Conflict

There are two hopeful signs for societies grappling with legacies of conflict. First, conflict has had transformational effects on the management of security, most notably the emergence of regional conflict prevention and management structures and corresponding notions of collective security. This reflects the realization that security problems cannot be adequately addressed within national borders, although these developments have not been unambiguously positive. Regional economic communities (RECs) such as ECOWAS, the Southern African Development Community (SADC), the Economic Community of Central African States (ECCAS), and the Intergovernmental Authority on Development (IGAD) have been increasingly diverted away from their original focus on economic integration and development, toward grappling with pressing issues of security. Given their lopsided capabilities, regional organizations have become more attuned to managing conflict instead of addressing broader and longer-term peacebuilding needs. Regional security complexes potentially pose their own accountability issues, and the emergence of "collective security" regimes has not necessarily transformed the way individual states deal with security issues or produced greater harmonization of national security systems. Regional states therefore remain a mishmash of idiosyncratic security arrangements.

Second, postconflict situations may provide strong motivation to overhaul the way security is produced, managed, and governed.[7] Hence, one of the paradoxes of postconflict SSR is that it can potentially result in countries leapfrogging other transitional political systems as well as more stable countries in security sector development and overall quality of security governance. It is not entirely surprising then, that among the countries with "best practice" security sector legal frameworks are countries such as South Africa, and to a lesser extent Sierra Leone, that recently emerged from conflict.

Rebuilding SSG in the Context of Peacebuilding

The reconstruction of the security services and the manner in which they are managed and governed are central to any peacebuilding strategy.[8] Indeed, issues of security and security governance have been at the core of the peace negotiations and subsequent peace agreements in Africa. In some contexts, such as South Africa and the Democratic Republic of the Congo (DRC), the provisions of peace agreements with regard to security governance have been further elaborated and entrenched in a new constitution. In others, for example Liberia and Sierra Leone, the old constitution has been retained but security sector policy and legislation have been overhauled. SSR and SSG exercises would appear to be logically related, and indeed a recent publication on security governance in West Africa has suggested, correctly, that "if democratic governance of the security sector defines the goal, then SSR represents the primary tool toward this objective."[9] Professional and operationally effective security forces are an essential foundation for improved security governance and improved delivery, but there are few security services in Africa that qualify.

Nonetheless, security sector governance has not frequently been a priority in approaches to peacebuilding, and security sector reform overall has had a poor track record in building institutions of accountability and oversight. This may not be manifest from the rhetoric, but it is nevertheless amply obvious from actual programming.[10] There are many reasons for this lack of focus on SSG,[11] on the part of both the donor community and national governments, including:

- References to civil oversight and good governance
  dimensions of security sector reform are relatively scarce
  in UN mission mandates, as is funding for the necessary

capacity building.[12] In addition, UN field officers often have scant appreciation of the principles of democratic governance of security,[13] and in any case the limited duration of the typical UN mission virtually precludes engagement with longer-term institutional reforms.

- National governments may not regard SSG as a priority.

- Legislatures and civil society, which constitute the usual sources of pressure for reforms in security governance, may have little effective voice or capacity to ensure that such reforms are actually delivered.

Capacity building for security oversight, limited as it is, has been largely left to independent national and international nongovernmental organizations (NGOs)[14] and in some cases, to quasi-official organizations, such as the National Democratic Institute (NDI), which has a long record of legislative engagement.

Building the capacity of security management organs has not been a consistent peacebuilding priority either. Civilian capacity to manage security issues is limited, and many civilian security ministries, particularly those of defense and interior, function as administrative adjuncts of the services rather than as instruments of political and policy direction. Similarly, strategic-level institutions such as national security councils may be more focused on operational issues and less on the development and implementation of a strategic framework. Since these functions, properly performed, also feed into and drive the work of parliament, their absence means that oversight is correspondingly compromised. With the exception of South Africa and to a lesser extent Sierra Leone, efforts to build the capacity of security management organs have been relatively scarce and selective.

The Peacebuilding "Gap": SSR, Rule of Law, and Transitional Justice

Another peacebuilding problem is the weak connection between security reforms and justice reforms. SSR assumes a context of rule of law. It is only when security agents are fully subject to the laws of the land, and only when all citizens have unimpeded access to due process and equal protection of the law, that security will be delivered accountably, equitably, and with due respect for human rights. SSR and the development of the rule of law should ideally occur in tandem, since systems of administration of justice are likely to be casualties of war. Weak rule of law contexts have largely been responsible for progression from a "war economy" to "criminal enterprise" in the aftermath of conflict.

Yet a consistent feature of peacebuilding is the low priority and lack of detailed attention often given to justice reform and rule of law issues. Indeed, as Call and colleagues have sought to demonstrate, justice reform has been particularly flawed in postconflict contexts.[15] There are several reasons for this:

- Formal rule of law traditions are weak or nonexistent in many transitional societies.

- Administration of justice is not seen as a priority by political authorities, in part because of the perception that a powerful judiciary constrains the power of government.

- Transformation of dysfunctional justice mechanisms is difficult and complex.

A similar chasm exists between SSR and transitional justice. Societies emerging from conflict face significant and interlocking imperatives of security sector reform and transitional justice. Many activities that occur under the rubric of "transitional justice" have profound direct or indirect impacts on SSR. These include the role of truth and reconciliation commissions in exposing abusive security institutions or personnel, curbing impunity, and building consensus for institutional reform and transformation, as well as underscoring the need for a culture of transparency, scrutiny, and oversight. At the same time, SSR serves the purposes of transitional justice by minimizing the possibility that human rights abuses by security institutions will occur in the future. However, transitional justice and SSR have tended to operate as separate streams of activity largely isolated from each other, with the exception of limited activities such as vetting of security forces by such organizations as the International Center for Transitional Justice (ICTJ).

Reaching beyond the State: Nonstate Providers of Security

The current approach of the international donor community to SSR reflects Westphalian assumptions: (a) the state is the sole or preeminent provider of security, and (b) it possesses sufficient control (or monopoly) over the means of coercion, in addition to the requisite legitimacy and other resources. This "Westphalian" perspective fails to recognize the state's complicated relationship with private organs of violence. This is manifested in two polar instances of the privatization of force: private military and security organizations, on the one hand, and community-based security and justice institutions, on the other. The delivery of security and justice in fragile and postconflict states is thus multilayered, involving multiple and overlapping (even competing) structures and agents, including "traditional" and "customary" institutions such as village chiefs, councils of elders, women's associations, age groups, and secret societies. There is some evidence that, where the state is weak, traditional, customary, or informal institutions may be responsible for up to 80 percent of service delivery at the local level. Indeed, a recent survey in the DRC found that only 11 percent of the population felt protected by the police. Community organs such as the *bashingantahe* in Burundi, the *gacaca* courts in Rwanda, and the *xeer* and *sharia* courts in Somalia may play important roles. Their resilience may provide a modicum of social order and security.[16] Indeed, they sometimes enjoy a legitimacy that is not always extended to the formal justice sector, which may be viewed as alien, inaccessible, and corrupt. Whereas the (imported) state may be fractured and in crisis, these local organs may sometimes function with relative coherence and vitality.[17] The single-minded focus on state organs of security in postconflict reconstruction thus ignores the realities on the ground in many postconflict countries.

Reframing the Paradigm: Prioritizing Local and Community Organs

On the basis of this analysis, a different peacebuilding paradigm is beginning to emerge. If the focus of pro-poor security and justice delivery is local customary and nonformal structures rather than the state, then it is at this level that reconstruction must begin. The key to expanding access to security and justice in fragile states is not so much in trying to create or re-create the imagined edifices of the Westphalian state, including rebuilding courthouses that no one would use, but focusing on community-level institutions that meet the test of the "four As": accessibility, accountability, appropriateness, and affordability. The approach would build from the ground up rather than the other way around, while still ensuring that the formal system itself is able to handle appeals as well as the range of responsibilities associated with a modern justice system. This would call for dialogue or negotiation to bridge the cleavage between customary institutions and nonstate networks, on the one hand, and the state sphere, on the other.[18]

Top-down, statist, and donor-driven approaches tend to mean that communities are relegated to the role of spectators and consumers of SSR, with little influence over the way reform is shaped or implemented. This is changing to some extent with the wider role that civil society organizations are playing in the process, whether through their own initiative or through limited donor support. However, civil society does not necessarily mean wider community involvement. The current emphasis on "local needs policing," "community policing," or "police de proximité" suggests some community involvement, but these practices do not guarantee adequate levels of local ownership and governance. At the same time, given the diversity of community and customary institutions in character and scale, careful mapping is required to determine appropriate mechanisms of inclusive governance.[19] This is not straightforward, as the processes and outcomes are bound to be contested.

Addressing the Gender Gap

Security is a highly gendered activity. Given the prevalence of sexual and gender-based violence in postconflict contexts, such as the DRC, Liberia, Sierra Leone, Burundi, South Africa, and Angola, special attention needs to be paid to the "gender gap" in reforming security delivery and governance at the level of local communities and at the state level. Although there are national variations, women on the whole have been underrepresented in the security services, as well as in security governance and management bodies and positions.[20] For instance, there was not more than a single female member in most of the nine parliamentary security committees surveyed in the ECOWAS area.[21] The dramatic exception was the defense committee in Liberia's House of Representatives, which was chaired by a woman. Although the gender balance appeared to improve at the level of parliamentary staff, men still dominated in terms of both numbers and seniority. There is some evidence, nevertheless, that conflict has sometimes improved the formal standing of women in legislatures generally and on parliamentary security committees in particular, for instance in South Africa and Rwanda.

Another manifestation of the gendered nature of (in)security is the failure of authorities and security agencies to take sexual and gender-based violence and other threats against women and people of different sexual orientation more seriously. "Engendering security" must go beyond elevating the presence and visibility of "women" in security institutions, toward eliminating the deeply cultural and ideological notion that some are qualified by their gender to be "protectors" and to enjoy the power and social preeminence associated with that role, while others are cast as congenitally "helpless" and in need of "protection," or as "booty" available for the taking by valorous warriors.[22]

The Case Studies:
Three Approaches to SSG in the Aftermath of Conflict

Experiences with security sector reform and governance in the aftermath of conflict have been far from unilinear, and lessons drawn from any particular case are not necessarily applicable elsewhere. As with peacebuilding generally, such experiences are highly contextual and path-dependent. This point can be demonstrated from the cases of security reforms and peacebuilding in Liberia, Sierra Leone, and South Africa. Each of these three countries has undergone (and is still undergoing) various degrees of security and justice reforms. Only the South African SSR process prioritized issues of SSG across the board. This difference can be traced to the issue of ownership, although "ownership" itself will have to be understood as a contested process involving complex local and national political dynamics, changing over time.

In sum, "ownership" refers to the ability to set and drive the agenda for security and justice reform. National ownership entails at least three related properties: (1) the commitment of national authorities and actors to a national vision of reform; (2) the technical and institutional capacity to manage a complex change process, or to manage those local and external actors entrusted with implementing or supporting such a change process, consistent with the national vision; and (3) the ability to mobilize indigenous resources to drive and sustain the reform process, complementing resources from bilateral and multilateral partners.

These elements existed in large measure in South Africa but not in Sierra Leone or Liberia. The peace agreements that launched security and justice reforms in the three countries already foreshadowed issues of "ownership." In both Liberia and Sierra Leone, peace negotiations involved a lead facilitating role for external regional and international parties. The resulting peace agreements assumed a prominent, even dominant, role for external actors in national reconstruction and peacebuilding. Control over SSR was initially ceded to bilateral and international partners. In the case of Liberia, clauses in the 2003 Comprehensive Peace Agreement (CPA) specifically requested the US to take a lead in restructuring the Armed Forces of Liberia (AFL). In the case of Sierra Leone, although the peace agreement itself did not cede as much control to foreigners, the tendency to identify national salvation with intervention by foreigners coincided with the UK taking a lead. As discussed below, these lead bilateral partners in turn placed their stamp on SSR in divergent ways, with important consequences for national ownership.

In South Africa, by contrast, the peace negotiations occurred entirely and directly between indigenous forces and political groups, with the representatives of the African National Congress (ANC) and the apartheid government as principals, but also involving a wide range of social movements and civil society organizations such as the United Democratic Front (UDF) and the churches. A UN observer mission would be subsequently dispatched to monitor the resulting peace agreement. Additionally, the South African National Peace Accord (NPA), in contrast to both the Lomé and Accra Accords, which were seen as finished documents, was designed as a prolegomena to the "real" national dialogue, opening the door to further, more localized and intensive negotiations and compromises between a wider range of local parties and actors.

The particular context at the end of the conflict is key to understanding security sector trajectories. Both Sierra Leone and Liberia, already two of the poorest societies in the world, emerged from devastating civil wars with widespread destruction of national institutions and infrastructure, with no clear victor or politically dominant force, and relatively weak civil societies. The postconflict governments that emerged had not themselves been direct parties to the war, but were confronted with the fact that formal security institutions had been destroyed or deeply discredited by war. The immediate policy objective was to promote security institutions that would meet minimal security needs of the population while protecting the fragile governments that emerged from the peace process. In both cases, reform was further undermined by the failure of the elected regimes that emerged from the peace process (Taylor in Liberia, Kabbah in Sierra Leone) to take SSR seriously, a factor that contributed to their downfall, as well as to the return to war.[23] "Civil control," "democratic security governance," and "oversight and accountability" were either notably missing or very much secondary priorities, to be pursued later.[24]

Even so, important differences emerged in the two West African countries, in large part attributable to the different styles of their main international partners, the United Kingdom in Sierra Leone and the United States in Liberia. In Sierra Leone, the United Nations Mission in Sierra Leone (UNAMSIL) and the International Military Assistance Training Team (IMATT) was combined with a robust bilateral lead by the UK government. After the unprecedented military action to dislodge the Revolutionary United Front (RUF) and its Armed Forces Revolutionary Council (AFRC) allies, the UK government stressed long-term partnership with the government of Sierra Leone, and comprehensive and ambitious governance and institutional reforms of security and justice based on evolving strategic policy frameworks. However, severely limited local capacity resulted in a tendency to draw on overly complex British models, such as in the design of the defense ministry, as well as the external management of many of these programs. This undermined local ownership. Also, notwithstanding references to "comprehensive and integrated SSR," initial reforms in Sierra Leone were selective and piecemeal, focusing on developing the national security office, technically a secretariat of the national security council but in reality functioning more as the nerve center for managing security and intelligence, the defense ministry, and the national armed forces and, to a lesser extent, the police.[25] Much more modest (and less coherent) attention was directed to the justice sector.

Nevertheless, there appeared to be a definite learning process, on the part of both the government of Sierra Leone and the UK agencies. Over time, the growing emphasis on local ownership and consultation, for example through the Security Sector Review of 2005, and attention to institution building and developing local capacity for strategic planning, led to a gradual rebalancing of this uneven partnership, with the Sierra Leonean government and local officials becoming more assertive.[26] The creation of the Office of National Security was the focal point for strategic planning and coordination of SSR. This was dramatically different from the situation in Liberia, where no priority was given to reforming the multitude of overlapping national security and intelligence organs inherited from the previous regime, and where central security management and coordination organs took time to emerge.[27] In Sierra Leone, regular and candid program reviews, principally through the UK's Department for International Development (DFID) "output to purpose" reviews, helped provide transparency and periodic corrections. Sierra

Leone has also been a pioneer in Africa in integrating SSR as one of the core elements of its poverty reduction strategy, although this may not be enough to generate dynamism for social and economic transformation.

Strikingly in Sierra Leone, though, although policy documents and pronouncements emphasized organs of accountability and parliamentary oversight, few resources were committed specifically to developing the capacity for oversight, especially in defense and internal and presidential affairs, as a component of SSR. The parliamentary oversight committees (respectively Presidential Affairs and Defence, and Internal Affairs and Local Government) suffered, like others in the Sierra Leone parliament, from a long list of constraints.[28] Very modest training has been rendered by two NGOs, Conciliation Resources and the Center for Development and Security Analysis.

In Liberia, the approach adopted by the US was markedly different. It focused narrowly on military reform and the rebuilding of the AFL, with limited support to police reform. The United Nations Mission in Liberia (UNMIL) took on the responsibility of rebuilding the Liberian National Police and the justice sector, though with markedly limited resources, as the original UN mandate had failed to provide the necessary resources. This focus left a large proportion of the amorphous security sector, such as the fire service, border security, and the many intelligence organs inherited from the regimes of Charles Taylor and his predecessors, out of the reform process, including those institutions specifically identified for reform in the CPA. The initial actions of the US diverged from the provisions of the CPA in two ways. The first was the decision, without consultation with the principals, to abolish and dismantle the AFL and rebuild it from the ground up, rather than "restructuring" it as provided in the accord.[29] The second was the privatization of the contract through Dyncorp International and Pacific Architects and Engineers, rather than relying on two sovereign partners, the governments of the United States and Liberia, envisaged by the CPA. This arrangement had considerable implications for transparency and accountability, since Dyncorp insisted that its contractual obligations were not with the government of Liberia but with the US State Department. To compound the confusion, Dyncorp widely adopted the term "SSR" to refer to its AFL recruitment and reform activities, contributing to a widespread misconception of the nature and scope of SSR. On the positive side, rebuilding the AFL from the ground up, including an exceptionally rigorous vetting process, created public legitimacy for the new force.[30]

An associated problem in Liberia was the initial lack of needs assessment or strategy framework on which to base decisions about the emerging security architecture. The initial targets in the rebuilding of the AFL, with a projected force of 2,000, were based on fiscal and cost considerations by the US embassy with little public consultation. A broad strategic assessment was not conducted until early 2006, when it was undertaken by the RAND Corporation, a foreign agency contracted by the US government, allegedly without the knowledge and participation of much of the Liberian security sector. The RAND Corporation's report directly questioned the logic that underlay the "SSR" initiatives, including the basis for deciding force levels in both the military and police, concluding that these were completely inadequate for the national security needs of Liberia. It also pointed out the lack of coherence and synergy between military and police reform planning objectives, the absence of a national security architecture to give coherence to the reforms, and the relatively narrow scope of "SSR," in particular the failure to address the issue of the large number of security organs inherited from the former regime.[31]

External actors in Liberia were not inclined to public consultation. A culture of consultation did not exist within the government of Liberia either, especially in relation to decisions on national security. At a workshop in Monrovia in November 2005, the Governance Reform Commission (later "Governance Commission") announced the launch of national consultations as the basis for the national security strategy, but externals complained that it would interfere with their timelines. Thus "external support . . . led to a decision-making process" that was "heavily top-down and, during the initial years, lacked consultation with local people"[32] and, under the lead of the US, gave rise to "overwhelming concern about lack of ownership of the SSR process in the country."[33] It was not until January 2008 that a draft national security policy framework was developed by the Governance Commission.

Scenarios unfolded quite differently in South Africa. That country emerged from its liberation war with three striking characteristics: the relatively unscathed and sophisticated structures of the apartheid state and economy; a popular liberation movement (the ANC) with a democratic mandate, around which a new state and new social relations could be conceived; and a vocal civil society and grassroots protest movement, constituting an independent democratic voice, committed as much to supporting the ANC as extracting accountability from the party, and regarding itself fully as a partner—not a bystander or political satrap—in the process of transformation. The immediate reality, however, was that the ANC had inherited a formidable war machine and security establishment that had been deployed against it over several decades of savage repression, and which remained intact, even in the face of the political defeat of apartheid. There was full awareness within the ANC and among its allies that subordinating the apartheid war machine to political control, particularly in the context of the early fears of a military coup by the right wing, was vital to the democratic transition and to its own political survival. This altered the political dynamics: "transformation," not "rebuilding," was the battle-cry. Thus the ANC had both the undoubted political imperative and, as it turned out, the political will to pursue transformation. The immediate and essential instrument for this was "civil" or "democratic control" of the defense and security establishments, along with an overhaul of the justice system. In the context of African SSR, this was a unique departure. And importantly, the South African NPA anticipated that this act of "transformation" would be executed by internal and not external agents.

The Roles of Civil Society Organizations and Parliament

Civil society and the legislature play essential roles in creating participation and broad-based ownership, and avoiding top-down SSR processes captured by the government and external actors. The political space for playing these roles differed in the three contexts.

In Liberia, government and external actors were less supportive of civil society engagement and parliamentary oversight. Civil society organizations and rebel groups played a commanding role in the Accra negotiations and hence in the drafting of the CPA, but their influence receded once the agreement was in place. The UN took over police reform, and the US government took over military reform. Although a civil society "SSR Working Group" was created, its influence in shaping SSR was marginal, in part due to a lack of effective organization and also because external agencies did not encourage local involvement. Similarly, the legislature was initially marginalized. The paradox is that the Liberian constitution grants extensive powers to Congress and its three defense and security committees, reflected in Article 34 of the 1986 constitution and the standing rules of both the House and Senate. However, the legislature had historically been dominated by the presidency and ruling party, and there was tight executive control of all matters relating to security. Although the various acts establishing the security agencies provided that all appointments by the president were subject to the approval and consent of the Liberian Senate, this provision was never seriously applied. To aggravate the situation, many parliamentarians were inexperienced, with low levels of education, and there was a high turnover among the members of the parliament.[34] The body was largely denied access to information relating to the military and police reform programs. There was no formal capacity building for the legislature as a component of the SSR programming. Training for the three defense and security committees was undertaken informally by a consortium of nonprofits consisting of the African Security Sector Network (ASSN), the Conflict Security and Development Group at Kings College, and the Geneva Centre for the Democratic Control of Armed Forces, which collaborated with the Governance Commission and the Civil Society SSR Working Group to develop a national security strategy framework and a limited review of the security sector.[35]

Nevertheless, the Liberian Congress has become increasingly assertive over time.[36] It rejected the draft Defense Act, successfully demanding that the government redraft it. It has summoned security personnel as well as the Ministers of Defence, and Justice, and the National Security Advisor for hearings on security and defense matters. This growing empowerment of the legislature reflects not only the salutary effects of the seminars conducted by the ASSN and partners, but also a weak presidency and the fact that, for the first time, the president's party did not command a majority in Congress.[37]

In Sierra Leone, though civil society organizations were active in peace campaigns, their role in both the Abidjan and Lomé negotiations was less direct than in Liberia. Nevertheless, under UK leadership, a large role was conceived for civil society participation in reconstruction and in the creation of structures of democratic accountability following the Lomé Peace Agreement. In contrast to Liberia, the formal SSR policy and strategy framework in Sierra Leone assigned roles to civil society organizations. In particular, the 2005 Security Sector Review and the mantra that accompanied it—"security is everyone's business"—afforded an opportunity for the participation of civil society. The new security paradigm sought to build civil society organizations into the security architecture, by recognizing their contribution to border security, intelligence, early warning, and conflict management and reconciliation. It granted civil society organizations limited representation on the district and provisional security committees, as well as on local policing partnership boards, and representation in the justice sector through a civil society coordinating group.

Nevertheless, one study argues that, for several reasons, "relations between the security sector and civil society are still limited" in Sierra Leone.[38] Sierra Leone emerged from the civil war with a legacy of bitterness and division between civil society, particularly women and youth, on the one hand, and the security sector, on the other, leading to initial reluctance to engage SSR. Deep suspicions inherited from the civil war, including negative national self-perception and self-confidence, also inhibited community action. Furthermore, strong UK bilateral leadership, high-profile involvement of the UN and IMATT, and the large number of international NGOs in the country, initially eroded possibilities for national ownership.

In South Africa, in contrast to both Sierra Leone and Liberia, security sector transformation was driven to an unprecedented degree by a popular coalition of civil society and community organizations, labor and church groups, NGOs, and elected representatives. The framework for political activism was the deliberate development of a substantial policy and legal framework for defense, public safety and security, and intelligence. The early hallmarks were a 1996 defense white paper and a 1998 defense review. The processes that led to the evolution of the defense white paper and defense review were highly participatory and consultative, drawing heavily on the work of civilian defense and other experts.[39] Nevertheless, parliamentary defense and safety and security committees and the Joint Standing Defence Committee retained a central role. Unlike in Liberia and Sierra Leone, the South African parliament engaged the reform process, carving out a muscular role for itself in developing a robust legal and policy framework for the security sector, monitoring the process and the institutions to ensure accountability, collaborating closely with defense officials, outside experts, and social movements, and relaying unmistakable messages about how seriously it intended to take its oversight role. The intervention of the South African parliament fundamentally reshaped the emergent debate in the defense arena, departing from the usual narrow "SSR" to the broader "SSG."[40] This meant deepening the concept beyond civilian control, usually meaning decision making by civilian government officials, to one of democratic control, in which a wide range of social actors could participate. At the same time, the transparency and performance of parliament itself was closely monitored, with extensive dissemination of debates, discussions, and proposed legislation on public media, and monitoring by civil society groups, including the parliamentary monitoring group.

The key to the process was the political leadership of the African National Congress, which included many powerful members of parliament of both genders. The ANC brought undoubted political capital and legitimacy. As an armed liberation organization, the party understood the dialectics of force. Ideologically too, the movement had a tradition of civilian political control of its military wing. Finally, there was a unique combination of "elite pacting" and popular mobilization, in which the ANC itself was a member of a complex alliance that included the Communist Party of South Africa, civil society organizations, labor unions, and churches. Yet the ANC as a party lacked intellectual and other resources required for security sector transformation. Arguably, in this curious paradox of hegemony and political weakness, the political leadership of the ANC *governed* rather than drove the security sector process. The multicentered and fractious alliance resulted in a broad-based ownership that made it impossible for the ANC to unilaterally impose its will or dictate the direction of events.

The Issue of Ownership

These three cases thus highlight key differences in terms of "ownership" in security sector reform processes. The conventional view is that ownership is essential to the success of SSR (as one publication pithily put it, "no ownership, no commitment").[41] Yet "ownership"—the ability to envisage, design, fund, manage, and oversee the implementation of a complex and multidimensional security reform process—is not a yardstick easily met by states and societies emerging from conflict. At the minimum, ownership implies the ability to make strategic decisions and deliver a clear set of priorities, and to ensure that these are respected by all partners, external and internal. However, even this minimalist definition may not settle the issue. As we have seen, ownership will remain mortgaged as long as countries are unable or unwilling to commit meaningful resources of their own to the process. External actors exercise an eventual veto through what they will or will not fund; hence, it is not unusual for crucial elements in independently crafted national "strategic plans" to wilt on the vine while less favored projects attract funding. What may be presented as "national priorities" have often been shaped by foreknowledge of what the donors would or would not fund.

It is not surprising then that SSR has been dominated by two contrasting narratives. On the one hand, there is the perception that SSR is donor-driven and, on the other, that reforming governments are unable to articulate a clear vision or set of priorities.[42] Both of these positions undoubtedly contain an element of truth. External support may be required to help build capacity in conflict-affected countries to enable these countries to exercise ownership. Unfortunately, this is contradicted by prevailing donor practices, such as an emphasis on quick results and outputs rather than outcomes, on piecemeal project funding rather than program funding, and on short-term rather than longer-term funding horizons, that undercut any possibility of meaningful ownership. Given the asymmetric relations that characterize SSR, "ownership" as a very concept will remain ambiguous and elusive.

Ownership is contested in a second and much more local sense. At home as much as in the global arena, "security" resides very much in the eyes of the beholder. Our individual and collective notions of security tend to be influenced by geography, social location, gender, ethnicity, and class. The question of whose ownership remains pertinent. It is thus essential that "national ownership" not be reduced to "government ownership." References to "national authorities" in the prevailing discourse on ownership are worrisome signs that this is commonly the case. Second, it is important that what is defined as security or security policy be the result of an inclusive national discussion that allows the concept and its ownership to be broadly shared. Indeed, wherever such a national debate/consultation has been undertaken, more democratic understandings of security have emerged that depart from previous militarized notions shaped by securocrats and the political class.[43] Transparent and accountable security governance is an essential counterpart to, and reflection of, notions of democratic security, but this requires ownership as a precondition.

Here too, though, ownership should not be reduced to a snapshot in time. Ownership by its very nature will remain contested and dynamic. The political space to debate security may begin to shrink; new security "threats," new forces and new actors may emerge that erode or force a rethink of the earlier consensus, and concerns about accountability and governance may yield to more muscular notions of crime control.[44]

"Ownership" was important to the respective outcomes in security sector reform in Liberia, Sierra Leone, and South Africa precisely because the multilayered discourse on global security merges a number of international and local security concerns, and it is not always clear whose interests are actually being served. In this discourse, "failing," or "fragile" states are seen not only as dangerous to their own citizens but also as a threat to international order (as defined by its most powerful states), fostering terrorism, international criminal rings, human and drug trafficking, piracy, money laundering, and a litany of other evils. It is for this reason that the European Defense and Security Policy and the US National Security Strategy point to Africa and other "fragile" states in the south as "security threats" and mandate muscular intervention mechanisms. The wholesale rush into "SSR" that we are witnessing today is not entirely altruistic.

Thus in the conflicting agendas that tend to characterize peacebuilding by the international community, "ownership" becomes crucial in determining not only who has voice but also who benefits from the complex calculations around peacebuilding and SSR. Such "ownership" meant, for instance, that indigenous forces in South Africa, not international actors, determined the objectives and modalities of peacebuilding. The protracted and sensitive negotiations that characterized the South African process would have been inconceivable if the international community, with its short attention span and multiple agendas, had been in command. The analytical intelligence and deep local knowledge brought to bear on the technical negotiations in the various committees and working groups were also important. The commitment to "ownership" did not come cheap, however. It meant hard policy and legal work, dedicated institution building, and substantial national resources.

National ownership, despite its benefits, is not a panacea, let alone a guarantee of inclusiveness. Security sector *governance,* much more than *reform,* explicitly requires the incorporation of the entire security sector, formal and informal, state and nonstate, modern and customary, into the scope of governance and regulation. It also requires full participation in the process by all the constitutionally mandated organs—the executive (policy), legislative (oversight), judicial (rule of law), and civil society and media (oversight and critical input). In the African context, it must build on traditional and customary practices for delivering and regulating security and justice; a robust connection between security on the one hand and justice and rule of law on the other; and "representivity" on the basis of gender, race, and ethnicity.

This is, of course, a highly idealized picture, particularly in countries emerging from conflict. The reality is that, for the foreseeable future, the provision of security is likely to remain segmented and take the form of hybrid security regimes, or what Eric Scheye calls "pragmatic realism."[45] This need not be a problem, as long as systems are increasingly infused with common norms, procedures, and human rights protections. Post-conflict peacebuilding provides an opportunity as well as an incentive to move toward greater synthesis and reconciliation. Nevertheless, one cannot avoid a note of skepticism. The problem with this "different strokes for different folks" approach is that nonstate systems may provide improved access to security and justice at the local level without providing the ability to curb the excesses of state institutions at the national level. Further, dependence on customary forums for justice is often a mark of vulnerability (and even exclusion), rather than empowerment. As one analysis of Sierra Leone's justice sector reforms argues, "Rural people are marginalized from and fearful of the structures of government and the formal legal system."[46]

A second concern relates to possible reversals. For instance, South Africa's efforts to create an inclusive and democratic system of security governance may be in jeopardy. As the African National Congress has moved to consolidate governmental power, more orthodox security dynamics have gradually begun to assert themselves, particularly in the aftermath of a defense procurement scandal, suspected involvement of the National Prosecution Authority ("Scorpions"), and the intelligence establishment in the intraparty intrigues within the ANC (the renaming of the "Ministry of Intelligence Services" as the "Ministry of State Security" has a chilling familiarity about it), and the increasingly strident "war on crime" rhetoric. Security sector reform is increasingly viewed through the prism of these wider contestations. Similarly, there is a diminished prominence of parliament and civil society. Although this may be explained in part by the routinization of governmental functions and the shift from legislation to implementation, and by the more technocratic style of government under Thabo Mbeki,[47] it arguably also points to possible shifts in the postapartheid political trajectory.

Another concern relates to "inclusivity." As the ANC has tried to fall in line with the dominant neoclassical global economic paradigm, while promoting black capitalist economic empowerment, it has been less successful in addressing mass poverty and deprivation, conflicts over land, violent crime, sexual abuse, vigilantism, "instant justice," witchcraft trials, and xenophobia that have tended to characterize the townships, squatter camps, and rural areas of South Africa. Hence, South African citizens, depending on who and where they are, are exposed to two very different worlds of "security" and "justice."

Notes

1. For a definition, see, for example, Hänggi, "Security Sector Reform." The security sector comprises all state and nonstate institutions, groups, organizations, and individuals that have a role in security and justice provision, including core security actors (armed forces, police, gendarmeries, paramilitary forces, presidential guards, intelligence and security services, coast guards, border guards, customs authorities, and reserve and local security units); security management and oversight bodies (the executive; national security advisory bodies; the legislature and legislative select committees; ministries of defense, internal affairs, foreign affairs; customary and traditional authorities; financial management bodies; and civil society organizations); justice and rule of law institutions (the judiciary, justice ministries, prisons, criminal investigation and prosecution services, human rights commissions and ombudsmen, and customary and traditional justice systems); and nonstatutory security forces (liberation armies, guerilla armies, private security companies, and political-party militias).

2. In addition to outlawing coups and "illegal changes of government," regional protocols such as the 2001 "Protocol on Democracy and Good Governance" of the Economic Community of West African States give a powerful impetus to democratic governance of security.

3. Many examples of such "asymmetric" forces can be found across the world in a variety of conflict contexts. In Africa, these include the alliances between the Sudanese armed forces and the "janjaweed" in Darfur; between the Congolese army and the "Mai Mai" rebels in the eastern DRC; and between the armed forces of the Republic of Sierra Leone (RSL) and the "kamajors." In the last case, the situation was further complicated by the fact that some soldiers of the RSL armed forces also defected to fight—often covertly—alongside the rebels. In the macabre wit that often accompanied the civil war in Sierra Leone, these were tagged "sobels," soldiers by day and rebels by night.

4. Preeminently for states, these include the need for force multipliers, tactical flexibility, and the political credibility and acceptance that local and indigenous forces bring to the table. See Byman, "Friends Like These"; Cassidy, "Long Small War."

5. See Thomson, *Mercenaries, Pirates, and Sovereigns.* African equivalents include the entanglement of the government of Sierra Leone with Executive Outcomes, and President Sirleaf-Johnson of Liberia inviting vigilante groups to assist with crime control in Monrovia and outlying districts.

6. This goes beyond the usual African meaning of "civilian government," or what I call "executive civilism," to denote the usually authoritarian mode of control of security by presidential cliques.

7. Unfortunately, given the weak rule of law context, they may also give strong incentives to use force to preserve impunity and war economies. One determining factor is how the operational capability of security and law enforcement is synthesized with the building of capable governance and justice mechanisms. Not all of this occurs in the state or formal sector. Community-level mechanisms may play a crucial and even more immediate role in securing both security and justice.

8. The country reports of the International Crisis Group (ICG) provide useful tracking of these efforts and provide evidence of the extent to which deficits in SSG can aggravate conflict and complicate peacebuilding.

9. Bryden, N'Diaye, and Olonisakin, eds., *Challenges of Security Sector Governance in West Africa*, 7.

10. Rees, *Security Sector Reform (SSR) and Peace Operations.*

11. The DRC, by contrast, has a large external and internal accountability component—the so-called Security Sector Accountability and Police Reform Programme (SSAPR) funded by DFID—as part of its SSR program. Yet weak political support, decades of neglect of the parliament, and lack of a sense of national ownership make the outcome uncertain at best. This is in contrast to SSR programming in Eastern Europe and the Balkans, where the North Atlantic Treaty Organization (NATO) through its Partnership for Peace, the Organization for Security and Cooperation in Europe (OSCE), and the European Union (EU) have tried to address issues of civil management and oversight of the military and (more tepidly) police and border security.

12. Hänggi and Scherrer, *Towards a Common UN Approach to Security Sector Reform;* Rees, *Security Sector Reform.*

13. Nicola Dahrendorf, referring to DDR/SSR officers in the United Nations Organization Mission in the Democratic Republic of the Congo (MONUC), in "MONUC and the Relevance of Coherent Mandates."

14. Examples of these are Conciliation Resources in Sierra Leone and the African Security Sector Network (ASSN) in Liberia.

15. Call, ed., *Constructing Justice and Security after War*, 395.

16. See, for instance, Thorne, "Rule of Law through Imperfect Bodies?"; Hill, Temin, and Pacholek, "Building Security Where There Is No Security."

17. For instance, research on conflict management in Guinea-Bissau points to the extraordinary vitality of local social and political institutions and processes of conflict management, involving diverse community organizations operating under different local rules. See "Local Strategies of Conflict Management in Guinea-Bissau," the report on collaborative research conducted by Bayreuth University and the Instituto Nacional de Estudos e Pesquisa (INEP) in Guinea-Bissau, funded by the Volkswagen Foundation.

18. One of the most challenging recent statements of this viewpoint may be found in Scheye, *Pragmatic Realism in Justice and Security Development.*

19. Sierra Leone's decentralized national security management system, modeled on a similar system in Ghana, and involving district and provincial authorities, attempts to engage chiefs and traditional authorities.

20. The extent of this is shown in evidence-based research by Women Peace and Security Network-Africa (WIPSEN-Africa) and the Geneva Centre for the Democratic Control of Armed Forces (DCAF) in West Africa. In particular, WIPSEN's recent survey of security institutions in Côte d'Ivoire carried out collaboratively with the UNDP speaks to how women, even while in the forces, continue to internalize gendered notions of the division of labor in security, such as the notion that actual combat is only for men. WIPSEN and UNDP, "Gender Assessment of Security Sector Institutions in West Africa."

21. African Security Dialogue and Research, "Feasibility and Needs Assessment of ECOWAS Parliaments."

22. Tracy Fitzsimmons expresses this sentiment more widely: "Too often, those responsible for constructing a domestic security system include one or two powerful, pro-women ideas, that is, changing divorce laws, allowing women to enter the police force,

offering psychological counseling to rape survivors. But without gendering the entire system, each of these changes makes very little impact." Fitzsimmons, "Engendering Justice and Security after War," 362.

23. In the case of Liberia, the security arrangements were molded by President Charles Taylor; the officers were drawn primarily from the ranks of his fighters and intended very much to be the praetorian guard of the regime, contrary to the understandings reached in the peace agreement.

24. It is not unusual to encounter the argument that effective operational forces must be put in place and the security situation normalized *before* worrying about institutions of accountability and oversight. For this notion of "sequencing" in the case of Burundi and Sierra Leone respectively, see Powell, *Security Sector Reform and Protection of Civilians in Burundi;* and Hewlett-Bolton, "Aiming at Holistic Approaches to Justice Sector Development." This argument is flawed, since it is precisely the absence of such organs of accountability and oversight that has led to abuses and nonperformance by security institutions in the past, and is responsible for the many documented cases of misconduct and fraud that have often characterized reconstruction operations, not least by US forces in Iraq and Afghanistan.

25. By contrast, key ministries like Internal Affairs (responsible for oversight of the police, prison service, immigration department) received little assistance and were described repeatedly in Sierra Leone Security Sector Reform Programme (SILSEP) reviews as "dysfunctional" and totally ineffective, with the result that "the [police] continue to operate within an accountability vacuum and other important departments receive inadequate policy or funding oversight." Biesheuvel, Hamilton-Baillie, and Wilson, *Sierra Leone Security Sector Reform Programme,* 17.

26. By the conclusion of SILSEP III, even though overall capacity building remained selective and confined to a limited number of institutions, Sierra Leonean government officials increasingly "owned" the conceptualization, design, and operationalization of SSR. They reversed earlier "imported" models that had proved inappropriate to local conditions, and became more independent and even critical of UK advice and practices. The SILSEP III review team reported as follows: "In our meeting with key SLMOD civilian and military staff, with no UK advisers present, we saw a self-confident, civilian-led team with a clear and well-coordinated line of argument. Their criticism of the UK input was couched in terms that we might once have used against them: lack of audit, poor communication, failure to learn lessons among others. Irrespective of whether the criticisms are justified, they show that the principles of accountability, civilian leadership, good management and acceptance of responsibility are being successfully transferred to local ownership." Biesheuvel, Hamilton-Baillie, and Wilson, *Sierra Leone Security Sector Reform Programme,* 1.

27. The closest approximation in Liberia was an SSR Task Force, comprising representatives from UNMIL, UNDP, ECOWAS, the US embassy, civil society (in the form of a "Civil Society SSR Working Group"), Liberian parliamentarians and government officials, and the Governance Commission (previously Governance Reform Commission), which was tasked after 2005 with developing a national security strategy and, against some resistance from donors and government officials, launched a broad public consultation process on SSR. The GC was seen in the CPA as a key instrument in reforming governance across the board, but was hampered by its ambitious mandate, lack of resources and uncertain government support. Another body was the Security Pillar, comprising all the major internal and external stakeholders involved in security matters in the country, and meeting regularly under the chairmanship of the minister of defense.

28. Jaye and Gbla, "Parliamentary Needs Assessment"; Hanson-Alp, "Civil Society's Role in Sierra Leone's Reform Process." See also Biesheuvel, Hamilton-Baillie, and Wilson, *Sierra Leone Security Sector Reform Programme*, 12.

29. This was a questionable tactic that had been attempted in Iraq and had dangerous consequences in throwing thousands of former fighters into the ranks of the unemployed.

30. Jaye, "Liberia"; ICG, *Liberia.*

31. Gompert et al., *Making Liberia Safe*

32. Jaye, "Liberia," 18.

33. Jaye, "Assessment Report on Security Sector Reform in Liberia."

34. Jaye, "Liberia," 12.

35. Jaye, "Expert Networks and Security Sector Transformation."

36. Ibid., 14. Comments by Senator Mobutu Nyankpen, of the Senate Committee on Defense, at a workshop for Ghanaian legislators in Elmina, Ghana, March 16, 2010.

37. Ibid.

38. Hanson-Alp, "Civil Society's Role in Sierra Leone's Reform Process."

39. As Elrena van der Spuys observes, "Academics and researchers played particularly important roles in setting the agenda for police reform." Van der Spuys, "Changing Fortunes of Police Accountability," 6.

40. According to Len Le Roux: "Whereas the defence establishment soon after April 1994 wanted to focus the defence transformation debate on issues of roles and force design (the size and shape of the military), the political leadership as particularly manifested in the JSCD [Joint Standing Committee on Defense], demanded that the issues of governance be addressed before they would entertain discussions on issues of roles, postures and hardware." Le Roux, "Governance of Defence in South Africa."

41. Nathan, *No Ownership, No Commitment.*

42. At a UN conference that I facilitated in New York in 2010, Burundi was cited as an example of this "disability." See United Nations, "African Perspectives on Security Sector Reform." However, other reports suggest that the Burundians were merely trying to gauge what donors would agree (or not) to fund before deciding what to present as their own "priorities."

43. Examples are the Defence Reviews in South Africa and Uganda, the Security Sector Review in Sierra Leone, and the popular consultations in Liberia. The revisions in South African security doctrine were particularly far-reaching.

44. An instance being recent attitudes to policing and anti-crime policy in South Africa.

45. Scheye, *Pragmatic Realism in Justice and Security Development.*

46. Open Society Justice Initiative, *Between Law and Society,* 19.

47. See Schoeman, "South Africa."

The Limits of Disarmament, Demobilization, and Reintegration

PAUL OMACH

THE DISARMAMENT, DEMOBILIZATION, AND REINTEGRATION (DDR) of ex-combatants and others associated with armed groups is widely accepted as an integral part of peacebuilding. International policy on DDR is influenced by the neoliberal discourse on the nexus of security and development. This discourse perceives poverty, underdevelopment, and poor governance to be at the root of violent crime and conflict. According to this view, conflict undermines development and deepens poverty, which in turn creates conditions for further conflict. This view justifies a range of programs to prevent, resolve, and recover from conflict, including DDR programs. Yet these programs, including DDR, can also be seen as tools to exert control over the global South and maintain global order.[1]

The desire to prevent conflicts and create stable conditions for sustainable development has led to the increased involvement of actors such as the United Nations (UN), the World Bank, international development agencies, donor states, and nongovernmental organizations (NGOs) in supporting DDR programs. Support has been given to an array of national and local actors, including signatories of peace agreements, national governments, provincial and local authorities, communities where the ex-combatants are reintegrated, and the combatants and others associated with armed forces. The contexts of such programs have varied. For instance, DDR has been implemented during peace support operations as part of peace settlements to end civil wars. It has been carried out as part of peacebuilding processes where wars ended in decisive military victory by one of the parties. DDR has also occurred in countries deemed to be at "peace," as part of military downsizing, normally as part of macroeconomic and institutional reforms supported by the International Monetary Fund (IMF) and World Bank. The objective of many of these programs is to reduce military expenditure and redirect resources to social sectors and poverty eradication programs.

Although the question of what to do about former combatants after the end of war is a question asked throughout history, more formal DDR programs have increased in number and in scope, and they have evolved over time. In 2004–5, UN agencies, departments, funds, and programs drafted a series of integrated DDR standards (IDDRS)—a set of policies, guidelines, and procedures for the planning, implementation, and monitoring of DDR programs in peacekeeping and nonpeacekeeping contexts. The IDDRS guidelines and their rather technocratic "to do" lists are adaptable to specific conflicts and country contexts to ensure that DDR processes are flexible.[2] Outcomes have varied, and determining the success of DDR programs has not been easy, given the complexity of conflict contexts and the conflicting objectives of the actors involved. Often, however, there is a disconnect between the approaches of the various international and national actors who use DDR programs for purposes that are at times out of touch with local realities and incompatible with peacebuilding. This makes it vital to analyze the approaches of various actors engaged in DDR, and to understand formal and informal processes of dealing with ex-combatants, including those that are rooted in traditional practices.

This chapter examines the discourse and practice of DDR programs in sub-Saharan Africa. It highlights the complex interplay of conflict contexts, DDR objectives, and the diverse approaches of various actors to DDR processes, despite the UN's seemingly universal integrated standards. The chapter begins by examining the different elements of DDR, and why DDR is considered vital for peacebuilding. It next analyzes the various actors engaged in DDR, their different approaches, and the coordination of their activities, and then examines the unintended consequences and shortcomings of DDR programs, including difficulties in defining the term *ex-combatant*. The chapter argues that local contexts matter for DDR programs, but they are often overlooked. The different interests and understandings that guide DDR processes are subject to reworking in different local contexts and this may lead to unintended consequences for peacebuilding.

DDR Programs and Peacebuilding

As the name indicates, there are three main components of DDR.[3] Disarmament is "the collection, documentation, control and disposal of small arms, ammunition, explosives and light and heavy weapons of combatants and often also of the civilian population" and also includes "the development of responsible arms management programs."[4] Disarmament is considered essential for reducing the number of weapons in society and restoring the monopoly of the means of violence to the state. The large number of weapons that remain after conflict is considered to be a threat to stability during the transition from war to peace and regional security.

There are many approaches to disarmament. It can be coercive, consensual and voluntary, or induced. Coercive disarmament is normally carried out after military victory by one of the parties, such as in Uganda in 1986, Rwanda in 1994, and Angola in 2003.[5] Members of the defeated force are forced to surrender their weapons. However, there is a risk that the defeated army may hide some of its weapons. Where disarmament is carried out as part of a peace settlement, the process is normally voluntary, such as in Mozambique in the 1990s. There is reliance on the goodwill and mutual confidence of the parties and on their commitment to the larger peace process. If the parties are not sure that the peace process will hold, the temptation to conceal some of their weapons will be strong. For example, it was widely observed that after the 1990 Bicesse agreement between the Movement for the Liberation of Angola (MPLA) government and National Union for the Total Liberation of Angola (UNITA) rebels, UNITA surrendered only obsolete weapons due to lack of faith in the agreement.[6]

Inducements may be offered to combatants to surrender their arms. This may take the form of gun "buybacks" through offers of cash or vouchers that can later be exchanged for cash.[7] This mechanism was used during DDR programs in Liberia in 2003 and Côte d'Ivoire in 2004. In Liberia, eligibility for benefits was determined by the willingness to hand over weapons. This was later expanded to include those who could produce at least 150 rounds of ammunition.[8] Alternatively, "weapons for development" programs, through which weapons are collected in exchange for development goods or services, are sometimes used.[9] Such programs were initiated in Mali in mid-1997 following a peace settlement between the government and rebel forces. Collected weapons were exchanged for development goods and services such as schools, roads, and wells.[10]

The cash inducement approach to disarmament has generated debate and controversy. Critics argue that the approach carries the risk of creating other security problems. If there are porous borders, weak controls, interlinked conflicts in neighboring countries, or endemic gun cultures, cash incentives may foment the illegal arms trade.[11] In Liberia, for instance, there was a large gap between the number of combatants who disarmed and the number of weapons collected, estimated at about one gun per four fighters, as weapons found their way to conflict zones in neighboring Côte d'Ivoire.[12]

The demobilization of ex-combatants entails reducing the size of armed forces, and in some cases dissolving opposition forces and integrating them into regular armed forces.[13] The process typically involves a survey of combatants; an assessment of their needs; medical examinations; assembly, counseling, and orientating; and discharging and transporting former combatants and their dependents to their former communities of origin or to their preferred destinations.[14] The demobilized become ex-combatants and may receive some form of assistance to facilitate transition to civilian life. This reinsertion assistance constitutes a "transitional safety net" to cover basic needs of ex-combatants and their families and may take the form of cash or kind, including clothing, food, shelter construction materials, and health services.[15]

Reintegration is a long-term process that takes place on multiple social, political, and economic levels.[16] Reintegration programs sometimes address the psychological impact of conflict on ex-combatants. In some cases, ex-combatants are traumatized by the brutal experiences of conflict and may experience depression, drug and alcohol abuse, violent behavior, or even suicide. In this regard, particular attention toward children affected by conflict is often seen as vital.[17] Reintegration involves the acceptance of former combatants and their families by the host community, as well as their engagement in productive livelihoods as civilians.[18] More recently, there have been efforts to ensure that support for ex-combatants does not create a feeling of unfair reward among other members of the community, which might generate discontent and undermine the peacebuilding process. According to Kees Kingma, rural people in Zimbabwe resented the demobilization and resettlement assistance given to ex-combatants and their dependents.[19] Group and community-based programs that benefit entire communities have sometimes been seen as more suitable, as they promote social reintegration and reconciliation.[20]

Since the late 1980s, DDR programs have become an integral component of international peacebuilding.[21] They have been regularly promoted by multilateral donors in the transition from war to peace, since they are seen to constitute a central element in security and development–oriented interventions.[22] International policy discourse on DDR views the often large number of former combatants who have no clear source of livelihood, alongside the widespread availability of weapons, as potential threats to stability in societies emerging from conflict. The "idleness" of ex-combatants is considered to be a source of violent crimes and insecurity. As Robert Muggah has observed, "The 'post-conflict' period is not as safe and secure as generally believed. Armed violence, particularly committed by ex-soldiers and informal militia, can reach epidemic proportions in the shadows of a ceasefire."[23] DDR of ex-combatants is thus viewed as essential in establishing favorable conditions for sustainable peace, recovery, and development.[24]

Sometimes DDR is viewed as a bridge between security and development. Then UN Secretary-General Boutros Boutros-Ghali, in his 1994 report *An Agenda for Development,* acknowledged the links between stability, recovery, and long-term development. He argued that development "cannot proceed in societies where military concerns are at or near the centre of life."[25] Emphasis on the reciprocal link between peace and development can also be seen in the development aid and foreign policies of international development agencies, Western donor states, and NGOs. These actors support DDR programs to address security problems associated with surplus soldiers and militias in societies emerging from conflicts, reduce expenditures on defense, to reduce fiscal deficits, and rechannel resources to social sector and poverty eradication programs.

In Africa, pressure on governments to implement neoliberal reforms or structural adjustment programs (SAPs), in exchange for foreign aid, created opportunities for the implementation of DDR programs. DDR was seen by many bilateral and multilateral donors such as the World Bank as an instrument to help rebuild the economic foundations for growth and development. A number of countries carried out DDR programs in the context of peacekeeping operations to end civil wars and to create conditions for sustainable security and development where conflicts had already ended. For instance, DDR programs were implemented in Namibia beginning in mid-1989, Angola between 1991 and 1992, Mozambique between 1992 and 1994,

Uganda from 1992 to 1995, Ethiopia in 1992, Eritrea beginning in 1993, South Africa after the April 1994 elections, and Zimbabwe after the 1979 Lancaster House Agreement.[26]

Actors and Approaches

Different global, regional, and local actors are involved in DDR in Africa. Most multilateral agencies and donors consider DDR as part of their overall framework for liberal reform, although different actors emphasize different DDR components. For instance, the World Bank has limited itself to demobilization and reintegration; it has not ventured into disarmament because its mandate prohibits it from engagement with militaries. The World Bank's Multi-Country Demobilization and Reintegration Programme (MDRP), and the Multi-Donor Trust Fund, are illustrative. The MDRP was implemented from 2002 to 2009 to support the demobilization and reintegration of former combatants in the Great Lakes and Central Africa region. At its height, it targeted approximately 300,000 ex-combatants in seven countries: Angola, Burundi, the Central African Republic, the Democratic Republic of the Congo (DRC), the Republic of the Congo, Rwanda, and Uganda.[27] The MDRP and Multi-Donor Trust Fund were designed such that contributions of the various donors, UN agencies, and NGOs would be based on their "respective comparative advantages," thus differing from country to country. The World Bank's contribution to the MDRP amounted to 30 percent of overall cost, but it funded only national programs.[28] Similarly, the United States Agency for International Development (USAID), which has supported DDR in Angola, Ethiopia, Mozambique, and Uganda, among other countries, has also confined itself to demobilization and reintegration, since USAID is prohibited from providing support to foreign militaries.[29]

Multilateral agencies and donors often collaborate with the African Union (AU) and subregional organizations in implementing DDR programs. For instance, the African Union Mission in Burundi (AMIB), deployed in April 2003, was mandated to support disarmament and demobilization and advise on reintegration. Although it achieved little, AMIB was a "holding operation" for the deployment of the United Nations Operation in Burundi (ONUB) in June 2004.[30] National governments and local NGOs also facilitate and support some components of DDR programs. For instance, in Liberia, following the peace agreement of August 18, 2004, the government established a national commission, comprising representatives of the warring parties, the Economic Community of West African States (ECOWAS), and the African Union, among others, to oversee the DDR process in the country.[31]

Local actors such as civil society–based organizations, including NGOs, cultural, traditional, and religious organizations, also facilitate DDR programs. In northern Uganda, even without a formal government initiative, the Gulu Support the Children—a local NGO, Ker Kal Kwaro—the Acholi Cultural Institution, Acholi Religious Leaders Peace Initiative and Caritas office in Gulu Archdiocese, among others have engaged in ad hoc reintegration processes since the 1990s. The initiatives of these organizations were given formal recognition in the Amnesty Act (2001) and the Government Peace Recovery and Development Plan, which was launched in October 2007 and implemented in July 2008.[32]

The global, regional, and local actors engaged in DDR programs have different goals and mandates, varying from the minimalist goal of improving security to a maximalist one of creating opportunities for development. Determining success is difficult, because of the lack of agreed-on measures. There is no agreement on whether to take a short-term view of success and focus on immediate outcomes or a long-term view that focuses on the ability of programs to provide sustainable peace and liberal development. Some actors, notably those engaged in humanitarian activities such as emergency assistance, take a minimalist and pragmatic view of DDR. The United Nations, for instance, tends to view DDR as serving a symbolic and confidence-building purpose.[33] Success is measured by the collection of weapons and the control and pacification of ex-combatants, so that the peace process is not disrupted. Other actors, like the World Bank and development agencies, lean toward a maximalist understanding of DDR as a means to create conditions for social peace and liberal development.[34]

However, although reference is often made to the goals of creating sustainable peace and development, resources devoted to DDR programs and immediate objectives tend to reflect short-term goals. A long-term perspective would mean that success is difficult to attain. The actual costs of DDR are also often very high. For instance, the cost of the MDRP was estimated at US$500 million. The strategy was designed on the premise that no single donor could address the complexity of DDR issues in the region. As Kingma has observed, "Savings as a result of demobilization are slow in coming and often not as expected."[35]

Coordination between different actors and multiple aspects of DDR programs is problematic because no single clear institutional mechanism exists. Coordination varies, and depends on "capacity and interests of institutions on the ground."[36] If DDR occurs within the context of a peacekeeping mission, typically the UN will coordinate. However, coordination and cooperation of the various agencies within the UN has not been easy. In Mozambique, for instance, the reintegration segment of DDR that was implemented under the UN peacekeeping mission in that country from 1992 to 1994 (UNOMOZ) was overseen by the United Nations Office for Coordination of Humanitarian Affairs (OCHA). It was not integrated with disarmament and demobilization, which were overseen by UNOMOZ and co-coordinated by the Special Representative of the Secretary-General (SRSG). OCHA reported directly to the UN's Department of Humanitarian Affairs in New York.[37] It is on the basis of these types of experiences that the UN developed the IDDRS guidelines to ensure better coordination and integration of DDR. The IDDRS guidelines stress that "the goal should be complete integration at the planning level and in the methods of the various entities."[38]

The implementation of DDR has varied. Some programs are planned and systematically implemented, while others are haphazard and spontaneous. In Uganda, for instance, the demobilization of former National Resistance Army (NRA) soldiers was well planned and systematically implemented according to a World Bank design.[39] The process entailed a baseline survey on the socioeconomic profile of the NRA, a study of opportunity structures for employment that led to a settling-in kit and long-term reintegration design, and the design for implementation structure. The Uganda Veterans Assistance Board was established through an act of parliament to implement the program. Soldiers identified for discharge were provided with discharge certificates, given pre-discharge orientation and "transitional safety net" packages, and transported to the districts of destination. However, in Mozambique and Namibia, the DDR programs were less systematic and not integrated.[40] In Mozambique, disarmament was not clearly specified in the peace agreement, but was implicit and tied to demobilization. The process was also marred by poor implementation, which contributed to the proliferation of weapons.[41] In Namibia, the program was "patchwork" rather than well planned,[42] and the mandate of the UN Transitional Assistance Group was limited to disarmament and demobilization. Reintegration was hastily designed and implemented later by Namibia's independence government and failed to effectively integrate ex-combatants into sustainable civilian livelihoods. The government subsequently implemented reintegration measures after protests by disaffected ex-combatants who had failed to integrate socially and economically into society.

There also tends to be a lack of integration between formal and informal DDR processes. The UN's IDDRS guidelines emphasize national institutions and processes, but this does not include informal processes, which are not even integrated with national DDR processes. Many people who take part in fighting do not go through formal DDR processes. They are not registered and are not entitled to benefits. Many fighters self-demobilize and do not disarm. Armies and guerrilla groups may gradually disintegrate due to low morale or the collapse of command structures, resulting in a large number of unregistered ex-combatants.[43] There are also many former combatants who go through traditional demobilization processes involving rituals embedded in cultural norms. Local communities may regard such rituals as a precondition or a symbol of acceptance into the community. Even ex-combatants who have gone through formal processes may also undergo these rituals. An example is the ritual of stepping on eggs and jumping over branches of olwedo shrubs among the Acholi of northern Uganda.[44] As Kingma has observed, in Uganda and Mozambique, ex-combatants underwent cleansing rituals in order to be accepted into their communities.[45] Such rituals may promote reconciliation and psychological reintegration according to local norms. Formal DDR processes tend to ignore or marginalize these important locally grounded initiatives.

Past experiences suggest that successful DDR requires good planning, effective logistics and management, and substantial resources.[46] In Uganda, where demobilization and reintegration of ex-combatants cost US$42.3 million, donors contributed over 90 percent of the funds.[47] In Liberia, the DDR process was marred by inadequate preparations. Some of the 15,000 peacekeepers of the United Nations Mission in Liberia (UNMIL) were not yet deployed when the DDR program started, and only one of the three cantonment camps was ready. There was also a lack of timely and adequate funding, which contributed to rioting and the suspension of the program to allow for reorganization.[48] A decentralized implementation mechanism for DDR is helpful, since DDR takes place in various parts of a country.

In 1996 the World Bank and other donors introduced a standard template for the demobilization and reintegration of military personnel in Africa, and outlined key factors for successful outcomes.[49] The Bank observed that "political will" is a "fundamental precondition" on which a DDR program needs to be built. Later, the UN's IDDRS guidelines similarly stated that "a genuine commitment of the parties to the process is vital to the success of DDR."[50] The experience of several DDR programs in Africa indicates that the goals of former belligerents may be different from the desires of donors and other international and regional actors. Parties are not always committed to peace. Their commitment may depend on the existence of security guarantees and political opportunities. Without a political solution and a secure environment, the chances of success are limited, as the example of Angola illustrates.[51] Where there is stronger commitment, as was the case in Namibia, there is a greater likelihood of success.[52]

More recently, based on the realization that many DDR interventions "have failed due to their narrow focus and short-term approach,"[53] the UN's IDDRS guidelines have emphasized the integration of security, wider recovery, and development programs. According to the guidelines, peacebuilding should be perceived as complementary to DDR, which should be entrenched in the peace agreement and in the overall national postconflict recovery and reconstruction and development strategy.[54] The guidelines and principles also recognize that context matters—each conflict is unique, and it is not possible to create a blueprint or model that fits all situations.

The IDDRS framework addresses some of the shortcomings of past DDR processes, such as the lack of integration of various components, especially between disarmament and demobilization on the one hand and reintegration on the other, and the lack of linkage with broader peacebuilding efforts. Yet the IDDRS framework assumes that such integration is possible and that outcomes will be favorable, which may not necessarily be the case. The IDDRS guidelines reflect a faith in the guiding framework of DDR—the nexus between security and development.

How and Why the Local Context Matters

Recent ideas about DDR, as expressed in the UN's integrated standards, acknowledge that context is critical. DDR should "be adapted to the unique needs of particular country (and region)."[55] Although there are similarities in the experiences of different countries, models are not necessarily transferable, and there is no universal format for sequencing. Traditional approaches that see DDR as a linear process or "natural continuum," implying that there is a gradual progression from where "disarmament terminates, demobilization begins" to where "demobilization ends, reintegration commences," do not often apply to the much more complex realities of transitions from war to peace.[56]

It does not always make sense to distinguish between the three phases of DDR and to carry out the program in sequence. Rather, activities should be viewed as interdependent and interconnected. Despite the importance attached to disarmament, it does not necessarily have to precede demobilization and reintegration processes or other peacebuilding activities. As Mats Berdal argued, there is no automatic or inherent relationship between disarmament and establishment of security.[57] Put differently, disarmament does not necessarily ensure a total collection of arms, since its importance may be symbolic.[58] There are circumstances during which it may be necessary to postpone the disarmament phase and embark on the reintegration process, especially when combatants are unsure of their security. Parties may hand in fewer arms, or obsolete arms, as was the case during the UN's peacekeeping mission in Mozambique, where "both Frelimo and Renamo ordered that weapons be hidden."[59]

Likewise, pursuing demobilization and reintegration simultaneously may be appropriate in conflicts where there are large numbers of parties and groups. In other situations, it may be necessary to find a political agreement first. Without a peace agreement, fighters have no guarantee that they will not be persecuted, and they will be reluctant to disarm and demobilize. Furthermore, former rebels who surrender their arms may be targeted by their former comrades.[60] Generally, without a well-planned recovery process, the viability of DDR will be questionable. As Mark Knight and Alpaslan Ozerdem have observed, "There is a symbiotic relationship" between peacebuilding and the DDR process. Successful peacebuilding is as important for successful disarmament, demobilization, and reintegration process as DDR is for peacebuilding.[61]

Aside from requiring variation in sequencing, contextual factors mediate the success and failure of DDR efforts in a number of other ways. These include local sociocultural factors, the nature of the state, the nature of the conflict, including the interpretation of the term *combatant,* and the economic context.

Local sociocultural factors may play a role in the outcomes of DDR programs. For instance, local attitudes toward the ownership of arms and toward disarmament may determine whether ex-combatants will be willing to give up their weapons. In weakly institutionalized states that lack capacity to provide security or protect rights, people may consider weapons as valuable tools for personal security and may view them as male "status symbols." In a socioeconomic environment where competition for resources is stiff and opportunities for development and means of livelihood are lacking, weapons are also used for securing economic interests. The symbolic association of weapons with masculinity may have political effects. Specifically, in relation to DDR programs, there may be barriers to effective disarmament through the ways in which masculine identities and roles have become conjoined with weapons possession.[62] In societies where the culture of gun ownership is well entrenched, emphasis should be put on "decommissioning" or ensuring that there are no abuses of guns, rather than on disarmament, which may be impossible to enforce. Failure to acknowledge sociocultural attitudes toward guns has contributed to the failure of various national disarmament programs in the pastoral areas of northeastern Uganda and northern Kenya, and played a role in the failure of DDR in Somalia.[63]

Identities created during times of conflict also have implications for disarmament. Conflict reinforces narrow and violent notions of masculinity where weapons are used as symbols and tools to contest other notions of masculinity. This is reflected in violence and civilian abuse. Chris Dolan's analysis of the conflict in northern Uganda, where abuse and humiliation of civilians by soldiers, militias, and rebels was frequent, is illustrative.[64] This has effects in postconflict societies. Thus, a gendered analysis that addresses the construction of masculinities and reinforces alternative notions of masculinities based on a culture of nonviolence may be important for successful disarmament and sustainable peace.[65]

There are other reasons why local contexts are so important in understanding the limits to DDR for peacebuilding. There may be a disconnect between the donors' DDR goals and national realities. As mentioned, the conceptualization of DDR programs is often guided by donors' strategic goals of liberal reform, stability, and development. Yet many African states lack a domestic political and social consensus over these goals. The military is often central in many African states, and many governments face challenges to their legitimacy and viability. Regimes may therefore rely on the suppression of opponents, the use of force, and political co-optation to remain in power. Leaders may prioritize the drive for military security,[66] sometimes at the expense of economic development, even though official rhetoric may stress development to its donor audience. Massive expansion of armies and internal security and their "operational" costs are central to the actual costs of maintaining security.

In these contested and factionalized states, political, economic, or administrative reform can be severely destabilizing. This makes DDR a sensitive and delicate process because of its relationship with power and security. Parties may agree to carry out DDR because of domestic political considerations or short-term political goals, yet these may be at odds with donor objectives and longer-term visions. For instance, during the early 1990s, the World Bank and other donors supported the demobilization and reintegration program in Uganda, in the context of reducing expenditure on defense and security and shifting resources to social services. The Ugandan government, however, used the program to achieve its short-term political objectives. It embarked on fresh recruitment, recalled some ex-combatants, and increased defense expenditures.[67] Similarly in Ethiopia, the transitional government, after achieving military victory over forces of the Derg in 1991, used its DDR program to control and restrict the movement of defeated Derg soldiers by confining them to transit centers before rapidly demobilizing them.[68]

Another problem is determining who is a combatant and therefore eligible for assistance. In interstate conflicts, combatants are individuals who are members of national armed forces that have an identifiable organization and a clear chain of command. They carry arms openly and conduct operations in accordance with the laws of war.[69] In intrastate conflicts, combatants are individuals who have taken part in fighting on behalf of the parties. Determining what exactly amounts to "taking part in fighting" and who qualifies for ex-combatant status is problematic, as was the case in Liberia, where almost "everybody fought."[70] This is because contemporary intrastate conflicts involve many civilians who carry arms and are somehow involved in fighting when the need arises or on part-time basis. Women and girls are especially unlikely to qualify as combatants if a restrictive definition of combatant is used. Some women may fight for brief periods and return to their communities. Women and girls also participate in conflict in different ways, including caring for the injured. In Zimbabwe and Namibia, female combatants and supporters of armed groups were generally excluded from formal DDR processes.[71] The UN's IDDRS guidelines emphasize the need to assess the roles of women and girls in conflict and to design gender-sensitive DDR programs in conformity with UN Security Council Resolution 1325.[72]

Soldiers and civilians in many African conflicts are therefore not necessarily fundamentally distinct and distinguishable. Given the nature of most African societies and economies, a soldier is very likely to engage in other activities, just like a professor or civil servant may be a part-time trader or farmer. Political and bureaucratic co-optation ensures the integration of the military into civilian life. As John Harbeson observed, civilians and military officers do not deal with each other at arm's length.[73] For example, in Uganda, where demobilization and reintegration exercises were conducted in the 1990s, the NRA soldiers were already an integral part of civilian society, not confined to living in army barracks. They were engaged in local politics, business, farming, and other activities alongside their civilian counterparts. Likewise, rebel armies are often made up of both full-time and part-time soldiers. Some rebel soldiers double as cultivators and traders.

Viewing civilians and soldiers as distinct can lead to the perception that ex-combatants are idle, potentially subversive, and dangerous. Ex-combatants may be associated with crime and the spread of disease, especially HIV/AIDS. As Lalli Metsola and Henning Melber's analysis of the ex-combatants of Namibia's South West Africa People's Organization (SWAPO) indicates, these individuals are perceived not as active agents, but as subjects in need of corrective action and reintegration assistance.[74] As Alex Vines argues, this view is contentious. He cites a study by the Refugee Studies Programme showing that in Maputo, the capital of Mozambique, there is little evidence to link former soldiers with armed crime.[75]

There is also a common misconception among donors that when ex-combatants are provided with skills and training, this will facilitate their reintegration into civilian society. This assumption overlooks the nature of the economy in many African societies that are emerging from conflict. Many states that suffer from intrastate conflicts have weak economic and political institutions with limited employment opportunities. There is therefore a risk of training people for jobs that do not exist. In Mozambique, for instance, expectations that agriculture would facilitate the reintegration of ex-combatants in the Zambezian region went unrealized, due to the collapse of agriculture, land shortage, and unavailability of goods in the rural areas. There were few employment opportunities for ex-combatants, let alone civilians.[76]

Thus the overall economic context for DDR should not be overlooked. Most postconflict reintegration efforts are undertaken without donor support, and ex-combatants and communities carry the heaviest burden of reintegration.[77] If there are multiple opportunities for sustainable livelihoods, ex-combatants are easily reintegrated in the economy. In Uganda, which is often cited as a successful story of demobilization and reintegration, ex-combatants received only token assistance from donors. Reintegration of ex-combatants was facilitated by the steady recovery of the economy, and support from family and community.

The regional context is also significant as many African armed conflicts are highly interconnected at the local, national, regional, and global levels. This creates a wave of security interdependence or formations where arms and combatants move across porous state boundaries with ease. Most DDR initiatives focus on national programs and are funded through bilateral cooperation, yet "regional conflict formations" mean that the conflicts, and therefore peacebuilding, are linked. For instance, the Great Lakes regional conflict formation, encompassing conflicts in Burundi, the Central African Republic, the DRC, Rwanda, Sudan, and Uganda, is a notable example.[78] Against this backdrop, the implementation of the previously mentioned Country Demobilization and Reintegration Programme was important. Similarly, the conflicts in Liberia, Côte d'Ivoire, and Sierra Leone are interlocked, with arms and combatants moving from one conflict zone to the next. Nonetheless, the DDR process in Sierra Leone lacked a subregional approach, even though it occurred at a time of widespread insecurity in the Mano River countries. Some combatants moved from Sierra Leone to conflict zones in Liberia and Côte d'Ivoire, influencing those conflicts.[79] DDR design and implementation need to take into account and address regional dimensions of conflict, since the success of DDR in one country may be dependent on peacebuilding in another part of the region.

The process of disarmament, demobilization, and reintegration is multidimensional, varied, and complex, involving a number of interrelated and interdependent processes. DDR tends to include global, regional, and local actors engaged in humanitarian, security, and development activities. The actors have different goals and mandates that are not always compatible. Success is difficult to determine, since different actors will have different yardsticks.

Along with other DDR donor initiatives, the UN's guidelines for an integrated approach to the planning, design, and implementation of DDR tend to be embedded in a wider, liberal project that links security with development. The experience of many African countries with DDR suggests that these approaches may not always be appropriate. For instance, donor-driven DDR programs often sideline important informal and traditional practices. Yet many people have confidence in informal processes rooted in particular cultural norms that resonate with the community. It is important to understand these informal processes because significant numbers of combatants are informally demobilized and reintegrated, and because sometimes combatants go through both formal and informal processes.

It is also important to understand the context of conflict, which affects the possibilities and limits of DDR in Africa. How a conflict ended, as well as the prevailing security situation, will shape the outcomes of any DDR program. A program that is implemented after military victory will be different from a program that is agreed upon during a negotiated settlement to conflict. Furthermore, donor-driven DDR programs may inaccurately interpret the motives of the parties involved in DDR. In the context of a fractured state and an insecure elite, willingness to sign a DDR agreement may not be an expression of a credible commitment to peace. Last, DDR programs often rest on the distinction between combatants and noncombatants. This is problematic in many African conflicts, where these categories are often largely artificial. Instead, programs that emphasize community livelihoods are needed, as well as a better understanding of the global, regional, and local economic relationships that often contributed to conflict in the first place.

Notes

1. Duffield, *Global Governance and the New Wars.*

2. United Nations, *Integrated Disarmament, Demobilization, and Reintegration Standards (IDDRS)*, Module 2.10, "UN Approach to DDR," 4.

3. Some programs, such as the Multi-Country Demobilization and Reintegration Programme (MDRP), which was launched in the Great Lakes Region in 2002, have been referred to as disarmament, demobilization, repatriation, resettlement, and reintegration (DDRRR). See World Bank, *Greater Great Lakes Regional Strategy for Demobilisation and Reintegration.*

4. United Nations, *IDDRS*, Module 2.10, "UN Approach to DDR."

5. See United Nations Office of the Special Adviser on Africa, *Overview: DDR Processes in Africa.*

6. See Dzinesa in this volume. See also Dzinesa, "Postconflict Disarmament, Demobilization, and Reintegration of Former Combatants in Southern Africa," 77.

7. Isima, "Cash Payments in Disarmament, Demobilisation, and Reintegration Programmes in Africa," 2–3.

8. Paes, "Eyewitness," 254.

9. United Nations Institute for Disarmament Research (UNIDIR), *Applying*

Participatory Monitoring and Evaluation (PM&E) Approaches to Weapons Collection and Weapons for Development Programmes, 4; Willibald, "Does Money Work?" 323.

10. Mugumya, *Exchanging Weapons for Development in Mali.*

11. Knight and Ozerdem, "Guns, Camps, and Cash," 505; Isima, "Cash Payments," 3–4; Willibald, "Does Money Work?"

12. Jennings, "Struggle to Satisfy."

13. Kingma, "Demobilisation, Reintegration, and Peacebuilding in Africa."

14. Colletta, Kostner, and Wiederhofer, *Transition from War to Peace in Sub-Saharan Africa,* 12–14.

15. Knight and Ozerdem, "Guns, Camps, and Cash," 511.

16. Colletta, Kostner, and Wiederhofer, *Transition from War to Peace,* 18.

17. United Nations Department of Peacekeeping Operations (DPKO). *Disarmament, Demobilization, and Reintegration of Ex-Combatants in a Peacekeeping Environment.*

18. Colletta, Kostner, and Wiedhoffer, *Transition from War to Peace,* 18.

19. Kingma, "Demobilisation, Reintegration, and Peacebuilding in Africa," 193–95.

20. Ibid., 194.

21. For a discussion of the evolution of the ideas of peacebuilding, see Curtis in this volume.

22. United Nations, "What Is DDR?"

23. Muggah, "No Magic Bullet," 241.

24. Colletta, Kostner, and Wiederhofer, *Transition from War to Peace,* 18.

25. Boutros-Ghali, *Agenda for Development.*

26. Kingma, "Demobilization, Reintegration, and Peacebuilding in Africa."

27. See MDRP website, http://www.mdrp.org/about_us.htm.

28. World Bank, *Greater Great Lakes Regional Strategy.*

29. Clark, "Demobilization and Reintegration of Soldiers."

30. Agoagye, "African Mission in Burundi," 13.

31. Knight, "Disarmament, Demobilization, and Reintegration and Post-Conflict Peacebuilding in Africa," 38–39.

32. Government of Uganda, *Peace, Recovery and Development Plan for Northern Uganda.*

33. United Nations, *Role of the United Nations Peacekeeping in Disarmament, Demobilization, and Reintegration, Report of the Secretary General.*

34. Willibald, "Does Money Work?" 319.

35. Kingma, "Demobilisation, Reintegration, and Peacebuilding in Africa," 182.

36. Clark, "Demobilization and Reintegration of Soldiers," 53.

37. Ibid., 52–53.

38. United Nations, *IDDRS,* Module 3.10, "Integrated DDR Planning: Processes and Structures," 10

39. Colletta, Kostner, and Wiederhofer, *Case Studies in War-to-Peace Transition.*

40. See Dzinesa in this volume.

41. Vines, "Disarmament in Mozambique"; Dzinesa, "Postconflict Disarmament, Demobilization, and Reintegration of Former Combatants in Southern Africa," 77–78.

42. See Vines, "Disarmament in Mozambique"; Dzinesa, "Postconflict Disarmament, Demobilization, and Reintegration"; Metsola and Melber, "Namibia's Pariah Heroes."

43. Nilsson, *Reintegrating Ex-Combatants in Post-Conflict Societies.*

44. The ritual is referred to as nyono tong gweno, which means "stepping on eggs," and kalo oboke olwedo, which refers to jumping over the leaves of the olwedo, a shrub common in the area.

45. Kingma, "Demobilisation, Reintegration, and Peacebuilding in Africa," 192.

46. Ibid., 183.

47. Colletta, Kostner, and Wiederhofer, *Case Studies in War-to-Peace Transition,* 309.

48. Jennings, "Struggle to Satisfy," 208–9.

49. Colletta, Kostner, and Wiederhofer, *Case Studies in War-to-Peace Transition.*

50. United Nations, *IDDRS,* Module 3.10, "Integrated DDR Planning," 14.

51. See Dzinesa in this volume.

52. Ibid.

53. United Nations Development Programme (UNDP), "Practice Note: Disarmament, Demobilisation, and Reintegration of Ex-Combatants," 18.

54. United Nations, *IDDRS,* Module 2.10, "UN Approach to DDR," 4.

55. Ibid. and Module 3.20, "DDR Programme Design," 14.

56. United Nations Department of Peacekeeping Operations, *Disarmament, Demobilization, and Reintegration,* 16.

57. Berdal, *Disarmament and Demobilization after Civil Wars,* 24.

58. Ozerdem, "Disarmament, Demobilization, and Reintegration of Former Combatants in Afghanistan," 965.

59. Vines, "Disarmament in Mozambique," 193.

60. Nilsson, *Reintegrating Ex-Combatants in Post-Conflict Societies,* 32–33.

61. Knight and Ozerdem, "Guns, Camps, and Cash," 501.

62. Cohn, Hill, and Ruddick, "Relevance of Gender for Eliminating Weapons of Mass Destruction."

63. Spear, "Disarmament and Demobilisation," 143.

64. Dolan, "Collapsing Masculinities and Weak States."

65. Farr, "Gendered Analysis of International Agreements on Small Arms and Light Weapons," 22; Myrttinen, "Disarming Masculinities," 44.

66. Sayigh, *Confronting the 1990s;* Ayoob, "State Making, State Breaking, and State Failure," 37–51.

67. The Ugandan government persistently complained about the conditions that donors attached to their assistance, especially the condition that Uganda's defense expenditures should not exceed 2 percent of gross domestic product. The government reasoned in a 2003 defense white paper that such a ceiling was "arbitrary" and not based on Uganda's security needs.

68. Colletta, Kostner, and Wiederhofer, *Case Studies in War-to-Peace Transition.*

69. Hague Convention IV and Regulation (1907), art. 1; Geneva Convention III (1949), art. 4 (2).

70. Cited in Jennings, "Unclear Ends, Unclear Means," 330.

71. See Barth, *Peace as Disappointment;* Sadomba and Dzinesa, "Identity and Exclusion in the Post-War Era"; Farr, *Gendering Demobilization as a Peace Building Tool;* Turshen and Twagiramariya, eds., *What Women Do in Wartime.*

72. United Nations, *IDDRS,* Module 5.10, "Women, Gender, and DDR."

73. Harbeson, "Military Rulers in African Politics."

74. Metsola and Melber, "Namibia's Pariah Heroes."

75. Vines, "Disarmament in Mozambique," 196.

76. Ibid.

77. Kees Kingma, cited in Nilsson, *Reintegrating Ex-Combatants in Post-Conflict Societies,* 24.

78. See Lemarchand in this volume.

79. Knight, "Disarmament, Demobilization, and Reintegration," 42.

PART TWO

Institutions and Ideologies

The Role of the African Union, New Partnership for Africa's Development, and African Development Bank in Postconflict Reconstruction and Peacebuilding

GILBERT M. KHADIAGALA

THE SEARCH FOR EFFECTIVE PEACEBUILDING STRATEGIES IN AFRICA since the 1990s is animated by the need to find durable mechanisms that contribute to sustainable peace and development.[1] Despite these efforts, debates abound about how to rebuild states, the operational limitations of peacebuilding, and the consequences of external engagement in postconflict reconstruction.[2] The African Union (AU), the New Partnership for Africa's Development (NEPAD), and the African Development Bank (AfDB), alongside multilateral institutions, have been at the center of intervention attempts to promote peacebuilding in complex political, social, and economic environments. In addition to dealing with differences among postconflict countries, African actors, just like international actors, have faced problems of sequencing humanitarian and development goals against the backdrop of limited internal and external resources.

This chapter seeks to understand the roles of the AU, NEPAD, and the AfDB in postconflict reconstruction and peacebuilding in Africa. The discussion is structured around three fundamental questions. First, how have the AU, NEPAD, and the AfDB conceptualized the notions of postconflict reconstruction and peacebuilding? Second, what strategies have these institutions adopted to deal with the challenges of peacebuilding in Africa? Third, are ideas and approaches to peacebuilding in Africa different from global ones? Answers to these questions are instructive in gleaning insights into the involvement of these institutions in postconflict African countries and the consequences of this involvement. The chapter contends that postconflict reconstruction and peacebuilding roles are novel to continental institutions that are struggling with issues of weak resource and institutional capacity and multiple mandates. Despite these weaknesses, however, continental initiatives remain critical in the mobilization of action and resources to complement international postconflict and peacebuilding efforts.

Postconflict Assistance and Peacebuilding in Africa

There have been significant debates about whether peacebuilding and postconflict reconstruction are complementary objectives. Aid agencies involved in humanitarian work, such as Oxfam, International Alert, and Doctors Without Borders, initially resisted efforts to integrate peacebuilding into postconflict assistance because of what they perceived as the dangers of injecting political objectives into their strictly "neutral" and apolitical sectoral work in postconflict contexts.[3] Viewing their work in strictly technical terms, these aid agencies resisted the integration of overt political goals into their reconstruction and development projects because it seemed to violate one of the cardinal rules of foreign assistance.[4] This skepticism has gradually given way to the recognition of the complementary nature of these objectives. This recognition stems from wide acknowledgment that the provision of security is an essential condition of peacebuilding and, furthermore, that the rebuilding of public institutions is a key to sustainable peace.[5] Hence, successful political and governance transition must form the core part of any postconflict peacebuilding mission.

Over the past decade, the experiences of many African countries, such as Angola, Burundi, the Democratic Republic of the Congo (DRC), Guinea, Liberia, Rwanda, and Sierra Leone, have affirmed that sustainable peacebuilding occurs within a broad context of political and economic reforms. Proponents of peacebuilding throughout the 1990s documented the failures of conventional approaches and challenged the assumption that aid in postconflict settings could be separate from politics.[6] In recent years, the thinking has gravitated toward the idea that postconflict contexts are distinct from conventional development settings and thus require separate strategies that integrate peacebuilding into postconflict assistance.[7] For instance, a number of donors, in particular the Canadian International Development Agency (CIDA) and the World Bank, have developed peace and conflict impact assessments (PCIAs) in the planning and execution of "traditional" development projects, underscoring the increasing donor interest in funding peacebuilding undertakings. The PCIA is a means of systematically evaluating the positive and negative impacts of development projects on peace and conflict in conflict countries.[8] Attempts to integrate peace and conflict concerns into development planning are particularly instructive in Africa, where civil wars have decimated economies, polities, and livelihoods, and where reconstruction involves the resuscitation of institutions of order and prosperity. These are the ideas about peacebuilding that undergird the AU, NEPAD, and the AfDB.

The Role of the AU and NEPAD

As the primary institution responsible for peace, security, and development on the continent, the African Union has prioritized the establishment of a peace and security management system that comprises several elements: the Peace and Security Council, the Panel of the Wise, the Continental Early Warning System, the African Standby Force, the Military Staff Committee, and the Peace Fund.[9] NEPAD is a program of the AU that focuses on the socioeconomic causes of conflict such as poverty, underdevelopment, and poor governance. While the AU's Constitutive Act articulates the centrality of the AU in the peace and security arena, NEPAD supports postconflict reconstruction and the mobilization of resources for the AU Peace Fund.[10] Given their novelty, both institutions confront questions of the effective harmonization of their roles. As part of harmonization attempts, NEPAD's Heads of State and Government Implementation Committee adopted a peace and security agenda in February 2003 that consists of eight priorities:

1. Developing mechanisms, institutions, and instruments for achieving peace and security in Africa.

2. Improving the capacity for, and coordination of, early action for conflict prevention, management, and resolution, including development of operational capabilities for peace support.

3. Improving early warning capacity in Africa through strategic analysis and support.

4. Prioritizing strategic security issues such as disarmament, demobilization, rehabilitation, and reconstruction (DDRR) efforts in postconflict situations and coordination of African efforts to prevent and combat terrorism.

5. Ensuring efficient and consolidated action for preventing, combating, and eradicating the illicit proliferation, circulation, and trafficking of small arms and light weapons.

6. Improving the security sector and the capacity for good governance as related to peace and security.

7. Generating minimum standards for application in the exploitation and management of Africa's resources (including nonrenewable resources) in areas affected by conflict.

8. Assisting in resource mobilization for the AU Peace Fund and for regional initiatives aimed at preventing, managing, and resolving conflicts on the continent.[11]

This collaborative framework is intended to contribute to peace and security by focusing on strategic planning of peacebuilding operations, including determining and defining priority interventions, identifying appropriate networks of partners, and consolidating the work of the various internal and external actors involved in postconflict reconstruction processes.[12]

The other important institution that the AU and NEPAD have developed to address the peace, security, humanitarian, development, and political dimensions of postconflict reconstruction and peacebuilding is an African postconflict reconstruction policy framework. Developed in 2005 through a consultative process facilitated by the NEPAD secretariat, this framework harmonizes the activities and programs of the AU, NEPAD, the regional economic communities (RECs), member states, civil society, and the private sector in Africa. As part of this initiative, the AU and NEPAD seek to develop a centralized funding mechanism to assist coordination of postconflict reconstruction. The framework also identifies the role of RECs and international donors in postconflict reconstruction.

The 2005 postconflict reconstruction framework recognizes that a country's transition from conflict to peace should be informed by its own particular circumstances, reflected in the programming features of peacebuilding interventions: composition, prioritization, timing, and sequencing.[13] Toward this end, the framework has identified five key areas of postconflict reconstruction: security; political transition, governance, and participation; socioeconomic development, human rights, justice, and reconciliation; and coordination management and resource mobilization.[14] In addition to these key areas, the AU and NEPAD stress the importance of building the capacity of postconflict states to enable them to gradually own the reconstruction process. According to the framework, "Externally driven post-conflict reconstruction processes that lack sufficient local ownership and participation are unsustainable."[15] Despite this intent, the AU and NEPAD have yet to successfully resolve the tension between externally driven strategies and priorities, and local ownership.

The AU strategy seeks to facilitate coherence in the assessment, planning, coordination, and monitoring of postconflict reconstruction systems by providing a common frame of reference and conceptual base for the broad range of multidisciplinary, multifunctional, and multidimensional actors that affect postconflict reconstruction. The main building blocks of the framework are as follows:

- *Country-level strategic framework:* To coordinate the various constituent elements of the postconflict reconstruction system around a common country strategy.

- *Monitoring and evaluation system:* To monitor progress in implementation of peacebuilding activities as well as setbacks and challenges encountered, enabling the various actors, sectors, and programs to adjust their plans accordingly.

- *"Special needs" strategic and programmatic component:* Certain groups or categories of internal actors require responses that cater to their specific needs. These groups include women, children, youth, the disabled, the elderly, female ex-combatants, child soldiers, internally displaced persons (IDPs), refugees, single-parent households, victims of sexual violence, and HIV–positive individuals.

- *Strategic coherence and coordination model:* To ensure that the peace, security, and development dimensions of crisis interventions are directed toward a common objective.

- *Aid harmonization:* To coordinate the external actors involved in postconflict reconstruction. This includes monitoring reporting and evaluation systems in recipient countries, as well as streamlining the interfaces between internal and external actors to limit their impact on host bureaucracies.

- *Synchronized delivery and assistance absorption:* To harmonize the delivery of postconflict aid by external actors with the absorption capacity of internal actors, primarily by incorporating assistance delivery into postconflict programs and aligning it with the needs of internal actors.[16]

Before the establishment of the 2005 policy framework, NEPAD's role in postconflict peacebuilding was to "support efforts at developing early warning systems [and] support post-conflict reconstruction and development . . . including the rehabilitation of national infrastructure, the population, as well as refugees and internally displaced persons."[17] These responsibilities remain a central part of the continental peacebuilding strategy, though it has evolved since 2005. In its 2004–7 strategic plan, NEPAD further elaborated on its goals with respect to peace and security: supporting the AU and the regional economic communities (RECs), supporting national focal points, coordinating and harmonizing the efforts of external actors, addressing the security needs in postconflict countries, supporting efforts toward justice and reconciliation, furthering the economic and social well-being of the citizens of postconflict countries, and working toward good governance and equalizing citizen participation.[18] Equally significant, NEPAD processes such as the African Peer Review Mechanism (APRM) also embrace some of the fundamental areas of postconflict reconstruction: good governance, political transition, human rights, justice, and participation. The APRM enables postconflict countries to assess their own development processes and receive objective recommendations for improvement.[19]

There are different views on the utility of a sequenced approach to the continuum of relief, rehabilitation, and development. Not only are conflict dynamics nonlinear, but effective sequencing can be difficult, particularly given the multiplicity of programs and actors converging in these efforts. According to the AU/NEPAD framework, postconflict reconstruction starts when hostilities end, typically in the form of a cease-fire agreement or peace agreement. In the same breath, however, the plan ambitiously states that peacebuilding involves actors undertaking a range of "interrelated" programs spanning security, political, socioeconomic, and reconciliation dimensions, and that peacebuilding "collectively and cumulatively addresses both the causes and consequences of the conflict" and establishes the long-term foundations for social justice and sustainable peace and development. Experience from most postconflict contexts, such as Burundi, the DRC, and Sierra Leone, reveals that various peacebuilding activities may not necessarily complement each other, as coordination and policy coherence becomes an arduous undertaking in these settings.[20]

Although its ultimate aim is to address the root causes of conflict and to lay the foundations for social justice and sustainable peace, in the short term the AU/NEPAD framework is designed to assist in stabilizing the peace process and preventing a relapse into conflict. The challenge here is that the processes involved in addressing the root causes of conflict are longer-term and more complex, involving difficult reforms in the governance and social realms.[21] According to the AU/NEPAD postconflict framework, interventions are undertaken through three broad phases: the emergency phase, the transition phase, and the development phase. The framework notes, however, that these phases should not be understood as being absolute, fixed, or time-bound, or as having clear boundaries. Other donors and development actors, such as the World Bank, the United Kingdom's Department for International Development (DFID), and the Canadian International Development Agency, based on their experiences in postconflict states in Africa, have acknowledged that it is more effective to identify a limited number of strategic objectives, grounded in solid analysis (including conflict assessments, political economy analysis, drivers-of-change studies, and capacity mapping) of the sources of fragility and the potential for change. In this regard, priority areas can be selected by mapping the goals of the intervention and then identifying the critical path for achieving them in the security, economy, and social spheres.[22]

Like most of the broad African security agenda, the initiatives encompassed under the AU/NEPAD postconflict reconstruction and peacebuilding agenda are still in their formative stages. Thus far, neither the AU nor NEPAD have engaged in any substantive activities toward peacebuilding. Part of this problem stems from the enormous resource constraints these organizations are facing. Thus, although the framework was articulated in 2005, it was not until 2008 that the AU and NEPAD made a formal request to donors for US$50 million over a three-year period for postconflict reconstruction and development.[23] Of this amount, none was to be sourced from Africa, but the AU and

NEPAD anticipated exploring new and innovative means of harnessing resources from other sources, including the private sector, southern partners, and the African diaspora. Although the US$50 million did not include the cost for other sectoral priorities, such as the continental peace and security architecture (including the early warning system), the African Standby Force, management of natural resources, and combating the spread of small arms and light weapons, it is difficult to envisage how the ambitious agenda of postconflict reconstruction could be realistically accomplished on such meager resources. In the context of the radical reduction of the AU's overall budget (estimated to be a 50 percent cut in the AU's operational budget) following the uprisings in North Africa in early 2011, it is unlikely that the AU will find new resources to finance peacebuilding efforts in the foreseeable future.

Even with a future generous injection of donor resources, the AU and NEPAD would face constraints and would need to focus on a few priorities. Realistically, external actors, including the AU and NEPAD, cannot do everything in postconflict countries, particularly given the scale of problems facing most of these countries. Establishing priorities is also a question of developing exit strategies that quickly wean postconflict countries from donor funds that focus primarily on humanitarian, relief, and postconflict capacity building toward standard development funding and financing.[24] The transition from postconflict reconstruction to economic development is a key puzzle that has received limited attention under the AU/NEPAD framework; however, it may take center stage as resources decline. Understandably, postconflict countries face unique problems in restoring political order and economic prosperity, but the disproportionate roles of external actors in reconstruction often comes at the expense of national ownership. Countries such as Angola, Eritrea, Liberia, and Mozambique made significant strides in shedding the stigma of a postconflict label through strong leadership and programs that privileged broad national ownership, domestic mobilization of resources, and creative bargaining with donors to establish priorities and plans that mitigated the creation of new economic and political dependencies.

The Role of the AfDB

In recent years, the African Development Bank has been involved in the planning and implementation of postconflict, peacebuilding, and reconstruction initiatives on the continent. Although its role in peacebuilding is limited compared to that of the World Bank, DFID, and the United

States Agency for International Development (USAID), the AfDB has increased the geographic reach of its operations, the size of its financial contributions, and the diversity of its programmatic support. In line with NEPAD's postconflict reconstruction policy framework and its emphasis on strengthening the peacebuilding capacity of the regional economic communities, the AfDB has tried to craft and implement regional strategies to prevent conflict and promote development. As it has emerged as a significant player in postconflict reconstruction, the AfDB has focused on strengthening the institutional capacity of postconflict states such as Burundi, Comoros, the DRC, Guinea-Bissau, Liberia, and Sierra Leone.[25] Most of these resources have been allocated to training of personnel involved in public sector management, budgeting, decentralization, and anticorruption.

In 2001 the AfDB established a set of policy guidelines for postconflict assistance that emphasized providing advice, financing, and advocacy to postconflict countries, as well as building their capacity. According to the AfDB, fragile states (including postcrisis and transitional countries) have their own special requirements. They need to be assisted in moving toward stable political and economic development and to reengage with the international community. In 2007–9 the AfDB approved two documents relating to fragile and postconflict states: the "Bank Group Strategy for Enhanced Engagement in Fragile States" and the "Operational Guidelines of the Fragile States Facility." The new strategy differentiates the Bank Group's support to postconflict and transitional countries from the support provided to other categories of fragile states along similar lines established by other international financial institutions.[26]

In order to be classified as a fragile state by the AfDB, a country needs to satisfy any one of three conditions: it must have a composite AfDB and World Bank Country Policy and Institutional Assessment (CPIA) score of 3.2 or less;[27] it must have low income and no CPIA score; or it must have hosted United Nations (UN) or regional peacebuilding, peacekeeping, or mediation operations on its territory during the preceding three years. Consequently, fragile and postconflict states are generally characterized by exceptionally weak institutional capacity, poor governance, political instability, and frequent conflict. Furthermore, these states are unlikely to have met the UN's Millennium Development Goals, usually in the face of huge and unaddressed socioeconomic needs.[28]

Over the past decade the AfDB has changed its policies regarding postconflict and fragile states. Prior to 2001, the AfDB embarked on a purely standardized lending program aimed at supporting macroeconomic reform, improving service delivery, building institutional capacity, and providing arrears and debt relief.[29] This program, however, was too broad, forcing the AfDB to establish a number of specialized facilities to assist member states. The AfDB's current approach involves a facility for fragile states, which also incorporates a facility for postconflict countries. The objective of the facility for fragile states is to provide a broader and integrated framework through which the AfDB can assist eligible states more effectively, in order to help them consolidate peace, stabilize their economies, and lay the foundation for sustainable poverty reduction and long-term economic growth.[30] To achieve this end, the facility has three windows of grant support for financing the recovery process in fragile states:

- *Supplemental support window:* These funds (US$272 million in 2008) are aimed at supporting governance, capacity building, and rehabilitation and reconstruction of infrastructure in fragile states.[31]

- *Arrears clearance window:* These funds (US$120 million in 2008) are essentially used as a onetime support mechanism for the clearance of arrears of eligible fragile states. The objectives of this window are linked to those of the facility for postconflict countries; however, its implementation is different.[32]

- *Targeted support window:* These funds (US$27 million in 2008) support capacity building and development of management knowledge in fragile states.[33]

Both the facility for fragile states and the facility for postconflict countries provide an array of financing options that enable eligible candidates to clear their arrears. The AfDB's arrears clearance program is closely linked with those of the World Bank and International Monetary Fund (IMF), as the facility for postconflict countries has helped candidates qualify for debt relief under the Highly Indebted Poor Country (HIPC) initiative and more recently under the Multilateral Debt Relief initiative.[34] Burundi was the first such beneficiary, gaining access to the HIPC initiative in September 2005 at an estimated cost of US$826 million. Access to this fund, which has supported resettlement of IDPs, development of infrastructure, and improvement of health care and education, has been important to maintaining stability in Burundi.[35] Other countries that have benefited from this facility include the Comoros, the DRC, and Liberia. Additional advantages of AfDB financing and loan provision for postconflict countries include jump-starting public spending programs that improve services to the population and provide jobs; helping countries return to a formal economy and build tax revenues; and improving domestic economic conditions to reverse capital flight. In Sierra Leone, the AfDB's frontal engagement in postconflict financing for the Bumbuna hydroelectric power project induced other donors to follow suit.[36]

There is no doubt that the African Development Bank has made significant provisions for supporting postconflict countries and addressing the specific needs of fragile states, particularly by emphasizing interventions in "priority areas": capacity building, employment creation, support for arrears clearance, and support for vulnerable groups—women, children, the elderly, and the disabled. Like its development counterparts such as the World Bank, however, the AfDB has been criticized for many shortfalls and limitations. First, some observers have noted that the AfDB tends to shy away from adopting a political "lens" to its postconflict interventions by not sufficiently considering the political and economic power dynamics in postconflict settings and their adverse consequences.[37] Instead, the AfDB's approach is primarily technical, focusing on economic variables and scores such as the CPIA. There are concerns that this may actually exacerbate income disparities, exclusion, and inequity, problems that drive instability.

Second, aid funds and donor-sponsored policy reforms can inadvertently strengthen elite dominance and patronage, fuel resentment among certain groups, increase exclusion, and increase the risk that such excluded groups may resort to violence to address their grievances. In most postconflict settings, systems of exclusion based on gender, caste, and ethnicity may be obstacles to sustainable reconstruction.[38]

Third, the AfDB's allocation system prioritizes performance over the needs of postconflict countries. Likened to the World Bank's CPIA, the AfDB's allocation system effectively penalizes poor-performing fragile states that have chronically weak policies, institutions, and governance. In this respect, the AfDB largely mirrors the World Bank in its approaches to postconflict reconstruction rather than evolving new ones that reflect African specificities. Furthermore, there is insufficient clarity on the meaning of local ownership, particularly in countries that have weak state institutions. Ownership may be rhetorical in contexts of insufficient domestic resources and inadequate capacity. Rather than acknowledging the tensions and dilemmas around ownership, the AfDB may be overlooking them in its programs. Moreover, operations in receiving countries are not always transparent. There have been reports of weak control of corruption and that the AfDB's facility for fragile states in some instances may be supporting undemocratic regimes.[39]

Fourth, although coordination has improved, the AfDB still needs to develop better mechanisms for coordinating with other donors and initiatives that stem from continental institutions and international actors. Coordination is critical because, unlike the AU and NEPAD, the AfDB has more expertise and experience in financing and implementation of development projects. In future peacebuilding initiatives, it may be prudent for external actors to funnel financial support to the AfDB to enable it to operate as the implementation and financial management arm of the AU and NEPAD. Such an arrangement would serve to enhance coordination between external donors and African institutions in peacebuilding.

African continental institutions have embraced postconflict and peacebuilding roles because of the importance they have attached to resolving conflicts, enhancing security, and laying firm foundations for sustainable development. As Africa's civil wars have ended, the AU, NEPAD, and the AfDB have elaborated various approaches and strategies to help with peacebuilding. These roles have also evolved as part of Africa's wider search for problem-solving mechanisms that draw from local initiatives and resources. In identifying the key strategies adopted by these institutions, this chapter has shown that although the broad articulation of strategies has often not translated into effective mobilization of resources or action, it has been important for African continental institutions to be involved in these efforts. The experience shows that thus far the AU, NEPAD, and the AfDB have expended modest resources in postconflict reconstruction and peacebuilding, depending for the most part on subventions from international actors. Yet since postconflict reconstruction roles are time-bound, future planning and strategies should accord more priority to helping countries to transition expeditiously from postconflict to development. Moreover, if African countries make significant steps to recover from civil conflicts, the need for additional resources for postconflict reconstruction and peacebuilding enterprises will no longer be as critical in the larger calculus of African continental priorities.

Notes

1. For a discussion of the concept of peacebuilding, see Curtis in this volume. For other wide-ranging discussions on peacebuilding and postconflict reconstruction, see Samuels, "Sustainability and Peace-Building"; Hagman, *Lessons Learned;* Grävingholt, Gänzle, and Ziaja, "Policy Brief," 3–4.

2. François and Sud, "Promoting Stability and Development in Fragile and Failed States"; Addison, "Conflict and Peace-Building"; Department for International Development (DFID), *Why We Need to Work More Effectively in Fragile States;* Milliken and Krause, "State Failure, State Collapse, and State Reconstruction"; World Bank, *Role of the World Bank in Conflict and Development;* Junne and Verkoren, eds., *Post-Conflict Development;* Rotberg, ed., *When States Fail.*

3. Menkhaus, *Impact Assessment in Post Conflict Peace Building,* 4.

4. Rafeeuddin, Manfred, and Khalid M., eds., *Role of the UNDP in Reintegration and Reconstruction Programmes,* 6; Schnabel, "Post-Conflict Peace-Building and Second Generation Preventive Action."

5. Dulic, "Peace Building and Human Security."

6. De Zeeuw, "Projects Do Not Create Institutions"; Samuels, "Post-Conflict Peacebuilding and Constitution-Making," 2.

7. Samuels, "Post-Conflict Peacebuilding and Constitution-Making," 2.

8. World Bank, *Role of the World Bank in Conflict and Development;* World Bank, *Framework for World Bank Involvement in Post-Conflict Reconstruction.* See also Menkhaus, *Impact Assessment in Post Conflict Peace Building,* 4–7; Bush and Opp, "Peace and Conflict Impact Assessment"; Bush, *Measure of Peace.*

9. For discussions on the AU's institutional structures, see Okumu, "African Union"; Moller, *Africa's Sub-Regional Organizations*

10. Murithi, "Towards a Symbiotic Partnership," 252.

11. African Union (AU) and NEPAD, *AU/NEPAD African Action Plan, 2010–2015,* 81–84.

12. Ibid.

13. New Partnership for Africa's Development (NEPAD), *African Post-Conflict Reconstruction Policy Framework.*

14. Ibid.

15. Ibid., 4.

16. Ibid., 11.

17. Murithi, "Towards a Symbiotic Partnership," 252.

18. NEPAD, *African Post-Conflict Reconstruction Policy Framework,* 12.

19. Ibid., 9.

20. For analyses of the experiences in Burundi and the DRC, see Lunn, *African Great Lakes Region;* Department for International Development (DFID), *Building the State and Securing the Peace.*

21. Murithi, "Towards a Symbiotic Partnership," 252.

22. See, for instance, Hanlon, "Bringing It All Together"; Snodgrass, "Restoring Economic Functioning in Failed States"; Bilgin and Morton, "From 'Rogue' to 'Failed' States?"; Trivedy, "Conflict Prevention, Resolution, and Management."

23. AU and NEPAD, *AU/NEPAD African Action Plan: Updated Final Draft Version*, 18.

24. On the challenges of making the transition from postconflict to development, see Addison and McGillivray, "Aid to Conflict-Affected Countries"; World Bank, *Breaking the Conflict Trap.*

25. African Development Bank (AfDB), *African Development Report, 2008–2009.* Launching this report, AfDB president Donald Kaberuka noted: "There is a critical role of sound economic policies for promoting post-conflict recovery and consolidating peace. The report underlines the importance of building strong national institutions for effective economic policymaking and peace building. In addition, state building must feature prominently in international efforts to help conflict-affected countries achieve lasting political stability and sustainable development." See also AfDB, *AfDB/Burundi.*

26. AfDB, *African Development Report, 2008–2009*, 61.

27. The CPIA score ranks countries against a set of sixteen criteria that focus on economic management, structural policies, policies for social inclusion and equity, and public sector management and institutions.

28. AfDB, *African Development Report, 2008–2009*, 61.

29. Ibid., 62.

30. Ibid., 70.

31. AfDB, *Strategy for Enhanced Engagement in Fragile States*, ii.

32. AfDB, *African Development Report, 2008–2009*, 70.

33. AfDB, *Strategy for Enhanced Engagement in Fragile States*, 2.

34. AfDB, *African Development Report, 2008–2009*, 63.

35. Ibid.

36. AfDB and World Bank, *Sierra Leone: Information Note on African Development Bank and World Bank Joint Assistance Strategy, 2009–2012.*

37. For some of these criticisms, see Moore, "Levelling the Playing Fields"; Le Sage, "Engaging the Political Economy of Conflict"; Holtzman, *Rethinking "Relief" and "Development" in Transitions from Conflict;* Goodhand and Hulme, "From Wars to Complex Political Emergencies"; Bojicic-Dzelilovic, "World Bank, NGOs, and the Private Sector in Post-War Reconstruction."

38. See, for instance, Luckham, *Politics of Institutional Design;* Ball, "Challenge of Rebuilding War-Torn Societies."

39. Duffield, "Political Economy of Internal War"; Moore, "Levelling the Playing Fields," 11–28.

SIX

Peacebuilding as Governance

The Case of the Pan-African Ministers Conference for Public and Civil Service

CHRIS LANDSBERG

THE AFRICAN CHALLENGE IS ESSENTIALLY A CHALLENGE OF development, and the African crisis is primarily a crisis of the state. Africans therefore have to respond simultaneously to a two-pronged problematic, brought about by decades of internal misrule and externally driven wars and exploitation: governance and development. As such, the state has to be set at the very center of African politics and development. African states have since the end of the Cold War and apartheid searched for their own post–Cold War, postapartheid interstate paradigm to address the consequences of decades of African bad governance and superpower rivalries and proxy battles at the continent's expense. Since 2002 with the formal establishment of the African Union (AU), the continent's most credible and legitimate interstate body, African states have pursued an "African Agenda" that spells out four areas of dynamic cooperation, or "calabashes": peace and security; stability, or governance; socioeconomic development; and international cooperation. Many continental and subcontinental actors and forums have emerged to embrace and champion this continental African Agenda. The Pan-African Ministers Conference for Public and Civil Service, established in 1994, is one such African interstate actor that has provided indigenous intellectual support and acted almost as a lobby group in support of a governance approach to peacebuilding and statebuilding.

It is one that many scholars and observers know very little about, yet one that can tell us a great deal about Africa's security-politico-development agenda and the peacebuilding challenges faced by the continent at the operational level.

This chapter deals with the little-known Pan-African Ministers Conference, which provides a forum for ministers who face weak governance infrastructures and massive public service delivery challenges, and helps them look outward to select global and continental postconflict tools and frameworks. It is an example of the continentalization of policy in Africa and demonstrates how government departments, other than the usual ministries of foreign affairs and defense, have staked a claim in foreign policy and security matters. The conference also potentially addresses two other problems. First, it can use postconflict reconstruction frameworks to address how political power is used and abused in continental affairs, and thus places the state and governance at the center of continental development. Second, it can address imbalances in the continent's relations with outside powers, notably those from the West. Typically, powerful industrialized states usurp the powers of African governments, to the point where these states lose much of their policy sovereignty. Thus, the Pan-African Ministers Conference can potentially reassert the role of national governments, and by extension the state, in the peacebuilding process.

Postconflict reconstruction and development (PCRD) are stated as key objectives of both the AU and the Pan-African Ministers Conference, but there are disagreements over what this means and which kinds of activities should be supported. Peacebuilding initiatives have typically taken, as their starting point, global institutions and their efforts to build peace in needy countries—an outsider-in approach. Scant attention is given to African or regional initiatives and efforts to ensure that external efforts dovetail with homegrown initiatives—an insider-out approach. But unless African efforts at statebuilding and development are made fundamental parts of the continent's postconflict peacebuilding efforts, little will come of these initiatives.

Since its first gathering in 1994 in Tangier, Morocco, the Pan-African Ministers Conference has prioritized postconflict reconstruction as a means of dealing with the question of the distribution of power, resources, and services. In that year, a regional conference on public administration was held in Windhoek in Namibia, with the aim of modernizing postconflict public services. The Pan-African Ministers

Conference was influenced by relevant resolutions of the United Nations (UN) General Assembly and by former UN Secretary-General Boutros-Ghali's 1992 report *An Agenda for Peace*. The ministers used these documents as a guide and subscribed to the idea that postconflict countries needed to embrace democratic governance and the notion of developmental states. Politics and development could not be separated.

This chapter specifically probes how the Pan-African Ministers Conference sought to engage postconflict reconstruction and development challenges on the continent, through an emphasis on statebuilding, governance, and public service delivery. In doing so, the chapter makes the case for developmental institutionalism and highlights the interesting ways in which national and continental peacebuilding and reconstruction initiatives are shaped by global ideas and approaches, but also how those ideas are interrogated and adapted to African conditions.

Toward Developmental Institutionalism?

Developmental institutionalism is derived from two separate concepts, developmentalism and institutionalism. Institutionalism emphasizes institutions as enduring and stable sets of arrangements that regulate individual and group behavior on the basis of established rules and procedures. Andrew Heywood argues that political institutions have a formal and often legal character, and imply explicit and often usually enforceable rules and decision-making procedures.[1] Developmental institutionalism refers to institutions that are meritocratic in character and are able to prioritize development by being goal oriented, and able to get key stakeholders to pull in the same developmental direction in society. The concept of developmentalism has been defined by Guy Mhone to mean an active approach by the state in a country's economy, which refers to the government having "a directive, promotive and facilitative role" in a country's economy.[2] A developmental state leads the market by directing market initiatives toward development and creating competitive advantage and fostering economic development. This is in stark contrast to the neoliberal view, which sees the state "not (as) an agent of growth, only an umpire, frequently an obstacle, and ideally not a major participant in development."[3] As the rest of this chapter will show, the Pan-African Ministers Conference offers an alternative approach to African peacebuilding that is anchored on developmental institutionalism.

The Pan-African Ministers Conference: A Background

With the formal cessation of the Cold War by 1990, and the end of apartheid in South Africa in 1994, African ministers of public service and administration came together to establish the Pan-African Ministers Conference for Public and Civil Service. The end of apartheid and white-minority oppression marked the continent's achievement of its objective of political emancipation. Africa's focus shifted to issues of socioeconomic emancipation.

Many African state actors emerged to play key roles in helping to shape the postapartheid governance and development architecture.[4] The Pan-African Ministers Conference is one such actor. It seized the opportunity to engage Africa's renewed pan-Africanism by committing to develop policies to enhance public and civil services and administration roles in political and socioeconomic development in Africa through its establishment as a common forum in 1994. Since its inception, the ministerial conference has demonstrated a commitment to move toward establishing standards and codes of practice for public administration in Africa. The ministers recognized that the continent is desperately in need of meritocratic civil services, and that the establishment of basic frameworks for public administration is central to the overall effectiveness of the state in realizing sustainable development.[5]

The ministers convened their first conference in Tangier, Morocco, June 20–21, 1994. While the goal was to have all African countries join this new club, states joined on a gradual basis. About 17 to 20 states participated on a regular basis, a far cry from the ambitious target of having all of the then 52 members of the AU participate directly.[6] The second Pan-African Ministers Conference, organized with the support of the UN's Department of Economic and Social Affairs, was held in Rabat, Morocco, December 13–15, 1998. Morocco, although not part of the African Union, continues to play a leading role, and it is because of this that the AU and the Pan-African Ministers Conference keep their relationship at an "informal" level.

The 1998 conference was a landmark event for Africa's public administration, as it seized the policymaking and agenda-setting initiative by laying the foundation for establishing a continental charter for the public service. In keeping with the recommendations of the conference, a ministerial working group, supported by a secretariat, was established to draft the charter. The Africa Public Service Charter (APSC) described below was adopted at the third conference, held in Windhoek, Namibia, February 5–6, 2001. The fourth conference took place May 6–7, 2003, in Stellenbosch, South Africa, where the ministers pledged to hold future conferences under the banner of the African Union Commission. This demonstrated their commitment to operating under the aegis of the continental body. Continental legitimacy was important to the Pan-African Ministers Conference, and the forum has met at least once a year since 2005 under the AUC.

The New Partnership for Africa's Development (NEPAD), a modernizationist blueprint that has been in operation since October 2001, mandated that its secretariat support the Pan-African Ministers Conference.[7] NEPAD's secretariat welcomed the fact that the ministers had set out to help meet the development mandates outlined by African leaders by linking the conference's work to the broader continental development agenda, showing again how this pan-African ministerial forum was engaging key continental initiatives. But very early on, it became clear that, even on NEPAD's score, there were serious challenges of implementation and operationalization. The experience of the ministers conference highlighted that although continental actors were good at crafting and developing policies, they often lacked the will to implement policies.

The Pan-African Ministers Conference also agreed to engage Africa's five key regional economic communities (RECs) on political governance and public administration questions because they form the building blocks of continental integration. These include the Southern African Development Community (SADC), the Economic Community of West African States (ECOWAS), the Economic Community of Central African States (ECCAS), the Intergovernmental Authority on Development (IGAD), and the Arab Maghreb Union (AMU).[8] One of the aims of the Pan-African Ministers Conference is to focus on strengthening these RECs through decentralization and the prioritization of provinces, municipalities, and local governments. Enhancing the planning capacities of these entities is a key issue. This is a novel, innovative policy idea. How to translate these ideas into action and to ensure that individual African governments implement them has been the Achilles heel of continental policy. One area neglected by the ministers conference is thus the issue of closing the policy-implementation gap in Africa.

Priorities

The ministerial forum has identified the Africa Public Service Charter as a key priority.[9] The charter signifies Africa's political will and commitment to good governance, ethics, and accountability, and commits ministers to help ensure transparency when making administrative decisions. The charter underlines common values while preserving diversity, and through sharing different experiences it could evolve into a powerful catalyst for reforming the public service of African countries. The Pan-African Ministers Conference also highlighted the importance of coordinating actions to combat corruption. This includes establishing a common definition of corruption, assessing its magnitude and costs, and developing an African position on how to fight it.[10] As early as 2006, then Nigerian President Olusegun Obasanjo revealed that corruption was costing African countries an estimated 25 percent of their combined national income per annum.[11] But the costs of corruption are not only financial; they are also developmental, as scarce resources earmarked for development went astray. The Pan-African Ministers Conference has noted that the devastating impact of corruption on development, governance, and service delivery processes should not be underestimated.[12]

The Pan-African Ministers Conference builds on numerous historical exchange initiatives across the continent to enhance governance and public administration effectiveness.[13] The initiatives were supported by organizations such as the African Training and Research Centre in Administration and Development, the Development Policy Management Forum, and the African Association for Public Administration and Management (AAPAM). These led to learning-exchange opportunities (conferences, seminars), training initiatives, and the development of research projects and publications.

The All-Africa Public Sector Innovation Awards constitute another priority area for the ministerial conference. Mauritius served as the lead government for this initiative and established a working committee made up of representatives of NEPAD and the chairperson's office to oversee its implementation, which comprises four stages: design, marketing, adjudication, and an awards ceremony.[14] The innovation award was introduced both to reward original work and encourage innovative approaches in the areas of governance and public service, but many African states have not taken up this opportunity to promote new and best practices in their own ranks.

The ministerial forum also initiated Africa Public Service Day, which highlights the major goals and objectives of the ongoing processes of civil service reform and emphasizes ideas of good governance, effective service delivery to citizens, particularly the most vulnerable and rural poor, and the dissemination of information on public service.[15] The African Public Service Day aims to attract attention to the enhancement of public services that adequately respond to citizens' expectations; this of course comes against the backdrop of assertions that governments and civil servants are often too far removed from the people they claim to serve. This state-society gap is one that has long bedeviled many African peacebuilding and democratization processes.

Cooperation with International Actors

Dialogue with donor agencies is another priority. A key objective is to foster greater cooperation between the continent and external powers on the basis of partnership, not paternalistic neocolonial links, while expecting external actors to respect African ownership and policy sovereignty. Over the past decade, most of Africa's development (or donor) partners, such as the United Nations Development Programme (UNDP) and the European Union (EU), have supported the emerging continental architecture around peace and security, governance and stability, development, and cooperation. The Pan-African Ministers Conference has made the case for the continent's development partners to coordinate their efforts more effectively among themselves, as well as with African partners. They insisted on synergy among donors and on efforts to dovetail with, and reinforce, African initiatives. The conference also expected donor partners to strategize more coherently for both short-term rehabilitation and long-term institutional development within the public sector. For instance, most national parliaments have enacted or are in the process of enacting legislation that specifically deals with corruption, transition, and development.

Although Africans have insisted on policy sovereignty and ownership, there has been a natural threat of dependency on donors and external partners exploiting the weaknesses of Africa's policy networks. Aid dependence can potentially undermine the quality of governance and public sector institutions, as well as development trajectories, by weakening accountability, encouraging rent-seeking and corruption, fomenting conflict over control of aid funds, siphoning scarce talent from the bureaucracy, and alleviating pressures to reform inefficient policies and institutions. It is thus important for donors to develop less costly and less intrusive ways of disseminating state-of-the-art knowledge on public sector reform and development agendas in countries emerging from conflict. Ultimately, Africans should guard ownership of their initiatives jealously, and foreign actors have to be seen to be supporting and bolstering continental initiatives.

Peacebuilding, Governance, Development, and the Pan-African Ministers Conference

The African Union's postconflict reconstruction and development strategy encompasses six indicative elements: security; humanitarian and emergency assistance; political governance and transition; socioeconomic reconstruction and development; human rights, justice, and reconciliation; and women and gender.[16] The pan-African ministers welcomed the AU's emphasis on "political governance and transition" as a key dimension of its postconflict reconstruction and development strategy, as they believe in the centrality of the state in constructing peace on the continent. The ministers thus promote the merits of a developmental institutional approach.

Typical postconflict reconstruction and development efforts consist of three main objectives: facilitating the transition from war to peace, supporting economic and social development and reconstruction, and consolidating political development through effective governance.[17] The pan-African ministers see consolidating development through governance as their particular focus. In most conflict situations, governance capacities are severely hampered by the loss of skills and experience associated with violence and displacement. The decision-making capacities of governments are compounded by postconflict political dynamics such as "sunset" arrangements, balance-of-power alliances and coalitions, and compromises.[18] To consolidate peace, a framework for effective and legitimate governance and the rule of law needs to be put in place, and constitutional order needs to be restored.[19] Many postconflict governments struggle to set up new administrations that are functional and effective.

Governance, peacebuilding, and development form a symbiotic relationship. As a 2008 report by the UN's Economic and Social Council (ECOSOC) noted, "It is now understood that the institutional and human capacities, governance and development are interdependent and in a relationship of reciprocal cause and effect." The ECOSOC report further posited that "in times of radical transformation and crises, new and renewed forms of governance and public administration capacities are needed to achieve sustainable, people-centred, pro-poor governance and development."[20] By placing governance at the center of their agenda, the Pan-African Ministers Conference contributes directly to peacebuilding. The challenge is whether African states will respond seriously to yet another interstate initiative and inculcate these ideas into their national programs.

There are, however, different definitions of governance. In 1995 the Commission on Global Governance defined governance as

> the sum of the many ways individuals and institutions, public and private, manage their common affairs. It is a continuing process through which conflicting or diverse interests may be accommodated and co-operative action may be taken. It includes formal institutions and regimes empowered to enforce compliance, as well as informal arrangements that people and institutions either have agreed to or perceived to be in their interests.[21]

The UN Development Programme (UNDP) has defined governance as "the exercise of economic, political and administrative authority to manage a country's affairs at all levels"[22] The World Bank identified three distinct aspects of governance: "(1) the form of political regime; (2) the process by which authority is exercised in the management of a country's economic and social resources for development; and (3) the capacity of governments to design, formulate and implement policies and discharge functions."[23] The Organisation for Economic Cooperation and Development (OECD) defined governance as denoting "the use of political authority and exercise of control in a society in relation to the management of its resources for social and economic development."[24] A 2008 United Nations report on governance states "governance and public administration capacities are essential for sustainable human development, in political, economic, social and environmental contexts."[25]

Despite some difference in emphasis, all the preceding definitions hint at the importance of power and resources. Focusing on power and resources emphasizes issues of inclusion and exclusion, and the privileged and marginalized: those who hold and are included in power and control resources, and those who are excluded from power and deprived of resources and are thus unable to shape formal power dynamics and even informal power relations.[26]

Peacebuilding as governance involves creating or re-creating structures and capacities in countries that have been reshaped by violent conflict and by the reconfiguration of political, social, and economic institutions. The Pan-African Ministers Conference for Public and Civil Service looks outward to global and continental instruments of peacebuilding in pragmatic and functional ways, to legitimize their activities to a wider audience. At the very least, they wish to see mutual reinforcement between their own perspectives and standards, on the one hand, and more conventional international perspectives on peacebuilding, on the other. The AU regards its PCRD strategy as a "flexible template that can be adapted to and assist regions and countries."[27] The Pan-African Ministers Conference has viewed this as a window of opportunity to flesh out the governance and public service dimensions of PCRD.

The AU's PCRD strategy framework argues that "successful PCRD is dependent on good political governance" and that "political governance involves the devolution and exercise of power from the national to the local level."[28] It encompasses the notion of democratic governance as called for in the AU's Constitutive Act of 2000. The Pan-African Ministers Conference has promoted a number of African initiatives and instruments over the past decade that recognize the importance of democratic governance. These instruments include the 2000 Lomé Summit of the Organization of African Unity (OAU), which adopted the Constitutive Act of the AU; the Inaugural AU Summit of 2002 in Durban, South Africa; the launch of NEPAD in October 2001; the adoption of the African Peer Review Mechanism (APRM) in 2003; and the Declaration on Political, Economic, and Corporate Governance of 2002. Other African governance instruments include the 2001 AU/NEPAD Foundation Document on Conditions of Sustainable Development in Africa; the 2002 Kananaskis Group of Eight (G8) Industrialized Countries–Africa Action Plan on Capacity Building and Conflict Resolution;[29] the coming into force in 2004 of the Protocol to the African Charter on Human and Peoples Rights; the 2005 Commission for Africa Report; and the 2007 Potsdam G8 Action Plan for Good Financial Governance in Africa. All these instruments promote the idea that democratic governance is associated with better appropriation and management of power. Nonetheless, many members of the conference, and African governments, remain tardy when it comes to operationalizing and implementing these instruments. Furthermore, while many pan-African ministers agree that improved investment and growth, government effectiveness and efficient bureaucracy, better economic performance, adult literacy, and the rule of law are associated with one another, a great many of them continue to undermine, or even violate such provisions.

The Pan-Africa Ministers Conference spoke directly to the question of power and the abuse of power, and aligned itself with the ideas of NEPAD, which highlighted the need to fight against "the abuse of human and peoples' rights resulting from policies of marginalization, identity-based discrimination, and perceptions of injustice."[30] Yet, since 2008, there has been a real ambivalence and reluctance by the successors of NEPAD's architects to embrace and take ownership of NEPAD as the continent's development program. Today, NEPAD is in limbo, and fast losing its status as a continental plan.

Given its emphasis on governance and the public service, it is not surprising that a key policy strategy of the Pan-African Ministers Conference is the "building of capable states," which the South Africa based NEPAD secretariat has been mandated to execute through its governance initiative. This particular initiative stresses three priorities.[31] First, it aims at assisting African governments in developing a capacity for self-reliance, particularly with regard to putting in place institutional and policy measures for mobilizing resources for development domestically. Second, it aims to build capacity within national governments for long-term strategic planning and continental integration. Third, it helps national governments develop institutional and policy measures for domesticating African democratic governance instruments. The point again is that the Pan-African Ministers Conference has made its contribution to articulating and designing sound policies; the problem has been in the realm of policy implementation. Another problem is that not all governments took the ministers conference seriously, and it was up to South Africa, Nigeria, Kenya, Algeria, and a few others to take the lead.

Likewise, while the Pan-African Ministers Conference has in recent years promoted the notion of the developmental state, there are problems putting this vision into practice. As explained previously, a developmental state assumes that some government intervention in the economy is desirable, and the regulatory and judiciary bodies, public enterprise, and other public administration institutions should be effective, efficient, fair, responsive, accessible, and accountable. The ministerial forum has encouraged the idea that decentralization of power and resources to local government is one way for governments to get closer to their citizens, increasing the scope of African citizens to influence priorities and service interventions. However, successful decentralization requires political commitment and leadership, adequate financial resources, and technical and managerial capacity for planning, budgeting, implementation, and monitoring in local governance.[32] These are still lacking in many African countries where local government elections do not always take place.

In 2006 the African Union called for the establishment of a think tank to provide advice on governance issues, since ideas about governance issues on the continent were dominated by Bretton Woods institutions, UN agencies, the African Development Bank (AfDB), and a host of think tanks based in the north. Such a think tank would serve as a policy initiator and clearinghouse for the Pan-African Ministers Conference, and help the ministers develop ideas and plans in the areas of public administration and governance that were specific and relevant to the African context. The interesting point to note is that the peacebuilding approach advanced by African institutions emphasizes the role and capacity of the state, whereas some international institutions such as the International Monetary Fund (IMF) and the World Bank either ignore or marginalize the state, or advance the idea of the minimalist state. The activist African state is thus pitted against the idea of a retreating state.

The statebuilding strategy developed by the Pan-African Ministers Conference is aimed at improving capacity for public service delivery. This strategy includes building state capacity, systems to deliver services, and anticorruption measures.[33] It embraced the ideas of the 2008 ECOSOC report, which noted that "organisationally, capacity development ensures the establishment of effective networks, teams and functional communities."[34] The individual dimension is also discussed, as the ECOSOC report suggests that "at the individual public servant level, capacity-building and development rely on effective leadership, career development and professional human resource management, responsiveness to community organisations and individual citizens, and active professional associations and functional communities of practice."[35] What is significant about the ECOSOC report is that it emphasizes both micro- and macro-organizational aspects of statebuilding.

The Pan-African Ministers Conference has recognized that one of the major weaknesses in many African states is that different government departments are poorly integrated with one another, making planning and implementation difficult. This contributes to problems with the monitoring and evaluation of outcomes of policies. Government-wide monitoring and evaluation systems are crucial for service delivery, yet these remain some of the most neglected elements in policy and governance processes. What is needed are greater levels of co-ordination and integration of policy initiatives.

Furthermore, one of the most serious challenges faced by many African states is the nonexistence, or poor operationalization, of national planning frameworks for the delivery of public services. In effect, service delivery requires all spheres in government, including national, provincial, and local, to act in unison and coordinate their work. Without a national framework, planning often remains unintegrated and improperly aligned with national strategic goals. Policy does not typically filter down to all echelons of government, and breakdowns in communications and service delivery tend to occur. Thus the Pan-African Ministers Conference has emphasized capacity building for service delivery in its efforts to create viable public administration institutions. Weak administrative capacities and deficits in human skills bedevil many African civil services, which continue to make the idea of developmental states in the continent mere pipe dreams, particularly for countries emerging from conflict.

State-society relations are typically weak in many African states, yet these states claim that their priority is to put citizens at the center of public service planning and operations. As many parts of the world move away from the old dispensation through which governments provided services "for" people and toward a new model of working "in partnership" with people, many African states face an uphill struggle. The Pan-African Ministers Conference has recognized that African governments face enormous challenges of transforming service delivery mechanisms to meet the needs of citizens. In order to address these challenges, there is need for a participatory strategy in which citizens have a stake and claim in governance and delivery models. Organized civil society must also engage with governments and the state. Unlike the majority of Africa's poor citizens, organized civil society has the resources to influence the state, and it too should become better connected with the poor so as to allow them the opportunity to have voice and influence. Citizens are empowered through access to information and services. Human and resource capacity constraints among African states often stretch the time lag between agenda setting, decision making, resource mobilization, and implementation. According to the AU, capacity-building strategies thus have to address these challenges at local, national, regional, and continental levels.[36]

Therefore, both the macro-organization of African states, including the systems of intergovernmental relations and public participation in policy formulation, as well as the micro-organization of African states, are on the agenda of the pan-African ministers. The challenge is to ensure that African states take these ideas seriously and move to implement and operationalize these ideas. Micro-organizational questions typically receive less attention, but they are vital spokes in the statebuilding hub. These include various structures and systems to enhance the delivery of services, including information communication technology, finance management, human resources, and electronic governance.[37] Electronic governance is not only about technology; it is about using information technology to make government services more accessible to citizens by increasing their effectiveness. The gains of electronic governance could include reduced cost of services, improved quality of delivery, increased capacity of government, and increased transparency and accountability.

Putting Ideas into Practice

The previous sections of the chapter have outlined the ideas, the framework documents, and plans set out by the pan-African ministers. In many ways, the pan-African ministers have been more successful in devising collaborative policymaking and harmonizing their rhetoric with those of other continental-level institutions than they have been in implementing their plans. At times, however, the pan-African ministers have tried to apply their ideas. For instance, recognizing that Burundi was experiencing a turbulent peacebuilding process, the ministers emphasized a peacebuilding approach that aimed to reduce the concentration of power in the centralized structures of state authority.[38] The key peacebuilding priorities continued to be those related to security, governance, and human rights.

External actors were encouraged to collaborate closely with the national authorities, the United Nations Integrated Office in Burundi (BINUB), the UNDP, and other partners in implementing the UN's action plan for the country. The pan-African ministers urged the various partners to rebuild governance and civil service administration and to restore confidence in government at the national, provincial, and local levels by building an effective balance of power and ensuring broad democratic representation. National and external actors were furthermore urged to support the promotion of a culture of accountability and transparency, including implementation of targeted anticorruption programs. Nevertheless, despite the efforts by the Pan-African Ministers Conference, Burundi remains fragile, public service provision is uneven, and violence could return, thus reversing the gains made since 2004.

In the Democratic Republic of the Congo (DRC), meanwhile, the peacebuilding process was slowed by the failure of transitional institutions to elaborate fundamental laws and to promote the reunification of the country through the appointment of provincial governors and vice governors. This affected the restoration of state authority throughout the country, including restructuring and integration of armies and security services.[39] Transforming and building the DRC's public services remain key priorities of the government in this unstable country. The pan-African ministers supported the government's agenda to reform the public service, which falls under the auspices of the DRC's Ministry of Public Services with the support of South Africa's Ministry of Public Service and Administration. The Technical Committee of Public Administration Reform was established within the DRC ministry to take overall responsibility for the coordination and integration of the public service reform process, which focused on developing a transitional strategy for human resources and institutional capacity building, including in the area of public administration. Just like with Burundi, however, progress in the DRC is slow and incremental at best.[40] Alongside the consolidation of peace, the government will have to show progress in the area of development and improving the quality of the lives of the citizenry. Thus, improvements in public service delivery are essential, but this can be done only alongside the consolidation of other peacebuilding initiatives. Statebuilding and development should thus be pursued simultaneously, but the difficulties in the DRC highlight the obstacles in translating the policy objectives of the pan-African ministers into actual reform and services that benefit people in countries emerging from conflict.

Peacebuilding in Africa requires statebuilding, which in turn requires developmentalism. We have thus posited the idea of developmental institutionalism, building strong, meritocratic institutions, which can help mobilize society around a clear and common development agenda, and through which the goals of growth, education, and health care can be pursued. Developmental institutionalism involves the strengthening of institutional capacities to make and execute effective policies. Africa has experienced a long battle to secure its policy sovereignty and to pursue policy agendas that suit and advance the continent's political and development interests.

The Pan-African Ministers Conference for Public and Civil Service is an example of a homegrown, continental initiative to tackle key challenges, and to devise solutions based on African needs and interests rather than serving the priorities of external foreign policy agendas. The forum has played an important role in thinking through the priorities in postconflict reconstruction and development in Africa, and has made a valuable contribution by advancing the idea of peacebuilding as governance and statebuilding. The Pan-African Ministers Conference is a novel example of how actors not traditionally associated with foreign policy and defense and security matters can become actively involved in this debate. To be sure, there have often been disagreements among the ministers on the best approaches to peacebuilding, with some stressing, for example, technical capacity building and training, some stressing anticorruption, and others emphasizing the macro-organization and re-organization of the state. Even more seriously, many conference members have violated the letter and the spirit of agreements entered into, and show little regard for *pacta sunt servanda;* they do not always honor commitments made by themselves, and in the name of their states. Despite ministers remaining determined to work together, because they face similar challenges despite different national contexts, many of their governments do not take seriously the cross-border and continental work they have helped to articulate.

As the Pan-African Ministers Conference has engaged in its postconflict peacebuilding work, it has aligned its mandate for effective and sustainable governance and service delivery within the AU's continental development and integration agenda. It is important that the ministers conference now raise its voice and impress on continental leaders, and those within leadership positions in the AU commission and other regional structures, to take seriously their agreements and implement the policies.

So, while the role of the Pan-African Ministers Conference offers an interesting alternative to dominant liberal peacebuilding models that marginalize the state, it also brings into sharp relief the gap between policy and implementation on the continent. The manner in which external powers and donor agencies intervene on the continent in the name of promoting peacebuilding speaks to the question of power. Given the hierarchy in power relationships between African and external actors, foreigners typically dictate policy terms and priorities, and Africans are left as mere implementation agents of external priorities. The need for international cooperation should be strongly emphasized, but it is important for Africans who work in the areas of governance and administration to take ownership of postconflict reconstruction and development initiatives and to identify priorities for success. African ownership does not mean that international actors are exonerated from their responsibilities toward the continent. External actors indeed have a vital role to play. What ownership does is to place the important question of African policy sovereignty squarely on the agenda.

The Pan-African Ministers Conference addresses the question of policy sovereignty in areas of key importance: the delivery of public services and the structure of the civil service. The ministers have recognized that there is much to learn from their colleagues in different African countries. As the work of the conference proceeds, ministers must continue to insist on the adoption of a regional approach that links Africa's governments, the regional economic communities, continental bodies, and civil society actors. The future debate over continental integration is likely to revolve around a devolutionary, confederalist model, through which the RECs would come to play a pivotal role. The Pan-African Ministers Conference should engage these actors in a decisive manner.

Continental institutions should insist that international agencies align their efforts with national, regional, and continental strategies, such as the AU and NEPAD's postconflict reconstruction and development plans, not the other way around. They should further implore that external powers and their agencies cease to undermine African efforts at governance, peace, security, and cooperation. Ownership should rest with Africans; it is unlikely to be offered to them on a silver platter. If Africans and their international partners remain faithful to respecting legitimate and credible African initiatives, including state-focused peacebuilding initiatives, then homegrown African models, driven by African agents, may prove to be more successful in ensuring sustainable peace. These African initiatives can take a myriad of forms, including the functional approaches discussed in this chapter for public service delivery. It is inconceivable in the medium to long run that international actors and their foreign agendas will disappear from the African political terrain. But it is incumbent on Africans to organize themselves more strategically and take greater ownership to ensure that international governments and agents engage the continent on terms that respect African interests and priorities rather than that Africans remain mere pawns in the chess game of foreign agendas. The current problem is not a lack of policies and agendas in Africa; it is rather the implementation and operationalization of such policies and ideas. A developmental institutionalist approach suggests that African states and civil society actors will have to increase their efforts in more deliberative and strategic fashion to help close the huge policy-implementation gap in Africa so as to ensure that peacebuilding and other governance efforts are more fruitful.

Notes

Some research and information for this chapter was accessed through work done for the German Technical Cooperation (GTZ) and the Pan-African Ministers Conference for Public and Civil Service, in South Africa, during 2007 and 2008.

1. Heywood, *Key Concepts in Politics*, 93.

2. Mhone, "Developmentalism and the Role of the State," 6.

3. Ibid.

4. For an assessment of Africa's emerging governance and peace and security architectures, see Akokpari, Ndinga-Muvumba, and Murithi, eds., *African Union and Its Institutions*.

5. Pan-African Ministers Conference for Public and Civil Service, report of the third ministerial bureau meeting.

6. There are fifty-four states in Africa following the independence in July 2011 of South Sudan.

7. For two contending views on NEPAD, see Landsberg, "Birth and Evolution of NEPAD," and Bunwaree, "NEPAD and Its Discontents."

8. Pan-African Ministers Conference for Public and Civil Service, Report of the Third Ministerial Bureau Meeting.

9. Pan-African Ministers Conference for Public Administration and Service, "Stellenbosch Declaration."

10. Pan-African Ministers Conference for Public and Civil Service, Report of the Second Ministerial Bureau Meeting.

11. BBC News, "Cost of Corruption in Africa," February 17, 2006.

12. See "Declaration of the Fifth Global Forum on Fighting Corruption and Safeguarding Integrity," Johannesburg, April 5, 2007.

13. Pan-African Ministers Conference for Public and Civil Service, Report on the Launch Conference of the African Management Development Institutes Network.

14. Pan-African Ministers Conference for Public and Civil Service, Report of the Second Ministerial Bureau Meeting.

15. Ibid.

16. African Union, *Policy Framework on Post-Conflict Reconstruction and Development in Africa*. For more detail on the African Union's PCRD policy, see Khadiagala in this volume.

17. World Bank, *Framework for World Bank Involvement in Post-conflict Reconstruction.* See also chapter by Curtis in this volume.

18. See chapters by Keen and Zaum in this volume.

19. See, for example, Samuels, "Post-Conflict Peacebuilding and Constitution-Making."

20. United Nations, "Strengthening Governance and Public Administration Capacities for Development," 1.

21. Commission on Global Governance, *Our Global Neighbourhood,* 2.

22. United Nations Development Programme (UNDP), *Governance for Sustainable Human Development,* 2–3.

23. World Bank, *Governance,* xiv.

24. Organisation for Economic Cooperation and Development (OECD), *Participatory Development and Good Governance,* 14. See also Isabelle Johnson, *Redefining the Concept Good Governance,* 11.

25. United Nations, "Strengthening Governance and Public Administration Capacities," 4.

26. Indeed, intra–civil society power dynamics and struggles for scarce resources can be as much of an impediment as state–civil society power dynamics, because some formal, well-funded, nongovernmental organizations may parade as civil society organizations and exclude poor people while monopolizing spaces for engagement.

27. African Union, *Policy Framework on PCRD in Africa.*

28. Ibid.

29. New Partnership for Africa's Development (NEPAD), "G8-Africa Action Plan."

30. See, for example, NEPAD, "Declaration on Democracy."

31. NEPAD, "Governance in Africa's Development."

32. See, for example, Julia Joiner, AU governance commissioner, opening remarks at the Sixth Conference of African Ministers of Public Service, Johannesburg, October 13, 2008.

33. Pan-African Ministers Conference for Public and Civil Service, "Framework for Pan-African Public Administration Involvement in Post-Conflict Reconstruction and Development (PCRD)," 6.

34. United Nations, "Strengthening Governance and Public Administration Capacities," 4.

35. Ibid.

36. Pan-African Ministers Conference for Public and Civil Service, Report of the Third Ministerial Bureau Meeting.

37. For an electronic governance perspective, see Government of South Africa, "South Africa's E-Government Experience."

38. Pan-African Ministers Conference for Public and Civil Service, "Framework for Pan-African Public Administration Involvement," 12.

39. Ibid., 13.

40. See Lemarchand in this volume.

SEVEN

The United Nations Peacebuilding Commission

Problems and Prospects

'FUNMI OLONISAKIN AND EKA IKPE

THIS CHAPTER EXAMINES THE CREATION AND OPERATIONALIZATION of the United Nations (UN) Peacebuilding Commission (PBC). We argue that while this institutional mechanism offers an improvement to the global approach to peacebuilding, its impact on and relevance to African security realities are marginal. The chapter begins with a discussion of the origins, mandate and structure, and substantive work of the PBC. This is followed by an examination of the prospects for the commission's success and then an analysis of the main challenges confronting the PBC. The chapter concludes with an assessment of how the commission might fare in African contexts that require a transformation of the conditions that sustain violent conflict.

Origins, Mandate and Structure, and Substantive Work of the Peacebuilding Commission

Applying the UN's tried, tested, and reinvented approaches in peacekeeping in the 1990s did not keep many armed conflicts at bay in Africa. The challenges posed by post–Cold War conflict environments led to a significant shift, from traditional peacekeeping to multidimensional peace operations.[1] Former peacemaking approaches had focused on stopping wars without tackling the underlying causes of the conflict. Typically, this involved keeping a fragile peace between warring parties while hastily organized elections were showcased as the end to a conflict, after which peacekeepers were withdrawn.

Current ideas about peacebuilding recognize the connections among the economic, social, and political spheres as well as the connections between different phases of violent conflict. For instance, Michael Doyle and Nicholas Sambanis frame peacebuilding as engaging with economic, social, and political institutions and realigning attitudes toward the prevention of violent conflict.[2] Charles Call and Susan Cook also see peacebuilding as encompassing conflict prevention, since they consider it to include all efforts to transform potentially violent social relations into peaceful ones.[3] The UN recognizes these different aspects of peacebuilding, yet its main peacebuilding focus remains on situations where social and political relations have degenerated into violence.

Origins

Conception of the Peacebuilding Commission began in 2003, when then–UN Secretary-General Kofi Annan tasked the High-Level Panel on Threats, Challenges, and Change to recommend necessary reforms on the UN's role in maintaining peace and security. Part of the panel's remit was to address the challenges of coordinating peacebuilding activities and to support the long-term efforts to consolidate peace in postconflict societies. There had been long-standing calls for increased coordination in international support for peacebuilding. UN peacebuilding was largely uncoordinated and took place within different branches of the organization, such as the Department of Peacekeeping Operations (DPKO) and the Department of Political Affairs (DPA), as well as the United Nations Development Programme (UNDP) and other agencies.

The High-Level Panel proposed the establishment of the Peacebuilding Commission, which would draw on the Security Council and the Economic and Social Council (ECOSOC) within the UN system, as well as on donors and national governments, to support countries in the transition from war to peace.[4] In addition, the commission would assist countries in preventing state collapse and conflict. Thus it was proposed that the new body would focus on conflict prevention and postconflict reconstruction. The High-Level Panel called for regional organizations and international financial institutions (IFIs), notably the World Bank and the International Monetary Fund (IMF), as well as the twenty largest economies globally, to support the work of the Peacebuilding

Commission. It also proposed the creation of the Peacebuilding Support Office (PBSO), to act as a secretariat for the commission.

The UN secretary-general supported the proposal for establishment of the Peacebuilding Commission in his 2005 report *In Larger Freedom*. However, in this incarnation, the commission was to engage with peacebuilding processes only in a postconflict context.[5] This recommendation was endorsed later the same year at the UN World Summit, where governments called for the establishment of the Peacebuilding Commission by the end of the year.[6]

At the time of the Peacebuilding Commission's creation in 2006, the UN was supporting a substantial number of postconflict peace processes following the signature of peace agreements. These included the Sudan peace process, following the signing of the Comprehensive Peace Agreement between the government of Sudan and the Sudan People's Liberation Movement/Army in January 2005, as well as the Liberian peace process, following the signing of the Accra Comprehensive Peace Agreement between the Liberian factions in August 2003.[7]

Another factor that influenced the creation of the PBC was the fact that the UN's reputation as the defender of global security had suffered substantially following the unilateral US military intervention in Iraq in 2003.[8] This led to questions about the credibility of the UN as a global institution that could respond to the interests of the broader global citizenry as opposed to those of the most powerful states.[9] The peacebuilding initiative can be seen in part as an attempt by the UN to restore its credibility and to reinforce the principle of universality that informed its work, by reasserting its primary role in consolidating peace and ensuring global security.

Mandate and Structure

The Peacebuilding Commission was mandated to bring together the relevant actors and resources in the early recovery period after conflicts, as well as to offer advice on comprehensive strategies to support peacebuilding processes.[10] The PBC was to focus attention on development and institution-building efforts in order to support postconflict recovery and avoid relapse into violence. In addition, the commission was expected to support the coordination of all relevant "stakeholders" in peacebuilding processes, both within and outside the UN system.

The PBC is made up of a thirty-one-member organizational committee appointed on the basis of two-year renewable terms. This committee consists of seven members of the Security Council (the five permanent and two nonpermanent members); seven members of the UN's Economic and Social Council, selected on the basis of regional groupings and experience with postconflict recovery; seven members elected by the UN General Assembly; five of the largest donor countries, based on assessed contributions to the UN's regular budget and voluntary contributions to UN funds, programs, and agencies; and five of the largest peacekeeping countries, based on number of troops and civilian personnel contributed.[11] Representatives from the IFIs, the IMF, and the World Bank are required to be present at all meetings of the organizational committee. This committee determines the agenda of the Peacebuilding Commission, and particular cases are assigned to country-specific configurations.

Substantive Work

The first four countries on the Peacebuilding Commission's agenda were African countries: Burundi, Sierra Leone, Guinea-Bissau, and the Central African Republic.[12] Liberia and Guinea have since been added to its agenda, in September 2010 and February 2011, respectively. The proverbial meat of the commission's work is found in its country-specific meetings.[13] In the country-specific meetings that support peacebuilding efforts, participants are the government representatives from the country in question, representatives from neighboring states, and the relevant regional organization.[14] These meetings also include representatives from IFIs and of UN officials in the field, as well as representatives from the particular donors and troop-contributing countries involved in the specific country. All actors in the various peacebuilding processes are brought together in formal and informal discussions.

The Working Group on Lessons Learned is a forum for generating learning from previous and current peacebuilding experiences.[15] Here a variety of experiences of postconflict engagements, at international and national levels, are addressed, with the view toward distilling lessons to guide ongoing processes. The Peacebuilding Support Office, acting as the Peacebuilding Commission's secretariat, obtains and analyzes relevant information on peacebuilding strategies and supports implementation of recommendations reached by the commission.[16]

In addition, the Peacebuilding Fund, managed by the assistant secretary-general for peacebuilding support, with the support of the PBSO, is funded on the basis of voluntary contributions administered by the UNDP's Multi-Donor Trust Fund.[17] As of February 2010, the Peacebuilding Fund's total portfolio stood at just over US$334 million, including pledges, commitments, and interest earned, with a total of just over US$196 million allocated to 115 approved projects.[18] As of March 2011 the portfolio stood at US$365 million.[19] The Peacebuilding Fund provides financial support both to countries on the PBC's agenda and to countries that are not (following eligibility approval from the UN secretary-general).[20] Funds are allocated through the Immediate Response Facility and the Peacebuilding Recovery Facility, to be used in response to imminent threats to ongoing peace processes, to support initiatives that contribute to peace agreements and political dialogue, to reinforce national capacity in order to promote coexistence and peaceful conflict resolution, to stimulate economic recovery in order to generate peace dividends, and to restore essential administrative services.

Prospects for Success

The Peacebuilding Commission is an improvement on previous global peacebuilding efforts. Despite some important limitations, there is added value in its remit and approach.

Ensuring a Balance between Security and Development

The PBC is set up to institutionally straddle the security and development divide. It is intended to bridge the operational gap between the security focus of peacekeeping, and the activities of development actors, including the IFIs, in supporting the rebuilding of war-torn economies.[21] This is evident in the Peacebuilding Fund's priority area of stimulating economic recovery in order to support progress toward tangible peace dividends.

An integrated security-development approach to peacebuilding is one of the PBC's strengths. For instance, to further the peacebuilding process in Sierra Leone, the commission supported a negotiations process for the inclusion of an energy provision as a priority in its strategic framework. This was justified on the basis of the impact of the energy provision on economic activity and the potential for negative economic fallout to undermine security gains in Sierra Leone.[22]

Undertaking a Contextual Approach to Peacebuilding

Another asset of the PBC is its case-study method of work. The commission is premised on the belief that dedication of time and resources to addressing peacebuilding processes in a single country case is important. Unlike in many other global institutions, the processes in the PBC are driven by context particularities.

For instance, in Burundi the commission has prioritized good governance, the rule of law, security sector reform, and community recovery, whereas in Sierra Leone it has prioritized youth empowerment and employment, democracy and good governance, and judicial and security sector reform. In Guinea-Bissau the commission has prioritized support for electoral processes, economic recovery, infrastructure rehabilitation, security sector reform, rule of law consolidation, addressing drug trafficking, and public administration reform, while in Central African Republic it has prioritized security sector reform, disarmament, demobilization, and reintegration, support for governance and rule of law processes, and development support.[23] In Burundi in particular, the PBC has been praised for its flexibility. It modified and extended a project that was supposed to focus on refurbishing courthouses, and instead worked to improve access to justice for the poor, as this was what the context required.[24]

Coordinating Peacebuilding Activities and Actors

The Peacebuilding Commission's role as a coordinating body, bringing together actors and resources to consolidate gains in postconflict reconstruction, has made it welcome in most countries. In Burundi, the commission has been commended for facilitating strong engagement with civil society as well as between civil society and the government, arguably after a troubled start.[25] Although this is a positive outcome, there is also a risk that the PBC will simply become an additional and largely irrelevant layer of bureaucracy, with only limited gains in increasing coordination. This point is reinforced by the 2010 review of the UN peacebuilding architecture, which suggests that there is a risk that the PBC will settle "into the limited role that has developed so far."[26] The efficacy of its coordinating role may be challenged by the location of the PBC at the UN secretariat in New York. Indeed it has been noted that less interactive processes such as video-linked meetings have not proven popular with some developing countries.[27] Some critics have therefore rightly argued that the commission's horizon "must be raised far beyond its New York base."[28] This is underlined by the 2010 review of the UN's peacebuilding architecture, which includes a recommendation for establishing field-based liaison committees for country-specific configurations.[29]

There is nonetheless some optimism that the PBC might improve the efficiency and coordination of various peacebuilding efforts. Jehangir Khan, former deputy director of the UN's Department of Political Affairs, argued that although the DPA had historically played the role of coordinator in peacebuilding activities, it was not set up to be operational. As such, the PBC could fill a much needed gap by enabling coordination on peacebuilding activities across the UN system.[30] The PBC's role as a coordinating body has provided a valuable umbrella for the activities being undertaken to support postconflict recovery and reconstruction, notably in driving deliberation on the inclusion of energy issues in the peacebuilding strategy in Sierra Leone and in negotiating a delicate impasse on continued funding from the IMF in Sierra Leone.[31] The commission's coordinating capacity was tested in Burundi, when the government called for the exit of the UN Executive Representative of the Secretary-General (ERSG) in December 2009.[32] The commission responded to these tensions by affirming its continued commitment to peacebuilding efforts in Burundi with the national authorities and the new UN representative.

Engaging Regional Actors

The Peacebuilding Commission provides an institutional site to engage with regional organizations. Specifically, the PBC mandates the membership of regional organizations and the relevant neighboring countries in country-specific meetings. It is still too soon to assess the added value or impact of the contribution of regional organizations to the work of the commission. This might become easier to gauge once many regional actors, for example the Economic Community of West African States (ECOWAS), have become regular participants in the PBC. Nonetheless, in the 2010 review of the UN peacebuilding architecture the point is well made that regional organizations may be best placed to intervene efficiently in highly sensitive situations.[33]

Challenges and Limitations

Notwithstanding its prospects for success, the PBC confronts a number of challenges that threaten to undermine its effectiveness and relevance in Africa. Fragile conflict-affected situations on the continent call for a much more fundamental shift in global and local conditions than the PBC can offer in the face of deep-seated conditions that perpetuate misery and insecurity for many ordinary people in Africa.

Conceptual Problems

The fundamental challenge to the work of the PBC has been its failure to define what peacebuilding should mean for transformation. The exclusion of preconflict peacebuilding work from the mandate and focus of the PBC is an important limitation, which has led to questions about its credibility and relevance to Africa's conflict environment. It is likely that future conflict in Africa will be primarily low-intensity and intrastate. Such conflict is unlikely to pose major threats to international peace and security but will remain a challenge for efforts to promote sustainable national development and human security on the continent.

Due to the nature of the threats faced by many Africans, peacebuilding should include preconflict peacebuilding and conflict prevention. Yet the PBC has excluded these activities from its focus because of resistance from some countries in the global South.[34] This exclusion, which was the result of political negotiations among global elites, does not reflect the interests of the broader African populace. Even the 2010 review of the peacebuilding architecture questions the static approach to addressing realities on the ground through its statement that "the Organization must adjust to the realities: the United Nations must continually reappraise its own structures and prioritize its approach to ensure they match needs on the ground."[35] The point is also made that the PBC needs to consider a preventive role in order to holistically engage with peacebuilding processes because "realities on the ground are not compartmentalized."[36]

Another challenge is that the PBC is broadly embedded in a notion of peacebuilding that aims at "transforming war economies to liberal market democracies," a notion of postconflict reconstruction and recovery to which most international actors broadly subscribe.[37] The PBC is fundamentally committed to this agenda,[38] as confirmed by its insistence on a strong role for IFIs that reflect this particular liberal ideal. As such, this "ideal" is pursued in many postconflict societies that are not effectively equipped to present homegrown visions based on their specific situational realities.

Limited Relevance to Africa's Strategic Environment

The particular scope of the PBC is driven by a faulty assessment of security threats in Africa. The focus on cases where conflict has escalated into large-scale fighting bears little relevance to the current and potential armed situations in Africa. When one takes the evolving security situation on the continent into account, two trends become apparent.

First, the large-scale regional armed conflicts of the past two decades in Africa have gradually mutated and, with some notable exceptions, have been mostly contained within national spaces. This is due in no small measure to the peacemaking and peacekeeping efforts of African regional organizations and the United Nations. There has been a de-escalation of the crises in the Mano River Basin (exemplified by the Parrots Beak problem in 1999), and of the large-scale armed conflicts in Liberia, Sierra Leone, and Côte d'Ivoire. As a result, there are fewer active wars in Africa that have the potential to inflict dire consequences on the region. Interestingly, what has emerged is not peace and stability throughout Africa's regions, but rather a situation of "no war, no peace" in which security and development remain volatile and unpredictable.

Second and related, the real challenge is low-intensity conflicts. These may not pose a threat to regional or international peace and security, but they pose great dangers to the population and harm the possibility of sustainable livelihoods for many people. Examples of such low-intensity conflicts are found in Nigeria's Niger Delta,[39] northern Ghana, northern Mali, northern Niger, Casamance in Senegal, and northern Uganda. They reflect the widespread structural instability in Africa, which predates many of the civil wars of the past two decades.

The reduction in large-scale armed conflict has created the space to address the structural underpinnings of armed conflict while responding to the challenge of low-intensity conflict. The ECOWAS region, for example, has begun to change its approach, through its articulation of a conflict prevention framework and its development of a subsequent implementation plan that is intended to actualize the objectives of the prevention framework, which aims at structural change rather than simply a reduction in armed conflict.[40] Likewise, the PBC must adapt itself to the needs of the continent. The African security environment is dynamic and will continue to mutate, albeit with (sub)regional variations for the foreseeable future. As such, conflict management and peacebuilding frameworks, not least the efforts of the PBC, must retain the flexibility to respond to "moving targets." Africa requires an effective transformation of its current structural environment into one having the stability and security to ensure sustainable and equitable development.

Arguably therefore, due to the way the PBC currently conceptualizes peacebuilding, its efforts are unlikely to be relevant to the low-intensity conflicts expected to play a central role in Africa's future.

Institutional Challenges

During the consultations surrounding the establishment of the PBC, some countries in the global South resisted the inclusion of conflict prevention or preventive diplomacy.[41] These countries feared that more powerful countries might use peacebuilding as a pretext for military interventions. All the country cases on the agenda of the commission are African cases, and the 2010 review of the UN peacebuilding architecture raises questions about the exclusive African focus on the PBC's agenda.[42] For some, the predominance of African countries on the agenda can lend credence to the view that there are important hierarchies and inequalities in the global system that result in countries from different regions being treated differently.

Furthermore, the creation of the PBC reflected institutional imperatives at the UN, and the perceived lack of an institutional process at the UN to engage countries in postconflict transitions.[43] It is therefore not surprising that the commission focuses on facilitating the UN's ongoing engagement with peacebuilding processes vis-à-vis other actors.

The composition of the PBC also reflects its institutional context, as the commission is dominated by the permanent members of the Security Council, the principal donors to the UN system, and the largest peacekeeping contributors, which make up almost half the central structure of the PBC, its organizational committee. This is especially pertinent given that many of these committee members are rich and relatively peaceful countries of the global North. Despite the two-year renewable terms, the country categories guarantee the continued membership of a small group of the most powerful Northern countries within the PBC's organizational committee. This pattern is to some extent redressed by the requirement that at least seven countries with postconflict reconstruction experience have membership in the organizational committee. This latter provision is almost the only guarantee for standing core participation from African countries, except Nigeria due to its role as a major troop contributor.

As of June 2010, African countries constituted 23 percent of the membership of the PBC's organizational committee; included were Angola, Burundi, Egypt, Ghana, Guinea-Bissau, Nigeria, and Tanzania.[44] Yet all the countries being considered for inclusion on the PBC's agenda are African. Although these are early days in the life of the PBC, this comparatively low ratio speaks to the challenges to Africa's participation in the activities of the commission, particularly as Africa seems to be its principal constituency.

These factors reinforce the notion of a "global apartheid" within the UN system, which can be described as a pattern of political power and socioeconomic inequalities, primarily between the rich countries of the global North and the poor countries of the global South, especially those in Africa, within the structure and workings of the UN.[45] Furthermore, some of the core partners of the PBC, such as the IFIs, are mandated to be present at all organizational and country-specific meetings, despite not being a core part of the UN system. This is especially pertinent when considering that the other key developmental body that is a core member of the PBC is the UN's Economic and Social Council, which has substantially less authority within the discourses and practices of global development. ECOSOC's limited impact is the result of its limited powers as delineated in the UN Charter, tensions between the developed and developing world within the body, as well as its continued subordination to the World Bank and the IMF.[46] However, ECOSOC has wider global membership than the World Bank and IMF, which have weighted voting systems and leadership structures that disproportionately represent the richer and more developed global North.[47]

These imbalances contribute to the Peacebuilding Commission's acceptance and prioritization of the IFIs' approaches, despite the long-standing critiques of these approaches. The extent of this prioritization in the work of the PBC was illustrated in the initial meeting about Sierra Leone's placement on the PBC's agenda in July 2006. In attendance were the PBC, the United Nations Integrated Office in Sierra Leone (UNIOSIL), the World Bank, and the IMF.[48] Curiously, the PBC is not under ECOSOC, but under the thumb of the UN Security Council (alongside the UN General Assembly), "where power lies."[49] The 2010 review of the UN peacebuilding architecture argues that the PBC's linkages with all three bodies are less than optimal, albeit with much emphasis on the relationship with the Security Council.[50] Without wholesale changes to the policies and the initiatives of the IFIs, their strong involvement with the Peacebuilding Commission will likely give preeminence to a market-driven development approach with scant regard for local contexts.[51]

The PBC may be compelled to adopt the approaches of the IFIs owing to the power of the latter within global development structures. The commission does not have the authority to require IFIs to modify their strategies even if they risk undermining peacebuilding efforts.[52] There are also other practical concerns. In the cases of Sierra Leone and Burundi, the commission pushed for the synchronization of mandates, roles, and responsibilities, but the IFIs and others have been unwilling to negotiate their autonomous and independent approaches.[53]

The IFIs, like the PBC itself, pursue peacebuilding only in the post-conflict stage. This is evident in the World Bank's activities in conflict countries, which the Bank labels as "pre-transition" countries, on the basis of aid support under the Country Policy and Institutional Assessments (CPIA) system. Broadly within this system is a "one size fits all" approach, as all countries are judged, within the same framework, on performance of policies and institutions regardless of need.[54] In addition, evaluations of country performance by the World Bank are based on its neoliberal ideological leanings, according to which the state is to have a minimal role and good performance is judged to present itself in the form of liberalized trade, "manageable" (read, low) levels of public expenditure, low ratios of debt to gross domestic product, avoidance of crowding out private investment, and prioritization of foreign debt servicing.[55] This insistence and reliance on the neoliberal agenda, especially in undermining public investment and expenditure when the latter are crucially required in the context of challenging conflict, effectively sidelines countries that have suffered breakdowns in their policy and institutional apparatus.[56]

Nonstate Actors

The Peacebuilding Commission's work in the country-specific process privileges the role of national actors. There have been criticisms of the PBC's engagement with civil society in Burundi and Sierra Leone, including the claim that state authorities selected the civil society actors that participated in proceedings.[57] In Sierra Leone, there was criticism of the "hand-picking" of certain organizations by the government that were not deemed best placed to put forward a grassroots position.[58] In addition, civil society groups claim that there is a lack of any clear system of their engagement in the monitoring of the PBC's activities.[59] In Burundi, despite the earlier-mentioned progress, capacity is a serious challenge, and civil society engagement with the PBC is declining because of the immense burden of the process as well as inadequate financial support to civil society groups.[60]

The role of civil society actors is yet to be clearly defined in the work of the Peacebuilding Commission, although General Assembly Resolution 60/180 notes that the commission is to consult with civil society, nongovernmental organizations, including women's organizations, and private sector actors as appropriate.[61] Although there are provisional guidelines for the engagement of civil society groups, their actual involvement remains very much at the discretion of the PBC and thus relies on the acceptance of commission members.[62] So far, the process for engaging civil society appears to be hampered by the vagueness of the guidelines, which raises questions about the notion of "local ownership" of the peacebuilding processes pursued by the commission.

This issue should not be taken lightly, given that there are often tensions between state and nonstate actors, especially civil society actors in many African contexts. In addition, the Peacebuilding Commission has to balance these tensions against the objective of strengthening public institutions as part of the peacebuilding process. These are dilemmas that may not be so easy to reconcile; nonetheless, the coordinating role of the PBC implies that it should help facilitate the representation of nonstate actors and their constituencies.

Other Contentious Issues

Another contentious issue is the question of which countries should be on the agenda of the Peacebuilding Commission. Countries are required to "put themselves forward" for the commission's support. Arguably, the PBC's initial approach was to support countries that were not experiencing the worst postconflict conditions, as the initial cases of Sierra Leone and Burundi seemed to show. However, the breakdown in stability in Guinea-Bissau in 2009, with multiple assassinations of the political and military leadership, tested the commission's commitment to the full spectrum of conflict conditions.[63] The PBC subsequently included Guinea-Bissau on its agenda, though, thus signaling its openness to a broader range of selection criteria for including countries on its agenda.

The work of the PBC as a resource mobilizer for peacebuilding activities has also been controversial. Financial commitments remain voluntary and as such the initial commitment to the Peacebuilding Fund was set at US$250 million.[64] However this has now been exceeded, with a total portfolio, including deposits, of just over US$334 million. A substantial proportion of these funds (approximately 80 percent of allocations) are earmarked for countries under consideration for inclusion on the PBC's agenda, with allocations to the first four countries (Burundi, Sierra Leone, Guinea-Bissau, and the Central African Republic) totaling US$106 million.[65] However, this is a limited fund, especially when compared to the costs of US intervention in Iraq and Afghanistan, where US$944 billion was spent in financial year 2009, with US$51.8 billion disbursed for reconstruction, embassy operation and construction, and aid programs.[66] Given the precarious nature of the PBC's finances, it is difficult for the commission to be perceived as a body that can procure predictable financing for the early postconflict phases.

The governments of Sierra Leone and Burundi have also raised some concerns. In Sierra Leone, local actors have highlighted the need for the PBC to take a longer-term and more strategic approach to peacebuilding on the political as well as the financial front, especially regarding structural issues such as youth employment priorities. There was a troubling perception that the short-term focus was being driven by electoral politics.[67] There was a lack of firm political process and dialogue for addressing governance and peacebuilding issues in the country, to accompany the allocation and disbursement of financial support from the Peacebuilding Fund. There was also some confusion over the Peacebuilding Fund's support to peacebuilding priorities vis-à-vis broader development initiatives, including Sierra Leone's Poverty Reduction Strategy Paper (PRSP) process.

With respect to Burundi, the PBC was said to have had "little impact on Burundian political trends. . . . It has been a 'sideshow.'" As in Sierra Leone, the PBC stands accused of focusing on financial drive while paying scant attention to the underlying political process, although this also suited the government of the day.[68] The pressure from New York drove the prioritization of the commission's focus in Burundi, with the goal of proving its relevance to the international community. In particular, the Peacebuilding Fund has been criticized as having a more development-driven agenda, to the exclusion of core peacebuilding issues, and of largely succumbing to the Burundian PRSP process, which is fundamentally a World Bank–driven initiative. Additionally, the list of projects undertaken by the PBC is influenced by donor interests, with projects added to or removed from the list simply on this basis alone. The quick disbursement priorities of the Peacebuilding Fund are not rooted in contextual realities, and artificial deadlines are set by committees thousands of miles away. The dominance of the opinions of elites within the agenda of the PBC has emerged as a key feature in Burundi, and there have been complaints about the overwhelming focus on government actors and political elites in its activities.

It is still too early to assess the performance of the United Nations Peacebuilding Commission with any degree of precision, but this chapter has raised questions about a number of issues that are likely to limit its effectiveness in African contexts. These limitations are related to the structure of the UN system, which is in part replicated in the PBC, where rich, powerful states still have a disproportionate influence. African elites and government representatives are often complicit in the consolidation of Western interests, which has led to the acceptance of neoliberal policy directions, with dire consequences for the global poor.

The failure to incorporate conflict prevention in the mandate of the PBC runs contrary to the expansive notion of peacebuilding and to realities and requirements in many parts of Africa. This limited mandate reflects concerns of member states regarding the possible violation of their sovereignty. This arguably reflects deeper structural challenges within a system whose less powerful members are unable to rely on the UN as a fair arbitrator in the face of its more powerful members.

Greater devolution to country teams, rather than the current format of the Peacebuilding Commission playing the overarching role and the country teams simply reporting back via video conferences or "flying visits," would also be an improvement. As the commission increases the number of countries considered for inclusion on its agenda, there will be increasing pressure to adopt a more formulaic approach to each case. It will be important to avoid any tendency to apply non-context-specific practices to different countries.

The sustainability of the case-by-case approach will need to be nurtured especially in light of the commission's inclination to "suggest" priority areas as a starting point in any peacebuilding strategy, thus giving the impression of a modeled approach.[69] The proposed priority areas—basic safety and security, support for political processes, provision of basic services, support for core government functions, and support for economic activities—are laudable objectives of peacebuilding processes, but framing them as standardized starting points risks the appearance of a "one size fits all" approach. Furthermore, there is the likelihood that a prescriptive understanding of these objectives will become entrenched, a prescriptive understanding that does not draw from the particular contexts, but rather borrows from dominant normative frameworks that are developed superficially.

The Peacebuilding Commission could benefit from the permanent presence of representatives of regional organizations, since many of these regional actors, such as ECOWAS, play substantial roles in peace-building. To be relevant in the long run to Africa's conflict and security challenges, the PBC might need to align itself to these regional and subregional structures and processes. The 2010 review of UN peace-building architecture reinforces this point by noting the vast experience of these institutions and recommending that "the Commission tap into this wealth of experience, in Africa and on other continents."[70]

The challenges posed by low-intensity conflicts, for which the PBC currently has no strategy, are among Africa's most important regional security concerns. In its present form, the Peacebuilding Commission will be at best marginally relevant to Africa, and at worst irrelevant, if it fails to overcome the limits that prevent it from contributing to a more transformative peacebuilding agenda.

Notes

1. For a discussion of the evolution of the concept of peacebuilding, see Curtis in this volume.

2. Doyle and Sambanis, *Making War and Building Peace,* 23.

3. Call and Cook, "On Democratization and Peacebuilding."

4. United Nations, *More Secure World.*

5. United Nations, *In Larger Freedom.*

6. United Nations, "Revised Draft Outcome Document of the High-Level Plenary Meeting of the General Assembly of September 2005."

7. For the text of these peace agreements, see http://unmis.unmissions.org/Default.aspx?tabid=515 and http://www.iss.co.za/Af/RegOrg/unity_to_union/pdfs/ecowas/liberiapeace.pdf. For details on the peace processes in Sudan and Liberia, see Srinivasan and Ero respectively in this volume.

8. See, for instance, "Iraq War Was Illegal and Breached UN Charter, Says Annan," *Guardian,* September 16, 2004.

9. Thald Deen, "UN Credibility at Stake over Iraq, Warn Diplomats," *Inter Press Service,* October 20, 2002.

10. United Nations, "Revised Draft Outcome Document."

11. Ibid. See also United Nations Security Council, "Peacebuilding Commission"; and United Nations Peacebuilding Commission, http://www.un.org/peace/peacebuilding/mem-orgcomembers.shtml.

12. Presently the PBC works only on a case-by-case basis. and hence, globally, much of the UN's peacebuilding efforts continue to take place in the Departments of Peace-keeping Operations and Political Affairs, the UNDP, and other relevant agencies.

13. United Nations, "First Session of the Organisational Committee of the UN Peacebuilding Commission."

14. United Nations Security Council, "Peacebuilding Commission"; United Nations Peacebuilding Commission, http://www.un.org/peace/peacebuilding/mem-orgcomembers.shtml.

15. United Nations Peacebuilding Support Office, "Chair's Summary on Peacebuilding Commission Working Group on Lessons Learned."

16. United Nations, "First Session of the Organisational Committee."

17. United Nations Peacebuilding Fund, "Peacebuilding Fund Brochure."

18. United Nations Peacebuilding Fund, "Key Figures as of 28 February 2010."

19. Comment by Mr. Eloho Otobo, Deputy Head, Peacebuilding Support Office (PBSO).

20. United Nations Peacebuilding Fund, "Peacebuilding Fund Brochure."

21. Rugumamu, *Does the UN Peacebuilding Commission Change the Mode of Peacebuilding in Africa?*

22. Center for International Cooperation and International Peace Institute, "Taking Stock and Looking Forward."

23. Otobo, "A UN Architecture to Build Peace in Post-Conflict Situations," 46–49.

24. Action Aid, CAFOD, and Care International, *Consolidating the Peace*, 26.

25. Ibid.

26. United Nations, *Review of the United Nations Peacebuilding Architecture*, 3.

27. Rugumamu, *Does the UN Peacebuilding Commission Change the Mode of Peacebuilding in Africa?*

28. Atwood and Tanner, "UN Peacebuilding Commission and International Geneva."

29. United Nations, *Review of the United Nations Peacebuilding Architecture*.

30. Cited in Ponzio, "United Nations Peacebuilding Commission."

31. Center for International Cooperation and International Peace Institute, "Taking Stock and Looking Forward."

32. World Federalist Movement—Institute for Global Policy, "Press Briefing."

33. United Nations, *Review of the United Nations Peacebuilding Architecture*.

34. Murithi, "UN Peacebuilding Commission."

35. United Nations, *Review of the United Nations Peacebuilding Architecture*, 9.

36. Ibid., 10.

37. Rugumamu, *Does the UN Peacebuilding Commission Change the Mode of Peacebuilding in Africa?* 32.

38. Biersteker, "Prospects for the UN Peacebuilding Commission."

39. See Oyefusi in this volume.

40. Economic Community of West African States, "ECOWAS Conflict Prevention Framework."

41. Murithi, "UN Peacebuilding Commission."

42. United Nations, *Review of the United Nations Peacebuilding Architecture*.

43. United Nations, *In Larger Freedom*.

44. Murithi, "UN Peacebuilding Commission."

45. Adebajo, "Ending Global Apartheid."

46. Jonah, "Security Council, the General Assembly, the Economic and Social Council, and the Secretariat."

47. Ibid.

48. Action Aid, CAFOD, and Care International, *Consolidating the Peace*, 12.

49. Pugh, "Political Economy of Peacebuilding."

50. United Nations, *Review of the United Nations Peacebuilding Architecture*.

51. Ibid.

52. Jenkins, "Organizational Change and Institutional Survival," 1327.

53. Rugumamu, *Does the UN Peacebuilding Commission Change the Mode of Peacebuilding in Africa?*

54. Within this there is access to a small window of support to some conflict countries judged to be beyond the realm of International Development Association (IDA) support and poor CPIA scorers, notably referred to by the World Bank as the Low

Income Countries Under Stress (LICUS) (this has since been transformed to the conflict-affected and fragile states group). There is a LICUS trust fund totaling US$25 million from 2002, benefiting a number of countries including Somalia, Sudan, Liberia (at the time), and the Central African Republic. International Development Association, "IDA 14."

55. World Bank, "Country Policy and Institutional Assessments: 2008 Assessment Questionnaire."

56. For more on the engagement of the World Bank in peacebuilding, see Harrison in this volume.

57. Rugumamu, *Does the UN Peacebuilding Commission Change the Mode of Peacebuilding in Africa?*

58. Action Aid, CAFOD, and CARE International, *Consolidating the Peace,* 16.

59. Ibid., 17.

60. Ibid., 27.

61. United Nations, "Peacebuilding Commission."

62. United Nations, "Peacebuilding Commission Guidelines for the Participation of Civil Society in the Meetings of the Peacebuilding Commission."

63. "Guinea-Bissau President Shot Dead," *BBC News,* March 2, 2009.

64. McAskie, "International Peacebuilding Challenge."

65. United Nations Peacebuilding Fund, "Key Figures as of 28 February 2010."

66. Belasco, "Cost of Iraq, Afghanistan, and Other Global War on Terror Operations since 9/11," 10.

67. Discussion in this and the next paragraph is based on Action Aid, CAFOD, and Care International, *Consolidating the Peace,* 12–13, 22 (quotation), 25, 30–32.

68. ActionAid, CAFOD, and CARE International, *Consolidating the Peace,* 22.

69. United Nations, *Report of the Secretary-General on Peacebuilding in the Immediate Aftermath of Conflict.*

70. United Nations, *Review of the United Nations Peacebuilding Architecture,* 32.

EIGHT

Financing Peace?

The World Bank, Reconstruction, and Liberal Peacebuilding

GRAHAM HARRISON

THE WORLD BANK AND THE INTERNATIONAL MONETARY FUND (IMF) have not been key players in peacebuilding. Quite explicitly, the Bank has defined peacebuilding and emergency relief as outside of its remit.[1] Rather, it has remained dedicated to its core function—larger-scale social and physical infrastructure lending and policy-based lending. Nevertheless, Africa's share of postconflict funds from the Bank has risen dramatically since the mid-1990s and the continent, as many chapters in this book recognize, has been the site of many of the world's civil conflicts in the post–Cold War period. Thus, although the Bank has put its greatest lump sums into postconflict states such as Kosovo and Iraq, it has also increasingly involved itself in some African countries including Uganda, Sierra Leone, Eritrea, and Mozambique.

The World Bank's and IMF's engagement in peacebuilding reveals many of the problems that characterize the relations between these international financial institutions (IFIs) and African countries. Peacebuilding has largely been an inevitable point of reference rather than a core operational theme for the IFIs. On a continent that has been so besieged by civil war, it has proven necessary for all external agencies to reconcile themselves to the challenges of engagement in "complex emergencies"[2] and the political economy of peace and reconstruction. For the World Bank in particular, peacebuilding has served as a rubric under which a series of reconstruction activities have been assembled with a view to the expedited and enhanced disbursal of (often soft) loans and grants. But this aspect of Bank activity is accompanied by another dynamic: the ongoing general orientation of macroeconomic policy-based lending as currently encapsulated in the Poverty Reduction Strategy Paper (PRSP) process and supported by the Bank. This chapter outlines the modalities of IFI involvement and explores the interactions between lending in postconflict situations and the political economy of neoliberal policy-based lending.

The World Bank and IMF have become central to African governance and development. Throughout the late 1990s and early 2000s, these sibling creditor organizations were the dominant external agencies in Africa, lending substantial amounts of money to governments and nongovernmental organizations (NGOs) with a focus on discrete projects, targeted sectoral initiatives, and also general budgetary support. In fact, the IFIs have always been involved throughout transitions from war to peace; it was simply that this transition was not named and packaged as such before the United Nations (UN) took up the specific challenges of "peacebuilding" beginning in 1994. A good example of this is Mozambique from 1992 onward following the signing of a general peace agreement after a protracted war. In this case, the IMF and World Bank had been very much involved in Mozambique's governance since 1986, and remained so throughout the transition to a multiparty postconflict political system. Although aspects of Bank lending were labeled as "reconstruction" (road building, for example), there was also a sense that the IFIs were pursuing an agenda that did not need to be significantly modified to tailor it to either the specific demands of war or the challenges of peacebuilding.[3] This was especially the case with the IMF, which drew substantial public opprobrium in Mozambique for its strict adherence to neoliberal conditionalities, even in the immediate postconflict period.[4] More generally, the IMF has remained—characteristically—indifferent to the specific circumstances that country context or states of war or peace present. For the IMF and to a large extent the World Bank as well, the solutions are universal: they set the answers to any developmental questions.[5] As such, the IMF has not developed a strong specific voice on peacebuilding.[6]

The IFIs and Conflict: A Very Short History

The World Bank established its Post Conflict Unit (PCU) in 1995. But before this, the Bank and IMF had been heavily involved in African countries that were either enduring war or implementing transitions to peace, such as Sudan (1978) and Uganda (1981). Throughout the 1980s and early 1990s, the IFIs cleaved narrowly to a neoliberal policy agenda that was realized through structural adjustment programs (SAPs). These programs, which went by various names in different countries, set fundamental economic dictates that reined in money supply, removed price controls and other forms of regulation, privatized state-owned enterprises, and opened up national economies to international trade and investment. The 1980s saw this agenda spread to practically all countries on the continent: by the end of the decade, thirty-six African states had implemented 243 adjustment agreements with the World Bank and IMF.[7]

And, of course, this universalization meant that SAPs became one of the tools that some countries used to manage war and transitions toward peace. It is worth reflecting a little longer on Mozambique, because of the importance of IFI involvement in the country and the extremely challenging circumstances of moving toward peace.[8]

Mozambique embarked on structural adjustment, known as the Economic Rehabilitation Programme (PRE), beginning in 1986.[9] The program contained within it conditionalities concerned with price liberalization and devaluation. This was seen, in the words of one researcher, as "bringing the war to the cities."[10] This is a telling phrase: it likens structural adjustment to the social disruption and hardship caused by war. And it was certainly the case that, during the war in Mozambique, the majority of the urban population experienced structural adjustment as additional social hardship and uncertainty—a result of the removal of price controls and retrenchment in particular.[11] The social damage done by the PRE was implicitly acknowledged by the World Bank in its second program, the Economic and Social Rehabilitation Programme (PRES), which included "safety net" expenditure items that would ease the transition from a statist to a market-based political economy.[12] Of course, underpinning both programs was the belief that economic liberalization would generate economic growth. In the context of a singeing war that had already destroyed so much of Mozambique's physical and social infrastructure, this belief seemed to many to be both fantastical and inappropriate.

So, to what extent did the transition to peace make a difference to the IFIs' involvement in Mozambique? One can make a rough distinction between two phases: the transition toward multiparty democracy and the multiparty period itself. From 1992 to 1994, Mozambique underwent a remarkable transition from war to peace. The Mozambican

National Resistance (Renamo), a former guerrilla organization, became a political party, and the UN invested very heavily in the demobilization of troops and the organization of elections.[13] International donors and NGOs eagerly arrived or increased their presence in order to contribute to the transition's social and economic components. The World Bank, along with the IMF, was at the heart of the reconstruction drive. It invested heavily in infrastructure such as roads, water supply, health, and education. Concurrently, the Bank maintained its macroeconomic focus on liberalization. Its strategy was to lend money to smooth a transition toward a liberal political economy, and this required maintaining its faith toward neoliberal basics throughout. "Normalcy" was defined as good adherence to neoliberal policies and a resumption of growth.

The 1994 elections saw the ruling party, the Liberation Front of Mozambique (Frelimo), maintain incumbency. Frelimo had been concertedly implementing aspects of the SAP agenda since the late 1980s and was now enjoying democratic legitimacy, civic peace, and close relations with the IFIs. As a result, Frelimo received strong support from the World Bank,[14] and the country's gross national income grew by a striking 11 percent in 1997 and maintained strong growth into the 2000s. It was the Heavily Indebted Poor Country (HIPC) scheme and the subsequent Poverty Reduction Strategy Paper process[15] that cemented Frelimo's support from the IFIs. The "normalization" constructed through these credit mechanisms was at the heart of the World Bank's contribution to peacebuilding in Mozambique.

Mozambique's experience is revealing; we can draw out salient aspects of the IFIs' involvement in transitions from war (with due recognition of nationally specific contexts). In essence:

- Structural adjustment continues throughout war and peace.

- The IFIs have generally seen their role during transitions to peace as lending for special and transitional social and infrastructural programs.

- The expectation is that there will be a transition to stability and normalcy, defined in neoliberal terms and underpinned by economic growth.

These key features could also be found in the IFIs' involvement in Angola, Liberia, Sierra Leone, and Rwanda during the 1990s, and these features persist in current peacebuilding endeavors. Clearly, in the cases of the 1990s, the trajectories of the conflicts and the IFIs' expectations did not match. SAPs were abandoned; conflict continued during and after elections; relations between states and the IFIs shifted drastically; and there was no straightforward stability and growth response. Indeed, in these more problematic cases, it might also be argued that the IFIs' involvement actually contributed to the instability and militarism that prolonged conflict or undermined moments of peace.

For instance, the government that prosecuted the 1994 genocide in Rwanda had maintained close relations with the World Bank up until 1994. The Bank, among many other donors, considered Rwanda to be a kind of success story, a success based in the strength of the government. Indeed, "the World Bank seemed to be the one with the strongest love affair with Rwanda."[16] The Bank's focus on working with an effective development partner meant that the increasingly violent and racist politics of the state were largely ignored.[17] In Sierra Leone, the World Bank and IMF led an attempt to liberalize the economy and roll back the state during civil war, as they did in Mozambique. Here, as David Keen details, state rollback exacerbated aspects of the civil war by making general social hardship more extreme and by supporting the National Provisional Ruling Council government, which was violating Sierra Leoneans' human rights on a large scale. Reminiscent of the kind of language that the Bank used in Rwanda in the early 1990s, the Bank stated that "the Government of Sierra Leone is carrying out a comprehensive program of economic growth aimed at achieving sustainable growth and reducing poverty."[18]

As an examination of other case studies would reveal, one can discern a paradoxical presence of the Bank and IMF in countries prone to or engaged in civil conflict. The Bank tends to depoliticize its relations with governments, looking only at issues of program implementation even when other radical and violent political practices might be present. But partly in contrast, the SAPs that are advocated by the Bank and IMF tend to undermine the ability of states to ensure forms of formal and informal social provision that tie together some sense of political order.[19] In this situation, states become vulnerable to radical instability of a kind that Chris Allen called "terminal spoils,"[20] or that William Reno identified as a violent kind of "shadow politics."[21]

Thus the Bank in its involvement in conflict situations has relied on core structural adjustment policies to guide its lending, regardless of the particular situation in a particular country. It has lent money to promote reconstruction, and this has been the main distinguishing feature of its lending to states recovering from civil conflict. But it is also the case that the "deep politics" of the Bank—its cleaving to a neoliberal agenda and its shyness about addressing state politics outside the modalities of implementation—have left it with an awkward relationship to conflict. This is critical to peacebuilding, since the policies promoted by the Bank may at times aggravate tensions. Furthermore, peace is not achieved through the signing of a cease-fire agreement and a political transition alone. Rather, low-level violence commonly remains; much of the social structures that in one way or another fueled conflict also often remain in place; and there is always the possibility that civil war, however defined, might break out again. We can see this clearly from Angola in the mid-1990s to Côte d'Ivoire in the early 2000s. The IFIs' (re)actions throughout the messy shifts between war and relative peace are extremely relevant.

The World Bank and Peacebuilding

Since the late 1990s the World Bank has demonstrated a willingness to engage with a range of development agendas that have emerged from other institutions, and this is the case with the peacebuilding agenda that has largely emerged from the UN. As ever, the Bank is careful to define its mandate: it has always been nervous about stepping into a "political" role when it officially declares itself as a nonpolitical organization. It is this "apolitical" premise that has led the Bank to define a division of labor between the UN system and the UN's remit to manage political transitions in various ways, and the "economic" demands of reconstruction. The Bank identifies for itself the following tasks: demobilization and reintegration, reconstruction, governance, and development.[22]

These tasks each need some unpacking. *Demobilization* refers to the need to fund the cantonment, disarming, auditing, and release of former soldiers after hostilities have formally ended. *Reintegration* follows from demobilization and comprises schemes to assist ex-combatants in ensuring livelihoods without the gun, most often involving a "package" of tools and seeds to recommence farming.[23] It also involves packages to manage the return of internally displaced people and returning refugees.[24] *Reconstruction* encapsulates the Bank's lending to repair and modernize destroyed infrastructure: sabotaged roads and rails, dilapidated electricity and water systems in besieged towns, and the like. It also might involve funding de-mining operations.

Governance and development are broader aims rather than project-related objectives. The premise here is that good governance and development will ensure the broader processes of a social transition toward a peaceful state of affairs. *Governance* encapsulates a well-known agenda of transparency, participation, partnership, and accountability. The order of specific reform objectives is rearranged to address transitions to peace: security, rule of law, tax administration, and state capacity as the "Weberian" starting points from which the more normatively explicit "good governance" might be constructed. In regard to the latter, the Bank's reports frequently make linkages between the "economic" factors behind conflict and their resolution through better forms of participation, social inclusion, and economic growth. This is where *development* comes in: transitions of peace must be underpinned by economic growth that is seen—to use a stylized phrase—as the solvent of social tensions. Of course, the substantial assumption behind this notion is that liberalized economic management and growth will generate socially beneficial outcomes, rather than intensified or new inequalities and social tensions. This is known in the critical literature as the "liberal peace" argument.[25]

The liberal peace model is central to recent Bank thinking on post-conflict assistance, so it requires more analysis. The premise of the liberal peace approach is that economic and political liberalization are complementary to peacebuilding efforts. This is precisely where the Bank can claim to be contributing to peacebuilding: "assistance must focus on recreating the conditions that will allow the private sector and institutions of civil society to resume commercial and productive activities."[26] Whatever context-specific peacebuilding measures might be required and implemented by other agencies, such as truth and reconciliation commissions and demobilization and reintegration, the movement away from these specific tasks to a "sustainable" peace is to be found within liberal governance and the free market.[27] This association is based on a belief that liberalization produces positive-sum and stabilizing effects on societies, a belief that pervades the Bank's development ideology.[28] But it is also the case that the Bank thinks through its worldview in the context of postconflict recovery in more particular ways.

At the heart of the Bank's lending in postconflict states is multi-sectoral lending, which largely connotes nonproject lending to rebuild states, capacity building and technical assistance in particular. Much of this lending appears to be the familiar governance reform that one might find in (relatively peaceful) Tanzania as much as in (relatively conflict-laden) Uganda over the past two decades.[29] But aspects of governance reform in postconflict states carry with them certain assumptions about liberal reform and peacebuilding.

The leitmotif of the Bank's multisectoral lending is normalization, which means directly (re)establishing relations with external agencies by clearing arrears, establishing working relations with the IFIs, and engaging on the processes embedded in HIPC, PRSP, and a range of other sectoral programs that address issues such as HIV/AIDS, agriculture, and so forth. The framework for normalization is commonly a postconflict needs assessment, which feeds into the creation of an interim PRSP.[30] But normalization also serves as a useful way to stylize more specific aspects of Bank lending in postconflict situations.

For instance, the Bank lends in order to support the rule of law in many countries. This requires a rehabilitation of police and military forces, a revived judiciary, a stronger legal protection of contracts, the establishment of property rights, and the rehabilitation of basic fiscal institutions.[31] The bulk of the Bank's State and Peacebuilding Fund (SPF), in its first objective, speaks to this agenda.[32] Ostensibly, this agenda seems perfectly sensible: it evokes ideas of social order and transparency, and the old and venerable liberal idea that property ownership promotes social stability.

But capitalism in Africa has rarely followed the liberal ideal. Indeed, aspects of capitalist development have generated conflict throughout Africa's colonial and postcolonial history.[33] Property rights are contested, or asserted through violence, in many places, and therefore any reassertion of rights might involve exclusion. The alienation of land and resources has been a driver of civil conflicts throughout the continent.[34] Whatever one's convictions about the nature of capitalism in Africa, it is reasonable to say that the Bank and other donors fail to, or cannot, recognize that the construction of regimes of property rights is necessarily political and contentious. In this sense, liberal reconstruction runs a risk of generating social sources of conflict. Institutions like the World Bank do not have the wherewithal to address this fact.

Institutions, Practices, and Programs

We have seen that IFI involvement in conflict and postconflict states has undergone a series of changes and that the IFIs have played a role in contexts of both war and peace in many countries. A salient feature of this involvement, throughout all of the turbulence and uncertainty of either failed or successful transitions, is structural adjustment and its progenies. As well, the World Bank has worked hard to develop a more detailed approach to peacebuilding, one that is less exclusively based on adjustment, and it is here that we find the liberal peace doctrine. The key argument is that the World Bank has developed a heuristic framework within which to engage in peacebuilding, in which neoliberal coordinates are married to the aspirations of liberal governance, are duly supported, and cautiously realized. So, how has the World Bank put its ideas into practice?

The Bank's establishment of its Post Conflict Unit in 1995 marked the inception of a dedicated unit to monitor conflicts, strategize early interventions, and liaise with other external donors and creditors. Throughout the 1990s, the Bank was concerned with maintaining its institutional identity vis-à-vis other agencies. The PCU functioned to coordinate donors' peacebuilding efforts, not to set a distinct World Bank agenda. The PCU was renamed the Conflict Prevention and Reconstruction Unit (CPRU) in 2001 as part of a moderate upgrading that involved a larger dedication of money.[35] The Low Income Countries Under Stress (LICUS) unit was created in 2004 with a remit that overlapped that of the CPRU. Both were effectively trust funds for discrete "exceptional" projects in states that were deemed to be suffering from, recovering from, or likely to fall back into conflict. As trust funds, the CPRU and LICUS disbursed money as grants. Though their activities were not well defined, the CPRU and LICUS were underpinned by an aim to move countries toward a "normalized" reconstruction process that would require mainstream International Development Association (IDA) and International Bank for Reconstruction and Development (IBRD) funding, closely followed by the broader frameworks of the HIPC scheme and PRSP process.

In 2008, the Bank's State and Peacebuilding Fund (SPF) was inaugurated with its own funding base (US$100 million for the period 2009–11 from the Bank, with additional funding from bilaterals) and its own strategic objectives. The SPF integrated the CPRU and LICUS, and signaled an increasing concertedness in the Bank's efforts to assist states in transitions out of conflict. The SPF aims to provide grants toward projects that promote state institutional stability and social reconstruction. The SPF has granted money for the same key areas already outlined, but reformulated to focus on improving governance and institutions, and reconstruction.[36]

The most salient aspect of the SPF is its integration of statebuilding and peacebuilding. These are seen as complementary and mutually reinforcing. The logic of the SPF is that effective neoliberal reform must be premised on a certain state infrastructure; this moves the Bank into a certain kind of state*building*, which cuts a contrast with the adjustment-related obsession with state rollback. States need to be strengthened in order to provide transparent governance, rule of law, social investment, and development of infrastructure. Peacebuilding is seen as the creation of a "peaceful, stable and sustainable" society.[37] Although this fits well with the liberal peace approach, the increasingly prominent suturing of statebuilding and peacebuilding is problematic. Whereas building states is concrete, building peace is abstract; peacebuilding does not signify a specific agency to build. What the SPF sets out is a readiness to work with NGOs and other donors to promote labor-intensive reconstruction projects, "safety net" funds, NGO reconciliation projects, and so on.[38] These projects might improve the lives of the target groups who benefit from projects, but it would be a stretch to define this as peacebuilding. An example of this targeted intervention would be the funding of public works programs for the demobilized.

The focus on statebuilding is complex.[39] Historically, strong states have ensured social peace through violence as well as through law and good governance. In the African context, where states have colonial origins and have been complicit in widespread violence against their citizenries, as is the case during civil wars, the assumption that building states will contribute to sustainable peace needs to be treated with caution. States are not simply institutions. They are also embodiments of modes of authority: they articulate ideologies, shore up ruling classes, and develop practices of governing that will at best involve aspects of liberal politics but will perhaps rely on more factionalized forms of authority and order. And states are historically embedded: rebuilding is not practiced on a tabula rasa.[40]

The SPF's remit shows no awareness of the difficult relationships between state strength and social peace. In fact, it rarely shows any awareness that protracted civil conflict has a profound effect on a country. One could cut all references to conflict out of SPF documentation and identify a fairly orthodox and generic World Bank program of neoliberalism and good governance. As with other "emergency" areas, the Bank has its solutions and largely sets these solutions to the problem at hand. The SPF seems likely to be a special fund to prepare postconflict states for the orthodoxies of the PRSP process.

In sum, the Bank has constructed a series of institutional innovations to put postconflict recovery more clearly at the heart of its operational strategy. But this does not indicate a significant policy innovation that tailors itself to the specific conditions of the transition from war to peace. Instead, we can identify that the World Bank has pursued three tasks. First, the Bank provides quick-release grants and technical assistance with a view to normalizing countries' relations with external agencies, most directly the IFIs. Second, the Bank provides grants for projects that are important for postconflict recovery, but these projects are also often of the kind that one might find in a nonconflict country that is borrowing from the Bank and the IMF. Thus the Bank's approach to postconflict engagement consists of expedited disbursal through dedicated trust funds, with a view to normalization within a very short period of time, after which the Bank's orthodoxies of governance, growth, and poverty reduction might take hold. Third, the Bank supports statebuilding through capacity building and lending to build up key institutions of governance in ways that efface the political issues that accompany these processes.

Africa appears to be enjoying a relatively peaceful moment, certainly compared to the period from the end of the Cold War to the mid-1990s. But many countries that have achieved formalized peace remain besieged by insecurities: low-intensity conflict, banditry, extreme poverty that makes "normalization" difficult to entertain, and political parties or organizations that remain only partially incorporated into liberal political practices. What does this mean for the World Bank and International Monetary Fund?

Perhaps the Bank should remove itself from conflict-prone states. If the basic public goods of peace and order are not in place, the Bank's policy-based lending will not work. This view represents a risk-averse point of view that allows the Bank to reduce its lending liabilities. It also reflects a debate about governance and aid effectiveness that took place in the mid-1990s, in which it was argued that lending should be concentrated in states that have demonstrated the "political will" to implement reforms. There are two problems with this argument. First, ethically, it means accepting that some of the world's most impoverished, brutalized, and desperate populations will be cut off from international concern. Second, it cuts off any discussions about *effective* intervention and *acceptable* risk, each of which might be achieved even within the Bank's own neoliberal terms of reference. For instance, in Mozambique, the Bank's social lending and support for the state, while hardly unproblematic, did play a part in the securing of peace and in the process of reconstruction, a process that, though limited, has been sufficiently effective to make a resumption of large-scale war extremely unlikely.

The realization that emerges from a study of Mozambique, as well as other relative successful peacebuilding cases, is that movement away from war and toward peace is both complex and largely nationally based.[41] Large amounts of external assistance can be marginal or even damaging if segments of a state or society are antagonistic toward peacebuilding. This has been the case with Sierra Leone recently.[42] Perhaps, then, the World Bank, and many other external agencies, should be more modest about the scope of their ambitions. A stronger sense of fallibility might enable more flexible forms of lending, which by itself can never ensure a successful transition to peace. Whether the World Bank's institutional culture might allow such a shift in mind-set is another question.

Notes

1. Kreimer, Eriksson, Muscat, Arnold, and Scott, *World Bank's Experience with Post-Conflict Reconstruction.*

2. Keen, *Complex Emergencies.*

3. In fact, the World Bank's first large "emergency" loan was in response to the floods of 2001, seven years after the end of the war in Mozambique. Before the mid-1990s, the Bank's project documentation generally conflated "natural" and conflict disasters.

4. Hanlon, *Peace without Profit.*

5. Fine, "Developmental State Is Dead"; Pincus, "State Simplification and Institution Building in a World Bank Financed Development Project."

6. In the IMF's words on fiscal reconstruction, "Advice was in many ways similar to what it recommends in countries without conflicts, but with important nuances." International Monetary Fund (IMF), *Rebuilding Fiscal Institutions in Post-Conflict Countries,* 4.

7. Chazan, Mortimer, Ravenhill, and Rothchild, *Politics and Society in Contemporary Africa,* 337.

8. Plank, "Aid, Debt, and the End of Sovereignty."

9. Mozambique's conflict, part insurgency and part external intervention by proxy from South Africa, lasted from 1977 to 1992.

10. Marshall, *War, Debt, and Structural Adjustment in Mozambique,* 1.

11. Hermele, "Guerra e estabilização"; Hermele, *Mozambican Crossroads.*

12. Hanlon, *Peace without Profit.*

13. For a discussion of disarmament, demobilization, and reintegration (DDR) in Mozambique, see Dzinesa in this volume.

14. Michailof, Kostner, and Devictor, *Post-Conflict Recovery in Africa.*

15. On the similarities and differences between SAPs and the PRSP process, see Gould, ed., *New Conditionality.*

16. Uvin, *Aiding Violence,* 46.

17. Storey, "Structural Adjustment, State Power, and Genocide."

18. Keen, "Liberalization and Conflict," 82. See also Andersen, "How Multilateral Development Assistance Triggered the Conflict in Rwanda"

19. Keen, "Liberalization and Conflict," 82.

20. Allen, "Understanding African Politics."

21. Reno, *Warlord Politics and African States.*

22. Taken from World Bank, *Post-Conflict Reconstruction.*

23. Spear, "Disarmament, Demobilisation, Reinsertion, and Reintegration in Africa."

24. For a further discussion and analysis of DDR in Africa, see Omach in this volume.

25. Heathershaw, "Unpacking the Liberal Peace"; Moore, "Levelling the Playing Fields."

26. World Bank, *Post-Conflict Reconstruction,* 25.

27. Castaneda, "How Liberal Peacebuilding May Be Failing Sierra Leone."

28. Harrison, "World Bank and Theories of Political Action in Africa."

29. Harrison, *World Bank and Africa: The Construction of Governance States.*

30. Kievelitz, Schaef, Leonhardt, Hahn, and Vorweck, *Practical Guide to Multilateral Needs Assessments in Post-Conflict Situations.*

31. IMF, *Rebuilding Fiscal Institutions.*

32. World Bank, *Establishment of a State and Peacebuilding Fund,* 8.

33. Cramer, *Civil War Is Not a Stupid Thing.*

34. Moore, "Levelling the Playing Fields."

35. Van Houten, "The World Bank's (Post-)Conflict Agenda."

36. World Bank, *Establishment of a State and Peacebuilding Fund.*

37. Ibid.

38. Projects highlighted by the SPF's 2009 progress report on Africa include "a youth employment and infrastructure project in Somalia; a programmatic, partnership approach to livelihood support in Zimbabwe; stabilization of electricity provision and of the state revenue generated from the sale of electricity in the Central Africa Republic; land reform in Liberia; two projects in Togo to strengthen the private sector and civil society." World Bank, State and Peacebuilding Fund, *Progress Report.*

39. See Zaum in this volume.

40. Englebert and Tull, "Post-Conflict Reconstruction in Africa."

41. Francis, ed. *Peace and Conflict in Africa;* Rigby, "Civil Society, Reconciliation, and Conflict Transformation in Post-War Africa."

42. Baker and May, "Reconstructing Sierra Leone"; Kandeh, "Rogue Incumbents, Donor Assistance, and Sierra Leone's Second Post-Conflict Elections of 2007"; Le Billon and Levin, "Building Peace with Conflict Diamonds? Merging Security and Development in Sierra Leone."

NINE

The International Criminal Court

A Peacebuilder in Africa?

SARAH NOUWEN

> Lasting peace requires justice—this was the decision taken in
> Rome by 120 States.
>
>> Luis Moreno-Ocampo, prosecutor of the International
>> Criminal Court, "Building a Future on Peace and Justice"

DOES A CHAPTER ON THE INTERNATIONAL CRIMINAL COURT (ICC)
belong in a book on peacebuilding in Africa? The ICC is definitely
relevant to Africa. Since the beginning of its operations in 2003, the
world's first permanent international criminal court has opened seven
investigations, each of them on the African continent. With European
states as the court's most fervent supporters and with its investigations
in Uganda, the Democratic Republic of the Congo (DRC), Sudan, the
Central African Republic, Kenya, Libya, and Ivory Coast, the ICC is
sometimes dubbed the "European Court for African Affairs."

But what is the relation between the ICC and peacebuilding? Is an
international court that was established to investigate, prosecute, and try
war crimes, crimes against humanity, and genocide a "peacebuilder"?[1]
How do peace and justice relate? More fundamentally, what is peace?
Is it the absence of war and violence ("negative peace") or the absence of
causes of violence ("positive peace")?[2] What is justice? Is it the enforcement of the rule of law ("legal justice"), the elimination of structural and
systematic injustices such as political and economic discrimination and

inequalities of distribution ("distributive justice"), or the addressing of the direct consequences inflicted on individuals ("rectificatory justice")? If the latter, should the focus be on the restoration of the position of the victim and of the affected relationships ("restorative justice") or on inflicting a penalty on the perpetrator ("punitive justice")?[3]

The complexity of these questions notwithstanding, the international criminal justice movement, a loose coalition of mainly Western nongovernmental organizations (NGOs), other Western-funded NGOs, and officials working in or on international criminal tribunals, has straightforward answers. The opening statement on the website of the Coalition for the International Criminal Court immediately reveals its conception of justice—"Together for Justice: Civil society . . . advocating for a fair, effective and independent ICC."[4] Justice in this context refers to ICC-style justice, which is individual rather than communal, criminal rather than distributive, and punitive rather than restorative. Victim participation and reparations remain subsidiary to the ICC's main focus on the criminal accountability of perpetrators. With respect to peace, the international criminal justice movement seems to focus on positive peace, arguing that impunity ultimately begets more violence. Without hard empirical evidence for the correlation, let alone a causal relationship, between ICC-style criminal justice and peace, the international criminal justice movement contends that "lasting peace requires justice," irrespective of the actual outcomes of the Court's actions. "No peace without justice" became one of the most dominant ideologies of the 1990s, and remains so today.

This chapter challenges the "no peace without justice" ideology on the basis of the ICC's experiences in Uganda and Sudan. The situation in northern Uganda was referred to the Court by the Ugandan government itself, while the situation in Darfur (Sudan) was referred to the Court by the Security Council.[5] The difference in how the Court became involved in these two cases allows for an analysis of the different interests involved. The chapter begins with a brief exploration of how criminal justice could contribute to peace. It then discusses the Rome Statute's vision of justice and peace, and subsequently, turns to how the Court became involved in Uganda and Sudan. With illustrations from these case studies, the chapter next presents four ways the Court's judicial work can influence peacebuilding efforts: as an instrument of obtaining peace by military means, as a facilitator or an obstacle to peace talks, as a substitute for peace efforts, and as a catalyst for discussions on questions of accountability in peace talks. Finally, the chapter identifies key obstacles to the ICC's functioning as an instrument for peace.[6]

Criminal Justice and Peace

The argument that ICC-style justice contributes to peace is based on similar sets of assumptions regarding national criminal justice and peace, yet extends this to the international level. Criminal proceedings against alleged perpetrators of conflict-related crimes may, for instance, have the following results:

- Provide justice to victims and prevent vigilante justice

- Establish or reestablish the rule of law

- Deter future crimes, by showing that those who have violated the law do not get away with impunity

- Delegitimize those who committed crimes and diminish their potential to act as spoilers, by "incapacitating" them through trial and sentences

- Provide a bulwark against revisionism and the ensuing tensions

- Avoid demonization of social groups and facilitate reconciliation, by showing that individuals, not entire groups, bear criminal guilt

- Provide a symbolic break with a violent past, by exposing and condemning past crimes.[7]

In comparison to domestic courts, an international court may have a stronger deterrent effect internationally and may promote the rule of international law. Yet the cultural and geographical distance of an international court to the society in which the crimes were committed dilutes the potentially beneficial effects of such proceedings on the establishment or reestablishment of the rule of law in the country concerned.

Peace and Justice in the ICC's Rome Statute

The Rome Statute of the ICC establishes and governs a criminal justice mechanism. It creates a permanent international criminal court, stipulates how the Court shall conduct its proceedings and outlines how states shall cooperate with the Court. The only explicit references to peace are in a preambular recital that recognizes that "grave crimes threaten the peace, security and well-being of the world,"[8] and where the Statute criminalizes attacks against missions mandated to keep the "peace."[9] Some provisions implicitly link peace and justice. For instance, the Statute allows the United Nations (UN) Security Council to refer a situation to the ICC Prosecutor as well as to defer ICC proceedings for a renewable period of twelve months.[10] In both instances, the Council must take its decision in a resolution adopted under Chapter VII of the UN Charter, a decision which aims "to maintain or restore international peace and security."[11] The Statute thus recognizes that both a referral of a situation to the Prosecutor and a deferral of ICC proceedings can be in the interest of peace.

The Statute's silences are equally revealing. Some delegations at the Rome Conference argued that the Statute should address the relevance of national amnesties for ICC proceedings.[12] The Statute, however, makes no mention of this, and national amnesties, which are a matter of domestic law, do not bind the ICC. Others have suggested that the ICC could and should play a role in rebuilding domestic justice systems,[13] through which the Court could contribute to the rule of law and in that way to peace. However, again, the Statute provides no legal basis for doing so.

As it is, the Statute provides only limited and narrow avenues for halting ICC proceedings if they appear to obstruct the achievement of (negative) peace. First, as mentioned, the Security Council can defer ICC proceedings if acting under Chapter VII of the UN Charter. The deferral is renewable every twelve months, but each instance is subject to a veto of a permanent member of the Security Council. As a result, peace negotiators and mediators cannot guarantee to negotiating parties that the ICC will not become involved again.

Second, the Statute allows the ICC Prosecutor to decide not to investigate or prosecute if this would not serve the "interests of justice."[14] When interpreted broadly, one could argue that this gives the Prosecutor discretion to refrain from proceedings if they threaten peace. But Luis Moreno-Ocampo, the ICC's first Prosecutor, has argued that an assessment of the interests of justice does not encompass the interests of peace. He has emphasized that his mandate is justice and that other institutions are responsible for peace.[15]

Third, a state can render an ICC case inadmissible by conducting genuine domestic proceedings, in accordance with the Court's complementarity principle. Pursuant to this principle, the Court may exercise

its jurisdiction in a case only in the absence of genuine domestic proceedings, whether past or present.[16] This avenue may be used to terminate the ICC's involvement in a case, but it cannot substitute ICC-style
justice. In order to render a case inadmissible on grounds of complementarity, criminal proceedings are required. If the state, prioritizing
the achievement of short-term negative peace, does not seek criminal
justice in a specific case, the ICC can assume jurisdiction in that case.

The avenues to terminate ICC proceedings in the interests of peace
are also exclusive. Only the Security Council can make the ICC defer
proceedings. No organ or person can legally compel the Prosecutor to
refrain from proceedings in the interests of justice. Only the Court's
Prosecutor and judges can decide on complementarity. The power to
decide on issues of justice and peace thus lies with international organs.
For persons affected by ICC proceedings, but not recognized as victims
of the crimes charged against a specific accused, there is no avenue to
express their views, let alone decide, on the meaning of peace and justice and how these aims should be pursued, balanced, sequenced, or
implemented.

The Referrals

Uganda

The first referral in the Court's history was made by the government of
Uganda in December 2003 and concerned its protracted conflict with
the Lord's Resistance Army (LRA). Uganda explained that it referred
the situation because

> without international cooperation and assistance, it cannot
> succeed in arresting the members of the LRA leadership
> and others most responsible for the above mentioned crimes.
> Furthermore, Uganda is of the view that the scale and gravity
> of LRA crimes are such that they are a matter of concern to the
> international community as a whole. It is thus befitting both from
> a practical and moral viewpoint to entrust the investigation and
> prosecution of these crimes to the Prosecutor of the ICC.[17]

On January 29, 2004, the Prosecutor and Ugandan president Yoweri
Museveni jointly announced the referral of "the situation concerning
the Lord's Resistance Army."[18] In light of NGOs' criticism that this

phrasing should not exclude the crimes allegedly committed by Uganda's national army (Uganda People's Defence Forces, UPDF) from the Court's investigations,[19] the OTP changed the referral's name to "the situation in northern Uganda."

The Court has issued arrest warrants against Joseph Kony and four other LRA commanders, alleging them to bear individual criminal responsibility for crimes against humanity and war crimes.[20] At the time of writing, none of the arrest warrants has been executed.[21]

Sudan

On March 31, 2005, the UN Security Council referred "the situation in Darfur since 1 July 2002" to the ICC.[22] Since the situation was referred to the Court in a resolution adopted under Chapter VII of the UN Charter, the Court can exercise jurisdiction over crimes committed by Sudanese nationals on Sudanese territory even though Sudan is not a state party to the Rome Statute. The Pre-Trial Chamber has issued arrest warrants for the then–minister of humanitarian affairs Ahmad Muhammad Harun, militia leader Ali Muhammed Abd-al-Rahman, also known as Ali Kushayb, and, for the first time in the Court's history, against an incumbent head of state, President Omar al-Bashir. All have been accused of war crimes and crimes against humanity.[23]

The arrest warrants remain to be executed. Even before the charges had been made against him, Sudanese president Omar al-Bashir swore "thrice in the name of Almighty God . . . never [to] hand any Sudanese national to a foreign court."[24]

The Prosecutor has also brought cases against three members of Darfuri rebel movements on three counts of war crimes committed during an attack on the peacekeeping force of the African Union (AU), the AU Mission in Sudan (AMIS).[25] They have appeared voluntarily before the Court.

The ICC as a Peacebuilder:
An Instrument to Defeat the Enemy?

If one were to classify the defeat of a warring party as peacebuilding, the ICC can be considered a "peacebuilder." Following this approach, the ICC Prosecutor has argued: "There is no tension between Peace and Justice in Uganda: arrest the sought criminals today, and you will have Peace and Justice tomorrow."[26] Similarly focusing on the potential of international criminal justice to incapacitate spoilers, he has argued with respect to Darfur that "arresting and removing Harun today will contribute to breaking the criminal system established in Darfur [and] will help peace, the political process and the deployment of peacekeepers."[27] In other words, international criminal justice can contribute to peace by delegitimizing and incapacitating spoilers, as the Nuremberg and Tokyo Tribunals have illustrated.

However, this potential of international criminal justice to incapacitate also makes it a powerful instrument of warfare that intensifies rather than mitigates conflict.[28] The Nuremberg and Tokyo Tribunals dealt with enemies that had already been defeated; the ICC, with jurisdiction over ongoing conflicts, provides parties with another battlefield on which to defeat their enemies. It is with this awareness of the ICC as another battleground that parties in Darfur and Uganda have co-opted the "no peace without justice" ideology when justice could lead to peace on their terms by weakening their enemy. Their opponents have rejected the Court precisely as a weapon used against them.

Take the Ugandan referral of (only) the LRA to the Court. The Ugandan government calculated that the ICC could turn the LRA from an enemy of the Ugandan government into an enemy of "the international community as a whole."[29] At the same time the referral could recharacterize the Ugandan government, the first government to refer a situation to the ICC, as a champion of international criminal justice. ICC supporters would no longer treat the LRA and the government as equal warmongers but would view Museveni's administration as a legitimate government fighting a criminal movement. Linking the arrest of the LRA leadership to the credibility of the ICC, European governments, staunch ICC supporters, would replace their criticism of UPDF abuses and of the government's failure to ameliorate the humanitarian situation in the north, with renewed support for the UPDF operations against the LRA "criminals."[30] Moreover, as the following statement of Amama Mbabazi, who was Ugandan minister of defense at the time, illustrates, the Ugandan government hoped that the ICC, with its international reach, might do what the UPDF had been unable to do: arrest the LRA. While conflating the ICC and the International Criminal Tribunal for the former Yugoslavia and ignoring the fact that enforcement is the weakest chain in the ICC's operations, he answered a parliamentary question:

> How does ICC operate? . . . They have the office of the prosecutor;
> they carry out investigations and actually the international

community supports them. So, for this Serbian, for example, there is an international force, which is hunting for that person. So, should Kony be indicted, and should he be indicted before we capture him, who will look for him in order to compel him to appear before this committee? It is not Uganda; if they ask us we shall lend a hand, but actually it will be international forces.[31]

In addition to rallying international assistance for the arrest of the LRA leadership, the referral would, so the Ugandan actors thought, convince the Sudanese government, wishing to be on the "good" side in the "war on terror" and under pressure on account of the conflict in Darfur, to discontinue its military and logistical support of the LRA.[32] In sum, concocted in the Ministry of Defense rather than Justice, the referral of the situation concerning the LRA to the ICC was part of a military and international reputation strategy.

At the same time, the use of the ICC as an instrument of war is not without risks; it may boomerang. In the example of Uganda, the ICC could equally prosecute state actors, for instance on charges of forced displacement, torture, and indiscriminate bombing. However, the Ugandan government knew the ICC's handicap of dependence on state cooperation in issues ranging from the issuance of visa for investigators to the arrest of the LRA leadership. By accusing state officials, the Prosecutor would risk the Ugandan government's cooperation in the case against the LRA.

To date, many of the Ugandan government's calculations have proved to be correct. The ICC's arrest warrants against the LRA leaders have helped the Ugandan government convince the DRC to allow the UPDF to pursue the LRA on Congolese territory. When the UPDF's military operation failed and only led to further dispersion of the LRA and the death and displacement of hundreds of civilians, there was hardly any international criticism. Indeed, the Security Council "welcome[d] the joint efforts . . . made [by states in the region] to address the security threat posed by LRA."[33] The Ugandan government has also proved right, so far, in expecting that the Prosecutor would not go after co-operative friends. The Prosecutor has not opened an investigation into alleged crimes by state actors, officially on the basis of (a dubious application of) gravity as a selection criterion.[34]

In Sudan, the calculations have been reversed. The government of Sudan rejects the Court as a Western instrument for regime change, and leaders of various rebel movements have embraced the ICC, grateful for "brother Ocampo's" legal attack on their enemy. The leaders of the Justice and Equality Movement (JEM) have increased their military activity since the Prosecutor's request for an arrest warrant against the Sudanese president in March 2009. Referring to the Prosecutor's advice to marginalize persons sought by the Court, the leader of one faction of the Sudan Liberation Movement (SLM) has refused to participate in peace talks, arguing that "war criminals" should not be negotiated with.[35] For the rebel movements, terms such as "war criminal" have become, in Mahmoud Mamdani's words, labels "to be stuck on your worst enemy, a perverse version of the Nobel Prize, part of a rhetorical arsenal that helps you vilify your adversaries while ensuring impunity for your allies."[36] Local leaders in camps for internally displaced persons have equally hinged their hopes on the ICC. "We need NATO, the EU and the ICC," they argue, listing the ICC as one of the powers that could militarily intervene in order to execute arrest warrants. In their view, international criminal justice could be an instrument to achieve peace, namely by achieving regime change.[37]

In the Darfur situation the Prosecutor has in fact brought charges against more than one side of the conflict. Yet, thus far, the charges against three members of rebel movements have not altered the positive attitude of rebel leaders toward the Court. The suspects are sought for acts that the major rebel leaders blame on a marginalized splinter group. Like the proceedings against government officials, proceedings against members of splinter movements serve the interests of the leaders of the mainstream rebel movements. The suspects themselves do not fear the Court either—they have appeared voluntarily before the Court, believing that the Prosecutor had insufficient evidence against them. One of them, Abu Garda, was proved right: the judges refused to confirm the charges against him. That decision came a week after the ICC's Appeals Chamber had ordered the Pre-Trial Chamber to reconsider its decision not to charge the Sudanese president with genocide.[38] The contrast between, on the one hand, the Court's pursuance of genocide charges against the President and, on the other hand, the Prosecutor's praise for the cooperation extended by rebel leaders and the judges' refusal to confirm the charges against one of them has in Sudan only reaffirmed the impression that the Court has taken the side of one of the parties against the other.

The ICC as a Peacebuilder:
A Facilitator or an Obstacle to Peace Talks?

Court officials have pointed to the Juba talks to substantiate their claim that the ICC spurs peace.[39] The talks between the Ugandan government and the LRA, under the auspices of the government of Southern Sudan, began a few months after the ICC had unsealed arrest warrants against the LRA leadership. These on-and-off negotiations between 2006 and 2008 resulted in the most comprehensive set of agreements between the Ugandan government and an LRA delegation in the two-decade history of the conflict.

When pointing to the Court's success in spurring these talks, the officials frequently ignore that other factors were equally if not more important in bringing the LRA to the negotiating table. The government of Sudan, which formerly had backed the LRA, had become less able and willing to continue doing so, not just because of the ICC's involvement.[40] The armies of Southern Sudan and Uganda, in turn, had increased their military pressure on the LRA. These developments threatened the LRA's long-term viability, thereby providing it with strong incentives to negotiate.

Moreover, rather than merely driving the LRA to the negotiating table, the ICC appeared to be an obstacle to the Juba talks insofar as its involvement made many states and international organizations that are supportive of the ICC reluctant to provide political and financial backing to the talks. They argued that their ratification or endorsement of the Rome Statute implied that they could not support negotiations that concerned persons sought by the ICC.[41] Whatever the outcome of the negotiations between the LRA and the Ugandan government, these states and organizations were committed to backing the ICC, a party that was not even present at the talks.[42] It was only when the security dividends of the talks became more tangible and the voice of the field offices, political advisers, and humanitarians gained the upper hand on the lawyers and human rights activists pushing the "no peace without justice" ideology at headquarters that donor countries and the UN began to provide financial, logistical, and political support for the Juba talks.[43] They adjusted their argument: if the ICC were circumvented by domestic trials, as ultimately envisaged in the Accountability and Reconciliation Agreement between the LRA and the Ugandan government, "no peace without justice" would still have prevailed.

The strongest argument against the claim that the ICC promoted the peace talks in Uganda is that LRA leader Kony has to date refused to sign the Final Peace Agreement. The separate parts of the agreement have been signed by the delegations of the LRA and the Ugandan government, but the LRA leadership itself never participated in the talks, partly out of fear of arrest and transfer to The Hague.[44] More fundamentally, the ICC's arrest warrants made it impossible for the LRA to achieve its desired outcome. From the outset, the LRA delegation had insisted that the ICC arrest warrants be "withdrawn," but the Rome Statute does not provide for simple withdrawal of the arrest warrants.[45] The only avenue open to Uganda for terminating the ICC's case against the LRA leadership would be to challenge the admissibility of the case on the ground of complementarity—that is, a challenge based on Uganda itself conducting criminal proceedings against the LRA. The 2008 Annexure to the 2007 Accountability and Reconciliation Agreement therefore envisages a special division of the Ugandan high court "to try individuals who are alleged to have committed serious crimes during the conflict" and a special unit to investigate and prosecute them.[46] Kony, however, referring to Charles Taylor's fate, the former Liberian president who was promised asylum in Nigeria and was nonetheless ultimately transferred to the Special Court for Sierra Leone, continued to demand guarantees for his security and further clarifications on the relation between the peace agreement and the ICC arrest warrants before he would sign any agreement.[47] A catch-22 situation emerged insofar as the Ugandan government wished to make representations to the Security Council and ICC with a view to deferring the proceedings and challenging admissibility only if the agreement was signed and Kony surrendered, whereas Kony would not sign "if the ICC indictments were not dropped."[48] Meanwhile, six years since the beginning of the negotiations, hopes for a peace agreement have been dashed.

All told, in the larger context of shifting regional politics, the ICC arrest warrants have served as a "double-edged sword,"[49] being, on the one hand, an additional incentive for talks but, on the other hand, an apparently insurmountable obstacle to the conclusion of an agreement.

In Darfur, too, the ICC's involvement at first seemed to facilitate peace talks. During the Abuja negotiations, the mediation team of the African Union readily took the agenda item "justice" off the table, arguing that the UN Security Council had delegated this issue to the ICC.[50] The rebel movements that had insisted on "justice" needed little convincing: they preferred the ICC to domestic proceedings, perceiving the ICC as a strong ally against their enemy. After seven rounds of negotiations during which the mediators presented the parties with a deadline to accept the Darfur Peace Agreement (DPA), they referred to the ICC in order to pressure parties to sign.[51] US deputy secretary of state Robert Zoellick, trying to address the movements' concerns about the draft DPA and to pressure the government to accept amendments in light of these concerns, referred to the ICC ("If you don't agree, I'll see you in The Hague") "to convey a sense of the stakes involved and the consequences."[52] But two of the most important rebel movements refused to sign. Indeed, they became even more reluctant to engage in peace talks when the ICC charged their ultimate opponent, the Sudanese president. He, in turn, was given extra incentives by the ICC arrest warrant to do everything possible to stay in power.

Involvement of the ICC may thus spur peace talks by putting pressure on rebel movements, as in Uganda, or by providing a reason to remove a breaking point from the agenda of peace talks, as in Sudan, but at the same time, the ICC's involvement can become an obstacle to the successful conclusion of such talks. First, whereas peace and reconciliation usually become possible once parties are convinced that they ultimately must live together again, international criminal justice can make them entrench in their positions, perceiving themselves as either legitimized or persecuted by an international court. Second, international donors have appeared reluctant to sponsor peace talks that concern persons sought by the ICC. Third, fearing arrest, persons sought by the ICC may refuse to participate in the talks, and the delegations they send on their behalf may have insufficient authorization to negotiate by proxy. Finally and perhaps most fundamentally, outsourcing issues to the ICC is not effective if disagreement remains. With respect to pressuring parties to sign an agreement, as Alex de Waal and Julie Flint have observed, "Pressure works if the party under pressure can agree with the end point. If that is life imprisonment, pressure only generates counter-pressure."[53] In the absence of a total defeat, parties will sign an agreement only if the ultimate outcome is acceptable to them. "The Hague" as an outcome is usually unacceptable.

The ICC as a Substitute for Peace Efforts

Rather than spurring peace, the ICC's involvement has sometimes replaced peace efforts. The position of Darfuri rebel movements and donors' initial stance toward the Juba peace talks, both recounted earlier, are two examples. Illustrative, too, are the UN Security Council politics involved in the referral of the situation in Darfur to the Court and a possible deferral of the ICC's Darfur proceedings.

Whereas the Prosecutor has claimed that the referral means that the Council has decided that justice is a critical component to achieving peace in Darfur,[54] the referral, rather than being a tested instrument for peace, may have served the Council as an instrument of therapeutic governance. Earlier condemnations, sanctions, and a peacekeeping mission had not been able to bring peace to Sudan. Despite report after report warning of widespread and systematic commission of crimes and despite powerful nongovernmental organizations calling on Western governments to "save Darfur" from "genocide," ten years after Rwanda, the Security Council seemed to be yet again a bystander. Irrespective of what happened and would happen in Darfur, with the referral to the ICC the Security Council could at least demonstrate its commitment to justice: "if not peace then justice."[55]

Soon after the referral, the first clashes between peace and justice appeared. The Government of Sudan refused to accept a Chapter VII peacekeeping operation, among other reasons out of fear that the mission would enforce ICC arrest warrants. Rebel movements became militarily more aggressive and reluctant to participate in peace talks. After the issuance of an arrest warrant against the Sudanese president, the government ousted thirteen international humanitarian organizations on allegations of cooperation with the ICC. For many human rights organizations, too, work has become more difficult, since they are suspected of handing over evidence to the Court.[56]

Arguing that the ICC's involvement threatened the chances for peace in Darfur, some states and organizations, most vocally the African Union, the Arab League, and the Organization of Islamic States, called upon the Security Council to defer its proceedings. The AU argued that "the situation in Darfur is too serious and complex an issue to be resolved without recourse to an harmonized approach to justice and peace, neither of which should be pursued at the expense of the other."[57] The AU worried about the ICC Prosecutor acting against an incumbent president. When conforming to foreign policy etiquette by signing on to the Rome Statute, AU members had not expected to endorse an "Amnesty International with legal powers."[58] More fundamentally, however, the AU was concerned with the ICC's impact on peace. Whether the potential escalation stemming from the ICC's involvement affects trade, refugees, proliferation of armed groups and weapons, or the security of their peacekeepers in Darfur, African states will bear the consequences of more violence in Sudan. Arrest warrants against members of the Sudanese government destabilize the government of an already fragile and conflict-prone state and region.[59]

However, the three Western permanent members of the Security Council have refused to defer proceedings. This is partially because Sudan has not taken the "meaningful steps"[60] or implemented a "radical and immediate change"[61] in its policies, which they had set as a condition for a deferral. But for the United Kingdom, France, and some Western nonpermanent Security Council members, the reluctance to vote in favor of a deferral is also inspired by a "no peace without justice" ideology. After the hard-won Security Council's referral of the situation in Darfur to the Court, these states do not want to be now seen as weakening the Court's position. Whereas the Council's *referral* of the situation to the Court was presented as depoliticizing the conflict, the Court's proponents argue that the Council's *deferral* of the ICC proceedings would politicize the Court, even though both actions are provided for in the Statute. In the field, representatives of organizations with pro-ICC policies at headquarters complained: "At headquarters, ICC politics are ruling over Darfur politics." To some extent the focus on the creation and survival of the ICC as an institution has led, to paraphrase David Kennedy, the work on building the Court to substitute for the work on achieving the aims that the Court was supposed to pursue—justice and, perhaps, peace.[62]

Court officials have argued that states and other international organs should prioritize compliance with ICC decisions. When accused of impeding peace negotiations, the Prosecutor claims that his mandate is justice, not peace,[63] and that other organizations are responsible for peace.[64] However, he has also argued that these other organizations must fulfill their responsibility within the framework of the Rome Statute.[65] In addition, the Prosecutor has questioned the wisdom of peace negotiations, arguing that persons sought by the ICC are unreliable.[66] Court officials thus argue that the ICC's mandate is justice and that the mandate of peace belongs to others, but at the same time they insist that others must implement the ICC's orders and not intervene in the Court's judicial mandate.[67] States parties to the Rome Statute may have agreed on this new normative framework by leaving the decision not to intervene "in the interests of justice" entirely to the discretion of the Prosecutor, but it does raise fundamental questions of power and accountability. Who can be held politically accountable for a decision pursuant to which the Court will (continue to) pursue punitive justice even if this seems to postpone (negative) peace?

The ICC and Domestic Accountability

On account of its principle of complementarity, the ICC at times spurs initiatives in favor of conducting domestic proceedings, which may help establish or reestablish the domestic rule of law and thereby contribute to (positive) peace. At the same time, the ICC may function as a court to which cases concerning conflict-related crimes are outsourced, limiting the extent to which the country concerned appears able to uphold the rule of law itself. Illustrations of the latter phenomenon are the Ugandan referral and AU mediators' taking the issue of accountability off the agenda of the Abuja peace talks once the ICC was involved. Over time, however, both the Ugandan government and the African Union realized that the ICC's involvement limited their leeway in negotiations. Since the only way to end the ICC's involvement was to conduct domestic proceedings, the ICC's involvement catalyzed initiatives to substitute another court for the ICC.

In Uganda, the ICC's involvement resulted in a paradoxical situation in which it was in the rebel movement's interests to insist on accountability instead of amnesty.[68] For the LRA, domestic accountability was the only way that the existence of the ICC arrest warrants against its leadership could be terminated. Seemingly aware of the complementarity principle, Kony argued that "the ICC should leave Uganda to handle the issue of accountability since Uganda has a functional justice system with jails in Luzira, Lugore etc."[69] However, rather than merely requiring the lifting of the ICC arrest warrants, the LRA delegation insisted that all sides to the conflict should be held accountable, including for crimes committed before the beginning of the Court's jurisdiction, July 1, 2002.[70] In line with the demands of some civil society organizations, the LRA also demanded transitional justice mechanisms other than criminal proceedings, such as a national truth and reconciliation commission and a compensation fund.[71]

The Juba talks, in turn, spurred a broader debate in Ugandan society about transitional justice. Adopting concepts used by international advisers to the Juba talks, the Ugandan government's Justice Law and

Order Sector has created its own "transitional justice" working group. Even though it remains to be seen to what extent the accountability agreements resulting from the Juba peace talks will be implemented now that Kony has refused to sign the Final Peace Agreement, the debate on transitional justice as such is a radical break with Uganda's past.

In Sudan, too, the issue of justice has returned to the mediators' agenda. In the same communiqué in which the AU Peace and Security Council requested that the UN Security Council defer the ICC proceedings against the Sudanese president, it "encourage[d] the Sudanese parties, with the support of the Joint Chief Mediator, to ensure that issues of impunity, accountability and reconciliation and healing are appropriately addressed during the negotiations aimed at reaching a comprehensive peace agreement."[72] The communiqué also established a High-Level Panel on Darfur, which considered the dropping of accountability from the Abuja talks "an error."[73] The Panel claimed that "external interventions will not, and cannot, of themselves, provide the answers to the range of difficult questions that Sudan faces."[74] Mirroring developments in Uganda, the AU has come to consider the ICC's involvement as an obstacle to peacemaking, has reconsidered its decision to leave questions of justice to an international court, and has identified the principle of complementarity as a way to undo the ICC's involvement. In doing so it has increased domestic and regional interest in criminal justice as an element of peacebuilding.[75]

Has the International Criminal Court been a peacebuilder in Africa? The ideology that is most often invoked as the Court's raison d'être, "no peace without justice," suggests that it should be. By giving teeth to international criminal law and by deterring crimes throughout Africa, the ICC may indeed contribute to building peace, but as with all criminal justice, it is difficult to establish whether the Court has indeed had these effects. With respect to the seven countries in Africa in which the Court has opened investigations, it is too early to tell whether the ICC has been a peacebuilder. But one can observe that in Uganda and Sudan conflicts are still ongoing, *despite* the ICC's involvement.

Some critics argue that conflicts are ongoing *because of* the ICC. In Uganda, the ICC's arrest warrants may have been a reason, or the decisive reason, for Kony's refusal to grasp the most promising chance for peace in northern Uganda. In Sudan, the ICC's charges against the

President have given him more incentives to cling to power. Furthermore, the Prosecutor's case against the President has given rebel movements sufficient ammunition to refuse to talk peace with a government of "war criminals." Rather than an instrument of peacebuilding, the ICC, operating in ongoing conflicts, is used as an instrument of war, with which to delegitimize and incapacitate enemies, thereby intensifying conflict. In theory, the Court, as an independent organization, could mete out justice on all sides. Yet because the Court depends on others for cooperation, these others can use the Court as an instrument to pursue their strategic aims.

To date, Court officials and Court supporters have used empirical and normative arguments to justify the "no peace without justice" ideology, constantly switching between consequentialist, deontological, and institutional justifications of criminal justice.[76] When empirical evidence, no matter how small, seems to support the claim, Court officials have presented the ICC as an instrument for peace, relying on a consequentialist justification. When the empirical evidence suggests that the Court obstructs peace, they have presented justice as an aim in itself, irrespective of its impact on peace, adopting a deontological approach. "No peace without justice" is then still invoked, for normative reasons. According to this view, ICC-style justice is the aim; peace may be a welcome derivative, but justice shall not be sacrificed to peace.[77] Alternatively, when justice seems to obstruct peace, ICC officials have put forward an institutional justification according to which the Court's mandate is limited to justice and other institutions are responsible for peace.

The problem with the deontological approach is that it is difficult to maintain that the sole purpose of the ICC is to punish crimes, irrespective of the consequences, even if these consequences undermine the very values that the law claims to protect, such as human life and physical integrity.[78] The problem with the consequentialist approach is that, as Eric Blumenson writes, it presents the Prosecutor with the "unavoidable but extraordinarily difficult task . . . to make decisions that invoke such magnificent hopes and terrible costs with so little predictive information."[79] Moreover, even if the Prosecutor had the information, how should he or she weigh consequences, for instance the short-term versus the long-term, the local versus the universal, the consequences for identified victims versus those for abstract potential victims? For instance, if it were established that impunity hampers the sustainability of peace (positive peace), should the Prosecutor then decide to start or continue proceedings even if this were to foreclose an immediate cease-fire (negative peace)? Should the Prosecutor prioritize his or her decisions on the basis of consequences for the communities where conflict is ongoing or where crimes were committed, or on the basis of consequences for the international legal order?

The institutional justification seems most convincing for the Court. In this view, the Court's mandate is "justice" (ICC-style), and others are responsible for "peace." Adopting this rationale, as they do, Court officials should stop presenting peace as the ICC's raison d'être. Moreover, this means that other organizations with a mandate to resolve conflict and promote peace should be allowed to fulfill their missions.

This division of labor reveals, however, a key problem that transcends the ICC. The "no peace without justice" ideology has spurred a justice bulwark, the ICC, but has created few institutional safeguards to promote peace if, in a concrete case, the two noble aims seem to clash. For the peace negotiator, justice is a powerful lever, but an "instrument" of peacebuilding over which it lacks control. The Security Council, in turn, can only *defer* ICC proceedings, and only for a maximum of one year at a time. Moreover, members of the Security Council that are committed to the "no peace without justice" ideology are reluctant to vote in favor of deferrals. The Court's proponents have successfully argued that such a deferral would be political interference in the judicial process of an independent court, notwithstanding the fact that the Statute provides for a deferral by the Security Council. For states wedded to the ICC ideology, supporting the seemingly clean, judicial ICC provides a safer moral high ground than supporting seemingly dirty, political peace deals. Encouraged by ICC officials, the ideology has even led some states to argue that they cannot support peace talks involving persons sought by the ICC. Is there any institution that still considers itself primarily responsible for peace? The ICC attempts to do justice in the fog of war. Persons in northern Uganda were stunned to learn that the Court issued arrest warrants against the LRA without providing the forces to execute the warrants and to protect Ugandans from LRA retaliatory actions.[80] No international actor claims responsibility for the consequences of justice on the security situation. States committed to the ICC shield themselves behind the Court, implicitly arguing "if not peace, then justice." Or they argue that peace will not be sustainable in the long term if accompanied by impunity. Meanwhile, those most directly affected by the consequences of ICC prosecutions on a conflict have "the weakest institutional channel" for influencing decision making by the ICC Prosecutor, the Security Council, or other external actors, and no means to hold them accountable.[81]

Given this institutional imbalance, the ICC Prosecutor would be wise to take into account the interests of peace when exercising his or her discretion of whether or not to open an investigation or prosecution. He or she could do so by interpreting the interests of justice to include the interests of peace.[82] Moreover, while the Statute suggests that the Prosecutor must investigate and prosecute when there is sufficient evidence and cases appear admissible and in the interests of justice, the Prosecutor has acknowledged that he factors in other considerations, such as the expected cooperation by states, when deciding whether or not to open an investigation.[83] Including the potential impact on peace would be a worthwhile other factor.

Notes

The material on which this chapter is based stems from research conducted for *Complementarity in the Line of Fire: The Catalysing Effect of the International Criminal Court in Uganda and Sudan* (Cambridge University Press, and Cambridge Africa Collection, Cape Town, 2012, forthcoming). The Gates Cambridge Trust, the Arts and Humanities Research Council, and the Smuts Fund for Commonwealth Studies have made this research financially possible. In Uganda, substantial research assistance was provided by Célina Korthals and Wendy Hanson. The author is also grateful to Hannah Richardson, the participants at the conference that led to this book, and the book's editors for comments on an earlier version of this chapter. Unless otherwise indicated, ICC documents are available at http://www.icc-cpi.int.

1. *Rome Statute of the International Criminal Court,* July 17, 1998, 2187, United Nations Treaty Series 90, arts. 1, 5.

2. See Galtung, *Peace by Peaceful Means.* See also Curtis in this volume.

3. On these different concepts of justice, see Mani, *Beyond Retribution.*

4. See http://www.coalitionfortheicc.org.

5. The third way by which the Court's jurisdiction can be triggered is by Pre-Trial Chamber authorization of a *proprio motu* investigation by the Prosecutor. The Court gave such authorization for the first time with respect to Kenya on March 31, 2010.

6. The analysis is based on empirical research, including three hundred semistructured interviews, conducted in Uganda, Sudan, the Netherlands, the US, the UK, Switzerland, and Germany, throughout 2006–10. For reasons of confidentiality and security, interviewees' names, exact locations, and dates of the interviews have been replaced by a general description of the person's position and a general indication of the place and date of interview.

7. See Kritz, "Coming to Terms with Atrocities"; Huyse, "Justice after Transition"; Landsman, "Alternative Responses to Serious Human Rights Abuses"; Orentlicher, "Settling Accounts"; Aukerman, "Extraordinary Evil, Ordinary Crime."

8. *Rome Statute,* third preambular recital.

9. Ibid., arts. 8(2)(b)(iii), 8(2)(e)(iii).

10. Ibid., arts. 13(b) and 16.

11. *Charter of the United Nations,* June 6, 1945, art. 39.

12. United Nations, *Report of the Ad Hoc Committee on the Establishment of an International Criminal Court,* UN Doc. A/50/22, 1995, 9, para. 46.

13. See, for instance, Burke-White, "Proactive Complementarity."

14. *Rome Statute,* arts. 53(1)(c), 53(2)(c).

15. International Criminal Court, Office of the Prosecutor (ICC-OTP), "Policy Paper on the Interests of Justice," 9.

16. *Rome Statute,* arts. 17, 20(3).

17. Government of Uganda, *Referral of the Situation concerning the Lord's Resistance Army Submitted by the Republic of Uganda,* December 16, 2003, para. 25. Thanks to Adam Branch, who found this submission at a workshop on the ICC in Kampala in 2004, and shared this document.

18. ICC-20040129-44-En, January 29, 2004.

19. For instance, Amnesty International, "Uganda."

20. See ICC-02/04-01/05-53, ICC-02/04-01/05-54, ICC-02/04-01/05-57, ICC-02/04-01/05-56 and ICC-02/04-01/05-55, July 8, 2005.

21. Two of the five persons are dead or presumed dead, and one is unaccounted for.

22. UN Doc. S/RES/1593, 2005, para. 1.

23. ICC-02/05-01/07-1, April 27, 2007, and ICC-02/05-01/09-3, March 4, 2009.

24. Hoge, "UN Gives Suspect List to Prosecutor."

25. *Summary of the Prosecutor's Application Under Article 58,* ICC-02/05–162, OTP, November 20, 2008.

26. Moreno-Ocampo, "Statement at the Eleventh Diplomatic Briefing of the International Criminal Court," 3.

27. Moreno-Ocampo, "Remarks by the Prosecutor of the International Criminal Court."

28. For an analysis of how warring groups have perceived the ICC as an instrument of warfare, see Nouwen and Werner, "Doing Justice to the Political."

29. Government of Uganda, *Referral of the Situation concerning the Lord's Resistance Army,* paras. 6, 25.

30. See also Branch, "Uganda's Civil War and the Politics of ICC Intervention"; Branch, "International Justice, Local Injustice."

31. "Statement: Defence Minister Mbabazi," *Hansard,* July 29, 2004.

32. "Uganda: Interview with President Yoweri Museveni," *IRIN,* June 9, 2005.

33. UN Doc. S/PRST/2008/48, 2008.

34. Moreno-Ocampo, "Statement on the Uganda Arrest Warrants," contended that "crimes committed by the LRA were much more numerous and of much higher gravity than alleged crimes committed by the UPDF." It could be argued that crimes committed by government officials against civilians, whom the government is supposed to protect, are by definition grave.

35. Author interview with a mediator, Nyala, December 2008.

36. Mamdani, "Politics of Naming."

37. Author interview with community leaders, Fasher and Nyala, December 2008.

38. ICC-02/05-01/09-73, February 3, 2010.

39. See, for instance, Kirsch, "Address to the United Nations General Assembly," referring to a statement attributed to the International Crisis Group.

40. After the attacks of September 11, 2001, and the US-led response in Afghanistan, Khartoum tried to be seen as aligned with the US in its "war on terror." The US had put the LRA on its "terrorist exclusion list," and Khartoum did not wish to be seen as

supporting terrorist groups. Moreover, Khartoum's support for the LRA became practically more difficult when the government of Sudan and the Sudan People's Liberation Movement/Army concluded the Comprehensive Peace Agreement that, among other things, outlawed all militias, provided for UN peacekeepers, and obliged the Sudanese Armed Forces, the LRA's most important supporter, to withdraw from Southern Sudan.

41. See, for instance, speaking notes for a European government minister regarding a phone call with a mediator of the Juba peace talks during which the minister stated: "I am not in a position to provide support—in whatever form to the peace talks, due to our obligations towards the ICC." On file with author.

42. As one official of a donor agency of a Western government observed: "If the ICC did not come out [of the Juba peace talks] smelling like a rose, the whole international justice project would collapse." Author interview, Kampala, October 2008.

43. Author interviews with persons involved in the Juba peace talks, the Netherlands, May 2008, and Kampala, September 2008.

44. Barney Afako, "Negotiating in the Shadow of Justice: The Juba Talks."

45. Wierda and Otim, "Justice at Juba," 23.

46. *Annexure to the Agreement on Accountability and Reconciliation [Annexure]*, Juba, February 19, 2008, clauses 7 and 10.

47. Author interview with persons involved in the Juba peace talks.

48. Frank Nyakairu, "Juba Talks Close As LRA Tables Fresh Demands," *Monitor,* March 2, 2008.

49. A term suggested in this context by Anton Baaré.

50. De Waal, "Darfur, the Court, and Khartoum," 33.

51. Author interview with mediators involved in the talks.

52. Author interview with Robert Zoellick, former US deputy secretary of state, Washington, DC, February 20, 2009, and e-mail correspondence with Zoellick's office, August 7, 2009.

53. Alex de Waal and Julie Flint, "To Put Justice Before Peace Spells Disaster for Sudan," *Guardian,* March 6, 2009.

54. Moreno-Ocampo, "Remarks by the Prosecutor." See also Moreno-Ocampo, "International Criminal Court," 223.

55. Elizabeth Rubin, "If Not Peace, Then Justice," *New York Times,* April 2, 2006.

56. For instance, see "Three Human Rights Activists Arrested in Sudan," *Sudan Tribune,* November 25, 2008.

57. "Decision on the Meeting of African States Parties to the Rome Statute of the International Criminal Court (ICC)," press release, Addis Ababa, July 14, 2009.

58. Author discussion with a participant in a session of the African Peace and Security Council, Khartoum, December 2008.

59. Alex de Waal and Abdul Mohammed shared these ideas in a discussion with the author in Khartoum, December 2008.

60. Daniel van Oudenaren, "US Will Veto Attempts to Defer ICC Move Against Sudan President: Official," *Sudan Tribune,* September 25, 2008.

61. Thijs Bouwknecht, "Sarkozy Proposes Darfur Deal," *Radio Netherlands Worldwide,* September 24, 2008.

62. Kennedy, *Dark Sides of Virtue,* 143, 279.

63. See, for instance, "Uganda: Kony Will Eventually Face Trial, Says ICC Prosecutor," *IRIN,* July 7, 2006.

64. International Criminal Court, "Statement of the Prosecutor of the International Criminal Court to the United Nations Security Council on the Situation in Darfur, the Sudan, pursuant to UNSCR 1593 (2005)," para. 30.

65. ICC-OTP, "Policy Paper on the Interests of Justice," 4.

66. See, for instance, "Joseph Kony Will Never Make Peace: ICC," *New Vision* (Kampala), July 14, 2009.

67. For the Court's discouraging contacts with persons sought by the ICC, see *Ninth Report of the Prosecutor of the International Criminal Court to the UN Security Council Pursuant to UNSCR 1593 (2005)*, para. 77. See also Moreno-Ocampo, "International Criminal Court," 221.

68. See Nouwen, "Complementarity in Uganda."

69. "Uganda: IDPs Unlikely to Meet Deadline to Vacate Camps," *IRIN*, December 26, 2006.

70. "LRA Position Paper on Accountability Truth and Reconciliation in the Context of Alternative Justice System [*sic*] for Resolving the Northern/Eastern Ugandan and Southern Sudan Conflicts," 1.

71. Ibid., 11–12.

72. AU Doc. PSC/MIN/Comm CXLII Rev.1 (2008), clause 11(iii).

73. AU Doc. PSC/AHG/2(CCVII) 2009, para. 173. See also para. 238.

74. Ibid., para. 245.

75. There are, of course, differences. In Uganda, the ICC's involvement became an obstacle when the LRA refused to sign any peace agreement until the ICC had dropped its case against the LRA; in Sudan, the ICC's involvement emboldened the rebels, leading them to refuse to negotiate with "war criminals." In Uganda, it was in the interests of the rebel movement to insist on domestic proceedings, and the government backtracked on outsourcing justice to the ICC; in Sudan, the rebel movements (still) prefer ICC proceedings and it is the mediating regional organization that tries to address the consequences of the ICC's involvement in the Darfur conflict.

76. On the consequentialist, deontological, and institutional justifications for the ICC, see Blumenson, "Challenge of a Global Standard of Justice." See also Nouwen, "Justifying Justice."

77. See, for instance, Kirsch, former ICC President, "Introductory Remarks," 4.

78. See, more elaborately, Blumenson, "Challenge of a Global Standard of Justice."

79. Ibid., 829.

80. Author interview with persons in northern Uganda, September 2008.

81. Blumenson, "Challenge of a Global Standard of Justice," 854.

82. See Schabas, "Prosecutorial Discretion v. Judicial Activism at the International Criminal Court," 731.

83. ICC-OTP, "Paper on Some Policy Issues before the Office of the Prosecutor," 2.

PART THREE

Case Studies

The Politics of Negotiating Peace in Sudan

SHARATH SRINIVASAN

MOST CONTEMPORARY ARMED CONFLICTS IN AFRICA END WITH negotiated settlements, and peace negotiations lay important foundations for peacebuilding. Yet peace negotiations straddle awkwardly the immediate desire to end violence and aspirations for forging a more lasting yet underdetermined "peace." The latter imperative assumes greater prominence in connection with outsiders' peacebuilding strategies, aimed ostensibly at transforming war-torn societies, in the supposed self-image of the outsiders, into strong and stable states as sites of peace, democracy, and prosperity. Peace negotiations thus prefigure ever-broader reformist agendas, and this leaves more at stake at the negotiating table. Consequently, negotiations now involve wider and more complex political contestations. External interveners and domestic actors, not limited to armed belligerents, all seek to shape the contours of what "peace" will mean through, or in spite of, the negotiating table.

The Comprehensive Peace Agreement (CPA) finalized in January 2005 between the Sudan People's Liberation Movement/Army (SPLM/A) and the government of Sudan provided a framework for national peacebuilding but also laid foundations for the secession of the Republic of South Sudan six and a half years later, in July 2011. These two adversaries had fought a bitter war since 1983, which had claimed more than a million lives and displaced millions more civilians. This also followed Sudan's first civil war, fought by southern separatists intermittently between 1955 and 1972. The so-called Government of National Unity, created by the CPA and comprising both signatories, failed to make unity attractive to southern Sudanese.

The CPA's promise of national democratic transformation and institutional reform, seen as key to peacebuilding in the country, also went mostly unrealized, and peacemakers' hope that the CPA would help in the resolution of the Darfur conflict—which escalated in 2003 while the exclusive bilateral negotiations for the CPA were under way—proved naively optimistic.

Rebellion in the western region of Darfur, aimed at the central government in Khartoum as much as being born of local intergroup conflicts, showed that the CPA was not at all "comprehensive," a bitter complaint expressed by various opposition groups across Sudan who had been excluded from the negotiations long before Darfur's crisis. Mediation efforts focused on Darfur between 2004 and 2011, first led by the African Union (AU) with strong support from the United States (US), and then followed by various initiatives that culminated in the Qatar-hosted joint AU and United Nations (UN) mediation. These negotiations were at times rushed, and failed to be wholly inclusive. They were also undermined by the way in which the post-CPA political arrangements constrained political space for compromise.

At the moment of South Sudan's naissance as a sovereign state in July 2011, violence escalated in the Nuba Mountains area of Southern Kordofan state, on the northern side of the new international border. Thousands of disaffected Nuba fighters who formed part of the SPLM/A demanded a better peace deal for their region than the CPA had delivered. This conflict soon spread to the neighboring Blue Nile state. This was another ominous reminder that the binary simplification of Sudan's wars into a north versus south, Arab versus African, Muslim versus Christian conflict, while it helped facilitate the CPA, did not come close to bringing peace to the region. Sudan is thus an example of partially failed peacebuilding with the negotiations process as a key element that severely limited the subsequent possibilities for peace.

At the heart of peacemakers' strategy in mediating the CPA was a belief that only by first ending the "north-south" war and then including provisions for national democratic transformation could Sudan's multifaceted political crises be addressed. Narrow, bilateral negotiations were not only expedient; they were considered the only way forward. Yet this causal logic was interpreted differently and actively resisted by groups who were excluded from the talks. Northern opposition groups and nascent rebel movements in Darfur feared that a bilateral deal would only strengthen the Khartoum government's power, rather than facilitate political change, and sought to access negotiations to influence the terms of constitutional and state reform. And they watched bitterly during these negotiations as control over power, wealth, security, and peace dividends accrued to the negotiating parties, who closely guarded their gains. This disenfranchisement of the opposition groups and rebel movements during the negotiations led to their further marginalization and disengagement in the post-agreement period, contributing to many opposition parties boycotting national elections in April 2010, which had been envisaged as central to the wider peacebuilding effort.

During the CPA negotiations, many SPLM/A leaders who still pursued a national liberation struggle, whether as an overriding objective or as a strategy for ensuring that southern objectives would be achieved, were also wary of a binary "north-south" solution. Well before the CPA was signed, the negotiations set in motion new political dynamics that would ultimately confound the peacebuilding and democratic transformation objectives of Western peacemakers. Instead of positive and sustainable political change, the uncertainties of the post-agreement period gave way to "stabilization" and conflict management in the foreign policy priorities of intervening states.

Negotiated peacemaking in Sudan could have been otherwise, and therefore it is important to understand how and why it took the particular course that it did. In the late 1990s and early 2000s, there was nothing certain about peace in Sudan. The possible political outcomes were many and diverse, and of grave national significance. Different peacemakers and diverse domestic actors all made distinct claims on the best way forward for the country, ranging from a narrow focus on violence in the south and southerners' aspirations to an inclusive national constitutional reform process. Much, then, depended on how those who prevailed in shaping the peacemaking process reduced these many futures to few, and then fewer still, focusing on a narrow and militaristic subset of Sudan's political elite to be the builders of peace. Peacemakers endorsed political opportunity born of violence, and Sudan's ongoing violent battles for peace became battles over the form and function of the institutions to deliver peace, with effects far beyond the negotiating table.

This chapter insists that peace negotiations must be analyzed within their wider politics. What is required is an examination not only of political actions at the negotiating table but also of the far-reaching political contestations through which the negotiating table is produced, reproduced, and reshaped. It is the institution of the negotiating table itself—whose form and constitutive parameters frame the bargaining of what "peace" might mean—that often becomes the primary object of political action. In the midst of a war, political actors with interests and choices construct negotiations that are unique, that could have been different, and that affect and are affected by the war as well as other political processes.

Applying this approach in broad strokes to the case of Sudan reveals how dynamics of war and their negotiated settlement are becoming interwoven with peacebuilding logics. The predictability of external intervention, combined with the likelihood that this intervention will involve efforts to forge institutions of civil peace, shapes discursive and coercive actions of conflict groups. Nonstate armed groups are often "asymmetrically" weaker than their state adversaries, and they strategize war with not just victory but also political settlement, and thus third-party peacemakers, in mind. The rise to prominence of power and wealth-sharing provisions as medium-term solutions has led many conflict groups to preempt such objectives in framing their political claims during war. Arguably this has served to increase numbers of armed insurgents strategizing for political advantage.[1] Similarly, nonarmed opposition groups seek to establish their legitimacy and credibility for being included in negotiation processes, often adopting consequentialist arguments that exclusion may threaten enduring peace. The leitmotif of war and violence during negotiating peace is reinforced rather than reduced.

The chapter proceeds in two parts. The first part introduces a schema for investigating the politics of negotiated peace, arranged around contestations over the institution's constitutive elements, that overcomes deficiencies in mainstream theorization of contemporary peacemaking. The second part examines recent experiences of peacemaking in Sudan, deploying this schema to account for the pathologies in external efforts to forge and foster peace, with implications for larger peacebuilding projects.

Analyzing Peace Negotiations

In Africa, negotiated settlement is lauded as civil war's new endgame. Military victory and defeat are now far less common. On one account, settlements outnumbered victories by seventeen to four globally between 2000 and 2005, and ten of these were in sub-Saharan Africa.[2] Peacemaking, these proponents tell us, is contributing to a more peaceful world.

Yet negotiations are not just civil war's endgame by other means; they are atypical sites of domestic politics where violent conflict has often constrained traditional domestic political space and enfeebled political institutions. Battles over what "peace" should mean are political contestations over the state, political authority, and society that are not limited to belligerents at the negotiating table.

A tension within the priorities of peacemaking and peacebuilding manifests itself in how negotiations articulate with national and local politics in unforeseen ways, sometimes sowing the seeds for future violence.[3] Although, in an era of liberal peacebuilding, negotiation agendas address wide-ranging societal issues,[4] external peacemakers are frequently motivated by a short-term priority of ending armed hostilities between belligerents, thereby rendering rights to participate as a product more of violence than citizenship. Negotiations between only armed political elites exert a pull on, yet exclude, a wider range of actors contesting "peace" than the belligerents alone.

Notwithstanding that Western peacemakers are often loathe to expand peace negotiations to a wide set of actors, they nevertheless seek to utilize the process of negotiations to lay foundations for efforts to change, shape, and strengthen state institutions and foster democratic "transformation." We should inquire into the effects that peacebuilding objectives have on a third-party peacemaker's actions in intervening in and shaping peace negotiations. We must also analyze how the normative appeal to reformist peacebuilding goals (such as institution building, democratic elections, rule of law, and security sector reform) serves as a justificatory rationale for specific mediation choices. Finally, the ways in which the objectives and logics of liberal peacemaking interventions are resisted, appropriated, and reshaped by national local actors require investigation.

The tensions and inconsistencies in how peacemakers pursue peace—between those who use leverage and strategy to wrestle the belligerents and the material and military dynamics of war to an end, and those who seek to intervene and build a sustainable peace in the twilight of violence—reflect basic divisions in theories and praxis of liberal peacemaking. Traditional "conflict management" approaches devise strategies for negotiations for striking rational bargains between armed adversaries to end hostilities.[5] A narrow instrumentalist logic dominates, and for some the content of peace settlements matters less than forestalling a resumption of violence.[6] Yet rationalist conflict management and mediation thought is increasingly inflected with normative proposals for reconstructing legitimate democratic governance and liberal state institutions to secure peace.[7] This shift reflects the increasing influence of the peacebuilding agenda on peacemaking thinking and practice.

Broader "conflict resolution" and peacebuilding frameworks are devised as something rightly to be "done" to transform violent societies. These frameworks are diverse,[8] but they have in common a normative orientation toward achieving some or another substantive conception of "peace" that goes beyond mediated bargains between belligerents. Conflict management's narrow focus on elite deals is criticized. They may help halt war, but, in Roger Mac Ginty's summation, they "minister to conflict manifestations rather than causes, reinforce rather than challenge intergroup division, attend to armed groups but neglect less vocal but more vulnerable constituencies . . . in short, they deliver poor quality peace."[9]

Conflict resolution approaches more readily identify normative standards for "good" peace settlements. Peter Wallensteen notes "increasingly established norms" for the content of "internationally acceptable peace agreements," including principles of democracy, human rights, criminal justice, reconciliation, and economic cooperation.[10] This normative turn is mirrored in increased scholarly attention to the elements of *jus post bellum,* the neglected third pillar in just war theory, which corresponds with postconflict peacebuilding.[11] How wars are justly ended bears upon the justness of going to war and how and to what extent war is fought, but these justificatory principles are being increasingly applied to legitimize when, how, and to what ends peacemakers should intervene.

Peace negotiations are a messy battleground. Whether the building of "just" peace should begin during the mediation of negotiated settlements poses particular dilemmas. Should peacemakers, for example, sanction a permanent cease-fire and general amnesties—possibly closing off the opportunity for agreement on more significant political reforms—in order to immediately end hostilities and human suffering? Conversely, might insistence that a wider group of political actors—including civil society groups—take the time to negotiate a "thicker" peace, one more widely accepted and in line with "established norms," come at the cost of prolonged war and more lives lost? Furthermore, how do the belligerents and other local actors view their stakes and how do they seek to influence the content and implementation of peace? These contradictions and tensions play out in local political dynamics, as political actors (armed and nonarmed) seek to pursue opportunities and secure advantages.

Despite significant differences, conflict management, conflict resolution, and just war theories are united by their focus on how to "best" contain and end war. There is a presumptive granting of virtue and legitimacy to peacemakers. An outsider-insider (mediator–conflicting parties) approach is taken, and mediation assumes a functional and technical identity. The embedded nature of negotiated peacemaking within wider politics is subsumed within analysis of conditions and techniques for, and obstacles and risks to, interventions for resolving conflict. The fact of whether and why third-party states intervene in African conflicts is sometimes analyzed in terms of their interests,[12] for instance security, material gains, or domestic political pressures, but there is a paucity of analysis on how the interests, power, biases, and ideological proclivities of the actors who intervene for peace affect the kind of peace promoted and its wider effects. It is evident that making peace is a "profoundly political endeavor," yet it is mostly analyzed within a depoliticized, problem-solving modality.

These deficiencies are more pronounced because of how peacebuilding imperatives increasingly guide the objectives and actions of third-party peacemakers. "Peace dividends" are combined with blueprints for constitutional and institutional reform to shape the positive peace that a negotiations process should be positioned to deliver. Beginning with the particular form and function of the institution created to achieve a mediated settlement, the contours of "positive peace" can be influenced by third parties oriented toward their objectives, especially institutional and political reform and security arrangements. Nonstate armed groups are supported with training and advice on preparing themselves to negotiate peace. Expert "technical" consultations are commonplace in matters such as wealth- and power-sharing and security arrangements, dealing not only with interim issues such as demobilization, disarmament, and reintegration of ex-combatants but also with issues such as electoral processes and institutions, decentralization, and judicial arrangements. Postconflict planning and financing processes begin during the negotiations themselves, and peacebuilding institutions seek protocol agreements and implementation arrangements to meet their needs.

Who defines the *what* questions—the "problem" of "war" and the "solution" of "peace"—generally and in any given case? How do certain actors' definitions prevail over those of other actors, and with what political effects? If different contestations over what "war" and "peace" mean are closely tied to ideas of how to address the conflict, then the choices over the institutional form of negotiated peacemaking are central to this political contestation. Peace is not a rational solution to the problem of war; rather, just as with war, it is a dynamic and contested process of social construction and action.

The institution for negotiations must therefore construct key elements of the war and the pathway to peace in ways that encourage a shift in the means of political action from violence to argumentative ideational politics. These "ideational" components include specifications for (1) *how to* (the scope of peacemaking, such as elite versus broad-based; rules of behavior in negotiations; organizational aspects, including sponsors, financing, mediator, location, international backing, experts, observers); (2) *end a war through reaching political compromises* (characterizing the political "conflict" that led to war with related possible solutions guided by ideas of "peace": a "problem/solution" nexus captured in the agenda for talks); (3) *between specific actors* (who are or are not to be included, and how their identities are depicted); (4) *who are resorting to violence* (the political naming of violence and the framing of war); (5) *to achieve political ends* (the ascribing of political ideology or purpose to the warring parties).

How these ideational components are specified significantly determines the territory of possible peace outcomes that negotiations might produce. The ideational components of the institution, taken together, also require sufficient logical coherence. For example, an expedient desire to restrict the number of negotiating parties to the fewest possible requires framing the conflict in more reductionist—ideally binary—terms. Yet such reductionism, given its powerful effects, is subject to real-time domestic contestations, creating a dynamic interaction between the process of creating the institution and the ongoing politics of conflict. Re-embedding analysis of mediation interventions within the politics to which they relate sheds a different light on them.

The Politics of Negotiated Peace in Sudan

The two Sudans of 2012 are still battling for peace, between and within themselves. Rather than giving all focus to how the negotiation of the CPA led to the independence of South Sudan, we should return to the period of the negotiations themselves and interrogate how the facilitation of this particular peace outcome was achieved and with what wider effects in Sudanese politics. The CPA negotiations between 2001 and 2004 were led by the Intergovernmental Authority on Development (IGAD), a regional organization,[13] with the heavy involvement of a "troika" consisting of the US, the United Kingdom (UK), and Norway. The CPA produced a singularly remarkable result, a peace process that despite many faltering moments remained intact and delivered for southern Sudanese full exercise of their rights to self-determination.

The agreement may be understood to be a tremendous success in this regard, but this would be as a success on its particular terms. Whether better or worse, peace outcomes in Sudan might have been otherwise, depending on the particular ways in which the prevailing institution to deliver peace was constituted. Moreover, in achieving this particular success, the CPA and the IGAD peace initiative also allowed a range of deleterious effects, especially in Sudan's north.

The IGAD initiative, which began in 1993, was only one among many regional and international peacemaking efforts to resolve the civil war. From the mid-1980s Sudan was on a seesaw between the battle of bullets and that of words. Major external peacemaking initiatives aside from the IGAD engagement included those led by former US president Jimmy Carter in 1990, Nigeria between 1992 and 1994, and Egypt and Libya between 1999 and 2002. The rejuvenated IGAD initiative between 2001 and 2004 prevailed over others and achieved far greater success for a range of reasons.

Despite a dominant rhetoric of neutrality and even passivity, third-party interveners in peace processes, whether mediators, facilitators, or observers, or more active (and coercive) peace enforcers, are influential interveners. In Sudan, most of the "peacemakers" involved in the IGAD negotiations had been engaged in proxy wars with Khartoum, were arming opposition groups, or had fractious diplomatic relations with Sudan. The type of peace they sought to make reflected their disposition toward the Sudanese state and aspirations for its future. The IGAD negotiations also presented a "ripe" opportunity for Western interveners—especially the troika but also a range of Western states in the IGAD International Partners Forum— seeking to advance their reformist political agenda in Sudan.

The four IGAD member states that sponsored the Sudan negotiations—Eritrea, Ethiopia, Kenya, and Uganda—each had its own interests in its neighbor's domestic politics and pursued ideas of peace in Sudan suited to its particular foreign policy. The Declaration of Principles for negotiations that they prepared in 1993 reflected their preferences with its tilt toward the SPLM/A's "New Sudan" aspiration of a secular democratic country and willingness to entertain southern independence.

After the talks broke down in 1994, Uganda, Ethiopia, and Eritrea increased military support to the SPLM/A and urged all opposition forces to unite under the National Democratic Alliance (NDA) banner (the NDA included northern opposition groups marginalized after the National Islamic Front/National Congress Party [NIF/NCP] took power in 1989; the SPLM/A joined and then led the NDA from the mid-1990s). Ethiopia took a particularly hard line against Khartoum after the attempted assassination on Egyptian president Hosni Mubarak in Addis Ababa in 1995, but relations recovered after the Ethio-Eritrean war of 1998–2000. Eritrea had become an earnest champion of the NDA and pursued confrontational strategies against Khartoum in spite of the IGAD negotiations, including arming and supporting the Darfur rebellion. Kenya, ultimately the key IGAD peacemaker, was the most impartial of all, but it viewed Sudan's wars, from its geographical vantage point and as host to many tens of thousands of southern Sudanese refugees, as being almost exclusively between south and north.

Sudan's wars were embedded within a vexed regional conflict complex, and contending regional peacemakers were engaged in efforts far removed from neutral and dispassionate peacemaking. The Egyptian-Libyan initiative between 1999 and 2002, in contrast with the IGAD negotiations, did not include the option of southern self-determination as a basic principle, did not mention religion and state, and involved the diverse northern opposition parties within its scope of negotiations. For Egypt, a reformed but united Sudan, with its Islamist government moderated, was a key foreign policy objective.

That the IGAD initiative prevailed as the focal negotiations forum had much to do with the heavy diplomatic endorsement it received from Washington, which had its own partisan position regarding Sudan. The oft-repeated phrase on Capitol Hill was that there was "no moral equivalence" between the SPLM/A and Khartoum, which had been on the US Congress's list of states sponsoring terrorism since 1993. Washington was not a neutral arbiter, but the domestic moral concern for an end to southerners' suffering motivated President George W. Bush's administration to engage Khartoum on peacemaking with the offer of focusing on ending the "southern war" (pulling back from previous demands for national political transformation or regime change) and counterterrorism cooperation, with the reward (albeit repeatedly postponed) of normalizing relations. Yet a tension remained between a more realist conflict management objective of striking a deal, on the one hand, and a wider peacebuilding imperative, on the other. According to one senior US diplomat, in 2003 President Bush linked democratization in Sudan, to be achieved through the peace process, with his wider Middle East strategy.[14]

In 2001 the US-UK-Norway troika began to seek an African-led peace initiative that they could significantly shape to include a broad transformative peacebuilding agenda. IGAD's Western backers agreed that "negative peace" required a deal between the primary belligerents, but along the way they hoped a more comprehensive "positive" or "liberal" peace deal could be urged that would include terms for multiparty democratic politics, security sector and judicial reform, and more equitable development. The IGAD initiative, with Kenya at the helm, was heavily dependent on its international backers for financial and technical support. This gave the international backers leverage to take a considerably interventionist stance toward the conduct of the negotiations.

Peacemakers, with their own interests in particular ideas of peace—ranging from imperatives for efficacy to aspirations for political transformation—thus also characterized the "problem/solution" nexus of the war in specific ways that played into domestic contestations over framing the war and the requirements of peace. Descriptive frames that oversimplified the conflict or distorted Sudan's sociopolitical makeup were not benign: they were active ingredients in the institutional practices of the negotiations that allowed for some possibilities of peace and foreclosed others. Frames, as Christopher Cramer points out in his discussion of the category "civil war," shape what is viewed and how what is viewed is interpreted.[15] Frames may be received, but they are actively reproduced and reshaped toward serving problem-solving policy action. As Stathis Kalyvas notes, the "serious semantic contestation" over the term *civil war* is often part of the conflict.[16] And the contestation takes on an altogether far more serious, and often violent, form when it is real, and between (often armed) domestic actors over a particular framing of a particular war that will determine political possibilities of peace.

The dominant frame for understanding Sudan's war in binary opposites was contested within Sudan and indeed lay at the heart of the conflict between the warring groups. Sudan's successive central governments were at pains to insist that the war with the SPLM/A was depicted and quarantined as the "southern problem" only, yet the SPLM/A pursued a national liberation struggle that attracted other marginalized groups within Sudan in addition to southerners. By the time of the negotiations, the SPLM/A included tens of thousands of fighters from predominantly Muslim groups in northern Sudan, and it had allied with other northern opposition groups to launch fronts in the east of the country, using Eritrea as a base. Although the latter was more a product of tactics and convenience, the many thousands of fighters from the Nuba Mountains, southern Blue Nile, and elsewhere in the north who joined the SPLM/A shared southerners' grievances that Sudan's political and economic elites held power to their exclusion and treated them as second-class citizens. In sum, the war had long ceased being only a "southern war."

Nevertheless, the binary simplification of the conflict aided an efficacious approach to structuring the negotiations. IGAD's constellation of peacemakers brought to an end Sudan's two-decades-long civil war, but this required the peace to be negotiated bilaterally and exclusively between Khartoum and the SPLM/A, who were deemed to represent the "north" and the "south" respectively. As the institutional parameters for negotiating peace became more fixed, this reality gave way to institutional rigidities. The Kenyan mediator for the negotiations, General Lazaro Sumbeiywo, when pressed on the narrow bilateral nature of the negotiations, stated: "I am interested in peace between north and south. That is my mandate, and I am sticking to it."[17] Before negotiations even began, the institution's ideational components had framed the political contest of wills that constituted the war, giving emphasis to some understandings of war and not others, and prefiguring the ideational possibilities of peace.

Domestic political actors, however, continued to challenge the institution's design on peace. The SPLM/A had been given the identity of "southern rebels" pursuing southern objectives. The SPLM/A from its inception consistently protested that the problem was national in scope and rooted in central government policies that had merely affected the south first and most egregiously. An influential part of the SPLM/A leadership, notably those close to its erstwhile leader John Garang, maintained this national outlook throughout the negotiations, even when many within the SPLM/A were more parochially focused on southern independence. It is thus somewhat unsurprising that when the negotiations increasingly looked as though they would box the SPLM/A into a deal for the south alone, Garang and his followers actively supported the nascent rebellion in Darfur.

The SPLM/A's support for rebel groups in Darfur accorded with Garang's national aspirations but also had immediate objectives, namely to put pressure on Khartoum and the peacemakers while the negotiations, especially those on partly SPLM/A-held areas in northern Sudan (the Nuba Mountains, southern Blue Nile, and Abyei), were going nowhere. Khartoum had refused attempts by peacemakers to address these areas in the IGAD institution, arguing, for example in late 2002, that "IGAD's mandate is to handle the southern Sudan question only, and we are not accepting any attempt (to include other areas) even if IGAD were to be dismantled altogether."[18] Khartoum finally acquiesced to such negotiations, but the SPLM/A failed to achieve its objectives for these areas and indeed undermined local aspirations for peace. This tracks well with the SPLM/A's success in laying symbolic claim to part of the Darfur rebellion as part of its self-identification as a wider national political movement but its ultimate failure to unify different rebellions within a common cause and achieve a decisive national settlement, let alone military victory.

Negotiations that were structured around a north-south axis but that held out hope for wider political transformation across Sudan exacerbated, in the short term, political violence rooted in the country's center-periphery dynamics of inequality and marginalization. Darfur's rebellion was not "caused" by the exclusive peace negotiations, but it was certainly emboldened by them. For the leader of one faction of the Darfur-based Sudan Liberation Movement/Army, Abdul Wahid al-Nur, the watershed Machakos Protocol of July 2002, which established the core elements of the CPA, was "not a solution. It put the country into a corner that the National Congress Party wanted. The SPLM was strong and they cornered the SPLM into the south. . . . For me, Machakos just divided the country, put our country in blocks, south and north, and just made things worse."[19] From late 2002 onward, as the situation escalated to all-out war in Darfur, his movement was in close contact with Garang's SPLM/A.

Equally, as growing political instability and violence in the Nuba Mountains region of Southern Kordofan throughout the post-agreement period foreboded, armed actors in this and other regions in Sudan's north could not and would not disappear simply because of a dominant historical narrative that framed a north-south peace that settled a north-south war. In turn, violence during the post-2005 period, notably in Abyei and the Nuba Mountains, prompted a reemphasis by external actors on security and stabilization priorities—above all, ensuring that the signatories to the CPA did not lapse back into direct military confrontation—that overshadowed peacebuilding efforts aimed at strengthening institutions of civil politics in Sudan's north.

How the "problem/solution" nexus was depicted was closely connected to the exclusivity of the negotiations and its effects. When the IGAD negotiations prevailed over other competing peace initiatives and peacemakers accepted defining Sudan's war as a "north-south war" and the "southern problem" was elaborated as first and foremost the need to "end the violence and civilian suffering in the south," then it was deemed sufficient to include only the primary belligerents depicted as representing "the north" and "the south" respectively, and to strike a deal *between* them that ended the war.

Despite the wider peacebuilding agenda being pursued by Western peacemakers, the expedient way forward in Sudan was not a broad inclusive negotiation. This would, to summarize various Western diplomats involved, "hopelessly complicate" the negotiations and jeopardize any agreement at all. The legitimacy of claims by various northern opposition forces—whose National Democratic Alliance had included the SPLM/A and had previously been championed by Western actors—to be included and heard in the negotiations was rejected. This policy decision was buttressed by deploying a cause-effect idea that only when the "southern war" was stopped would national political reform that addressed wider grievances be possible.

This causal logic proved fallacious. Early exclusion laid the basis for enduring exclusion and disenfranchisement, and this ensured that the advantage granted to the Khartoum government in focusing on the "southern problem" persisted during the post-agreement period. Peacemakers repeatedly deferred inclusion of northern opposition parties in the negotiations on the promise of subsequent inclusion in a constitutional review process and their right to freely contest scheduled democratic elections. However, the parties to the negotiations secured their preferential position at the expense of those excluded. The CPA, running to over 250 pages of detailed prescriptions for the political and security arrangements of the post-agreement period, largely predetermined the shape and structure of the interim national constitution and ensured the dominant role of the signatories to the agreement in any further reforms.

The disaffection of the northern opposition parties with the constitutional review process was followed by their frustration with how the ruling NCP managed the elections process, which led many parties to ultimately boycott the (delayed) national presidential elections in 2010. By 2011, when it was clear that the southerners wished to secede, a new opposition coalition in the north was again calling for an inclusive national constitutional review process. Worryingly, the wholesale failure to achieve meaningful political reform in Sudan's north during the interim period laid foundations for a new war between a largely unreformed NCP in control of the "center" in Khartoum and the north's new "peripheries" of Darfur, South Kordofan, Blue Nile, and Eastern Sudan.

A narrow emphasis on resolving violence in southern Sudan within the CPA negotiations also necessitated depoliticizing violence elsewhere, lest the negotiations appear manifestly ill-conceived and in need of reform that might jeopardize the chance of an imminent deal. When, in 2003 and early 2004, both the Sudan government and IGAD and Western peacemakers were concerned that Darfur might spoil the CPA negotiations, all benefited from downplaying the violence in Darfur and naming it "local," "intertribal," and "between farmers and pastoralists." This obviated the need to address this violence within the IGAD institution: the "southern war" remained distinct.

In different ways and during different time periods, both of these actor groups actively supported such frames. In 2003, notwithstanding that the rebel movements had released political manifestos, Khartoum mostly referred to the rebel groups as "bandits" with no political agenda, "armed criminal gangs," "gangsters," "highwaymen," or "outlaws." Also in 2003, UK government ministers referred to the tribal and historical nature of the conflict in Darfur when fielding questions in parliament, notwithstanding the increasingly evident national political dimensions of the rebellion. When the US State Department spoke out on Darfur for the first time in late 2003, it specifically noted that Darfur was "not linked to the ongoing peace talks between the Government of Sudan and the Sudan People's Liberation Movement/Army in Kenya."[20]

Yet peacemakers and the Khartoum government also knew of the SPLM/A's involvement in supporting the rebels. This knowledge was unutterable, lest it make clear that violence in Sudan was deeply interlinked, and that the neat simplicity of IGAD's "north-south" negotiations was problematic. On one occasion, in mid-2003, the SPLM/A's leader reveled in the enabling and constraining features of the politics of naming violence. Accused by Khartoum of supporting the Darfur rebellion during a crisis in the negotiations, Garang noted to a reporter that Khartoum could not, on the one hand, describe the situation in Darfur as armed plunder and, on the other hand, accuse the SPLM/A of being involved. Khartoum, he added, "must first define the matter clearly" and understand its "political content."[21] But to do so, he well knew, would be to jeopardize the whole basis of the IGAD negotiations as aiming to solve Sudan's "southern problem." The SPLM/A's involvement in the conflict in Darfur proved useful leverage as it negotiated a more favorable deal for itself in the CPA. The war in Darfur and the CPA negotiations were thus entwined in complex ways, and these political developments during the negotiation of the agreement cast a shadow over the post-agreement period.

Many of the challenges that plagued postconflict peacebuilding efforts in Sudan after the CPA had their origins in how peace was negotiated in the first place. The achievement of southern self-determination and the independence of South Sudan was the CPA's towering success; however, the process of arriving at this point also left open the possibility that Sudan's wars would, for the foreseeable future, be without end. This ensured that an array of new and equally vexing peacebuilding challenges would face Sudan and South Sudan despite the CPA process having in a formal sense neared finality.

Bloody front lines of the war prior to the CPA included those in the Nuba Mountains and Blue Nile regions of central Sudan, and these areas experienced renewed instability after the culmination of the CPA peace process failed to deliver secure and meaningful political change that addressed local grievances. Northern opposition groups that were marginalized during the negotiations and dissatisfied with opportunities for political engagement in the post-agreement period remained fractious and continued to agitate for wholesale change in Sudan. The conflict in Darfur, despite an agreement reached in Doha, Qatar, between one of the rebel movements, the Liberation and Justice Movement, and the government of Sudan, in July 2011, appeared poised to worsen, given that the dominant National Congress Party now sought to reassert its claim to rule the new "north" Sudan in the wake of the secession of South Sudan. By early 2012, an alliance between the "SPLM-North" and the main Darfur rebel movements had been formalized.

Meanwhile, the dominant SPLM/A, in near-exclusive control of the state in South Sudan, faced its own challenges from discontented armed and nonarmed political factions that seemingly had been waiting for the South's secession before seeking to settle old scores. This was portentous of a new peacebuilding challenge to build inclusive and plural civil politics within the militarized and war-ravaged new state. It also remained to be seen whether these latent and manifest conflicts could be contained to those already developing within the two new sovereign states or, far more worryingly, whether dynamics had been established that might lead to a new interstate war. The unresolved dispute between the two states over the oil-producing region of Abyei, as well as disputes over oil export revenues and fees that led to South Sudan shutting down production and over the demarcation of the new international border, presented ample trigger points for such confrontation. Finally, in April 2012, major military confrontation broke out between the two states, forcing the AU and UN Security Council to scramble into "conflict management" mode once again.

The particular course that negotiated peacemaking took in Sudan owed considerably to how the IGAD institution was constituted to pursue a particular strategy for peace in the country. The manner in which the peace was devised in ways that sought to simplify and distort the underlying reality of the conflict to make it easier to achieve a bargain, or to leave that complexity to be resolved sequentially in the post-agreement peacebuilding period, had dynamic consequences well before the agreement was reached. The negotiations, given the power they held over Sudan's future political arrangements, became a target of political contestation within wider Sudanese politics. Such contestation left a legacy of renewed political struggle, disenfranchisement, and violent contestation that squarely undermined the ambitions of peacemakers and peacebuilders for the post-agreement period.

Notes

1. Tull and Mehler, "Hidden Costs of Power-Sharing."

2. See Human Security Centre, *Human Security Brief 2007*. See also Centre for Humanitarian Dialogue, *Charting the Roads to Peace*.

3. See Keen in this volume.

4. See Curtis in this volume.

5. Representative studies include Stedman, "Negotiation and Mediation in Internal Conflicts"; Zartman, *Negotiation and Conflict Management*; Rothchild, *Managing Ethnic Conflict in Africa*; Fortna, *Peace Time*; Hartzell and Hoddie, *Crafting Peace*; Walter, *Committing to Peace*; and Sisk, *International Mediation in Civil Wars*; and collections such as Crocker, Hampson, and Aall, eds., *Leashing the Dogs of War*; Stedman, Rothchild, and Cousens, eds., *Ending Civil Wars*; and Brown, ed., *International Dimensions of Internal Conflict*.

6. Virginia Page Fortna argues that peace agreements without adequate peacekeeping enforcement are mere "scraps of paper." Fortna, "Scraps of Paper?"

7. See Zaum in this volume.

8. See, for example, Ramsbotham, Woodhouse, and Miall, *Contemporary Conflict Resolution*; Darby and Mac Ginty, *Management of Peace Processes* and *Contemporary Peacemaking*; Wallensteen, *Understanding Conflict Resolution*; Galtung, *Transcend and Transform*; Lederach, *Building Peace* and *Moral Imagination*.

9. Mac Ginty, *No War, No Peace*, 5.

10. Wallensteen, *Understanding Conflict Resolution*, 11. See also Jarstad and Sisk, *From War to Democracy*.

11. See, for example, Bass, "Jus Post Bellum"; Orend, "Justice after War."

12. See, for example, Maundi et al., *Getting In*.

13. IGAD comprises six Horn and East African states: Sudan, Somalia, Eritrea, Ethiopia, Kenya, and Uganda.

14. See Nielsen, "Sudan Experience Project: Interview #7, 1 June 2006," 20. This is an anonymous interview with a US ambassador who led the State Department's Sudan Programs Group.

15. Cramer, *Civil War Is Not a Stupid Thing*.

16. Kalyvas, *Logic of Violence in Civil War*, 17.

17. Quoted in Martin, *Kings of Peace, Pawns of War*, 141.

18. Associated Press, "Sudan Denies Violating Cease-Fire, Says It Is Fighting Eritrea's Aggression," October 18, 2002.

19. Author interview with Abdul Wahid al-Nur, Paris, July 2008.

20. Richard Boucher, "Sudan: Situation in Darfur," press statement (Washington, DC: US Department of State, December 16, 2003).

21. Ahmad Zayn-al-Abidin, "Interview with SPLM Leader John Garang, 14 August 2003," *Al-Sharq al-Awsat* (in Arabic, English translation by World News Connection, NTIS, US Department of Commerce), 2003.

ELEVEN

Peacebuilding in the
Great Lakes Region of Africa

RENÉ LEMARCHAND

IN NO OTHER PART OF THE CONTINENT IS THE MULTIFACETED TASK of peacebuilding facing more daunting challenges than in the Great Lakes region of Central Africa, an area comprising the eastern part of the Democratic Republic of the Congo (DRC), Rwanda, Burundi, and Uganda. Nowhere else has the effort enlisted the participation of such a wide array of domestic and international actors, ranging from advocacy groups, local nongovernmental organizations (NGOs), churches, international think tanks, regional organizations, special envoys, individual statesmen, the Bretton Woods organizations, as well as the European Union (EU) and United Nations (UN). No wonder the sheer multiplicity of interveners is often seen as part of the problem rather than the solution.

As the centerpiece of peacebuilding operations in the DRC, the United Nations Organization Mission in the Democratic Republic of the Congo (MONUC) carried the heaviest load. Nowhere else has a UN peacekeeping operation mobilized the energies of a larger number of civilian and military personnel (from 5,500 at its inception in 1999 to some 20,000 by 2012), at greater cost for the international community (US$1 billion per annum), and with more ambivalent results. This is a commentary on the scale and complexity of the crisis. It brings into focus the devastating impact of the two Congo wars (1996–97 and 1998–2003)—the pivotal events in the Congo's slide into chaos and a catastrophe for which there are no precedents anywhere on the continent.

There is, however, an instructive precedent for the UN engagement, traceable to an earlier crisis when, in the years immediately following independence in 1960, Cold War pressures threatened to bring the new state to the edge of collapse. As the mineral-rich Katanga province declared its independence from the central government, Stanleyville (now Kisangani) became the bastion of a left-leaning breakaway faction headed by Antoine Gizenga. What became known as the United Nations Operation in the Congo (ONUC) effectively brought to an end the Katanga secession, through the use of force, and laid the groundwork for a government of national unity headed by Cyrille Adoula.[1] ONUC, unlike its more recent avatar and though claiming approximately as many men on the ground (20,000) as MONUC, was significantly more limited in terms of its goal (ending the Katanga secession), its activities (political and military), and its duration (1960–63), and, not surprisingly, it was considerably cheaper. MONUC (later MONUSCO),[2] by contrast, covers a significantly larger area; it involves a plethora of auxiliary activities (such as disarmament and reinsertion of ex-combatants, civil and political affairs, refugee relocation, public health issues, and so forth) and claims a longer life-span. Unlike what has all too often been the case with MONUC/MONUSCO, its predecessor did not shun the use of force when diplomacy proved unavailing. There is evidently more than a change of acronym separating the two UN interventions.

The extension of conflict on a regional scale, drawing into its vortex an ever-increasing number of participants, with easy access to automatic weapons and mineral resources, helps explain its deadly impact on civilian lives. According to the International Rescue Committee (IRC) the death toll in the DRC between 1998 and 2008 was estimated at nearly 5.4 million.[3] Although the figure has since been revised downward, it is probably a fairly conservative estimate if one adds the human losses in Rwanda and Burundi since 1993.

What peacebuilders are up against in the Great Lakes is a long-term, multifaceted, interlinked crisis. It is best described, in Braudelian terms, as a *longue durée* phenomenon rooted in the historicity of domestic and interstate conflicts, a crisis made even more intractable by the obstacles inherent in the regional environment. There is no room in this context for quick-fix solutions; nor can the continuing significance of major historical events be ignored, any more than their tragic repercussions among the people of the region.

Before turning to a discussion of the strategic shortcomings that have plagued peacebuilding efforts in the Great Lakes, something must be said of the contrasts and paradoxes inscribed in the geopolitics of former Belgian Africa.

The Regional Environment: Contrasts and Paradoxes

The most obvious contrast is between the enormity of the area covered by the DRC, the second largest state on the continent (950,000 square miles), and the Lilliputian size of its neighbors to the east, Rwanda and Burundi, each approximately a hundred times smaller (10,000 square miles).[4] No less striking are the disparities of mineral wealth. It is not for nothing that the early Belgian colonizers, upon discovering the Congo's huge deposits of copper, cobalt, diamonds, and gold, called it "a geological scandal"—a situation in stark contrast with resource-poor Rwanda and Burundi, both heavily dependent on the export of tea and coffee cash crops. It is hardly a matter of coincidence, therefore, if much of the violence sweeping across the region is often referred to as a "resource war," if the rewards held up to ex-combatants for returning to civilian life seem all too modest compared to the benefits reaped from diamond and gold smuggling, and if continued access to the Congo's wealth is perceived by Rwanda as a major goal of its regional foreign policy.

The differences in the countries' social landscapes are equally clear. The extreme diversity of communities and social systems found in the DRC has relatively little in common with the more hierarchical, biethnic social patterns characteristic of Rwanda and Burundi, or indeed with the sharply divergent restructuring of their respective social systems brought about by recent upheavals. It is worth emphasizing that Rwanda and Burundi are not the only states inhabited by Hutu and Tutsi. Uganda, Tanzania, and the DRC claim sizable minorities of Hutu and Tutsi elements, which together could number anywhere from 10 to 12 million; only in the DRC, however, has the Kinyarwanda-speaking, or rwandophone, minority played a more decisive role in the country's destiny.

Other paradoxes come to mind. Although the DRC's treasure trove translates into a uniquely promising potential for economic development, 80 percent of its population lives in abject poverty. Rwanda, in contrast, once described as among the poorest of the poor, shows one of the highest rates of economic growth on the continent (7 percent). More surprising still, the Rwandan army, estimated to number around

75,000 personnel, has developed into the most formidable military machine in the region. Rwanda has the capacity effectively to project its military force anywhere into eastern DRC, as it has on several occasions in the past. The key to the paradox lies in the magnitude of the financial aid provided by the international community in the years following the 1994 Rwanda genocide, reaching the unprecedented level of over US$500 million in 2004, as if to atone for its inaction during the genocide and redeem itself in the eyes of the victimized minority. The height of irony is that some of the most intractable issues faced by peacekeepers in the wake of the 1996 anti-Mobutist insurgency, including the repeated human rights violations committed by the Rwandan army or its surrogates in the DRC, could not have happened without the enormous amount of international financial aid channeled into the coffers of the Rwandan regime.

Rwanda's military capabilities have led to cost-free access to the DRC's mineral wealth, at which point Rwanda's military involvement in eastern Congo became self-financing. Even more surprising in view of the overwhelming circumstantial evidence pointing to Paul Kagame's direct involvement in the crash of the Rwandan president's plane on April 6, 1994—the precipitating factor behind the genocide—is the fact that this evidence has done little to diminish his prestigious aura in the eyes of his principal benefactors, the United Kingdom and the United States. Nor has his utter disdain for democracy dented his image as the man who brought the genocide to an end—never mind that he helped provoke it.[5]

The Historicity of Conflict

Extreme brutality is the defining characteristic of the conflicts that have ravaged the region; their cumulative impact on the life of local communities has been little short of devastating. The savagery of the Rwanda genocide, resulting in the deaths of over 600,000 people, mostly of Tutsi origins, needs no elaboration. What is not always appreciated is that Rwanda is not the only venue tainted by genocide. In a classic replay of victims turned killers, tens of thousands of Hutu refugees in eastern DRC were massacred by units of the Rwandan Patriotic Army (RPA) in 1996 and 1997, when search and destroy operations directed at the génocidaires morphed into a wholesale massacre of Hutu civilians.[6] Burundi, likewise, suffered a terrifying bloodletting—better described as genocide—in 1972, when, in response to a localized uprising, between 200,000 and 300,000 Hutu civilians were killed in cold blood by the

Tutsi-dominated army. Nor did the litany of horrors, begun with the abortive, Hutu-sponsored coup of 1965, stop in 1972.[7] After the election of Melchior Ndadaye, a Hutu, to the presidency in Burundi in 1993, the Tutsi-led army swiftly proceeded to reverse the verdict of the polls: his assassination unleashed an extremely bloody civil war, causing possibly as many victims among Hutu as among Tutsi. Not until 2005, following multiparty elections and the adoption of a power-sharing constitution, would the country experience a modicum of peace. But after the decision of most of the opposition parties to boycott the 2010 elections, thus giving the ruling party unfettered control of parliament and government, the future of Burundi's consociational democracy is anybody's guess.

How did such sustained, deliberate violence affect local communities? Although the answer is by no means self-evident, this question goes to the heart of the problems facing peacebuilders: how to come to grips with the multiplicity of local tragedies brought about by massive refugee flows, the looting of property, the theft of cattle, the expulsion of millions of internally displaced persons from their traditional homelands, uprooting of traditional authority figures, the spread of sexual abuse, the emergence of armed bands, and so forth. As had been noted time and again by outside observers, most notably Séverine Autesserre,[8] failure to take into account the critical importance of local issues goes a long way toward explaining the inability of peacebuilders to live up to their mandate.

These local issues did not just happen; they are the consequences of broader conflicts. To be more precise, there is a circular connection between regional or interstate conflicts and their spin-off effects at the local level, so that bottom-up pressures feed into top-down confrontations and vice versa. To take the most obvious example: local-level grievances were certainly instrumental in mobilizing the Congolese masses against the Mobutist state in 1996–97, but the collapse of the regime created the institutional void out of which a flurry of local militias emerged, and these in turn were quickly recycled on behalf of, or against, new regional enemies, again with disastrous consequences among rural communities.

How local conflicts spilled over national boundaries to bring about wider confrontations is perhaps best illustrated by the role played by the Banyamulenge[9] in paving the way for Mobutu's demise. The projection of the Hutu-Tutsi conflict into the Congo is indeed the key to understanding the circumstances that led to the collapse of the Mobutist state. Though previous Hutu-Tutsi frictions were not unheard of, it was not until 1994, after the Rwanda genocide, that the "Banyarwanda" label dissolved into full-blown Hutu-Tutsi enmities. Almost overnight the lines were clearly drawn between the Mobutu-backed Hutu refugee community and the pro-Rwanda Tutsi minority, the latter including both the long-established so-called Banyamulenge ("the people of Mulenge") in South Kivu, and the ethnic Tutsi of North Kivu. Many were the Congolese Tutsi who joined the Rwandan Patriotic Front (RPF) in the early 1990s, and their open display of sympathy for Kagame's RPF confirmed the suspicion of many Congolese that their loyalties were to Rwanda. Lingering distrust of the Tutsi quickly turned into hatred as a million Hutu refugees from Rwanda poured across the border into eastern Congo, soon followed by thousands of Hutu from Burundi fleeing the avenging arm of the Tutsi-dominated army. By mid-1996 the Banyamulenge minority of South Kivu had become the target of chronic violence; soon they were served notice that unless they returned to the land of their ancestors (Rwanda) their lives would be in peril. It took little prodding for Kagame to endorse the cause of the Banyamulenge, and even less to harness their support in the destruction of the Hutu refugee camps. This, in a nutshell, is the background to what has been called Africa's first world war.[10]

In masterminding the anti-Mobutist insurrection, under the guise of a disparate coalition of forces known as the Alliance of Democratic Forces for the Liberation of Congo-Zaire (AFDL) under the nominal leadership of Laurent Kabila, with the Rwandan army acting as the senior partner, Kagame was able to achieve three major strategic goals: rally the solid support of the Banyamulenge minority, destroy the Hutu refugee camps strung along the border with Rwanda and Burundi and thereby eliminate a major security threat, and overthrow Mobutu—no small feat when one considers the odds. Not only was eastern Congo safe for Rwanda, but so too was the ruling authority in Kinshasa, or so it seemed in the heady days that followed the AFDL victory. By August 1998, however, the fragile coalition stitched together by the AFDL leader was in a shambles. Thus began the second Congo war, with Rwanda backing the Banyamulenge-dominated Rally for Congolese Democracy (RCD) and Kabila throwing his weight behind an odd assortment of recycled Mobutist soldiers, Mai-Mai warlords, and Hutu refugees.

Taking a closer look at Kagame's military prowess, the least that can be said is that it came at a heavy price for the Congolese people. His alliance with the Banyamulenge resulted in the more or less systematic removal of previous incumbents from the urban and provincial institutions of North and South Kivu and their replacement by Banyamulenge elements, many of them unqualified to hold these positions. What came to be known in diplomatic language as the "closure" of the refugee camps was the signal for a massive manhunt of Hutu refugees throughout North and South Kivu, and beyond. While causing an untold number of casualties among civilians, contrary to official statements from Kigali (approvingly relayed by US embassy officials),[11] the Rwandan search and destroy operation failed utterly to wipe out the génocidaires—ex–Armed Forces of Rwanda (FAR) and Interahamwe. In time the Hutu survivors would reemerge as the Democratic Liberation Forces of Rwanda (FDLR), one of the most violent of the renegade factions spawned by the war. It is noteworthy that the anointment of Laurent Kabila as the new king of the Congo involved, among other quid pro quos, the promise to the kingmakers that he would do his utmost to block an impending UN investigation into the killings of Hutu refugees, a task of which he acquitted himself with exemplary zeal. But the worst was yet to come. In August 1998, after realizing that the costs of his dependency on Rwanda exceeded the benefits, Kabila finally grasped the nettle; no sooner had he sent his Tutsi advisers packing home than began a long and vicious civil strife.

Reflecting on "how to rebuild Africa," Stephen Ellis notes that "outsiders tend to ignore the historical roots of today's conflicts."[12] Nowhere is this more evident than in the Great Lakes region, where the twists and turns of its tortured history are the key to an understanding of its present agonies.

The history of the region helps explain why peacebuilding in Rwanda and Burundi operates within a radically different set of parameters from that of the Congo. Rwanda is a prime example of a historically rooted trade-off between democracy and statebuilding. In contrast to the Congo, where threats to the peace are in large part a reflection of the extreme fragility of the state, the Rwandan state is by far the strongest of all states in the region, and the most oppressive. Immediate and long-term threats to the peace have little to do with the fragility of the state apparatus; if there is such a thing as a clear and present danger to long-term stability, it stems from the stubborn unwillingness of the Kagame government to meet the demands of the Hutu majority. Effective repression rather than political participation is the key to peace and stability. Burundi, in contrast, exemplifies the reverse phenomenon, that is, a situation where peacebuilding depends to a large extent on the effective workings of a power-sharing arrangement that allows a modicum of political participation to all groups in society, not just Hutu and Tutsi but the pygmoid Twa (representing about 1 percent of the population). The key question is whether the Burundi form of conso-ciational government can survive the crisis of confidence engendered by the refusal of the major opposition parties to take part in the 2010 elections, resulting in their virtual exclusion from the country's political life. The current trend is toward the strengthening of the state under a one-party dominant system of government, which suggests an ominous parallel with Rwanda.

On an altogether different plane, what the historicity of the regional conflict underscores is the massive intrusion of external forces into the Congolese arena. No fewer than eight countries were at one time or an-other involved in the Congo's civil wars. Besides having been the locus classicus of proxy wars by African states, the eastern DRC has become a major sphere of Rwandan influence, through direct or indirect interven-tion. Failure to take full measure of the Rwandan connection has been a constant source of confusion and miscalculation for peacebuilders.

Vital as it is, the problem goes beyond the political dynamics of the regional context; it also involves a fair amount of confusion and inco-herence among the many well-meaning do-gooders in their collective efforts to restore peace to the region.

Peacebuilding: A Surfeit of Good Intentions

That peacebuilders sometimes overcrowd the field and end up work-ing at cross-purposes with each other is seldom taken into account by analysts; nonetheless, the phenomenon must be recognized for what it is—a thoroughly counterproductive state of affairs, frequently moti-vated by internal rivalries and competition for access to domestic actors.

The case of Burundi is a prime example. In perhaps no other state have so many humanitarian NGOs, international organizations, spe-cial envoys, and think tanks been so heavily involved for so long in such a small space, and with more limited results.[13] The reason for such modest achievements lies in part in the plethora of peacebuilders, each guided by a different reading of the nature of the conflict. The result, at best, has been *immobilisme,* and at worst a parallel diplomacy leading to further fragmentation of the political chessboard.

The point is persuasively argued by Fabienne Hara, a close observer of the Burundi scene in the years following the assassination of Melchior Ndadaye in 1993: "The profusion of players in Burundi, each with its own agenda and favored solution, has undermined the coherence of the international community's response and led to competition among various Burundian factions and NGOs for recognition and support."[14] More damning still is her indictment of the role of special envoys, and the struggle for influence among Western states:

> The sheer number of special envoys reflects the diversity of their agendas and motivations, and tends to jeopardize the official claim that the international community wants peace, or at least the same peace, for the region. . . . Amid the various popularity contests between the nations of the region and the superpowers, the struggle for influence between France and the United States, and the geopolitical and economic interests of the countries in the region, all official mediators have been suspected of partiality.[15]

Hara goes on: "Various attempts to impose drastic solutions, to hurl them forward with no consideration of political logic, and to claim effectiveness based on symbolic rather than concrete results have resulted in failures, slowly eroding the local populations' faith in the international community."[16]

Hara's arguments have wider applicability in the region. The DRC offers a number of examples where peacebuilders developed their own agendas and ended up pulling in different directions. High-level disagreements among interveners have had particularly serious consequences throughout the region,[17] but nowhere with more disastrous effects than in the DRC. In 1996 and 1997 in the wake of the AFDL and Rwandan attacks against the refugee camps, the media reported a humanitarian disaster of alarming proportions. Much of the area in the vicinity of Kisangani was swamped with tens of thousands of hapless Hutu refugees fleeing westward. Howard French, an eyewitness to the scenes of apocalypse, described them as "people who had walked for seven weeks through some of the world's most inhospitable territory, with killers in their midst and more killers on their trail."[18] Despite the urgency of a swift humanitarian intervention, the international community proved utterly unable to reach a consensus on how to cope with the situation. Whereas the French and the European Union favored a UN-authorized force to secure a humanitarian corridor, the US and UK, all too eager to comply with the demands of their Rwandan ally, categorically opposed any such move, thereby sealing the fate of hundreds of thousands of human beings.[19]

One of the more persistent impediments to coordinated action among peacebuilders refers to their radically divergent views of Rwanda's role in fueling conflict in eastern Congo. Not all interveners shared the sympathy displayed by the US and UK toward Kigali, but most of the time the latter's influence prevailed. Thus, despite overwhelming evidence of Kigali's responsibility in providing military, logistical, and financial assistance to its Congolese clients—ranging from the RCD in the late 1990s to Laurent Nkunda's National Congress for the Defense of the People (CNDP)—there was little inclination on the part of MONUC to rein in their moves, even when these constituted manifest threats to the peace, as happened in Kisangani in 2002, in Bukavu in 2004, and in much of Masisi during Nkunda's antics from 2006 to 2009.[20]

Pro- or anti-Rwandan posturings, and pro- or anti-Tutsi sentiment, are not the only elements that have informed the divergent perspectives of outside peacebuilders. A recurrent source of discord has been between those advocating military intervention on humanitarian grounds, and those favoring a more cautious approach, based on regional diplomacy or "talking through" problems. Whereas the latter has been characteristic of African mediators, appeals for military intervention, as one observer noted, have been typical of the attitude of the NGO community in moments of crisis.[21] But the problem goes beyond such differences, and involves competing definitions of the roots of conflict and how best to deal with them, including disagreements over systemic versus proximate causes, whether to apportion responsibility of local or regional actors, whether the key issues are human rights violations or the denial of political participation, and the absence of democracy or presence of the wrong type of democracy (e.g., majoritarian versus power-sharing formulas). Behind many of these conceptual divergences lies a conflict of priorities.

Resetting Priorities

Building peace can start from the ground up, so as to restore a modicum of normality to communities whose lives have been torn asunder, or it can proceed from the top down, on the assumption that agreement among leaders is a precondition for peace. The latter has been the standard approach in much of the Great Lakes, with the disastrous results that Séverine Autesserre has so convincingly described.[22]

Although these are not mutually exclusive, there is reason to believe that the unending series of setbacks met by peacebuilders is in large part a reflection of the low priority placed on resolving local issues. These cover a wide spectrum, ranging from chieftaincy disputes to wrangles over taxes or conflicting claims to landed property. Land issues are indeed the most critical. Food security and local livelihoods depend on access to land. As some observers have recently emphasized, "Recent research has pointed to the direct links between access to land and food security in conflict environments: it is recognized that land access constitutes one of the more problematic and volatile facets of societal relations during and subsequent to armed conflict."[23]

This is where the massive population movements generated by ethnic confrontations carry a frightening potential for conflict. A classic example is the district of Masisi in the DRC, which has been and remains to this day the focus of endless litigations over land rights, some going back to colonial days. In recent times, land has passed back and forth from one group of owners to another, from Hunde (the original owners) to Hutu and Tutsi, from Tutsi to Hutu, and now back to Tutsi refugees returning from Rwanda with their cows. Behind these bewildering changes of occupancy lie a number of historical watersheds: the arrival of Tutsi refugees from the 1959–62 Hutu revolution in Rwanda, the outpouring of Hutu refugees from the 1994 genocide, the expulsion of Tutsi landowners in 1996 and their flight to Rwanda, and now, following the conclusion of the 2009 peace deal between Kagame and Kabila, which resulted in the removal of Nkunda from the political scene,[24] the border-crossing of some 60,000 Tutsi along with their herds (derisively called "cows without borders"). This latest twist in the district's complicated and violent history casts an ominous shadow on the future of peace in North Kivu.

Whereas the Masisi imbroglio shows how wider conflicts can percolate to the grassroots, the case of Ituri is illustrative of the reverse phenomenon: how a local dispute over land can suddenly burst into a regional conflagration out of all proportion to the triggering event. This is shown in admirable detail by Thierry Vircoulon and Florence Liégeois in their discussion of what they term *un conflit ultra-local* in the Djugu district: in a matter of days, violence mutated into a "tribal war" between Hema and Lendu, spreading to the whole of Ituri and causing some 60,000 deaths from 1999 to 2003.[25] Regardless of whether local issues stem from the top down or from the ground up, they develop a dynamic of their own and therefore need to be dealt with in these terms, as conflicts intrinsic to the communities from which they have arisen. This is where peacebuilding efforts have been most conspicuously wanting.

Another misplaced priority has been the overemphasis on the domestic roots of conflict at the expense of their transnational ramifications. Although the DRC has been a privileged arena for proxy guerrilla movements,[26] their sponsors have operated with almost complete impunity. Their role as spoilers has generated relatively little concern from the international community. This is particularly true of Uganda's ceaseless meddling in the politics of Ituri. But if any state has played and will continue to play a determining role in the fortunes of the DRC at minimum cost to itself and probably with some benefits, it is Rwanda. The "Rwanda connection" has had a multiplier effect on many of the most violent confrontations recorded in the history of eastern DRC. Examples include the repeated incursions of the Rwandan army into North and South Kivu after the Lusaka peace deal, the logistical and military assistance given by Kagame to the Hema-dominated Union of Congolese Patriots (UPC), the support extended to the two renegade Tutsi officers of the Congolese armed forces, General Laurent Nkunda and Colonel Jules Mutebutsi, during and after their military takeover of Bukavu in June 2004,[27] and more recently, the web of economic, financial, and political ties radiating from Kigali to Nkunda's CNDP. The extent of this network, disclosed by the UN Group of Experts in late 2009,[28] was indeed instrumental in prompting Kagame to disown his erstwhile client. But one cannot underestimate the proddings of the US State Department,[29] the clinching factor behind the fragile Kabila-Kagame peace deal that led to their joint operations against the FDLR. If the interstate dimension of threats to the peace cannot be left out of the accounting, neither should the remedies be confined to the domestic scene.

Nor should the quest for short-term solutions mask the necessity of long-term strategies. The urgency of a change of perspective is nowhere more evident than in the alarming demographic explosion in Rwanda and Burundi. With a total population that has increased from 2 to 8 million in half a century, neither state can sustain the extraordinary pressure on the land. And yet little is being done to defuse this time bomb and convey the gravity of the situation to policymakers. Just as imperative is the need for long-term economic planning. If economic scarcity is one of the motivations behind the readiness of the young to join armed factions, it is also the main reason why so little success has been achieved in reinserting ex-combatants into civil society.

MONUC on Trial

Inclined at first to vindicate MONUC, recently a growing number of observers have voiced criticisms of its performance.[30] Among its many shortcomings, its inability or unwillingness to protect human lives has been singled out as its greatest failing. This was made clear on a number of occasions, but at no time more dramatically than during the attack on Bukavu in 2004, the mass slaughter in Gatumba (Burundi) in August of that year, and in Kiwanja in November 2008. It was in that latter locality of North Kivu, during Nkunda's advance toward Goma, that MONUC's performance was at its most shameful: with a peacekeeping force only half a mile away, it did nothing to prevent the killing of 150 people by the CNDP. In a blistering indictment, a Human Rights Watch (HRW) report noted that although MONUC had one of its largest field bases in Kiwanja, with 120 peacekeepers, "it failed to keep the CNDP from taking Kiwanja and Rutshuru on October 29 and failed to prevent the killings and other abuses by CNDP and Mai-Mai combatants in early November."[31] It is noteworthy that the Kiwanja tragedy occurred shortly after Lieutenant-General Vicente Diaz de Villegas y Herreria handed in his resignation as MONUC's head of military operations, reportedly being taken aback by the organization's "lack of a coherent strategy, lack of a mandate and lack of resources needed to get the peacekeeping job done."[32]

No less shocking has been the attitude of UN peacekeepers during what one journalist described as a "four-day frenzy of rape" in Luvungi from July 30 to August 2, 2010.[33] Although dozens of MONUC soldiers were stationed "just up the road," nothing was done to stop the rapists, most of them identified as members of FDLR and Mai-Mai groups. At least 179 women were sexually abused. The UN special representative to the UN, Roger A. Meece, subsequently tried to explain the MONUC's appalling performance: "At the time there was one alleged rape and no reason to believe that this was happening on a mass scale as was later reported."[34] For his part the UN Under Secretary General for Peacekeeping Operations, Alain Le Roy, invoked the "limited resources" at the disposal of blue helmets: "The expectations on the blue helmets are often unrealistic given our limited resources. Yes, some 18,000 peacekeepers are deployed in the Congo, but there are more than 60 million people in an area the size of Western Europe. If all peacekeepers were in eastern Congo alone, there would be just 18 peacekeepers per 10,000 civilians."[35] Though persuasive up to a point, the argument carries little weight in light of other limiting factors.

According to its mandate under Chapter VII of the UN Charter, MONUC has the authority to use of force "to ensure the protection of civilians, including humanitarian personnel under imminent threat of physical violence," but only rarely has it done so.[36] Though some have suggested the need for additional troops, the roots of MONUC's poor performance run deeper. It stems in large part from self-inflicted disabilities.[37]

In a wide-ranging critique, Thierry Vircoulon points to a dual process of "congolisation" and "bureaucratization" as key factors. MONUC, he writes, "has been contaminated by the corruption and impunity inherent in its environment, while at the same time suffering from the characteristics of a heavy bureaucracy projected in a war zone."[38] Many of the more distasteful traits, from sex scandals to trafficking in gold and diamonds and other forms of corruption, have gravely tarnished its image. A former deputy chief investigator with the UN Office of Internal Oversight Services in the Congo from 2005 to 2007 describes illegal deals between Pakistani peacekeepers and local militias: "We found corroborative information that senior officers of the Pakistani contingent secretly returned seized weapons to two warlords in exchange for gold, and that the Pakistani peacekeepers tipped off two warlords about plans by the UN peacekeeping force and the Congolese army to arrest them." He concludes that MONUC "cannot close its eyes and ears to evidence of misconduct. Such behavior undermines peacekeeping efforts everywhere."[39] Another critic confirms these accusations, pointing the finger at "the illegal buying of gold from the FDLR, the use of a UN helicopter to fly into the Virunga National Park to exchange ammunition for ivory, trading UN rations for gold, the purchase of drugs from rebels, and a general failure to support the disarmament of the group."[40] None of such damning evidence of wrongdoing ever surfaced in any of the official UN reports.

MONUC's preferred strategy of dealing with crises through "peace diplomacy" has spawned a flurry of auxiliary operational units, committees and subcommittees, regional conferences, and emissaries and special envoys. Out of this heavy institutional scaffolding has developed what Vircoulon calls an "international action system" notable for its bureaucratic inertia: "Absent a unified command, a plurality of decision-making centers has emerged, involving a mosaic of international bureaucrats, thousands of military and civilian personnel, consuming billions of dollars, and mobilizing a world-wide net of activists, developers, diplomats, journalists and army men."[41] Although this cumbersome machinery helps explain MONUC's inability to respond quickly and efficiently to crisis, the contrast between the size of its presence on the ground and the modesty of its accomplishments is directly related to its image problem: for many Congolese, MONUC is everywhere, except where it should be—at the front lines.

Hardly more effective in dealing with ground-level emergencies, the creation of the UN Peacebuilding Commission as a coordinating agency within the UN bureaucracy has attracted scathing criticisms from outside observers: though well-meaning, this initiative proved sadly inadequate to deal with the complex political dimensions of post-conflict transitions.[42] By downplaying or ignoring such crucial dimensions, the UN has cast considerable discredit on itself while unwittingly ensuring that the crisis would become self-perpetuating.

———————

The Congo crisis defies simple solutions. Contrary to the impression conveyed by MONUC's Public Information Division, peacebuilding cannot be reduced to a set of techniques or procedures. Nor is it greatly improved by adding one more operational unit to an already top-heavy bureaucracy, or by invoking time and again the mantra of R2P (shorthand for Responsibility to Protect). It is a telling commentary on the practical limitations of the much-touted formula that its progenitor's book-length disquisition on that theme appeared in print in 2008,[43] precisely when tens of thousands of civilians were forced out of their homes in the wake of the one of the most devastating outbursts of violence to rage across North Kivu. In the language of the MONUC they were the latest additions to a flow of internally displaced persons (IDPs) that by 2009 had reached half a million in North Kivu, and almost as many (419,000) in South Kivu.

IDPs: the acronym is emblematic of many such aseptic renderings of human tragedies, which tend to obscure their magnitude and downplay their cruelty. The searing experience of displacement and dislocation, the destruction of homes and property, the fear and despair etched on people's faces, their seemingly endless march to nowhere, such are the grim realities encapsulated in "IDP." There are many variations on this theme—such as the use of the neutral term "closure" to refer to the systematic destruction of refugee camps in 1996–97, the indiscriminate shooting of civilians, their flight into the forest, and the ensuing manhunt. The result, invariably, is to conceal the unsettling realities of war in eastern Congo.

If peacebuilding is to be more than a technical exercise, it is important to grasp the full dimensions of the appalling human wreckage attendant on the crisis: the horrific price paid in lives extinguished, properties destroyed, land alienated, social ties sundered. Though often masked by the language of peacemaking, these are the human dramas that bear testimony to the lethal consequences of lack of attention to local issues. Many are the fallout of wider conflicts; but more often than not they serve as the detonators that generate even more devastating confrontations. Festering hatreds feed into revanchist attitudes; past injuries are rarely forgotten, nor are collective wrongs easily forgiven. Countless examples could be cited of local disputes, largely ignored by peacemakers, in time becoming the ignition points of more serious clashes. From Ituri to Minembwe, from Masisi to Rutshuru, there is ample evidence pointing to local conflicts becoming the vehicles of more extensive intergroup conflicts. Putting them in proper historical perspective is essential if meaningful solutions are to be found.[44]

What the historicity of local and regional issues also demonstrates is the highly counterproductive role played by external actors in intensifying or expanding conflict: by failing to control their domestic enemies, or by themselves becoming the critical vectors of violence in eastern Congo, Uganda and Rwanda must be seen as chief villains in the Great Lakes crisis. While the Lord's Resistance Army (LRA)— responsible for the continuing horrific mayhem in Ituri, as well as in the Central African Republic (CAR)—dramatically illustrates the spillover of Uganda's domestic problems into the DRC, Rwanda's repeated interventions—ranging from armed aggression to the manipulation of proxies, with the Hutu *génocidaires* often used as a ploy in a carefully orchestrated game of bluff—shows just how close is the imbrication of domestic and international conflict arenas. That so little should have been done by peacebuilders to come to grips with this situation, directly or indirectly, diplomatically or otherwise, is little short of astonishing, unless one bears in mind the consistent tilt of key donors, notably UK and US, on behalf of their privileged clients.

If only because of its self-perpetuating nature, the crisis in the Great Lakes will remain at the top of the agenda of domestic and international actors for years to come. At no other time has the need for developing an effective and sustained peace strategy been more pressing, but if the past is any index, the prospects for such a collective effort getting under way are not encouraging.

In part because of the complexity of the issues that stand in the way of peace, in part because of what has been described as the lack of an effective approach to peacebuilding, there is no light at the end of the tunnel. But the more obvious reason lies in the absence of something resembling a functioning state system. Only in Rwanda has significant progress been made in this direction, but at the cost of democratic participation and widespread human rights violations. By denying the Hutu, representing 80 percent of the population, the right to control their political destinies, President Kagame is sowing the seeds of future confrontations. Although Burundi has dealt more constructively with ethnicity, through a power-sharing formula, there is an ominous convergence between the two states in their shared distrust of opposition groups and their pitiless repression of dissidents. Recent events in the DRC indicate a similar trend, but without the benefit of a strengthening of the state.[45] Fifty years after independence the Congo resembles nothing so much as its Mobutist clone, with this difference: that the level of devastation after years of civil strife is without precedent.

Thus the three states that make up most of the Great Lakes region are illustrative of the contradictions between statebuilding and democracy promotion, the two principal goals of peacemaking. The dilemma is pithily captured by Francis Fukuyama: "Before you can have democracy you must have a state, but to have a legitimate and therefore durable state you eventually must have democracy."[46] While the case of Rwanda shows how the construction of a powerful state is likely to thwart democracy, the Congo exemplifies the opposite phenomenon, how multiparty elections run counter to the building of a strong state. Burundi, unsurprisingly, doesn't quite fit into either model: a democracy of sorts has been achieved through a power-sharing arrangement, but the pressure of the coercive state is far too strong to allow a full flowering of liberal democracy.

As has been argued time and again, the reconstruction of the state is a precondition to peace, just as peace is a sine qua non for economic and social development, yet there is no indication that the critical first step toward that goal, that is, the creation of a reliable and efficient constabulary, is being seriously considered. In the absence of a professional army, Kabila's strategy has been to recruit former rebels, thus paving the way for further human rights abuses and defections. Similarly, the exigencies of creating a modicum of trust within the government have given rise to a clientelistic system that bears all the trademarks of the Mobutist era. And just as under Mobutu ethno-regional ties provided the glue that held the system together, so also under Kabila, whose closest advisers are from his home province, Katanga. This is hardly the most propitious scenario for peacebuilding. Unlike what happened in the 1960s, however, when China was actively involved in supporting anti-Mobutist insurgents, Beijing has emerged as a key actor in promoting Congo's economic rehabilitation and reconstruction.[47] Although observers differ as to how to assess the costs and benefits of the "deal of the century," between China and the Congo, it cannot be seen as an alternative to peacebuilding.

How to create sustained, complementary partnerships among domestic and international actors, how to set new priorities for channeling assistance, how to achieve better coordination and a more effective division of labor among donors, and how to harness governmental capacity to the exigencies of economic and social development—these are the fundamental tasks awaiting the new generations of peacebuilders. They've got their work cut out.

Notes

1. For an excellent, wide-ranging account by the head of ONUC from 1960 to 1961, see Dayal, *Mission for Hammarskjöld*. For a more recent and succinct, comparative treatment, see Willame, "De l'ONUC à la MONUC."

2. After resisting President Kabila's insistence that the MONUC's mandate be terminated, on May 28, 2010, the UN Security Council adopted a resolution extending the presence of the UN peacekeeping force until June 30, 2011, renamed the United Nations Organization Stabilization Mission in the Democratic Republic of the Congo (MONUSCO, an acronym that appropriately rhymes with "fiasco").

3. For a more detailed commentary on the IRC findings, see Coghlan et al., "Mortality in the Democratic Republic of the Congo." For more recent figures, see http://www.theirc.org/special-reports/congo-forgotten-crisis. The figure of 5 million deaths has been challenged by the Human Security Report 2009–10, which suggests that the IRC overestimates the total number of lives lost by 50 percent.

4. This section draws freely from Lemarchand, *Dynamics of Violence in Central Africa*.

5. Whether Kagame must be seen as responsible for the crash of Juvénal Habyarimana's plane remains a highly controversial issue. The case against Kagame has been argued at length and with considerable persuasiveness by a former high-ranking officer of the Rwandan Defense Forces (RDF), Abdul Joshua Ruzibiza, in *Rwanda: L'histoire secrète*. For a summary of the arguments against Kagame, see Lemarchand, "1994 Rwanda Genocide." The notion that the crash was the outcome of a plot concocted by extremist members of Habyarimana's entourage, the so-called *akazu* (meaning "the little hut" in Kinyarwanda) has been set forth by Gérard Prunier in a number of publications, most recently in *Africa's World War*.

6. For a sustained discussion, see Reyntjens and Lemarchand, "Mass Murder in Eastern Congo."

7. I have discussed the 1972 genocide in Burundi in a number of publications, most recently in Lemarchand, "Burundi 1972."

8. Autesserre, "Trouble with the Congo."

9. The term *Banyamulenge* refers to a Tutsi-related, Kinyarwanda-speaking minority of South Kivu whose roots in eastern Congo are traceable to precolonial migrations. They are culturally distinct from ethnic Tutsi from North Kivu. Their number is impossible to determine with precision. One observer suggests 300,000 (see Matloff, "Crisis in the Heart of Africa," 7) but 50,000 seems like a more reliable estimate. Reyntjens suggests a combined figure of between 120,000 and 130,000 for Tutsi elements indigenous to North and South Kivu.

10. For an extended discussion, see Reyntjens, *Great African War.* For a more discursive and less succinct treatment, see Prunier, *Africa's World War.*

11. For evidence of the support of the US embassy to Kagame, including his role in "neutralizing" Hutu refugees in eastern Congo in 1996–97, see Reyntjens, *Great African War,* 68–74.

12. Ellis, "How to Rebuild Africa," 141.

13. For a partial listing, see Lemarchand, "Genocide in the Great Lakes."

14. Hara, "Burundi," 135.

15. Ibid., 143.

16. Ibid., 144.

17. For an illuminating discussion of the discords generated by UN Secretary-General Boutros Boutros-Ghali's proposal, in August 1994, to send a preventive multinational standby force into eastern Zaire in anticipation of a Rwanda-like bloodbath in neighboring Burundi, see Evans, *Responding to Crises in the African Great Lakes,* 56–61.

18. French, *Continent for the Taking,* 144.

19. For a fascinating account of this episode, during which the late Sergio Vieira de Mello served as UN humanitarian coordinator for the Great Lakes, see Power, *Chasing the Flame.*

20. For an outstanding analysis of Nkunda's meteoric rise, see Stearns, "Laurent Nkunda and the National Congress for the Defence of the People (CNDP)."

21. For specific examples, see Evans, *Responding to Crises,* 49.

22. Autesserre, "Penser les conflits locaux."

23. Lecoutere, Vlassenroot, and Raeymaekers, "Conflict, Institutional Changes, and Food Insecurity in Eastern DR Congo," 50.

24. See Lemarchand, "Reflections on the Crisis in Eastern Congo."

25. See Vircoulon and Liégeois, *Violences en brousse.*

26. See Prunier, "Rebel Movements and Proxy Warfare."

27. See Tull, "Congo Facing a Third War?" 1–3. The Bukavu tragedy dramatically illustrates the impotence of MONUC in the face threats to the peace, and the complexity of the overlap between domestic and transnational issues. While Nkunda and Mutebutsi would not have attacked Bukavu without Kigali's approval, what happened next provides a dramatic illustration of the unanticipated consequences of their action. After the recapture of Bukavu by government troops, an estimated 25,000 panic-stricken Banyamulenge, fearing retribution, fled to Burundi, and hundreds were relocated by the United Nations High Commissioner for Refugees (UNHCR) in the border town of Gatumba, where 163 were murdered on August 13, 2004. The carnage appears to have been carried out by Mai-Mai militias from the DRC and elements of the National Forces for the Liberation of Burundi (FNL), a radical Hutu-dominated party.

28. United Nations Security Council, *Final Report of the Group of Experts on the Democratic Republic of the Congo Re-established Pursuant to Resolution 1857*.

29. Author interviews with US officials and HRW members.

30. See, for example, Lebor, *Complicity with Evil*, 216–19; Matthias Bassanisi, "Keeping an Eye on Peacekeepers," *New York Times*, May 23, 2008, A23; Vircoulon, *Réformer le "peace making" en République Démocratique du Congo*. Among MONUC critics Linda Polman deserves pride of place for her withering criticisms of peace-keeping operations in the Congo and Rwanda: see *Crisis Caravan* and *We Did Nothing*.

31. HRW, *Killings in Kiwanja*, 22.

32. Jeffrey Gettleman and Neil MacFarquhar, "Congo Rebels Advance; Protesters Hurl Rocks at UN Compound," *New York Times*, October 28, 2008, A6.

33. Jeffrey Gettleman, "4-Day Frenzy of Rape in Congo Reveals UN Troops' Weakness," *New York Times*, October 4, 2010, 1.

34. Josh Kron and Jeffrey Gettelman, "UN Officials Knew of Rapes in Congo, Messages Show," *New York Times*, September 1, 2010, 6.

35. Alain Le Roy, "Brutality in Congo: Who Can Stop It?," in a letter to *The New York Times* editor, October 7, 2010.

36. One such occasion occurred in November 2006, after Nkunda attacked the town of Sake in North Kivu. "For the first time," writes Jason Stearns, "UN peacekeepers reacted forcefully against Nkunda with attack helicopters and infantry, killing between 200 and 400 insurgents." Stearns, "Laurent Nkunda," 252.

37. Emily Paddon makes the convincing point that part of the challenge faced by the UN in protecting civilian lives stems from the tension between that obligation and supporting or extending the authority of the state when the state is itself complicit in the violence against civilians. Personal communication to the author.

38. Vircoulon, *Réformer le "peace making,"* 9.

39. Matthias Basanisi, "Keeping an Eye on Peacekeepers," *New York Times*, May 23, 2008, A23.

40. R. Escobales, "UN Peacekeepers 'Traded Guns with Rebels,'" *Guardian Weekly*, February 2, 2008, 6.

41. Vircoulon, *Réformer le "peace making,"* 10.

42. See Del Castillo, *Rebuilding War-Torn States*. See also Olonisakin and Ikpe in this volume.

43. Evans, *Responsibility to Protect*.

44. The historicity of intergroup conflicts is excellently brought out in Roger Kasereka's doctoral dissertation, "Dynamiques locales et pressions extérieures dans la conflictualité armée au Nord-Kivu: Cas des territoires de Beni-Lubero," esp. chap. 4.

45. Sadly illustrative of this trend is the assassination of the human rights activist Floribert Chebeya, head of the NGO *La Voix des Sans Voix* (Voice of the Voiceless), on June 1, 2010. Despite official statements to the contrary, and gruesome attempts to camouflage the circumstances of his death, that he happened to be one of the most outspoken critics of the many abuses committed by the Kabila government is the most obvious explanation for his murder. See "Repression in the Congo," *Economist*, June 12, 2010, 54.

46. Fukuyama, "Stateness First," 88.

47. See Marysse and Geenen, "Les contrats chinois en RDC."

TWELVE

Peacebuilding through Statebuilding in West Africa?

The Cases of Sierra Leone and Liberia

COMFORT ERO

When conflict broke out in Liberia on December 2, 1989, commentators did not forecast the subsequent instability, political crisis, and civil war that would consume neighboring Sierra Leone in 1991 and Côte d'Ivoire in 2002. The Economic Community of West African States (ECOWAS) led the first regional peacekeeping mission to Liberia in August 1990. It was later joined by the United Nations (UN) in efforts to end violent conflict and begin the complex process of rebuilding in all three neighboring countries. After two decades, regional and international actors in these West African countries have contributed to new trends and practices in the global peacebuilding enterprise.

This chapter examines the wide-ranging international peacebuilding initiatives that have spanned two West African countries, Sierra Leone and Liberia. By exploring a subcomponent of the peacebuilding experience in West Africa, namely statebuilding, the chapter considers the tensions, dilemmas, and successes at the heart of the peacebuilding endeavor in both countries. Although commonalities exist in the cases of Sierra Leone and Liberia, they provide different insights into postconflict statebuilding. As I argue here, the process of statebuilding in West Africa provides a cautionary tale of the limitations of the global peacebuilding enterprise. International intervention was aggressive and robust in Sierra Leone and Liberia.[1] At one level, intense partnerships between national actors in Sierra Leone and Liberia and the international donor community resulted in significant progress in rebuilding some aspects of the state in both countries. Yet at another level, tensions between national, regional, and international actors often led to local elites either resisting or rethinking and reorienting external ideas and partnerships. The experience of statebuilding in both countries demonstrates the limitations of external intervention, especially when there is a clash between national ideas and practices, and regional and global programs and strategies.

The State, Statebuilding, and Conflict in West Africa

Central to the peacebuilding enterprise is the attempt to establish conditions that prevent the return to conflict. Following the end of the Cold War, large-scale international efforts took place to help bring peace to countries emerging from conflict. Key lessons learned from international peacebuilding efforts in the 1990s, of which Liberia and Sierra Leone were recipients, was that the quick-fix approach to ending conflicts and holding national elections was insufficient to prevent the recurrence of conflicts. By the late 1990s and early 2000s, major discussions on improving the performance of the UN and other multilateral institutions for peacebuilding had evolved. It was agreed that if durable peace was to take hold in countries emerging from conflict, international peacebuilding strategies required radical reorientation. This reorientation focused on a more "macro-level approach" that placed greater emphasis on constructing or strengthening the state and its institutions. It was a departure from the "micro-level approach" of earlier peacebuilding efforts, which focused on technical quick fixes and the supervision of elections. As Dominik Zaum notes in chapter 2 of this volume, and as Roland Paris and Timothy Sisk have noted elsewhere, this macro-level statebuilding approach is not synonymous with peacebuilding, nor is it an attempt to supplant peacebuilding. Statebuilding is a subcomponent of the peacebuilding enterprise,[2] which is part of a "larger effort to create the conditions for a durable peace and human development in countries that are just emerging from war."[3]

Statebuilding is a complex project in the African context. Historically, African states were created to serve the political and economic interests of colonial forces. The survival of the colonial territories was reinforced through authoritarian governance, leading to the subjugation and exploitation of the population. Colonial authorities relied on force and violence to protect their imperialist objectives. Colonialism also created alliances between local elites, co-opted to solidify colonial power and administration over territories. Consequently, the "state" was largely an alien construct, lacking the legitimacy to mobilize or extract cohesive groups from among the indigenous populations.

Independence in Africa did not bring a fundamental transformation in the structure of the state. Instead, many states assumed characteristics of the colonial state—existing primarily to serve the interests of small but powerful elite groups. The state retained its forceful authoritarian character. Like the colonial leaders they took over from, many of Africa's independence leaders failed to establish legitimacy over their territories or extend formal control across their countries. New African leaders relied on the sovereignty that underpinned the international system for legitimacy and sought protection from their Cold War patrons, instead of seeking legitimacy from the societies they governed. When they required internal support, again, like their colonial predecessors, they established alliances, especially with local chiefs to control the country-side, to collect revenue, and to win votes. To shore up its survival and its extractive role, the postindependent state controlled the production and distribution of national resources. The state became an instrument of accumulation and patronage, in which leaders built networks, often on ethnic (or regional lines) and bestowed rights and privileges, often economic, as a means to ensure its continued existence. Politics became a frequently violent struggle for access to the state and control of "the national cake."[4]

This violent struggle and competition for power has characterized politics in Sierra Leone and Liberia since their founding. State forma-tion in Sierra Leone and Liberia has generally followed the previously described patterns. In the case of Sierra Leone, founded in the eigh-teenth century by British antislavery activists as a haven for freed slaves from Britain and the New World, the peninsula later came under Brit-ish colonial rule from 1808 until it gained independence in 1961. In 1896, the British established a Protectorate to regulate the entire population in the upcountry interior, who lived under indigenous structures and institutions. Rather than establish a unitary state structure, the colonial-ist power established "a strong administrative distinction between the Colony (Freetown and the Western Area) and the Protectorate (rep-resented by three modern provinces)."[5] Britain operated a bifurcated system of governance in which Freetown and the Western Area had its own local government under the British legal system and where Creole settlers enjoyed extensive rights and privileges, while the Protectorate was established as "a sphere of indirect rule in which chiefs were central to the maintenance of law and order."[6] Over time, the powers of the local chiefs, particularly over land and labor, including the allocation of mineral licenses in diamond areas, were strengthened. At the same time, rivalry intensified between the Creole region and the hinterland. This rivalry was later replaced by competition between two main ethnic and regional groups in the country—the Temne and other northern-based ethnic groups, and the Mende, predominantly in the south and east.

When the newly independent state emerged, neither ethnoregional group, both of which had evolved into political parties—the northern-based All People's Congress (APC) and the southeastern-based Sierra Leone People's Party (SLPP)—was large enough to win elections. As a result, they developed alliances with other ethnic groups by buying favors from local chiefs or other local strongmen. Gradually, local chiefs began to wield immense influence over local politics with considerable unchecked powers of abuse. Like their colonial predecessors, the two dominant parties—the SLPP, which governed from 1961 to 1967, and the APC, which ruled for over twenty years (1968–92) following a military coup—relied strongly on the support of chiefs to impose order on rural communities. This eventually led to resentment. Indeed, a feature of Sierra Leone's civil war of March 1991 to January 2002 was the deliberate killing of chiefs or alienation from their communities.

The period of rule under the APC's first leader, President Siaka Stevens (1968–85) sowed the seeds for conflict. Rather than build formal state institutions, he governed through a network of patronage and used state resources to compensate allies. His control of the informal sector enabled him to entrench his patronage to local elites, including chiefs, and Lebanese commercial traders. Critical state institutions, such as the security sector, eroded and were unable to function because essential revenues were diverted. In 1985 when Stevens handed power over to Joseph Momoh, who was then commander of the Sierra Leone Armed Forces (SLAF), the state was no longer able to control deep societal resentments and divisions. The ground was ripe for the Revolutionary United Front (RUF) rebel invasion in 1991, and a coup led by disgruntled military elements who formed the National Provisional Ruling Council in 1992. The years of war that followed reproduced the logic that had governed postindependence political life in Sierra Leone. War was essentially a violent competition and collusion for control of the country's resources.[7]

The case of Liberia is unique, because the country lived under the protection of the United States for over a hundred years, though it was never colonized. Nonetheless, Liberia shared many hallmarks of postcolonial African states. Like Sierra Leone, it was founded as an entity to house freed slaves. In 1847, freed slaves from the US, who had settled mainly in Monrovia and along the coastal front, declared the new Republic of Liberia. Paradoxically, the settlers, commonly defined as America-Liberians, were no different from their plantation slave masters, who had treated them with a brutish and domineering hand. Efforts to create a new republic did not bring the settler community closer to the indigenous population. State power remained largely centralized under the True Whig Party (TWP), the party of the America-Liberian settler community that dominated the country for 133 years. Under the TWP, Liberia suffered from poor governance, injustice, and economic mismanagement. These factors created the basis for political and social dissension among the indigenous people in the 1970s.

The overthrow of the America-Liberian oligarchy by Master Sergeant Samuel K. Doe in April 1980, following the murder of the last True Whig leader, President William Tolbert, unleashed a ferocious contest between America-Liberian elites and political parties representing indigenous groups.[8] Yet the indigenous people were not a unified force, and when conflict broke out from 1989 to 1997, the fight for power was a contest not only between America-Liberians and indigenous political groupings, but also between these indigenous political forces. The July 1997 presidential election delivered only a temporary respite from the war. Under the warlord-turned-president Charles Taylor, whom some indigenous groups deemed as politically closer to America-Liberians, the state was unable to resuscitate already crumbled state institutions. His government could not provide basic public services or essential infrastructure; national institutions were broken, and state functionaries who had been unpaid for years were left to fend for themselves. The country became a haven for international smugglers who collaborated with Liberia's desperate elites, which in turn helped to fuel and sustain Liberia's war and, with it, a warlord economy.[9] But the collapse of the Liberian state predates Charles Taylor's 1997–2003 presidency. Indeed, his government was a microcosm of what existed prior to his assault on the Doe government. When regional and international forces intervened in August 2003, governance consisted of coercion by three brutal armed groups—the government of Liberia's forces and those of two rebel groups, Liberians United for Reconciliation and Democracy (LURD) and the Movement for Democracy in Liberia (MODEL)—who divided the country into enclaves in the north (LURD), the center, including the capital (the government's forces), and the south (MODEL).

Thus in Sierra Leone and Liberia historical processes and political competition and fissures led to weak and fractured central governments. Another common thread was the interlocking nature of the conflicts in the region. The sociopolitical and cultural ties between the three countries that composed the Mano River Basin (Sierra Leone, Liberia, and Guinea) largely determined the role each country played in the conflicts that emerged. Long established cross-border affiliations and networks between state officials and dissent groups also greatly shaped the fighting. At the same time, competition for regional influence by various ECOWAS member states (for example, Nigeria versus Côte d'Ivoire at the onset of the Liberian crisis), sometimes with the involvement of other Africa actors (Libya) or international actors (Britain in Sierra Leone, France in Liberia (and Côte d'Ivoire), and the US in Liberia), also exacerbated and influenced the character of conflict. In part because of the interlocking nature of the conflicts in Liberia and Sierra Leone observers called for a regional involvement, including peacekeeping and peacebuilding. The regional body, ECOWAS, and the UN focused on a political and security framework to stabilize regional civil wars as a foundation to the longer-term goal of sustaining peace in these two countries, as well as in the region.

The Success, Limits, and Clash of Ideas of Postconflict Statebuilding

Although regional and global peacebuilding strategies have increasingly focused efforts on constructing legitimate, effective state institutions, the record of these strategies has been mixed. Although some significant successes have been registered, the degree of vested interests and resistance to change by political elites has exposed the dilemmas of the statebuilding enterprise in Sierra Leone and Liberia. Further, as the cases show, the partnership and cooperation required to ensure an effective outcome have resulted in tensions between local national actors and their external partners. Both groups often desired the same stated outcomes, namely achieving national ownership and restoring sovereignty, but clashed over priorities, practices, and policies to attain these ends. Equally, the statebuilding strategy employed by external actors sometimes contradicted the views of national actors. But national actors were not a homogeneous group that articulated a common view; while they sought ownership, their interests and agendas varied and often clashed.

Sierra Leone: Consensus and Resistance to Statebuilding

In early 2009, Sierra Leonean freelance journalist Lansana Gberie published an article in which he remarked that his country had "passed a significant milestone."[10] The milestone was the successful completion, without UN peacekeepers, of national elections, five years after the civil war had ended. The incumbent governing party, the SLPP, and its candidate, Solomon Berewa, accepted defeat and handed power over to the rival APC and its leader, Ernest Koroma.[11] In praising his country's achievement, Gberie singled out the role of the reformed national electoral commission for the management of the elections, but left much of the praise to the army and police for securing a peaceful outcome.[12] Significantly, these security forces reversed a historical trend of interfering in national politics. This, Gberie opined, was a "refreshing sign of maturation." Credit, he argued, should also be given to the SLPP for its commitment to guaranteeing a democratic process and to the significant strides made to consolidate peace and rebuild basic state institutions.[13]

This defining moment in Sierra Leone's consolidation of peace must be understood within the context of the five years of partnership and cooperation between the government and its donor partners. It was a partnership underpinned by intensive regional and international intervention to restore peace to the country.

DEFINING THE PRIORITIES FOR STATEBUILDING

At the heart of this partnership was an immediate coalescing around the core fundamental reform issues that President Ahmad Tejan Kabbah had outlined in his speech at the opening of parliament on May 22, 1998, as critical to rebuilding the Sierra Leonean state. The most salient reform issues included reform of the security sector, namely the army and police; regulation of the diamond sector to end illegal smuggling; decentralization of government, including reestablishment of local councils and election of Paramount Chiefs; strengthening of the administration of justice; and maintenance of a sound macroeconomic framework.[14] Donors such as the United Kingdom's Department for International

Development (DFID) and the European Commission (EC) supported this approach, which formed the basis of the government's framework of action with various international partners. Yet although there appeared to be a shared vision in implementing this action plan, there was still a glaring disjuncture between international rhetoric and the reality of international engagement in Sierra Leone. In 1998, the UN's presence and significant international financial support to help rebuild Sierra Leone were largely missing. International involvement was mostly limited to the military intervention of the regional body, ECOWAS.

It was not until the resumption of conflict in late 1998, culminating in the Lomé Peace Agreement in July 1999, that any significant international effort was put in place to end the conflict. The major turning point came in May 2000 when RUF fighters took 500 UN troops hostage. This placed pressure on the UN Security Council to strengthen the peacekeeping mission in the country, and on Britain, the former colonial power, to intensify its engagement. Between 1999 and 2001, the United Nations Mission in Sierra Leone (UNAMSIL) was strengthened from 6,000 (October 1999) to 11,100 (February 2000) to 13,000 (May 2000) and finally to 17,500 (March 2001) to expand the remit of the mission and enable it to play a more robust role throughout the country.[15]

The British military took a hands-on-approach in restructuring the design, formation, and training of the Sierra Leonean army, including the organization of the Ministry of Defense. Overall, considerable human and financial resources were expended by Britain to reform the army. Police reform unfolded at a much slower pace, but by May 2003 the British inspector-general had handed over leadership of the Sierra Leone police to his national successor. Reform of the intelligence agencies also formed an important part of the security reform agenda, with Britain helping to establish a national security office. This supported government efforts to define a national security strategy. It also enhanced planning and coordination of national security among the key security agencies in the country.[16]

Regulating the diamond sector, addressing corruption, and strengthening local governance through decentralization were also critical to Sierra Leone's statebuilding strategy. These three areas were considered key components of the country's peacebuilding strategy by the Kabbah government. Aggressive campaigns against "blood diamonds" by local civil society groups such as the Network Movement for Justice and Development, and by international groups such as Partnership Africa

Canada, Global Witness, and Amnesty International, soon forced the US and UK to give greater attention to the diamond sector. The US and UK devised programs that guaranteed government regulation of diamond fields and financial transparency in the management of revenue collection. They also improved working conditions of the large number of laborers involved in artisanal mining. Regulation of the diamond sector was set within the wider campaign against Sierra Leone's historically institutionalized corruption at all levels of state. In 2000, Britain supported the government's initiative to set up an anticorruption commission.[17]

There was a consensus among local and international actors that establishing security was a prerequisite for future peacebuilding activities. This "security first" approach helped stabilize the precarious situation in the country, although maintaining it was not always easy. For example, there were significant and near paralyzing tensions between the United Kingdom and UNAMSIL in 2000 following the hostage crisis. The decision of President Kabbah to seek a Special Court for Sierra Leone in response to the RUF's violations of the Lomé Peace Agreement caused further fissures between the UK (and the US) and Nigeria, as well as in the wider subregion, where it was felt that the pursuit of war crimes could undermine efforts to persuade the RUF to reengage in the peace process.[18] Also, the restoration of the Paramount Chiefs and new local councils under the decentralization program caused disagreement between rural communities, the government, and its donor partner, DFID. The latter saw the restoration effort as critical to demonstrating the return of security to Sierra Leone's provinces, but it exacerbated local grievances, especially among the youth, who expressed resentment at the unrepresentative and unaccountable power the local chiefs wielded.[19] But despite tensions about how to achieve security, there was common agreement globally, regionally, and locally that security, including security sector reform, control of the diamond sector, and restoration of Paramount Chiefs, underpinned by a more robust UN peacekeeping force, was vital to supporting future peacebuilding initiatives and statebuilding.

RESISTANCE TO REFORM:
THE POLITICAL REALITIES OF STATEBUILDING

But consensus was difficult to reach on how to address the other statebuilding priorities outlined by President Kabbah in his speech to parliament. Statebuilding efforts soon foundered as tensions between the government and external actors emerged over contentious governance issues like corruption, public finance management, and service delivery. Resistance to reforming these politically sensitive areas revealed the limitations of donor influence and international engagement when key vested elite interests were threatened. For example, the slow implementation of a ten-year memorandum of understanding (MOU) agreed to in 2002 by the governments of Sierra Leone and the United Kingdom (under the auspices of DFID)[20] laid testimony to the difficulties of achieving commitment to address the issues of corruption and governance that President Kabbah had stated were critical to rebuilding the Sierra Leonean state. By 2005, the government appeared largely resistant to change, causing donors to conclude that old habits would die hard, or were resurfacing again to shape postwar Sierra Leone.[21] The unity of purpose and harmony that was singled out to explain Sierra Leone's steady progress had dissipated. Donors were left frustrated, with one former DFID official concluding that this state of affairs had largely shattered the myth that international partners, in particular the UK, had considerable influence over the government in shaping Sierra Leone's statebuilding agenda.[22]

This reluctance to change was not surprising. Gberie, who formed part of a team of two consultants assigned by DFID to review progress in implementing the MOU, says that there was a lack of consultation with the government in designing the benchmarks underpinning the MOU and little agreement on more politically sensitive issues relating to the UK's call for the downsizing of military personnel within a year. This latter requirement caused alarm for a government that believed that a similar suggestion to immediately roll back the national army may have contributed to the May 1997 coup.[23] The Sierra Leonean government therefore lacked ownership of the governance dimension of the statebuilding reform agenda, even though it was premised on the objectives articulated by President Kabbah in 1998. Furthermore, the state was constrained in its ability to deliver on its proposed reform agenda.[24] Critically, the progress of reform and change was hindered by the fact that postwar Sierra Leone remained dominated by the same old political forces (despite their political party affiliation) that "reinforced their traditional power basis and manipulated the reform agenda."[25]

THE UN PEACEBUILDING COMMISSION IN SIERRA LEONE

For the United Nations, placing Sierra Leone under the purview of its newly established entity, the Peacebuilding Commission (PBC), demonstrated that Sierra Leone had reached a major milestone.[26] In December 2005, UNAMSIL left the country, claiming that stabilization had been successful, and the work of the UN shifted from peacekeeping to peacebuilding. Through the establishment of the United Nations Integrated Office in Sierra Leone (UNIOSIL), the PBC was mandated to foster closer collaboration and consensus between local and international efforts in addressing the more difficult political aspects of Sierra Leone's longer-term statebuilding agenda. However, a 2007 assessment by three international nongovernmental organizations (INGOs)—Action Aid, CARE, and CAFOD—provided sobering reflections on the PBC. The report criticized the slow start and lack of political focus, analysis, and strategic direction of the PBC, as well as the lack of coherence and coordination between donors.[27] The review further highlighted a perennial problem in international endeavors in statebuilding: the failure to appropriately link the US$35 million in funding received from the Peacebuilding Fund (PBF) to the need to reach political consensus with local actors on tackling challenges to peacebuilding. The PBF financial support was granted prior to securing the political will of the government and, more worryingly, ahead of the 2007 elections. This gave the unfortunate impression that the funds were aimed at bolstering the fortunes of the incumbent SLPP party.[28] This perception was made more real by the fact that the vice president and presidential contender, Solomon E. Berewa, was cochair of the PBF's steering committee. Another concern was that the Peacebuilding Commission's involvement in Sierra Leone suffered from a lack of "an informed debate on the meaning and politics of post-conflict peacebuilding" that resulted in the commission's adopting a technical approach at a time when securing the political commitment of the government was vital to consolidating peace in the country.[29]

After the 2007 elections, a strategic framework premised on the original four priority areas of the previous government—youth empowerment and employment; democracy and good governance; justice and security; and capacity building—was developed by the government in collaboration with the UN. In September 2008, UNIOSIL departed from the country, leaving the PBC as the main UN instrument in Sierra Leone. Its task of maintaining consensus and the commitment of Sierra Leone to the objectives of postwar reconstruction could succeed only if these objectives remained politically acceptable to the government. Yet the fact that Sierra Leone's political landscape remains largely unaltered should be cause for concern. The voting patterns that saw the APC winning, overwhelmingly, in the northern half of the country and the Western Area (including Freetown), and the SLPP maintaining its control of the southern and eastern provinces, reflect the old order. As UN Secretary-General Ban Ki-moon observed, this exposed a deepening political schism and highlighted the increasing dominance of ethnicity and regionalism in the politics of Sierra Leone, a fact that if not addressed "could have a negative impact on peace-consolidation efforts in the country."[30] These examples highlight the tensions in Sierra Leone between the external statebuilding agenda that encourages new ways of conducting politics and new political actors, and the national ownership agenda.[31]

Liberia: Securing Legitimate Elections and State Control

The Liberian experience highlights that security is essential for statebuilding.[32] Lessons from previous rounds of regional and international peacekeeping from 1989 to 1997 provided a stark reminder that security is a primary ingredient for guaranteeing longer-term peacebuilding. Consequently, in their second intervention in Liberia beginning in August 2003, regional and international actors provided robust security coverage throughout the country. The mandate of the United Nations Mission in Liberia (UNMIL) was designed to correct past mistakes that focused on elections, believing that this was sufficient to ensure stability.[33] Similarly, ECOWAS as guarantor of the Comprehensive Peace Agreement of August 2003 that brought an end to Liberia's civil war played a more prominent political and security role with UNMIL in shaping the country's postconflict environment. Effective statebuilding in Liberia required both security and a break with the predatory and warlord politics of the country's past political history. Former president Charles Taylor's removal from political power and his exile in August 2003 following the unsealing of his indictment by the Special Court for Sierra Leone for war crimes in June was a vital first step for Liberians and its international partners to alter the basis for politics in the country.[34] Neutralizing other potential spoilers was the next critical step on the path to holding viable elections and constituting a legitimate state.

NEUTRALIZING SPOILERS

For many Liberians and international partners, namely ECOWAS, UNMIL, and the International Contact Group on Liberia,[35] there was consensus that external intervention should support efforts that contribute to changing the political landscape of the country. Inevitably this goal of creating a new postwar state faced resistance from a coalition that sought to cling to the status quo. This coalition of status quo forces was spread across the spectrum of Liberia's elite class, most notably the transitional government and business community. It brought under its umbrella all the leaders of the Americo-Liberian settler hegemony as well as the top echelons of the three major armed factions (former members of government, LURD, and MODEL forces) that had held the country in a stranglehold for a quarter of a century. Their goal was to prevent the implementation of changes that would destroy their individual careers or reveal the extent of their involvement in previous state predation and plunder.

The coalition employed various tactics to derail the peace process and thereby prolong the life of the transitional government, in order to enable its members to loot the vestiges of an already bankrupt state. One such attempt was to forestall national elections in October 2005. To achieve this, the coalition sought to delay the signing into law of an electoral reform bill that would lay the procedural and operational foundations for running elections. Another delaying tactic was to prevent completion of the disarmament and demobilization process, which was critical to securing the country ahead of national elections.[36]

UNMIL attempted to build partnerships at various levels to break the power base of the coalition that did not want to change the status quo. The coalition was not a homogeneous entity, and international partners therefore encouraged splits. Another vital factor was that the CPA stipulated that members of the transitional government could not contest for political or elective positions in the postwar elections. This excluded the principal political leaders of the armed factions from participating in the post-transition government.

Against this powerful coalition resisting change was another constellation of actors who desired reform. These people sought support from, and often aligned themselves with, Liberia's international partners, although the relationship was at times strained. The coalition brought together human rights activists, prodemocracy movements, different faith groups, and some national NGOs, including women's groups. It provided a domestic anchor in society that helped UNMIL and its international partners navigate the difficult road to creating a new political space to contest elections.

FREE AND FAIR ELECTIONS

The nationwide democratic elections provided for in the CPA took place on October 11, 2005, in a remarkably peaceful environment. Twenty-two aspirants had registered as presidential candidates along with thirty registered political parties. The multiplicity of registered political parties exposed many of the deep-seated problems in the Liberian political system, in that many of the parties, beyond the established groups, were not national in character, but tended to represent regional or ethnic identities.

Ellen Johnson Sirleaf and her Unity Party (UP) won the presidential elections in a second round run-off against George Weah and his Congress for Democratic Change (CDC). But postconflict politics were shaped and influenced by interactions between three major political forces that emerged during the elections: the "conservative/status quo forces," the "nativist caucus," and the "progressive nationalist movement."[37] The conservative forces were made up of the remnants of the previously dominant Americo-Liberian political class, represented by Varney Sherman under the Coalition for the Transformation of Liberia (COTOL). Weah and his CDC embodied the aspirations of the nativists' goal of indigenous rule. President Johnson Sirleaf's UP represented the progressive nationalist movement.

The outcome of the elections reflected the historical resentment toward the Americo-Liberian hegemony and others associated with the dominant political class and the status quo. The voice of the dispossessed and disenchanted youth, who constituted a potent majority of Liberia's population and who overwhelmingly supported Weah, emerged as a force to challenge the status quo. Yet Sirleaf's ultimate victory may be interpreted as a rejection of the ethnic jingoism that characterized the Weah camp. It was also a repudiation of attempts to entrench the historical division of society along an indigenous versus Americo-Liberia fault line. What emerged was a progressive nationalist movement that represented a rejection of a throwback to the past. Sirleaf's government wanted to forge an inward-oriented and focused pan-Liberian force that encompassed social, political, and economic liberalism as a basis for policy, and to negotiate the terms of political and economic engagement with Liberia's international partners.

Yet the hope that warlords would not feature in the new postwar electoral climate was dashed. The race for seats at the National Assembly ushered in factional leaders, some of whom were on the UN's sanction lists, including Jewel Taylor, the wife of former president Charles

Taylor, and other Taylor allies such as militia leader Adolphus Dolo and former warlord Prince Johnson, a self-proclaimed born-again Christian. It was, therefore, inevitable that uneasy relations would develop between the executive and the legislature and dominate Liberia's political landscape. For the first time in Liberia's history, the ruling party did not dominate the legislature. Yet while we must take caution not to overstate the emergence of a new democratic process, the success of the elections significantly altered the context in which the political process was evolving. It would also affect the nature of Liberia's peacebuilding agenda because the executive, led by a confident sovereign, would clash in the early years with a legislature that wanted to carve a prominent role for itself in determining the country's progress. The administration of President Johnson Sirleaf outlined an extensive array of reform initiatives necessary to buttress the new democratic dispensation, premised on integration and nationalism, or "Liberianization," meaning ensuring Liberia's ownership of various processes. Her vision and accompanying policies would come to shape the postconflict peacebuilding process, including Liberia's relations with various international partners.

POSTELECTION STATEBUILDING:
REDEFINING INTERNATIONAL AND LOCAL RELATIONSHIPS

The immediate task of the new government after its inauguration on January 16, 2006, was to consolidate the country's hard-won peace, embark on various reform initiatives, and put in place mechanisms to address long-term development and economic recovery. The role of ECOWAS, UNMIL, and other international partners was to complete the unfinished aspects of the CPA and provide the new government with the political space it needed for elaborating longer-term peacebuilding strategies. The international mantra of "partnership" and "ownership" was tested in the early months of the new democratic dispensation, as international actors were confronted with a confident head of a sovereign state, who, while pragmatically negotiating the terms of political and economic engagement with Liberia's international partners, also displayed strong "nationalist" leanings. It became quickly apparent that President Johnson Sirleaf would vigorously seek to "Liberianize" all donor interventions. For ECOWAS, UNMIL, the International Contact Group on Liberia and other external partners, it became immediately clear that the robust and rigorous style of diplomacy adopted by international partners during the transitional period would have to be tempered.

Soon after her election victory, Sirleaf and Liberia's regional and international partners (under the auspices of the International Contact Group) met to discuss an internal paper that set out what these partners considered as key priority areas. The document encouraged the new administration to open a dialogue with the people of Liberia and the legislature in order to set clear priorities and benchmarks for action and change at national and local levels. It further advised that dialogue focus on priority policy and institutional reforms pivotal to the political stability and economic progress of Liberia.[38] Sirleaf did not find any of these identified priorities objectionable. The meeting, however, provided an opportunity for the president to articulate her goals and outline her priorities for rebuilding Liberia. More critically, she emphasized the importance of Liberians taking ownership of the destiny of the country, while collaborating with international partners. In the immediate months following her election, Sirleaf set out her reform and development agenda, and in March 2006 she announced the government's 150-day action plan, which was jointly elaborated with the support of Liberia's donor partners. The plan had four interrelated parts: security, economic revitalization, rule of law and governance, and basic services and infrastructure. The government also established the Liberia Reconstruction and Development Committee (chaired by the president) to coordinate external aid, and to oversee the 150-day action plan, which later evolved into a set of government activities to be accomplished under an interim poverty reduction strategy.[39] A key hangover, however, from the transitional period and a major governance problem for the Sirleaf government, was how to deal with the history of corruption and the hemorrhaging of state funds. Continued donor and international support, especially from the US, the European Union, and international financial institutions, was contingent on proper financial management of state revenue and a strong anticorruption program. Sirleaf's vision of ownership of Liberia's affairs and how she would ensure an outcome that was favorable to Liberia was immediately tested.

The implementation of the Governance and Economic Management Assistance Program (GEMAP) tested donors' commitment to partnership and ownership. GEMAP was negotiated and signed under the transitional government in response to the troubling revelations of corruption concerning public officials at all levels.[40] Although President Sirleaf was committed to the ideas behind GEMAP, her party as well as other Liberian political parties perceived the program to be a highly intrusive form of international assistance that directly challenged Liberia's sovereignty. The requirement to deploy international experts with cosignatory authority in the financial machinery of the Liberian state was considered the epitome of intrusion.

Pragmatically, however, Sirleaf encouraged GEMAP, because she agreed with the core elements of its agenda, especially management of public finances. In accepting the recommendations of GEMAP and the foreign experts, the president, in her inauguration speech, committed her administration to ensuring competency and integrity in managing the country's resources but demanded that international partners pursue an integrated capacity-building initiative "so as to render GEMAP inapplicable in a reasonable period of time."[41] Tensions were inevitable in implementing such a controversial and intrusive program. Although Sirleaf chaired the oversight GEMAP Economic Governance Steering Committee (EGSC) made up of donors and other international partners, its technical arm was still led by the US government. A special retreat between the Liberian government and its international partners was convened in April 2007, during which President Sirleaf raised concern about the lack of teamwork, collegiality, and partnership that was supposed to underpin relations between the internationally recruited GEMAP experts and the management of those GEMAP-assisted government agencies. Another concern was that without a more robust plan of action for capacity development, the objectives of GEMAP could not be sustained. A consensus was reached that Liberia would begin to assume full control of GEMAP processes.[42]

The implementation of GEMAP provides revealing insights into the mind-set of the new government, especially the president's, over the issue of "ownership." The flip side of the ownership debate was made visible in the implementation process. Indeed, it was apparent to President Sirleaf that limited capacity in government ministries to deliver and meet the expectations of the country meant that much of what she wanted to achieve could not be done without international assistance. Liberia's partnership with the international community in the pursuit of peace could therefore be characterized as an "awkward relationship" in which Liberians were proud of their independence but needed to reconcile that pride with the fact that they lacked the necessary capacity to rebuild their country.

Statebuilding is an immensely complex and expensive endeavor that is dependent on an intense partnership between international, regional, and local actors but that contains a number of important tensions and contradictions. Based on the two case studies presented in this chapter, we can draw out four observations. First, an often repeated phrase is that there is no "one size fits all" approach to statebuilding. Rather, a key lesson is the need to think boldly about ways to tailor statebuilding approaches to individual postconflict situations. Second, the strategy of ensuring security first is a necessary step, but not sufficient for peacebuilding. The region, the UN, and the international donor community have made important contributions to helping Sierra Leone and Liberia achieve stability. However, while both countries have achieved increased security, the more deeply complex political tasks of statebuilding have proven to be problematic. In particular, it has been difficult to achieve transformation that leads to a fundamental change in the political landscape, although developments in Liberia point to a realignment of political forces. Overall, there is a tension between the transformative aspirations underlying the statebuilding enterprise and the demands for local ownership.

Third, where states are weak, fractured, and with limited functional capacity, external assistance is more likely to be highly interventionist and assertive, as witnessed in the early phase of international intervention in Sierra Leone and Liberia. Yet when a strong government emerges as in Liberia, states will resist or seek to limit international attempts to determine or dictate the statebuilding agenda, especially on contentious issues where the sovereignty of a state is at stake. This once again highlights the problematic nature of the peacebuilding enterprise and the conflicting imperatives of transformative statebuilding and national "ownership."

Finally, the long-term objective of helping to build legitimate and effective state institutions is contingent on creating processes and institutions such as coordinating bodies or policy forums that enable dialogue over contentious issues between government and external actors (and even among the latter). This does not mean that tensions between local, regional, and international actors can be overcome. Indeed, as the examples in this chapter suggest, it may be impossible to resolve such tensions. However, processes like the Economic Governance Steering Committee and the Liberia Reconstruction and Development Committee bring internal and external partners together in

Liberia to discuss and debate priorities in statebuilding programs and may enable or encourage consensus building. The Liberia case shows that coordination mechanisms between international actors and the national authority can be helpful in defining priority actions. Further, the UN's approach of encouraging a shared vision of a peacebuilding framework is a useful strategy for consensus building on the way forward to statebuilding, as seen in Sierra Leone. This does not guarantee a convergence of ideas between national and external actors; indeed, the politics of postconflict peacebuilding remain hard to navigate. External actors often have limited reach in altering the underlying structures, patterns, and political dynamics that created violence and civil wars. Nonetheless, the importance of peacebuilding processes over time should not be neglected. Although coordination mechanisms do not eliminate difficult relations between national and external actors, there are certain important ingredients, including reinforcing trust and respect, and encouraging a shared vision of the way forward, that are mutually beneficial.

Notes

1. This is in part due to the devastating effect of the conflicts on the state and society in both countries.

2. Paris and Sisk, "Introduction: Understanding the Contradictions of Postwar Statebuilding," 14.

3. Paris and Sisk, *Managing Contradictions*, 1.

4. See Reno, *Warlord Politics and African States.*

5. Brown et al., "Sierra Leone," 3.

6. Ibid.

7. See Thomson, "Sierra Leone," 2–3.

8. See Ero, "UN Peacekeeping in West Africa," 286.

9. See Reno, *Warlord Politics and African States.* See also reports since 2001 by the UN Panel of Experts concerning Liberia, available at http://www.un.org.

10. Gberie, "Rescuing a Fragile State," 1.

11. Ibid.

12. Ibid., 9.

13. Ibid.

14. See Thomson, "Sierra Leone," 5–6.

15. UNAMSIL was established on October 22, 1999, under United Nations Security Council Resolution 1270. It replaced a smaller 200-strong United Nations Observer Mission in Sierra Leone (UNOMSIL) that had been established in July 1998.

16. For an assessment of Britain's early security sector reform program, see Thomson, "Sierra Leone," 12–14.

17. However, progress was slower than anticipated because of a delay in the arrival of the British advisory team and administrative problems in the anticorruption commission. Thomson, "Sierra Leone," 17.

18. See Ero, "UN Peacekeeping in West Africa," 295.

19. In light of the criticisms, DFID reviewed its chieftaincy program. See Thomson, "Sierra Leone," 5–6.

20. This was known as the "Long-Term Partnership Agreement between the UK Government and the Government of Leone." This MOU was based on the state reform agenda articulated in President Kabbah's 1998 speech to parliament.

21. See Thomson, "Sierra Leone." I was working in Sierra Leone during this period (2001–4) and observed frustrations among several donors, most notably the European Commission and the World Bank. See International Crisis Group, *Sierra Leone after Elections*.

22. Thomson, "Sierra Leone," 30.

23. The May 1997 coup was partly as a result of government's desire to downsize the national army, which many in government and the wider population felt had been ineffective in fighting against the rebel RUF and AFRC, while at the same time bolstering the budgetary allocation of the civil defense forces (CDFs). Grievances within the army over preference given to the CDFs led to tensions with the government.

24. Gberie, "Rescuing a Fragile State," 10.

25. Ibid.

26. For an analysis of the UN Peacebuilding Commission, see Olonisakin and Ikpe in this volume.

27. Action Aid, CAFOD, and CARE International, *Consolidating the Peace*, 12–15. See also Street, Smith, and Mollet, "Experiences of the United Nations Peacebuilding Commission in Sierra Leone," 36, 38–39.

28. Street, Smith, and Mollet, "Experiences of the United Nations Peacebuilding Commission."

29. Curran and Woodhouse, "Cosmopolitan Peacekeeping and Peacebuilding in Sierra Leone," 1063.

30. Quoted in Gberie, "Rescuing a Fragile State," 19.

31. See Zaum in this volume.

32. This section is based on the author's work in Liberia between 2004 and 2007.

33. The United Nations Security Council established UNMIL on September 19, 2003, under United Nations Security Council Resolution 1509.

34. The SCSL prosecutor had indicted President Taylor in March of the same year, but the indictment remained sealed. It was eventually unsealed on June 4, when Taylor traveled to Accra, Ghana, for the start of peace talks on Liberia. In May 2012, the SCSL convicted Taylor for war crimes and sentenced him to fifty years in prison.

35. The ICGL was established in 2002. Initially it comprised ECOWAS, the European Commission, the UN, Nigeria, Ghana, Britain, and the United States. It was later expanded to include the World Bank and Germany.

36. The disarmament process began on December 1, 2003, but was postponed soon after the UN encountered difficulties largely because of the overwhelming numbers of combatants. There was also some misunderstanding concerning the benefits ex-combatants were to receive, which led to disturbances. The program resumed in April 2004.

37. These three terms were coined by the Political, Policy, and Planning Section of UNMIL, in which I worked from 2004 to 2007.

38. The priority areas outlined included constitutional change, security sector reform, economic recovery, growth and poverty reduction, rule of law and the administration of justice, human rights and national reconciliation, basic services, and public sector reform.

39. The interim strategy was launched in March 2007. In August, the government launched the next phase of its development reform agenda, the poverty reduction process, which concluded in March 2008 and commenced implementation the following June.

40. See United Nations, *Seventh Progress Report,* paras. 2, 7–10.

41. The text of the inauguration speech is available at http://www.emansion.gov.lr. The specific quote on GEMAP is in the section on corruption.

42. A decision was made at the April 2007 retreat that Liberia should gradually assume the chair of the technical committee as well as of the EGSC.

THIRTEEN

Oil and Peacebuilding in the Niger Delta

ADEROJU OYEFUSI

It is true that some of the boys have taken to criminality, but there are no jobs, no schools for them; no water to drink, no electricity, and they see their parents as helpless. How many of their parents are lifting crude oil? How many of them get oil blocks? When did the Nigerian National Petroleum Company (NNPC) become a prerogative of a certain section of the country, whereas the people who own it (that is the oil) are not involved in the administration of the place? The federal government should not treat the people as conquered people.

> Edwin Kiagbodo Clark, "The Niger Delta Crisis," *Guardian* (Lagos), June 12, 2009

We are but products of government's intransigence on the Niger Delta question, victims of the political class' extreme lust for power and rabid ambition, children of necessity of the high-handedness and violent suppression of the Niger Delta struggle by the Joint Task Force, fall-outs of mercenary elders who feed fat from the struggle of the Niger Delta people. . . . If the so-called militants are criminals, then all these parties are also criminals and therefore need their own amnesty.

> A militant in the Niger Delta, and his representative, quoted in *Guardian,* June 12, 2009

The very reason for militancy is because of injustice. Fiscal federalism is among the things that will silence our guns. A simple reversal to fiscal federalism will save you the trouble of another future ceremony where you are made to receive piles of worthless paper.

> Movement for the Emancipation of the Niger Delta (MEND), in a letter to Nigeria's president, *This Day* (Lagos), June 6, 2009

THE PRODUCTION OF CRUDE OIL AND THE MANAGEMENT OF ITS RENTS
have been recurring sources of conflict in Nigeria, sub-Saharan Africa's largest producer. The politics of oil led to an unsuccessful attempt at secession by the Ijaws, the largest ethnic group in the oil-producing Niger Delta, in 1966. It also contributed to an outbreak of civil war following the declaration of independence by the eastern region in 1967, and has since generated continuous unrest in Nigeria. This has placed the country in a situation that can be characterized as between war and peace.[1] After two decades of a fragile postwar peace, an insurrection by military officers from the South-South region and the Middle Belt in April 1990 led to a resurfacing of fundamental questions on resource management and statehood, and provided the occasion for fresh outbreaks of community and ethnic uprisings in the Niger Delta region.[2] Violent unrest in the region reached alarming levels after that. Between May and June 2009, in an outbreak of violence between government forces and militant groups, oil production plummeted to as low as 800,000 barrels per day (about 30 percent of normal output level) as foreign oil companies were forced to shift operations offshore.[3]

Following the 2009 round of violence, the government introduced and implemented an amnesty package for militants that included a disarmament, demobilization, and reintegration (DDR) program. The peacebuilding program is unique in that it was primarily homegrown and managed by the Nigerian government and people. Though it succeeded in bringing some measure of peace to the Niger Delta region, many believe that the fundamental issues underlying the crisis remain largely unresolved, such as property rights to oil and an appropriate revenue-sharing formula between the Nigerian government and producing regions. This chapter discusses ten key issues and questions arising from oil resource management and peace efforts in the Niger Delta, and the challenges they raise for local and international peacebuilding. It argues that contracts for the extraction of natural resources ought to be based on a relationship of trust between governments, host communities, and extractive firms, but there are serious obstacles to this.[4]

Economic Justice in Oil Ownership and Rent-Sharing

A major factor underlying the Niger Delta crisis is the question of ownership or property rights to oil and the appropriate formula for sharing oil rents. Before the outbreak of the 1967–70 Nigerian civil war, communities had property rights over land even though the British colonial government's mineral ordinance of 1914 (amended in 1925, 1950, and 1958) meant that it had vested ownership of all mineral resources in the country. The independence constitution provided for 50 percent of revenues from natural resources to be returned to the producing region on the basis of the derivation formula. However, just before the end of the civil war, in 1969, the federal government introduced the Petroleum Act, which gave it total control of the oil industry and oil revenue. It also enacted the Land Use Act in 1978, which vested ownership of all land within a state to the governor. These steps were associated with a gradual reduction in the derivation formula to 45 percent in 1970, 20 percent in 1975, 2 percent in 1982, and 1.5 percent in 1984, before an increase to 3 percent in 1992.[5]

The acquisition of absolute rights to oil by the central government undermined the establishment of appropriate institutional arrangements to regulate oil exploration and production activities and safeguard host communities from the negative impact of oil activities on the environment from which communities derive their livelihood.[6] As the International Crisis Group notes, over five decades of oil activity has resulted in extremely high levels of air and water pollution, thousands of oil spills, and a notorious record of gas flaring.[7]

Absolute central government ownership and control of oil resources has also led to the extreme dependence of the Nigerian government on oil revenue. There is a marriage of interest between the state and the major multinational oil companies, such as Shell and Chevron, operating in the country. As a result, the administration of justice in cases of oil-related disputes has been biased in favor of Western companies, and the state has been excessively repressive toward host communities.[8]

In addition, developmental initiatives by the federal government in the Niger Delta region, such as the establishment of the Oil Mineral Producing Areas Development Commission (OMPADEC) in 1992, and the Niger Delta Development Commission (NDDC) in 2001, have followed a top-down approach. The federal government has starved the developmental agencies of funds, thereby incapacitating them. For example, the government and oil companies have habitually defaulted on their statutory financial commitments to the NDDC. Between 2001, when the agency was created, and December 2007, the total funds owed to the commission by the government had accumulated to a staggering 300 billion naira.[9]

In 1999, the derivation formula was increased from 3 to 13 percent. However, this has failed to pacify oil-producing communities, as it was viewed as an inadequate response to over four decades of neglect. Virtually all the committees set up by the government since the return to civilian rule in 1999 to recommend lasting solutions to the Niger Delta crisis have suggested an increase in the derivation formula to at least 25 percent. In particular, the Technical Committee on the Niger Delta, set up in September 2008, suggested a framework in which the additional funds should be invested in new infrastructure and sustainable development in the oil-producing region. It also suggested the need for greater involvement of host communities. In October 2009, the federal government muted the idea of transferring 10 percent of equity held in joint-venture contracts to oil-producing communities.[10] However, it did not clarify exactly how this was to be done. Although the idea that economic issues are an important component of peacebuilding is widely accepted, the Niger Delta experience shows that in practice there are profound disagreements about this.

Legally Enforceable Responsibilities of Stakeholders

The federal government of Nigeria operates two contractual arrangements with oil companies, a joint-venture contract and a production-sharing contract. Under the joint-venture arrangement, the NNPC, representing the government's interests and multinational oil companies, set aside part of its oil earnings to finance development activities in host communities. One of the oil companies is appointed to operate the venture. I have argued elsewhere, however, that the reliance on oil companies to operate community development programs has encouraged governments at all levels to abandon their statutory responsibilities.[11] It has also allowed multinational firms to play a disproportionate role in community governance and service provision and increased the space for conflict between the latter and host communities.

In 2005, a survey of eighteen communities in the Niger Delta region showed, for example, that 39 percent depended on oil companies for electricity, which was often rationed. The survey also revealed that the demand on companies for the provision of basic amenities fueled up to 40 percent of identified conflict episodes, and contests among communities, and between groups for benefits from companies, ignited another 36 percent.[12] There is a need for a clearly defined concept of corporate "social responsibility" and the delineation of responsibilities of the government toward host communities in a legally enforceable resource extraction contract.

External Guarantees and Involvement

The role of guarantees by external actors in preventing resource-related violence has been examined in the existing literature, but the focus is often on the use of external military deterrence to discourage potential insurgents.[13] This is one-sided, and there is a need to examine how external actors could compel governments to take action to prevent conflict.

Nigeria's former president, Alhaji Umaru Yar'Adua, strongly supported the creation of an external force to guarantee stability in the Gulf of Guinea. This enthusiasm toward military deterrence was followed up with military training and technical assistance by some foreign countries, such as the United States and Britain.[14] However, the same countries have not adequately pressured the Nigerian government to address the causes of the Niger Delta crisis. There has also been no pressure from other countries within and outside sub-Saharan Africa, nor from international organizations such as the United Nations (UN) and the African Union (AU).

As many analysts have observed, Nigeria did not walk into the Niger Delta crisis blindfolded. Apart from the Willinks Commission's report of 1958, which first noted the possibility of an outbreak of rebellion in the region, Nigeria has organized at least fifteen other conferences, summits, and forums to examine the crisis and provide recommendations for a solution.[15] However, successive governments never implemented their core recommendations. In fact, official copies of some reports are said to have disappeared from government archives.[16]

This lack of commitment on the part of the federal government to resolve the Niger Delta crisis was, therefore, at least partly responsible for the continued violence in the region. For example, the Movement for the Emancipation of the Niger Delta (MEND)[17] was formed some months after the failure of the National Political Reform Conference of 2005 to satisfactorily address the Niger Delta question, and the perceived deliberate assault against the Ijaw people almost immediately thereafter. Similarly, over a year of peace initiatives in the region were shattered by the government's failure to publish or implement practical recommendations that had emanated from a technical committee it had set up in September 2008 to study all previous reports and position papers on the Niger Delta crisis. In fact, in what appeared to be a confusing signal, government troops bombed one of MEND's camps in Rivers state while the committee was still working, thereby triggering another round of violence.

Multinational oil companies operating in the Niger Delta region have also contributed to the unrest and violence. Oil companies have traditionally supported, and even instigated, violence against protesters and communities. They have sometimes set communities, families, and individuals against each other, through the way in which they offer selective compensation or damages for land and developmental assistance.[18] More recently, however, oil companies have made some efforts to improve their practices. For example, in 2006, the Shell Petroleum Development Company introduced a new approach (the Global Memoranda of Understanding) aimed at improving the way it engages with communities, by allowing clusters of communities to determine what projects are carried out under the joint-venture arrangement.[19] Some oil companies have also begun to advocate for greater participation of host communities in exploration activities through ownership of oil assets as a way of preventing attacks.[20]

The actions of foreign oil companies are therefore critical to peacebuilding in the Niger Delta, as the conflict cannot be viewed as separate from international processes. Yet regional and international actors have not exerted strong political pressure on the Nigerian government. The argument here is that strong political pressure by regional and international actors would be helpful, but the presence of strategic mineral resources and so many competing interests have made this unlikely.

Political Marginalization and Power-Sharing

There has been continuous agitation by many of the ethnoregional groups in Nigeria for a "true" federal political structure where each region has significant autonomy and control over its destiny. Among the grievances expressed by the Niger Delta people is the claim of political marginalization. Until 2007, no Ijaw or any other person from the Niger Delta region occupied the country's highest political offices, which were dominated by persons from the northern, western, and eastern regions. With the outbreak of violence in the Niger Delta region in 2004, President Olusegun Obasanjo, a Yoruba from the West, made a political arrangement within the ruling People's Democratic Party (PDP) whereby an Ijaw was to run as vice president in the 2007 election. With the victory of the PDP in the elections, Goodluck Ebere Jonathan became the first person from the Niger Delta to assume political office at that level of government.

This raised the prospects of peacebuilding in the Niger Delta, as the new president, Alhaji Umaru Yar'Adua, extensively relied on his vice president to reach out to militants in the region and facilitate discussions on how to resolve the lingering crisis. But early efforts by the vice president to avert the disasters that occurred during the military action against the Ijaws in May 2009 were rebuffed by the president, who was reported to have denied his vice president audience for three days. The apparent "inability" of the vice president to avert or minimize the large-scale assault or to convince the federal government to take action to minimize civilian casualties or provide relief for victims demonstrated that power and political office sharing are not necessarily synonymous. This prompted some groups, such as MEND and the Warri Ijaw Peace Monitoring Group, to ask for his resignation. Many felt his office had, in any case, been reduced to that of a "house boy," and there was nothing the Niger Delta region stood to benefit from his appointment.[21]

In November 2009, President Yar'Adua was rushed abroad for medical treatment. On February 9, 2010, the National Assembly adopted a motion empowering the vice president to assume the office of president in an acting capacity. On becoming acting president, Goodluck Jonathan took some steps to assert or consolidate his authority. The first was replacing the national security adviser. The second was the dissolution of President Yar'Adua's cabinet. The new cabinet reflects a major change in the allocation of ministries among the various ethnic groups in the country. Two of these changes (the appointment of Deziani Allison-Madueke, an Ijaw, as the new minister of petroleum resources, and the elevation of Peter Godsday Orubebe, another Ijaw, to that of substantive minister of Niger Delta) are particularly important for the Niger Delta crisis. Following the death of Yar'Adua on May 5, 2010, Jonathan was made president and commander in chief of the armed forces of the Federal Republic of Nigeria. He was reelected president in 2011 for a term of four years. However, militants in the Niger Delta have shown that they do not desire a Jonathan presidency as an end in itself. They say that violence in the region will not abate unless the president addresses the issue of economic justice. The above developments suggest that power and political office sharing must remain an integral part of peacebuilding efforts where ethnic divisions run deep, but that economic justice remains central.

"Democracy," Electoral Violence, and Peacebuilding

In May 1999, Nigeria experienced a transition to civilian leadership after sixteen years of brutal military rule. This transition reshaped the nature of the Niger Delta crisis. Oil availability raised the stakes associated with winning political office, since attaining the latter meant almost unhindered control of this flow of wealth.

Between 1999 and 2007, the oil city of Warri, in Delta state, as well as parts of Rivers state, including the state capital, Port Harcourt (regarded as Nigeria's oil capital), suffered violent conflicts. Two groups—Tom Ateke's Niger Delta Vigilante (NDV) and Alhaji Mujahid Asari-Dokubo's Niger Delta People's Volunteer Force (NDPVF)—fought over control of oil-bunkering routes and control of tribal chieftaincy titles in communities with access to patronage from government and oil companies.[22] Highly placed federal government officials from the ruling People's Democratic Party are reported to have provided logistical support and political protection to Ateke to help counter the influence of the opposition All Nigeria People's Party (ANPP) during the 2003 state and federal elections. In exchange, they would receive free rein to carry out profitable bunkering activities.[23] Former Rivers state governor Peter Odili is alleged to have provided financial backing to assist Asari-Dokubo in securing the presidency of the Ijaw Youth Council. Asari-Dokubo is reported to have subsequently used this position to exploit divisions between the Ijaws in different states, and to recruit youths to help ensure Odili's reelection in 2003.[24]

These events show that while democracy and elections can contribute to peace by providing opportunities for representation, they can also trigger violent expression of grievances and competition, especially in environments with weak institutional arrangements and weak rule of law. Some Niger Deltans believe that one of the underlying factors in the crisis in the region is the fact that elections tend to be flawed.[25] The manipulation of frustrated youths by political leaders has been identified as another important factor.[26] The international community's role of observing elections fails to adequately address electoral malpractices.[27]

Peace Negotiations

The issue of who should preside over negotiations to resolve the Niger Delta crisis has been controversial. Former President Yar'Adua consistently rejected the suggestion that a non-Nigerian lead a mediation process, and largely relied on his vice president, Goodluck Jonathan, to reach out to militants. The Ijaws and most militant groups considered this as "an attempt to saddle the Vice President with the sole responsibility of solving 'his peoples' problem, so that he can be charged with responsibility for failure."[28]

In 2008 there was disagreement over who should chair a proposed Niger Delta summit. Many within and outside the region had suggested an experienced and well-respected African figure, like former UN Secretary-General Kofi Annan of Ghana or Archbishop Desmond Tutu of South Africa, both Nobel Peace laureates. The federal government, however, opted for Ibrahim Gambari, a seasoned diplomat of northern affiliation who had served under previous military regimes and as a former ambassador to the UN. The federal government argued that the Niger Delta crisis was a domestic problem and Nigerians were best qualified to solve it, but many Niger Deltans believed that the choice of Gambari represented the pursuit of sectional interests and a hidden government agenda.[29] Following the threat by the Federation of Ijaw Youths not to participate, the idea of a summit was eventually jettisoned. In the wake of the military onslaught against Ijaw communities in May–June 2009, the Nigerian Bar Association called for the establishment of a truth commission composed of "neutral persons," and headed by a distinguished international figure, to mediate between government and militants, but this call was ignored.

Apart from the controversy over who should facilitate peace negotiations, activists in the Niger Delta have repeatedly complained that national negotiations between the Nigerian government and "representatives" of the Niger Delta have always been closed, and have involved delegates appointed by the federal and state governments, most of which are believed to lack public credibility in the Delta.[30] These meetings are viewed as avenues for government to buy the loyalty of participants. Delta militants have also requested that "resource control negotiations" between the government and representatives of each of the Niger Delta ethnic groups take place in any of the major cities in the Niger Delta rather than in Abuja.[31]

Nigeria's experience suggests it may be difficult to achieve consensus between all groups in relation to the choice of a mediator between parties to a conflict. Mediation by international figures or agencies may be resisted by some parties for political reasons.

Lack of Coordination within the Niger Delta

Efforts to negotiate a peaceful settlement have also been complicated by the lack of unity among different groups in the Niger Delta. There are many armed groups in the region, with the government officially identifying sixteen in 2003. Although most groups collaborate in some areas, the issues of hierarchy and representation remain sources of disharmony. The loose formation among militant groups and the considerable latitude they exercise in choosing what kinds of operations they carry out have encouraged various acts of criminality, such as kidnapping for ransom and other forms of violent extortions. This has made peacebuilding efforts by government and other stakeholders more difficult, since they cannot readily identify a command structure to negotiate with. Many groups, such as the Ijaw Youth Council, the Ijaw Youth Leadership Forum, the South-South Governors Forum, the Delta State Elders, Leaders, and Stakeholders Forum, the Conference of Ethnic Nationalities of the Niger Delta, the Ijaw, Isoko, and Itsekiri Leaders Forum, the Niger Delta Ethnic Nationalities, and the Niger Delta Peace and Development Forum, attempt to mediate, and many more seek relevance, thereby complicating any peace process. There is a problem of cohesiveness within the militant groups. For example, during the implementation of the amnesty program introduced by the federal government in August 2009, some members of different groups publicly embraced the amnesty even when their organizations either had not stated their position or had publicly rejected the offer.

Divisions between militant groups are replicated among the various ethnic groups in the Niger Delta. Frequent squabbles over positions and rents have encouraged both the government and oil companies to employ divide-and-rule tactics in the Delta.[32] For example, the violence in the city of Warri, Delta state, between 1997 and 2003, involving the Ijaws and Itsekiris, and later the Urhobos, illustrates how rent-seeking contests brought very lucrative benefits to the leaders of ethnic militias.[33]

As a result of ethnic rivalry and a lack of coordination, militancy in the Niger Delta has come to be viewed as an Ijaw struggle, and there have been efforts by other groups to discredit the agitations. For example, during the 2009 face-off between the Ijaws, the federal government, and oil companies, an Itsekiri community publicly applauded the efforts of a multinational oil company, Chevron, which had written a memorandum of understanding with them. Some other non-Ijaw communities praised government troops for "helping to maintain order and peace" in their communities, and called for continuous occupation.[34]

There has been some measure of cooperation lately, especially with requests for greater control of oil resources by host communities and states, but the issue of fractionalization between and among ethnic groups in the Niger Delta remains a significant impediment to peacebuilding.

Disarmament, Demobilization, Reintegration, and Amnesty

At different times in the conflict, the Nigerian government has granted amnesty to militants in the Niger Delta. More than four decades ago, the government granted amnesty to some Ijaw youths who had taken up arms against the state and proclaimed a "Niger Delta Republic."[35]

The Obasanjo government also granted amnesty to Asari-Dokubo and Ateke, leaders of two prominent militant groups, in October 2004, following their agreement to lay down their arms. The agreement, which included an arms-for-cash deal, was aimed at disarming Asari-Dokubo's NDPVF, Ateke's NDV, and their affiliated cult and youth-group members. It also provided for the reintegration of these groups into society, and the creation of jobs for youth.[36]

These efforts failed to bring lasting peace to the region. Despite the much-talked-about plan to create jobs for youth, there were no specific and concrete proposals to accomplish it. The 2004 disarmament process also failed to collect all the arms. Reports indicated that very old weapons were traded for financial rewards, while newer and more sophisticated weapons were retained by militants.[37]

The federal government granted another amnesty to militants in the Niger Delta, subject to each militant signing a "renunciation of militancy" form within sixty days of August 6, 2009, when the amnesty was to take effect. The government also announced the creation of twenty-seven rehabilitation and reintegration centers across the region, and a budget of 50 billion naira for the implementation of the amnesty package, including the rehabilitation and reintegration of militants (government officials later claimed that the amount actually earmarked for the program was just over 10 billion naira, not 50 billion).[38] Under the program, militants were to receive a monthly income of 20,000 naira, in addition to a daily allowance of 1,500 naira for meals, as a form of reintegration assistance, but there were no payments for arms returned by militants. Approximately 10,000 militants spread across sixty camps in the region were expected to benefit.

The attorney general and the minister of justice considered the government's initiative "the boldest step taken in the history of Nigeria towards tackling the Niger Delta question," but the amnesty package did not find universal acceptance among Nigerians, Niger Deltans, or even militants. Nobel literature laureate Wole Soyinka described the gesture as a "cynical use of rhetoric to douse an epic conflagration."[39] Soyinka and others believed that the amnesty package would fail because the government had not committed itself to addressing the causes of unrest in the Delta, such as inadequate compensation for environmental damages, failure to develop the region, denial of the right to oil control, and government repression. Some viewed the requirement for militants to fill out renunciation forms as laughable, and others believed that the amnesty package was a scheme to round up militants in the region.[40]

Most militants were not positively disposed toward the amnesty plan, especially at the initial stages. For example, Asari-Dokubo believed that it was the Nigerian government that needed amnesty, and he attempted to bring the government to court for criminalizing him by including his name on the list of persons to be granted amnesty.[41] MEND spokesperson Jomo Gbomo consistently reminded the government that his group did not ask for amnesty, because its members were not criminals. He described MEND as "a movement challenging the current status of the nation," whose members do not need amnesty but an armistice, meaning an "enabling environment that allows a cessation of hostility by all parties and facilitate[s] meaningful dialogue on the Niger Delta debacle."[42]

Other militants had earlier expressed doubt over the sincerity of government, citing the cases of Soboma Jackree, Asari-Dokubo, and Henry Okah, who were arrested by the government while they were in the process of negotiating peace or after the granting of amnesty. In exchange for their participation in the amnesty deal, the militants requested that the government guarantee their safety, expunge their names from all criminal records in order to facilitate their rehabilitation to normal life, and shield them against prosecution by future governments.[43]

Although the government tried to persuade militants to embrace its "magnanimity" in offering amnesty to all militants, it also employed subtle threats. For example, senior security officials warned unrepentant militants to be prepared for "anything" after the government's sixty-day ultimatum.[44] Nevertheless, militants continued to destroy oil facilities. On July 9, 2009, the government decided to release Henry Okah, the alleged leader of MEND, who had been incarcerated since 2008 and whose release had been one of the conditions demanded by MEND. On July 14, MEND unilaterally declared a sixty-day cease-fire two days after attacking the Atlas Cove Jetty, an oil facility in Lagos state, killing five workers in the process.[45] On August 3, 2009, militants articulated their conditions for implementing disarmament, demobilization, and reintegration. They demanded 300,000 naira for each AK-47 and two magazines of ammunition surrendered.[46] They also requested that the government construct a three-bedroom apartment "of relatively good comfort" for each of their members in places of their own choice within the Niger Delta, the cost of which would be paid back by each of the beneficiaries over a ten-year period.[47] They promised to hand over seven oil wells within the first week of the federal government's agreeing to these terms, and to end all hostilities.[48] The federal government did not make any official response to these demands.

On August 6, 2009, when the amnesty took effect, there were reports that some purported militants embraced the government's package and handed in their arms. "Boyloaf," one of the MEND commanders in charge of the Bayelsa axis, met with President Yar'Adua in the Federal Capital Territory in Abuja, and accepted amnesty.[49] At the same time, the Nigerian police raided Asari-Dokubo's arms depot, carting away arms and ammunition.[50] The sixty-day period for militants to accept the government's amnesty ended on a note of seeming victory when, a few hours before the expiration of the deadline, in a televised, carnival-like program, Government Ekpemupolo, also known as Tompolo, who had been declared wanted by the government "dead or alive" after the destruction of Camp 5 in Delta state in May 2009, embraced the government's amnesty.[51]

The amnesty board was disbanded on October 18, 2009, but post-amnesty efforts to secure peace continued, as there was an alleged meeting between President Yar'Adua and a MEND negotiating team that included Wole Soyinka and a former chief of general staff from the Niger Delta. A post-amnesty committee was also established.

In July 2010 the federal government began the rehabilitation and reintegration aspect of the peacebuilding program. This involved exposing ex-militants to nonviolence transformational training and counseling in a camp setting in Obubra, Cross River State. The training was facilitated by the Foundation for Ethnic Harmony in Nigeria (FEHN) and involved American instructors from Emory University in Atlanta, Georgia.[52] This was to be followed up with skills-acquisition training and formal education. In 2010, the Ministry of the Niger Delta began construction of nine skill acquisition centers across the country, which were to complement existing facilities such as the Petroleum Training Institute and Scotchville in Warri, Delta State, Pendaxia in Lagos State, Peugeot Automobile in Kaduna, and the National Institute for

Freshwater Fisheries Research in New Bussa, Niger State.[53] The government also revealed plans to sponsor at least 13,000 ex-militants to various tertiary institutions both in Nigeria and abroad using the platform provided by the Ministry of the Niger Delta.[54]

The actual deployment of ex-militants to training centers began in August 2010. In March 2011, the Presidential Amnesty Office sent twenty former militants, including one female, to South Africa for aviation training as pilots.[55] One of the ex-militants who embraced the amnesty program and underwent nonviolent education and skills acquisition, Abraham Ingobere, was elected into the Bayelsa State House of Assembly in the 2011 election. According to Ingobere, this demonstrates that ex-militants can have a part in the political administration of the country.[56] In June 2011, thirty-six Niger Delta youths were sponsored to Israel for training in agriculture.[57]

The apparent commitment of the federal government to the post-amnesty and peacebuilding program has not gone unnoticed. There are reports, for example, that the United Nations may adopt the Nigerian DDR/peacebuilding model in other conflict areas, if it proves to be successful.[58] Other militants who had earlier expressed doubts as to the sincerity of government and workability of the program have since been encouraged to turn in their arms. In June 2010, about one hundred ex-militants stormed Abuja in fourteen buses, demanding to be included in the Federal Government Amnesty Programme.[59]

Throughout the process, the government continued to issue warnings saying it would not condone "any act of sabotage whether from the ex-militants and beneficiaries of the post-amnesty scheme or stakeholders under whatever guise" and that it has a robust plan to move the Nigerian youths to "greater heights."[60] In October 2010, the government instigated the arrest of Henry Okah in South Africa and instituted charges of treason against him for bomb explosions around the "Eagle Square" in Abuja for which MEND claimed responsibility. In a solidarity visit to Abuja to commiserate with the president and the nation over the incident, a group of ex-militant leaders (including many former commanders of MEND) attempted to impress upon the nation that the militant phase of the Niger Delta struggle was over and that MEND as a movement died with their embrace of the federal government amnesty.[61] In response to a federal government directive, the Joint Task Force (JTF) in the Niger Delta launched a major offensive on the hideouts of regrouped militants in Bayelsa, Delta, and Rivers State in

November 2010 during which it captured fourteen militants and recovered various arms and ammunitions. It also attempted to capture John Togo, leader of the Niger Delta Liberation Force, a newly formed militant group.[62] These efforts led to the destruction of over forty houses in Ayakoromo and other communities in Burutu Local Government Area of Delta State, the killing of over sixty civilians and displacement of over a thousand persons in December 2010.[63] In May 2011, there were reports that John Togo and his Niger Delta Liberation Force (NDLF) had declared an end to militancy, which according to the spokesman of the group, was born out of a desire to avert further killing of civilians in rural communities in the Niger Delta. However, many believed the group was only seeking a way out. There are also unconfirmed reports that John Togo had been severely injured in a military assault by the JTF and had died of the wounds.[64]

Notwithstanding these developments, the DDR and peacebuilding program have not been without flaws. For example, in an interview with Al-Jazeera, Henry Okah said that the peace process could unravel because of the government's focus on buying off important militants rather than addressing the fundamental issues behind the crisis.[65] These claims are corroborated by accusations by some ex-militants that the government is applying double standards in dealing with those who have embraced amnesty, and is focusing only on the "big boys." MEND had earlier accused the federal government of "enticing every militant camp with one billion naira to support the amnesty plan."[66] John Togo attributed his renewed offensive to "the refusal of the federal government to dialogue with the real freedom fighters" and the practice of "lobbying some handful of disgruntled elements with money and oil contracts."[67] In Edo state there were protests by ex-militants complaining of neglect. There have also been cases of armed robbery involving alleged ex-militants.[68] MEND considers the five-day to two-week training in nonviolence as laughable and has asked rhetorically why the American prison system is "over-burdened with about 2.3 million inmates" if it is that easy to transform people by a two-week training.[69] A threat by the group to bomb the Eagle square in Abuja, the proposed venue for the 2011 independence anniversary celebration, made the government cancel the entire arrangement. In February 2012, the group attacked and destroyed the trunk line of the Nigerian Agip Oil Company (NAOC) in coastal Brass, Bayelsa State, and threatened to cut off the country's oil production and to attack South African companies operating in the country over what it described as the "interference" of its president, Jacob Zuma, in "the legitimate fight for justice in the Niger Delta." It also accused President Goodluck Jonathan of "squander[ing] public funds on tribalistic sycophants and thugs calling themselves ex-militants," rather than addressing the "serious issues facing the nation and its citizens."[70] The system of paying ex-militants their allowances through their former commanders also created problems. There were complaints that some ex-commanders failed to remit payments to ex-militants over long periods. Such accusations may have contributed to the assassination of some former commanders, such as Sagboma George in August 2010 and Ebi Albert in June 2011.[71]

The DDR program has also proved to be expensive. Ex-militants are paid 65,000 naira monthly as part of the reintegration program.[72] This is similar to the income they are reported to have earned as militants.[73] By comparison, the current minimum wage in Nigeria was raised in July 2011 to 18,000, up from 7,500 naira. Given the country's high youth unemployment, it is not surprising that the DDR program became a honey pot. By January 2011, the government became concerned about a "bloated figure" of ex-militants by the Presidential Amnesty Committee headed by the ex-minister of the interior, General Godwin Abbe.[74] By October 2009, the deadline for militants to turn in their arms, the committee had registered and documented up to 20,192 "repentant Niger Delta Militants," more than double the initial estimate. By May 2010, there were an additional 2,971 ex-militants from more than eleven different "militant groups" seeking inclusion and documentation in the post-amnesty program.[75] The government has had to buy the support and loyalty of key militant leaders with huge amounts of money, oil-related contracts, and other benefits.[76] These developments show that a DDR program involves heavy financial costs.

Between Justice and Peace

The Niger Delta crisis offers insights into the much-debated issue of a possible trade-off between justice and peace in postconflict peacebuilding. There have been calls at various times and by various persons and organizations for the government to take "strong" action against the perpetrators of violence in the region. For instance, Human Rights Watch (HRW) expressed concern that the granting of amnesty to individuals responsible for serious human rights abuses will contribute to the culture of impunity and jeopardize the prospects for peace in the region.[77]

There have been similar condemnations by international agencies investigating the May–June 2009 onslaught against Ijaw communities. For example, the Conference of Ethnic Nationalities of the Niger Delta threatened to drag the federal government into the court of the Economic Community of West African States (ECOWAS) over the onslaught, while the Federation of Ijaw Women (FIW) petitioned the UN Human Rights Commission against the blockage of waterways across the Niger Delta in the Ijaw areas of Delta state during and after the attacks, describing it as a "wicked attempt to eliminate the Ijaw race through starvation and sickness."[78] The allegations are corroborated by Amnesty International, which accused the federal government of displacing innocent people and denying them health care.[79]

MEND also called on the United Nations to investigate alleged extrajudicial killings and rape by troops of the Joint Task Force during the military confrontation. It also called on the International Court of Justice (ICJ) to try former president Obasanjo for alleged crimes against humanity and ethnic cleansing against the Ijaw people.[80] The Nigerian government has so far ignored the allegations and threats of legal action.

The federal government's dilemma over what to do with the documents discovered in Camp 5, one of the camps operated by MEND, in May 2009, aptly demonstrates the complexity of pursuing both justice and peace in the Niger Delta. The documents were said to contain a list of "militants' sponsors," minutes of meetings held between militants and politicians, details of attacks on oil facilities and who was responsible, including insiders within the oil companies, details of bunkering money paid to prominent people, names and addresses of foreign contacts, documents of arms purchases and names of Nigerian middlemen, and a plan by militants to acquire "sophisticated military hardware, including armored cars and jets" as well as "gun-ships, bombs, and rocket-launchers from an East European company."[81] The discovery of the documents confirmed what many believe to be the intricate relationship between political violence and oil theft, and caused a stir in government circles.[82] Although some people, including some serving senators, asked for the publication of the documents and the trial of those implicated, the federal government felt that this could create a security backlash and complicate the ongoing peace efforts.[83] Some officials also expressed concerns that public knowledge of the revelations could distract the government from the key issues at hand.

What Peace?

The cost of the crisis in the Niger Delta is astonishing. Between 2006 and 2008 alone, the country is said to have lost US$61.6 billion due to attacks on its oil installations as well as oil theft, and another US$3 billion lost to oil bunkering within the first seven months of 2008.[84] Violence between militants and government troops also cut down the nation's oil production.[85] In addition, at least one thousand people are reported to have been killed in conflicts involving militants and security forces between 2006 and 2008, with up to three hundred hostages taken.[86] There is other unaccounted human misery connected to the violence, such as rape, physical assault, loss of property, and disruption of socioeconomic activities. The death toll in the May–June 2009 violence has not yet been officially determined, but there are indications it may be well over a thousand.[87]

The conflict has sparked huge spending on security and defense by both the Nigerian government and oil companies. For example, the nation's budgetary allocation to defense in 2008 was a staggering 445 billion naira, while multinational oil companies are reported to have jointly spent about US$3.7 billion on security in 2007 alone.[88] According to the chairman of the Technical Committee on the Niger Delta, the nation has never spent so much on military hardware and security and related aspects, not even during the civil war. The director-general of the National Institute for Policy and Strategic Studies, located in Kuru, Jos, noted that the state's management of the Niger Delta struggle has largely militarized the region, turning it into "a huge garrisoned command" and making it "the most large-scale and prolonged military operation" the country has experienced.[89] Oil is still being produced at gunpoint all over the Delta.

Rather than addressing the issues underlying the Niger Delta crisis, oil companies and governments at various levels have paid militants to keep their constituents under control and to guarantee the safety of companies' operations and staffs.[90] This has predictably promoted distrust, divisions, and violent rent-seeking contests between groups. It has contributed to the criminalization of the Niger Delta crisis.[91]

The most striking element of the peacebuilding efforts in the Niger Delta is its primarily homegrown nature involving many sections of Nigerian society, including civil society groups, labor unions, women's organizations, the Nigerian Bar Association, and religious leaders.[92] Yet international actors have also had an impact on the crisis in the Niger Delta, including the ambiguous involvement of multinational oil companies operating in the region.

There is broad agreement on explanations for conflict in the Niger Delta. The national question and the division of resources have remained unresolved since 1966, when the first republic was violently brought to an end by the military. Addressing these issues would involve the creation of an equitable federal structure and the promotion of economic justice. Even the most outspoken critics of militancy and criminality in the Niger Delta region agree that there are underlying grievances that the federal government must address. There is also considerable agreement that the report of the Technical Committee on the Niger Delta (TCND) addresses some of these challenges and provides the government with practical steps that could help resolve the crisis.[93]

There is a paradox in that international private oil companies are involved and also have interests in the Niger Delta region. Many of the activists and militants in the region wanted international actors to be directly involved in peace discussions and negotiations, and petitions were sent to international and regional organizations such as the United Nations and ECOWAS. Although some Western countries are worried about the effect of the Niger Delta crisis on oil prices and have at times pressured the Nigerian government to take steps to avert a major crisis, there has been no deliberate international engagement to bring lasting peace to the Niger Delta.[94] There have been only smaller-scale efforts, such as in 2004 when the US government allegedly pressured President Obasanjo into negotiating with Asari-Dokubo and his NDPVF, and at times when US courts have entertained litigations by Nigerians against multinational oil companies operating in the Delta.

There is much at stake in the Niger Delta, for local, national, and international actors. President Goodluck Jonathan has made the resolution of the Niger Delta crisis and the problems of the power (energy) sector the focus of his administration. But the reality is that peacebuilding is not straightforward given the complexity of the conflict, the high stakes involved, and the fluid boundaries between opposing sides.

Notes

1. Rustad, "Between War and Peace."
2. Ihonvbere, "Critical Evaluation of the Failed 1990 Coup in Nigeria."
3. "Nigeria's Lost Trillions," *Newswatch* (Lagos), May 4, 2009, 12–21.
4. Oyefusi, "Trust and the Breakdown of Civil Order in Nigeria's Delta Region."

5. United Nations Development Programme (UNDP), *Niger Delta Human Development Report,* 36–37.

6. See Frynas, *Oil in Nigeria,* 87; Oyefusi, "Oil-Dependence and Civil Conflict in Nigeria."

7. International Crisis Group (ICG), *Fuelling the Niger Delta Crisis.*

8. Oyefusi, "Trust and the Breakdown of Civil Order."

9. In 2008, after an early promise to pay the debt, President Yar'Adua shockingly declared that the money had "lapsed." At the same time, he allocated a budget of about 445 billion naira for annual defense spending. *Tell,* July 14, 2008, 5.

10. *Nation* (Lagos), October 22, 2009, 1–2.

11. Oyefusi, "Oil-Dependence and Civil Conflict in Nigeria"; Oyefusi, "Trust and the Breakdown of Civil Order."

12. Oyefusi, "Trust and the Breakdown of Civil Order."

13. See, for example, Collier, Hoeffler, and Rohner, "Beyond Greed and Grievance."

14. "Yar'Adua Canvasses Regional Security Force," *Punch* (Lagos), April 11, 2008, 7; "Beyond Okah's Trial," *Tell,* July 14, 2008, 26–28; "Yar'Adua, British PM Set to Fight 'Blood Oil,'" *Nation,* July 17, 2008, 1.

15. For more on the Willinks Commission's report, see UNDP, *Niger Delta Human Development Report,* 29–30.

16. "Niger Delta: Whither Technical Report?" *Vanguard,* May 26, 2009, 47–48.

17. MEND's objective is to achieve total resource control for the Niger Delta or the control of not less than 50 percent of oil revenues from the region by its people, something similar to what it obtained at independence. Convinced that dialogue and peaceful engagement with the Nigerian government is not likely to achieve results, it seeks to draw attention to its demands by attacking oil installations and facilities across the country.

18. For case studies, see Frynas, *Oil in Nigeria,* 54–56, 170–81; HRW, *Price of Oil;* HRW, *Nigeria: Crackdown.*

19. "Sweet Crude," *Vanguard,* August 2009, 3.

20. "Way Out of Militant Attacks, by Oil Firms," *Vanguard,* June 24, 2008, 1, 5.

21. "Clark Flays Federal Government over Attacks," *Nation,* May 20, 2009, 2.

22. See ICG, *Fuelling the Niger Delta Crisis.* The phrase "oil bunkering" denotes the stealing of crude or refined petroleum products by tapping directly into oil pipelines, or extracting crude oil, which is piped into river barges that are hidden in small tributaries and then transported to ships offshore for sale in other countries. Militants in the Niger Delta neither deny nor hide their involvement in the activity, which they consider a legitimate way of taking that which belongs to them.

23. See HRW, "Rivers and Blood."

24. Ibid. See also ICG, *Fuelling the Niger Delta Crisis.*

25. "Confusion over Amnesty," *Tell,* July 28, 2007, 7–28.

26. See HRW, "Rivers and Blood."

27. See Von Gienanth et al., "Elections in Post-Conflict Countries."

28. "Yar'Adua's Hidden Agenda," *Tell,* July 14, 2008, 18–25.

29. Gambari is reported to have attempted to justify the "judicial murder" of the "Ogoni nine" by the ruling military junta on November 10, 1995, describing them as "common criminals." He is thus largely regarded as an "enemy" by many Niger Deltans.

30. See ICG, *Fuelling the Niger Delta Crisis.*

31. Ibid.

32. See Frynas, *Oil in Nigeria,* 54–56, 170–81. See also HRW, *Price of Oil;* HRW, *Nigeria: Crackdown.*

33. For more details, see HRW, *Nigeria, the Niger Delta.*

34. *Vanguard,* July 25, 2009, 39, 47; "Niger Delta Hero, Boro, Resurrects on Screen," *Guardian,* May 28, 2009, 60.

35. Adaka Boro Centre, "Boro."

36. ICG, *Fuelling the Niger Delta Crisis;* HRW, "Rivers and Blood."

37. Ibid.

38. "A Call to Disarm: Government Grants Amnesty to Militants," *Guardian,* June 26, 2009, 1–2; "Amnesty to Cost N10b," *Nation,* October 9, 2009, 1–2.

39. "Soyinka Accused Yar'Adua of Insincerity," *Punch,* July 24, 2009, 1.

40. Ibid.

41. "Season of Amnesty," *Guardian,* June 26, 2009, 51.

42. "Militants Prefer Truce, JTF Denies Killing Monarch," *Guardian,* July 6, 2009.

43. "Season of Amnesty," *Guardian,* June 26, 2009, 51; "Yar'Adua, Amnesty, and Diplomatic Deadlock," *Guardian,* July 10, 2009, 1–2.

44. "Okiro Warns: Be Prepared for Anything After 60-Day Amnesty Period," *Vanguard,* July 16, 2009, 1.

45. About a week after the attack on the Atlas Cove Jetty, the United Kingdom allegedly issued a security alert based on intelligence reports that Niger Delta militants might soon begin to hijack planes. *Punch,* July 29, 2009, 1.

46. "Amnesty: Militants Demand N3bn for Arms," *Vanguard,* August 4, 2009, 5. According to some sources, MEND expressed personal disinterest in any arms-for-cash deal, saying it would voluntarily give up arms once the government addressed the real issues behind its grievances, *Vanguard,* August 7, 2009, 1. It is not clear, however, whether this reflected the disposition of all members.

47. The latter demand might have been informed by the plan of the Ministry of Niger Delta (a ministry created in September 2008 amid controversy) to construct 360 housing units in the nine states of the Niger Delta as part of a federal government plan. "Yar'Adua Set to Receive Repentant Militants," *Nation,* June 17, 2009, 2.

48. "Amnesty: Militants Demand N3bn for Arms," *Vanguard,* August 4, 2009, 5.

49. MEND reacted by denouncing him. "MEND Denounces Boyloaf for Embracing Amnesty," *Nation,* August 7, 2009, 1.

50. "Police Raids Asari-Dokubo's Arms Depot," *Nation,* August 7, 2009, 1.

51. Government Ekpemupolo is said to be the richest, most dreaded, and perhaps most influential of the militant leaders in the Niger Delta. See "Camp 5 Invasion: The Morning After," *This Day,* June 6, 2009, 60–63; "Carnival as Tompolo Finally Gives Up Arms," *Guardian,* October 5, 2009, 1.

52. "670 Ex-militants Graduate in Second Batch Training," *Nation,* September 8, 2010. According to reports, up to 800 of the over 1,000 11th batch of ex-militants at the Obubra Non-violence and Reformation camp were women. "Excitement in camp as female ex-militants put to bed," *Nation,* January 10, 2011, 6.

53. "FG Sends 779 Ex-Militants on Two-Year Training," *Nation,* August 22, 2010.

54. "FG to Sponsor 13,000 Ex-Militants to Tertiary Institutions," *This Day,* July 14, 2010, 5.

55. "Amnesty: 20 Ex-Militants for Pilot Training in South Africa," *Nation,* March 28, 2011, 1.

56. "Hope for Ex-Militants as One Emerges Legislator," *Nation,* June 18, 2011, 3.

57. "Govt Serious about National Security, Says Jonathan," *Guardian,* June 21, 2011, 1.

58. "Post-Amnesty: FG Warns Repentant Militants, UN to Adopt Nigeria's Model," *This Day,* 6 July 6, 2010, 5.

59. "In Abuja to Protest, Militants Get a Hearing," *This Day,* July 8, 2010, 1.

60. "Post-Amnesty: FG Warns Repentant Militants," *This Day*, July 6, 2010, 6.

61. "Jonathan, Ex-Militant Leaders Meet, Denounce Abuja Bomb Blasts," *Guardian*, October 6, 2010.

62. "14 Militants' Camps Captured, John Togo Flees," *Vanguard*, November 19, 2010, 1.

63. "Scores Missing after Fresh Attack by JTF," *Nation*, December 3, 2010. John Togo and his group had earlier engaged the JTF in a six-hour gun battle and stalled an attempt by the task force to overrun his camp. The federal government later delivered relief materials to the victims and promised to resettle them. "Militants' attack: FG to Relocate Affected Ijaw Community," *Nigerian Tribune*, December 24, 2010, 6.

64. "Press Statement: Niger Delta Group, NDLF, Led by John Togo Declares 'End Of Militancy,'" *Sahara Reporters*, May 16, 2011.

65. *Nation*, October 18, 2009, 40.

66. See "Militants Hit Shell's Facility in First Blow to Amnesty," *Nation*, June 30, 2009, 1; "JTF, MEND Differ on Militant Leader's Arrest," *Guardian*, 23 November 2010.

67. "14 Militants' Camps Captured, John Togo Flees," *Vanguard*, November 19, 2010, 1.

68. "Militants Hit Shell's Facility in First Blow to Amnesty," *Nation*, June 30, 2009, 1

69. "MEND: Niger Delta Region Rebels Vow to Resume Attacks and Reject Gov't's Amnesty Initiative," *Sahara Reporters*, June 8, 2011.

70. "MEND Attacks Agip Facility, Threatens MTN, SacOil," *This Day*, February 6, 2012.

71. "Soboma: Military on the Alert in N'Delta," *Nation*, August 30, 2010; "Repentant Niger Delta Militant Leader Assassinated in Bayelsa," *Sahara Reporters*, June 11, 2011.

72. "In Abuja to Protest, Militants Get a Hearing," *This Day*, July 8, 2010.

73. Watts, "Petro-Insurgency or Criminal Syndicate?"

74. "The Untold Story of the Rage By Ex-Militants in Abuja," *Nation*, July 11, 2011.

75. Ibid.

76. It would appear that the governments of the Niger Delta states have also financially supported the DDR program. For example, the Rivers state government is reported to have recently increased annual funding for rehabilitation of repentant militants from the state to N1 billion from N500 million ("N1b for Rivers Ex-Militants' Rehab," *Nation*, September 24, 2010).

77. See HRW, "Rivers and Blood."

78. "Ethnic Nationalities Threaten Legal Action," *Nation*, May 28, 2009, 5; "Ijaw Women Protest JTF Blockade of Waterways," *Vanguard*, May 26, 2009, 6.

79. "Amnesty Accuses JTF," *Vanguard*, May 22, 2009, 5.

80. "MEND Seeks UN Probe of Niger Delta Crisis," *Nation*, June 8, 2009, 3; "MEND Wants Obasanjo Tried," *Nation*, July 10, 2008. The reference is to the destruction of two Ijaw communities, Odi and Odioma, during Obasanjo's tenure as president. MEND actually meant the International Criminal Court.

81. "Militants Shopping for Armored Cars, Jets," *Nation*, May 29, 2009, 1; "Yar'Adua Gets List of Niger Delta Militants' Backers," *Nation*, June 2, 2009, 1.

82. The report of a special security committee on oil-producing areas that was set up in 2001 noted that a "cartel or mafia," composed of "highly placed and powerful" persons, was stealing crude oil and finished produce from pipelines in the region, and that many of the militant youth groups "could be enjoying the patronage of some retired or serving military and security personnel." ICG, *Fuelling the Niger Delta Crisis*.

83. "Fed Govt in Dilemma over List of Militants' Backers," *Nation*, June 8, 2009, 1–2.

84. "Nigeria's Lost Trillions," *Newswatch*, May 4, 2009, 12–21.

85. "Nigeria Oil Revenue Cut by Half in 2009," *This Day*, July 24, 2009, 1.

86. "Nigeria's Lost Trillions," *Newswatch*, May 4, 2009, 12–21.

87. *This Day*, July 24, 2009, 1; *Vanguard*, July 29, 2009, 6.

88. *Tell*, July 14, 2008, 5; *Punch*, April 10, 2009, 2; *Newswatch*, May 4, 2009, 12–21.

89. *This Day*, June 1, 2009, 20–21.

90. For example, Shell and Chevron, the two multinational oil companies operating in the Gbaramatu territory of Delta state, and the state government are said to have been making monthly payments to "Tompolo," the erstwhile commander of Camp 5, in order to buy peace. He was also alleged to have collected protection fees from cargo ships passing through the Escravos river to Warri ports; "Camp 5 Invasion: The Morning After," *This Day*, June 6, 2009, 60–63. An obscure group, the Ika Revolutionary Movement (IRM), in July 2008 threatened to embark on a violent rampage if it was not given a share of the 100 million naira (about US$950,000) monthly allocation that it claimed was been given to other militant groups in the Niger Delta. *Nigeria/Africa Masterweb*, July 17, 2008.

91. See Oyefusi, "Oil-Dependence and Civil Conflict in Nigeria"; Oyefusi, "Trust and the Breakdown of Civil Order."

92. On the role of women in conflict resolution and peacebuilding in the Niger Delta, see Ukeje, "From Aba to Ugborodo"; Ikelegbe, "Engendering Civil Society."

93. For details on the recommendation of the TCND, see "Niger Delta: Whither Technical Report?" *Vanguard*, May 26, 2009, 47–48.

94. The UNDP claimed to have played a vital role in the latest peacebuilding exercise in the Niger Delta; *Guardian*, October 29, 2009, 8. But it is not clear, concretely, what this involved.

Disarmament, Demobilization, and Reintegration in Southern Africa

Namibia, Angola, and Mozambique

GWINYAYI A. DZINESA

UNITED NATIONS (UN) PEACEKEEPING FORCES SUPERVISED disarmament, demobilization, and reintegration (DDR) of former combatants in Namibia, Angola, and Mozambique. In all three southern African countries, DDR aimed at creating sustainable, secure, and peaceful frameworks of transition. In Namibia, the United Nations Transition Assistance Group (UNTAG) successfully executed its disarmament and demobilization mandate. In Angola, disarmament and demobilization, monitored by four UN peace missions—three incarnations of the United Nations Angola Verification Mission (UNAVEM), and the United Nations Observer Mission in Angola (MONUA)—foundered, leaving no room for reintegration. The United Nations Operation in Mozambique (UNOMOZ) departed without completing its disarmament mandate. Focusing on the interplay between local, regional, and international actors in the crafting and implementation of DDR, this chapter examines the factors that led to the different outcomes in these three countries.[1]

Namibia

Namibia demonstrates that synchrony between local, regional, and international stakeholders neutralizes the challenges to effective implementation of DDR. Following protracted colonial occupation, liberation politics, and prolonged involvement by the League of Nations and the United Nations, the New York Accords of December 22, 1988, facilitated the implementation of Namibia's independence in line with UN Security Council Resolution 435 (1978) and the establishment of UNTAG.[2] The accords, mediated by the United States, were signed by Angola, Cuba, and South Africa. In 1989–90, UNTAG—one of the first multidimensional UN peace operations—successfully supervised Namibia's transition to independence. Critically, UNTAG had a specific mandate to disarm and demobilize the country's armed groups, as part of the overall strategy to create secure conditions for Namibia's transition to independence.

The mission, with the cooperation of South Africa and the South West Africa People's Organization (SWAPO), was required to follow a clearly crafted plan for disarming and demobilizing the following: SWAPO's military wing, the People's Liberation Army of Namibia (PLAN), and indigenous forces established by colonial South Africa to fight against PLAN alongside the South African Defense Force (SADF), such as the South West Africa Territorial Force (SWATF), citizen and commando forces, and the counterinsurgency unit Koevoet ("Crowbar"), which terrorized Namibians.[3] UNTAG was also tasked with supervising the SADF's withdrawal from Namibia. As the time-specific UNTAG did not have a mandate to assist with the long-term and important reintegration of the demobilized combatants, this was left to the devices of the independence government. Therefore, Namibia's DDR was not an integrated process, as it experienced a gap between disarmament/demobilization and reintegration. There were no steps to ensure continuity through UNTAG's postwithdrawal synergy with relevant local bodies.

Despite its well-stated disarmament and demobilization schedule, UNTAG experienced an inauspicious complicated start, partly because of the bureaucratic nature of the UN's institutional framework. The implementation of Resolution 435 and effective deployment of UNTAG were delayed by the Security Council's powerful Western countries, which clamored for downscaling the mission's budget and its disarmament and demobilization military component. Although the tripartite New York Accords had been signed on December 22, 1988, the UN Security Council did not approve UNTAG's budget of US$416 million until February 1989.

The delay in UNTAG's full deployment meant the mission was not ready to monitor the movement of armed groups and their confinement to bases on April 1, 1989, when the cease-fire was to come into effect. On this day, South African forces clashed with PLAN combatants who had crossed the border from Angola into northern Namibia. UNTAG later confirmed PLAN's explanation that it had been engaged in establishing military bases inside Namibia that would be monitored by the UN mission, only to be ambushed by South African forces. However, at the time, South African forces, authorized by the Special Representative of the Secretary-General (SRSG), Martti Ahtisaari, to deploy and enforce the cease-fire, engaged in a major onslaught against the outnumbered and less well equipped SWAPO combatants, in which more than 375 PLAN combatants were killed.[4] The clash reflected the sensitive security atmosphere that had been created by mutual distrust and suspicion between the parties. An urgent joint commission meeting at Mount Etjo, involving the external parties—the United States, Russia, Cuba, and Angola—calmed the potentially explosive situation, which threatened the UNTAG mission through a possible resumption of war, and secured the parties' recommitment to the peace process.[5] The ultimate consensus among local, regional, and international actors for promoting Namibia's independence process at the end of the Cold War was important.

In addition to resolving the cease-fire violations, external actors—including the Contact Group,[6] which comprised the United States, the United Kingdom, West Germany, Canada, and France—supported the Namibian peace process. UNTAG was well funded. The Frontline States—Angola, Mozambique, Tanzania, and Zambia—also gave constructive and important support to the independence plan, particularly to the mediation and confidence-building activity between the South Africans and SWAPO in the aftermath of the clash between their forces.

UNTAG's operational and logistic capacity was expeditiously boosted to enable it to establish a firm nationwide strategic presence and authority over and above South Africa and SWAPO to credibly carry out its clear disarmament and demobilization mandate. The parties' crucial commitment to Namibia's independence process and amenability to UNTAG pressure facilitated significant disarmament and demobilization. This mitigated widespread skepticism about whether the in-country and global affairs were indeed effectively transformational.

UNTAG had a strong institutional framework. Its military component reached a maximum strength of 4,493, consisting of 300 military monitors and observers, three infantry battalions, and logistics units. This made it credible and increased the chances of its success. The peace operation deployed one military observer for every six fighters, enabling effective monitoring of disarmament and demobilization.[7] UNTAG subsequently demobilized SWATF and the citizen commando forces. The arms, military equipment, and ammunition collected from these units were deposited in "double-locked" drill halls guarded by UNTAG infantry.[8]

The UN, determined to ensure effective disarmament, exerted pressure on the South African administrators, which led to the demobilization of 1,600 ex-Koevoet members that South Africa had tactically "infiltrated" into the South West African Police (SWAPOL),[9] under UNTAG supervision by October 30, 1989. Their arms were retrieved and sent to Windhoek.[10] This effectively brought the menacing unit under UNTAG's control and eased the transition process. The remaining 1,500-strong "Merlyn Force" was withdrawn after certification of the independence elections on November 21, 1989, completing the withdrawal of the SADF and its concomitant military equipment. Most of the heavy weapons that were collected during the disarmament process were transported to South Africa by the SADF under UNTAG observation.[11] In essence, UNTAG engaged in limited weapons collection and disposal programs in Namibia.

The disarmament of PLAN was implemented in Angola. PLAN troops who were in Namibia after April 1, 1989, were assembled at designated camps before being escorted under UNTAG supervision to assembly points north of the 16th parallel in Angola. Despite a slow start, more than 5,000 combatants were ultimately confined to bases in Angola[12] where their disarmament and demobilization was supervised by a small team of thirty-one military monitors known as UNTAG A (Angola).[13] Difficulties such as the absence of accurate information on PLAN's force posture did not derail the process, and by the end of November 1989 many PLAN combatants had been disarmed and demobilized, and the assembly camps had been closed.

The success of the disarmament and demobilization was undermined by the Namibian independence government's failure to proactively plan and implement comprehensive reintegration programs. Since Namibia had no army at independence, one of the priorities of the new government was the establishment of an integrated Namibian Defense Force (NDF). Against a backdrop of mistrust and suspicion, establishment of the NDF was informed by the political imperatives of using the new military as a vehicle in the nation-building project while ensuring stability and consolidation of state power.[14] Together, the NDF and the transformed Namibian police absorbed between 8,000 and 10,000 combatants, offering them and their dependents some stability.[15] However, this accounted for only a fraction of the more than 50,000 total demobilized. Preoccupied with the swift formation of the NDF, Namibia's government embarked on stopgap reintegration measures for the additional former combatants. This created a time bomb that would explode, close to a decade after the war had ended, in nationwide protests by ex-combatants disaffected by their poor socioeconomic status.

In terms of reintegration, ex-SWATF members were better placed than their ex-PLAN counterparts, as they continued to receive salaries from South Africa after their discharge, until Namibia's independence. This was designed to facilitate their reintegration into civilian life, and to retain their loyalty to the SADF in case Namibia's transition to independence collapsed.[16] In 1991–92, South Africa implemented a compensation scheme consisting of "a once-off payment of 12,000 Namibian dollars (US$2,600) to former *Koevoet* and SWATF forces as a gratuity to tide them over until they found employment."[17] Their prior achievement of the standard education criteria required for entry into SWATF also gave them good standing for civilian employment and reintegration.

The same cannot be said of former PLAN combatants, whose employment prospects were restricted by their lack of formal qualifications. The majority, unable to be absorbed into limited public sector employment, remained part of the mainstream unemployed population years into independence. This was at a time when the transition to independence was accompanied by a neocolonial economic structure and a small private sector that was not immediately restructured to facilitate economic growth and job creation. The country recorded a small growth of real gross domestic product (GDP), of 0.2 percent, in 1990, which was 23 percent lower than in 1980.[18] Low mineral prices, overexploitation of fishing resources, prolonged drought, and financial mismanagement were some of the factors behind the depressed economic performance. The government also did not develop the potential of the informal sector to meet the reintegration goals of creating jobs and alleviating poverty among unattached former combatants.

Former PLAN combatants were each paid a small, onetime gratuity of 1,400 rand in 1991. This followed demonstrations by former combatants in Windhoek who demanded compensation for their liberation war efforts. The plan was that this gratuity would be complemented by the succeeding two-year (1991–92) Development Brigade (later Development Brigade Corporation) training program, which was designed to impart practical agricultural and construction skills for sustainable postgraduation income-generation to the unemployed ex-combatants. However, this did not quite work out as planned.

The Development Brigade was strategically placed under the Ministry of Lands, Resettlement, and Rehabilitation, as land reform was to be central to its success. However, Namibia's slow and cumbersome land resettlement program resulted in the perpetuation of skewed landownership patterns. Access to land was problematic, in particular for former combatants who were not treated as a specific preferential target group under the snail-paced national land reform program. Other institutional and operational problems, including a lack of funding, a lack of technical expertise and qualified personnel, as well as inappropriate training, resulted in the Development Brigade program failing to acquire self-sufficiency and being unable to wean the trainees into productive employment or viable projects. Bilateral donors such as the Swedish International Development Cooperation Agency (SIDA) and later the European Community withdrew sponsorship on the basis of negative evaluation reports on the performance and viability of the Development Brigade. The dependency syndrome among brigade members, who believed that the government had to indefinitely guarantee their welfare and employment, aggravated the situation. The Development Brigade project also confined former combatants together and reinforced their separateness, thereby undermining their reintegration into society.

Namibia's initiatives failed to facilitate the reintegration and guarantee the postwar human security of former combatants. This presented a potential threat to national stability and security, as demonstrated by the public disruption and rioting by unsuccessfully reintegrated and neglected former combatants in the mid-1990s. In order to avert full-scale instability, the government reactively institutionalized the "Peace Project," aimed at affirmative job placements, mainly in the public service, for about 11,950 unemployed and registered former combatants. A larger civil service was the price that the Namibian government had to pay for the earlier botched reintegration. Instead of mollifying the disgruntled and riotous former combatants in the short term with monetary payoffs, the Peace Project enhanced prospects for the long-term reintegration of its beneficiaries, and for some time did manage to prevent new security threats posed by former combatants. In a significant step, Namibian president Hifikepunye Pohamba, within a year of taking office, established a stand-alone Ministry of War Veteran Affairs in October 2006 to take care of war veteran matters.[19]

In addition to the absence of a generalized comprehensive reintegration strategy, Namibia illustrates the potential harm of failing to address the concerns of particular groups, such as women, the disabled, and psychologically distressed former combatants. Although about 10 percent of the former combatants suffered from physical and psychological disabilities, governmental rehabilitation programs were limited. The Evangelical Lutheran Church in Namibia (ELCIN) ran a rehabilitation center at Nakaye in Ovamboland for the wartime injured and mentally stressed PLAN veterans who required specialized treatment and training. It was the only such rehabilitation center. Operating on a shoestring budget, the rehabilitation center could accommodate only 180 former combatants under "unacceptable" living conditions with inappropriate training programs.[20] Not surprisingly, within a year, in July 1990, the number of interns had plummeted to 71. However, these individuals could not secure employment, and the rehabilitation center could not profitably use their skills.

The government later took charge of most rehabilitation activities, including the ELCIN center, which opened its doors to the broader disabled population. Significantly, the Namibian government made a policy shift—from institutional rehabilitation of people with disabilities, to "community-based rehabilitation" involving provision of assistance to the disabled as part of the mainstream society into which they were supposed to reintegrate.[21] This aimed at facilitating grassroots-oriented rehabilitation and raising the awareness of the community about the struggles involved in dealing with disability. The community-based approach, however, did not single out disabled former combatants as a special target group, making it difficult to evaluate the impact of this approach on their rehabilitation.

Further targeted assistance for disabled former combatants was put in place in 1998. This came in response to pronounced protests by ex-fighters for jobs and welfare assistance. In June 1998 the government cobbled together a temporary program for unemployed veterans with severe disabilities that entitled them to receive a monthly allowance of 350 Namibian dollars for twelve months. A monthly allowance of 500 Namibian dollars per disabled ex-combatant was subsequently formally administered by the Ministry of Health and Social Services. Similar allowances were also granted to older former combatants who could not be absorbed under the government's ex-fighter employment programs. The former combatants, however, claimed that the allowance was not substantial enough to cater for their basic needs.

There were also no specific reintegration programs for female ex-combatants who faced the challenge of readjusting to traditional and feminized civilian life. The patriarchal society of postconflict Namibia was disinclined to accommodate difference or promote equality in the treatment of female former fighters, politically or socioeconomically. Female former fighters had to swiftly lose their military identity, slip into "gender-appropriate civilian attire, and were sent to refugee rather than demobilisation camps, where they received no benefits, retraining or psychological counselling to assist them in their reintegration."[22] The reintegration process essentially relegated most female former freedom fighters to official oblivion against the backdrop of a conservative society.[23] Ex-PLAN single mothers faced greater difficulties in sustaining themselves and their children in the absence of dedicated support initiatives.[24] It is thus not surprising that female former combatants were active participants in postindependence protests calling for government assistance. For instance, a list compiled by the jobless former combatants who demonstrated at Okahao in 1998 indicated that there were 115 women, 65 men, and 7 children gathered at the northern town.[25] Although the "Peace Project" absorbed female ex-fighters, some complained of being allocated arduous jobs such as road work. Despite these difficulties in the reintegration of ex-combatants, local, regional, and international actors had collaborated to ensure that disarmament and demobilization was reasonably successful.

Angola

Angola illustrates how local, regional, and international actors can collude to undermine the potential for DDR to contribute to durable peace. Failed attempts at DDR twice contributed to the resumption of armed conflict between the military factions of the Movement for the Liberation of Angola (MPLA) and National Union for the Total Liberation of Angola (UNITA). DDR was first undertaken between 1991 and 1992 as part of the larger peacekeeping initiative monitored by the UN's second verification mission in the country. UNAVEM II was established in accordance with the bilateral Bicesse Agreement of May 31, 1991, between the MPLA and UNITA, with a mandate to end

Angola's sixteen-year civil war. The comprehensive agreement was an outcome of Portuguese mediation observed by the United States and Soviet Union. It provided for, among other things, a cease-fire, cantonment, disarmament, and demobilization of about 200,000 soldiers from the opposing forces, alongside the formation of new unified armed force of 50,000 and a neutral police force, within an inflexible time frame.[26] Joint political and military commissions—made up of MPLA and UNITA members and observers from Portugal, the United States, and the Soviet Union[27]—were established to ensure the parties' compliance with the Bicesse Agreement.

The UNAVEM II–supervised disarmament and demobilization process was undermined by questionable confidence in, and political commitment to, the process—particularly on the part of UNITA—as well as by the mission's poorly designed mandate and the international community's failure to allocate it a substantial budget. UNAVEM II, with an inadequate mandate to verify implementation of the Bicesse Agreement by the MPLA and UNITA, was essentially an adjunct to the Angolan disarmament and demobilization process.[28] The UN deliberately aimed at establishing a resource-stringent "small and manageable" mission and accepted a minimal and passive monitoring role.[29] Using the analogy of a sporting contest to describe the excessive power of the MPLA and UNITA in the arrangement, former UNAVEM II chief military observer Major-General Michael Nyambuya noted that "the parties were the players and referees themselves."[30] This made the disarmament and demobilization process susceptible to manipulation by either party in the absence of effective external supervision.

UNAVEM II, and by extension its supervision of the disarmament and demobilization process, was inadequately funded and poorly equipped. Notwithstanding that UNAVEM II was established two years later than UNTAG, and for deployment in a more complicated context, it was allocated US$132.2 million compared with UNTAG's US$416 million. This shortage of funds was aggravated by the considerable insecurity and mistrust between the long-term warring parties. Both the MPLA and UNITA bypassed the disarmament process and maintained contingency fighting capabilities.[31] UNAVEM II military observers lacked verification equipment like sensor mechanisms to authenticate the parties' caching of arms.[32]

The lack of an appropriate security infrastructure meant that the storage and control of weapons that had been collected from the armies was ineffective. The recommended "double key" system, whereby one key to a depository building remains in the custody of local hands and the other in UN hands, was not feasible in Angola, as tents and grass huts used as safe houses could not be padlocked.[33] UNAVEM II, with only 350 military observers, was understaffed, and cases abounded of five-person UNAVEM teams monitoring about 30,000 troops each.[34] That UNTAG deployed one military observer for every six soldiers is an illuminating contrast. Typical financial limitations and hardships were a powerful disincentive for combatants to disarm and demobilize, and many deserted the poorly secured cantonment areas. These inadequacies combined to foster the disappearance of arms. In the run-up to the 1992 election, only 65 percent of MPLA and 26 percent of UNITA troops had been demobilized, while only 8,000 had been integrated into the Angolan Armed Forces.[35] The MPLA also reputedly and clandestinely mobilized a crack paramilitary unit of demobilized soldiers, whose strength ranged from 1,500 to 10,000 "ninjas."

The loopholes in the disarmament and demobilization process allowed the opposing armies to retain or return to combat readiness and easily resume fighting in the aftermath of UNITA's rejection of the election outcome.[36] Even without a limited mandate, it is hard to conceive that UNAVEM II could have put DDR back on track when UNITA was not committed to the peace process and desired to fight on. The result was the destructive war of October 1992 to late 1994, which caused at least 300,000 human deaths (3 percent of the population), as conservatively estimated by Human Rights Watch.[37]

Similar obstacles to UNAVEM II's DDR were replayed under the subsequent UNAVEM III–led peace process. The latter multidimensional mission, established on the basis of the comprehensive Lusaka Protocol of November 20, 1994, was given responsibility for the "overall supervision, control and verification" of the cease-fire, as well as for the disarmament and demobilization process.[38] UNAVEM III's comprehensive and clear mandate was not underpinned by a commensurate budget, personnel, or logistics, with predictable results. Former UNAVEM III chief military observer Philip Sibanda noted that the Security Council authorized a military component of half the requested 15,000 troops, a situation that was compounded by the provision of a few fixed-wing and rotary aircraft, in a country with transport infrastructure devastated by prolonged war.[39] UNITA largely continued its trend of circumventing DDR. It maintained its elite fighting force while about 12,000 of its almost 68,000 personnel who had registered for DDR systematically deserted, leaving only about 55,000 in the camps, including 7,000 underaged soldiers.[40] In addition, then–UN Secretary-General Boutros Boutros-Ghali reported that the military equipment surrendered by UNITA had mainly been of mediocre quality.[41]

In Angola, in contrast to the facilitative regional consensus for UNTAG's success, certain governments and nationals of neighboring states abetted UNITA's sanction-busting activities through lucrative "diamonds for military-aid" arrangements.[42] This ensured UNITA firepower, thus undermining DDR and prolonging the conflict. In return for diamonds and cash, Zaire's president, Mobutu Sese Seko, allowed UNITA to use his country (now the Democratic Republic of the Congo [DRC]) as a base for stockpiling weapons, in addition to providing the movement with Zairian end-user certificates, thereby facilitating UNITA's procurement of weapons.[43] Burkina Faso allowed its territory to be used as a transit point for military hardware procured by UNITA from Eastern Europe. Congo-Brazzaville was a major "sanctions-busting hub" for UNITA between May and September 1997, and in one incident facilitated the purchase by UNITA of 10,000 military uniforms. Individual South African nationals also aided UNITA's military equipment procurement from other countries outside South Africa. Togolese president Gnassingbé Eyadema reportedly became UNITA's chief provider following Mobutu's ouster in 1997, with Togo and UNITA allegedly cultivating a lucrative arrangement under which Togo retained a share of the military equipment that was imported for UNITA. The collusion of these regional states and individual gunrunners in sanctions-busting galvanized UNITA's military capacity and spoiled Angola's chances for stable peace.

The UN's smaller observation mission in Angola, MONUA, whose military component comprised 2,650 personnel, replaced UNAVEM III on June 30, 1997. UNITA exploited MONUA's ineffective surveillance, coupled with an abortive sanctions regime, and invested returns from illicit diamond trading into a substantial remilitarization program.[44] Regional and international countries were complicit in UNITA's sanctions-busting and arms-purchasing. It continued its illegal trade in "blood diamonds" with Europe through the DRC, Congo-Brazzaville, and other conduits such as South Africa, Namibia, Rwanda, and Zambia, earning about US$420 million annually, which it could invest in arms.[45] Diamond revenue was invested in the purchase of weapons from a range of suppliers, including Albania and Bulgaria, with UNITA using most of the above-mentioned countries as transit zones. The Angolan government, for its part, used revenues from oil, mining concessions, and bank loans to obtain military equipment. MONUA's failure to complete Angola's on-and-off DDR ended in remobilization and forced conscription by both sides, followed by the return to war.[46] This effectively dealt the Lusaka peace process a death blow and was the epitaph of the series of failed UN-led DDR attempts. Following the MPLA forces' military defeat of UNITA in 2002, the government lent primacy to a largely domestically managed DDR of the vanquished.

Mozambique

The General Peace Agreement (GPA) for Mozambique of October 4, 1992, signed in Rome between the ruling Liberation Front of Mozambique (Frelimo) and the opposing Mozambican National Resistance (Renamo), ended Mozambique's seventeen-year civil war. The GPA was the culmination of mediation by a host of regional and international actors: the Catholic Church of Mozambique, Sant' Egidio Community (a Catholic lay organization associated with the Vatican), African states including Botswana, Malawi, South Africa, Kenya, and Zimbabwe, as well as Western countries, namely Italy, the United States, the United Kingdom, and Portugal. The Italian government supported the negotiations logistically. Rome also contributed about US$35 million, between 1990 and 1994, to help fund Renamo's continuing commitment to the peace process and its transformation into a political party.[47]

The mediation process had been aided by "the radically changed peaceful conditions in Southern Africa, especially in neighboring South Africa, a country that had previously stoked the wars in the region and in Mozambique."[48] This came at the end of the Cold War and apartheid in South Africa. On the basis of the GPA, the UN Security Council, through Resolution 797 (December 16, 1992), established a mission in Mozambique, UNOMOZ, whose military tasks included monitoring and verification of the cease-fire, DDR of the parties, withdrawal of foreign forces (Malawian and Zimbabwean contingents) from Mozambican territory, and disbanding of private and irregular armed groups. The mission was ten times larger than UNAVEM II, as the Security Council authorized 7,000 peacekeepers and allocated a budget of US$500 million.[49] A cease-fire commission, chaired by UNOMOZ and also comprising representatives from the Frelimo government, Renamo,

Portugal, Italy, France, the United Kingdom, and the United States, was responsible for disarmament and demobilization in approved troop-assembly areas.[50]

The last foreign forces departed from Mozambique on June 9, 1993, almost seven months past the agreed-upon deadline, but disarmament was complicated by the lack of reliable data on the number of troops and weapons on both sides. Estimates of the number of weapons imported into the country during the civil war range from 500,000 to 6 million.[51] The Frelimo government also allegedly distributed 1 million AK-47 rifles to civilian defense units in the 1980s.[52] By December 1995, only a modest number of the total weapons had been collected by the UNOMOZ-chaired cease-fire commission.[53] Most of the surrendered arms were of poor quality, as both sides retained their high-quality weapons. To aggravate matters, UNOMOZ initially gave in to politically motivated demands by the government to abandon the original plan of sending weapons collected from assembly areas to regional depots pending their destruction.[54] Fragile security in the assembly points later resulted in the parties agreeing to transfer weapons to the UNOMOZ-guarded depots. Although there are no accurate statistics, a large proportion of the 190,000 weapons collected and not destroyed during the UN operation recirculated locally and regionally.[55] This inflated the estimated millions of uncontrolled firearms that were not collected by UNOMOZ, with serious implications for national and regional security. Furthermore, from being initially identified as a prerequisite to holding elections, the "disarmament train . . . was allowed to derail" as elections took precedence.[56] UNOMOZ departed soon after the October 1994 elections, without completing the verification of disarmament carried out at assembly points. The parties had also made it impossible for the mission to carry out its disarmament mandate outside the assembly areas.

Recognizing the security threats posed by the proliferation of illicit arms after the departure of UNOMOZ, Mozambique's security forces, at times in partnership with neighboring governments, conducted weapons control exercises.[57] The governments of Mozambique and South Africa—erstwhile enemies for over a decade—significantly demonstrated the political and operational will to cooperate in dealing with the security threat posed by redundant weapons. In a series of significant joint seek-and-destroy missions code-named Operations Rachel, between 1995 and 2001, South African and Mozambican police forces used various incentives and other methods—including cash rewards and modest buyback programs—to persuade local communities to pinpoint known arms caches throughout Mozambique.[58] Other supplies, even sweets, were also used to reward the increased number of women and especially children informers. The confidence nurtured between the police forces and local communities, together with the substantial numbers of re-covered weapons, demonstrated the ineffectiveness of the UNOMOZ disarmament exercise, which had resulted only in a continued and abundant presence of illicit arms.

Mozambique's demobilization and reintegration process, which was managed by UNOMOZ during the transition to the October 1994 elec-tions, was not immune to the potential of collapse. Demobilization was delayed as the government and Renamo respectively withheld 5,000 and 2,000 troops as "insurance."[59] In the assembly areas, at one point, the extent of the mutiny by former combatants, due to poor conditions and uncertainties with the lengthy process, threatened the entire peace process.[60] The revolts included blocking main roads, with combatants demanding swift demobilization. Notwithstanding the delays, about 93,000 soldiers were eventually demobilized between 1992 and 1996.[61]

The General Peace Agreement emphasized the need for reinte-gration support for former combatants to guard against immediate post-agreement threats to peace posed by unsuccessfully reinstated fighters. However, the agreement lacked a specific implementation strategy, which resulted in a limited focus on long-term reintegration and created a gap between the latter and disarmament and demobili-zation. Whereas UNOMOZ had been tasked with disarmament and demobilization, the country office of the United Nations Develop-ment Programme (UNDP), the UN agency mandated with sustainable human development, managed the reintegration support scheme. This scheme, a two-year cash compensation program financed by donors through a US$35.5 million UN trust fund, was the major component of the subsequent reintegration strategy and succeeded in "paying and scattering" the demobilized soldiers.[62] The quick-fix cash compensa-tion scheme was not supplemented effectively by other mechanisms and did not guarantee the human security of the demobilized, who had difficulty with long-term employment-related reintegration. Mozam-bique's war-torn formal economy was unable to absorb the majority of former combatants who also had low levels of education. It is esti-mated that about half of the former combatants took up unprofitable, small-scale agriculture.[63] Mozambique's average GDP growth after the conflict was impressive: 6.7 percent from 1993 to 1997, 10 percent from 1997 to 1999, and 7.7 percent from 2003 to 2007.[64] However, this growth did not address structural economic inequalities and largely failed to benefit the informal economy.[65] As a result, the reintegration of former combatants suffered.

Two ex-combatant associations were later established to represent the interests of their members, and since then former combatants have expressed their discontent on a number of occasions.[66] Even though one of these groups, the Mozambican Demobilized Soldiers Association (AMODEG), insisted that members engage in peaceful protests, violent demonstrations were common in Zambezia and Sofala provinces. In 1996, former combatants engaged in sporadic riots against unemployment and in favor of war pensions. In 1997, a UNDP study revealed that 29 percent of demobilized combatants considered themselves not reintegrated, while 5 percent feared they would never be integrated due to war trauma.[67] By April 1999, only 5,000 of the subsequently registered 22,000 Renamo former combatants were eligible for pensions.[68] Due to ineffective DDR, some former high-ranking combatants have since been involved in criminal enterprises such as illicit arms trading, contract assassinations, money laundering, and drug trafficking. Other associated violent crimes have included raping women at gunpoint and burglary by armed thieves.[69]

In contradiction to this frequent portrayal of ex-combatants, however, the case of Mozambique also shows how some war veterans may serve as advocates against violence and as agents for change. In 1997, Frelimo and Renamo ex-soldiers joined to establish PROPAZ (For Peace), whose volunteers, working in six provinces of the country, helped local communities solve conflicts without using violence.

Targeted assistance for special groups such as women and the disabled was largely absent in Mozambique. Female ex-combatants constituted a mere 1.48 percent of the total recognized demobilization caste, and expressed sentiments of being used for political purposes and being neglected during the transition and postconflict periods.[70] The low numbers of female ex-combatants who formally demobilized can be explained by a narrow definition of "combatant" that did not formally recognize the different roles and participation of women in the war.[71] As in Namibia, against a conservative and patriarchal backdrop, female former freedom fighters in Mozambique were expected to "simply return to their fields and get cultivating" in accordance with the "proper role of women."[72] Female ex-combatants have told stories of "renegotiation of roles, responsibilities and issues surrounding access to and control of household resources. Marital relations have been under strain and some marriages have not survived. There has been an increase in domestic violence and women have been exposed to infection by STDs and perhaps HIV/AIDS, considering the risk factor involved with the use of astringents in the vagina."[73] Sally Baden quotes a researcher who "witnessed many women losing their independence within their homes, their livelihoods; some women [became] even more burdened with work as they were abandoned by their war-husbands and, even more tragically, some women became victims of violence within their own homes, long after the fighting had stopped."[74] At the same time, protests, such as roadblocks, by disabled ex-combatants housed in assembly areas manned by UNOMOZ, showed the lack of attention toward their special needs.[75]

Local institutions assisted with contextualized psychosocial support, healing, and reconciliation. In addition to policies, strategies, and programs implemented by the government and local and international nongovernmental organizations,[76] traditional healing and reconciliation practices were used to facilitate the reintegration of combatants, especially young soldiers, into their communities.[77] A study of the life outcomes of thirty-nine male former child combatants conducted between 1988 and 2004 found that "the majority of this group . . . have emerged from violent childhoods to become trusted and productive adult members of their communities and nation."[78] The children's recovery was attributed to a "combination of rehabilitation programs, community sensitization campaigns, community projects, and traditional ceremonies."[79] Community-based strategies such as ritual cleansing and appeasement or "treatment" ceremonies, through which a person's identity as a demobilized soldier dissolved,[80] were irreplaceable rites of passage. Some of these reintegration ceremonies also included a civic education component meant to assist former combatants adjust to civilian livelihoods.

Disarmament, demobilization, and reintegration is a political endeavor, yet it is critical for peacebuilding. Favorable outcomes depend as much on local and regional politics and initiatives as on international grand plans. At the local level, there can be no substitute for the parties' unquestionable political will and commitment to DDR. In Namibia, the parties were willing to implement and support the DDR process, whereas in Angola the protagonists were not. For their part, the Mozambican parties subverted the process by exploiting the loopholes occasioned by the UN operation's preoccupation with holding the country's October 1994 postwar elections regardless of progress in disarmament.

International actors and neighboring states either facilitate or impede DDR through the demonstration of constructive commitment and support or willful violation of their obligations. The international community and particularly the UN Security Council's powerful Western countries were more prepared to financially underwrite UN operations in Namibia and Mozambique with a significant positive impact on DDR, especially in the case of the former. Angola's neighboring states and international gunrunners poured arms and ammunition into UNITA's hands, helping the rebel movement effectively skirt its DDR obligations. In Mozambique's case, the postwar government and its post-apartheid South Africa counterpart engaged in collaborative post-UNOMOZ weapons collection exercises to rid Mozambique of some of its superfluous arms and ammunition.

Although DDR may be the flip side of the logically strategic establishment of the unitary and legitimate national defense forces that are crucial for postconflict peace- and statebuilding, it should not be crafted as an afterthought, because effective DDR guarantees the human security of superfluous fighters. It is essential that stakeholders constructively coordinate the resolution of tensions that may threaten the process. Any institution trying to design contextually relevant DDR programs without doing harm in postconflict situations should consider the specific needs of the demobilized combatants according to age, sex, and physical condition. Local institutions can certainly be harnessed to assist with the macro-management of DDR as the case of Mozambique shows. This is important for the long-term success of DDR, given the usually time-specific external engagement with the process.

Notes

1. For a discussion of the concept of DDR, see Omach in this volume.

2. See Dzinesa, "Comparative Perspective of UN Peacekeeping in Angola and Namibia," 648.

3. United Nations, *Blue Helmets*, 209–10.

4. See Dzinesa, *Swords into Ploughshares.*

5. See Saunders, "UN Peacekeeping in Southern Africa," 271.

6. The Contact Group attempted to implement its proposed settlement of the Namibian situation in the 1970s, with the involvement of the UN, South Africa, SWAPO,

and the Frontline States. The group's 1978 settlement plan was endorsed by the Security Council following a positive report on Namibia by a UN survey mission and laid the basis for UNTAG.

7. Dzinesa, "Comparative Perspective," 653.

8. United Nations, *Blue Helmets,* 221.

9. Dzinesa, *Swords into Ploughshares,* 5.

10. Ifejika, "Namibia," 23.

11. Howard, "UN Peace Implementation in Namibia," 116.

12. Ibid., 109.

13. Dzinesa, *Swords into Ploughshares,* 5.

14. See Dzinesa and Rupiya, "Promoting National Reconciliation and Regional Integration."

15. Dzinesa, *Swords into Ploughshares,* 5.

16. Ibid.

17. "Namibian War Veterans Protest for Jobs," *Financial Gazette* (Harare), July 10, 1997.

18. Du Pisani, *Rumours of Rain,* 12.

19. Gwinyayi Dzinesa, "Attention to the Welfare of War Veterans Can Prevent Threats to Stability," *Cape Times,* July 15, 2009.

20. Preston, "Integrating Fighters after War," 468.

21. Author interview with Frans Tsheehama, Permanent Secretary, Ministry of Lands, Rehabilitation, and Resettlement, Windhoek, November 12, 2004.

22. Farr, *Gendering Demilitarization as a Peacebuilding Tool,* 23.

23. Shikola, "We Left Our Shoes Behind," 147–48.

24. Ibid., 146.

25. "Poverty Grips Former Combatants," *Namibian,* July 23, 1998.

26. United Nations, *Peace Accords for Angola,* annex.

27. See also Omach in this volume.

28. Boulden, "Rules of Engagement, Force Structure, and Composition in UN Disarmament Operations," 147.

29. Ohlson and Stedman, *New Is Not Yet Born,* 109.

30. Author interview with Major-General Michael Nyambuya, Zimbabwe National Army (former UNAVEM II Chief Military Observer), Harare, August 29, 2002. See also Dzinesa, "Comparative Perspective," 651.

31. Dzinesa, "Comparative Perspective," 656.

32. Potgieter, "Price of War and Peace"

33. Anstee, *Orphan of the Cold War,* 49.

34. Ibid., 38.

35. Paris, *At War's End,* 66.

36. Gamba, *Small Arms in Southern Africa,* 16.

37. Human Rights Watch, *Selling Justice Short,* sec. 7.

38. MacQueen, "Peacekeeping by Attrition," 407.

39. Sibanda, "Lessons from UN Peacekeeping in Africa," 119–20.

40. *Angola Peace Monitor* 2, no. 3 (1996).

41. Dzinesa, "Postconflict Disarmament, Demobilization, and Reintegration of Former Combatants in Southern Africa," 77.

42. Dzinesa, "Comparative Perspective," 656.

43. For details on this event and others discussed in this paragraph, see United Nations, *Report of the Panel of Experts on Violations of Security Council Sanctions Against UNITA,* UN Doc. S/2000/203 March 10, 2000.

44. Dzinesa, "Postconflict Disarmament, Demobilization, and Reintegration," 77.

45. Dzinesa, "Comparative Perspective," 57.

46. Dzinesa, "Postconflict Disarmament, Demobilization, and Reintegration," 77.

47. For a detailed account of the mediation process see Hume, *Ending Mozambique's War*.

48. United Nations, Office of the Special Adviser on Africa, *Overview*.

49. See Saunders, "UN Peacekeeping in Southern Africa," 275.

50. See Jeong, *Peacebuilding in Postconflict Societies*, 44–52.

51. Gamba, *Small Arms in Southern Africa*, 42.

52. Spear, "Disarmament and Demobilization," 169.

53. See Baptista-Lundin et al., "Reducing Costs through an 'Expensive Exercise,'" 204.

54. McMullin, "Reintegration of Combatants," 632.

55. Gamba, *Small Arms in Southern Africa*, 43.

56. See Potgieter, "Price of War and Peace."

57. See Baptista-Lundin et al., "Reducing Costs through an 'Expensive Exercise,'" 205.

58. For a detailed discussion of Operations Rahel, see Hennop, *Operations Rachel 1995–2001*.

59. Spear, "Disarmament and Demobilization," 169.

60. Kingma, "Demobilisation, Reintegration, and Peace-Building," 141.

61. Willett, "Demilitarisation, Disarmament, and Development in Southern Africa," 421.

62. McMullin, "Reintegration of Combatants," 629.

63. Willett, "Demilitarisation, Disarmament, and Development," 421.

64. Kotze, "Democratisation and Development," 230.

65. Ibid., 232.

66. Kingma, "Demobilisation, Reintegration, and Peace-Building," 142.

67. Spear, "Disarmament and Demobilization," 170.

68. Kingma, "Demobilisation, Reintegration, and Peace-Building," 142.

69. Rehn and Sirleaf, *Women, War, and Peace*, 114.

70. Baden, *Post-Conflict Mozambique*.

71. Dolan and Schafer, *Reintegration of Ex-Combatants in Mozambique*, 44.

72. Ibid., 44–45.

73. Baden, *Post-Conflict Mozambique*, 76.

74. Ibid.

75. Kingma, "Demobilisation, Reintegration, and Peace-Building," 142.

76. See Máusse, "Social Reintegration of the Child Involved in Armed Conflict in Mozambique."

77. See Omach in this volume. See also Dzinesa, "Participatory Approach to DDR," 41; Boothby, Crawford, and Halperin, "Mozambique Child Soldier Life Outcome Study"; Honwana, "Children of War."

78. Patel, De Greiff, and Waldorf, eds., *Disarming the Past*, 195.

79. Ibid.

80. Dolan and Schafer, *Reintegration of Ex-Combatants*, 59.

FIFTEEN

Peacebuilding without a State

The Somali Experience

CHRISTOPHER CLAPHAM

THE SOMALI STATE HAS BEEN COMPREHENSIVELY DESTROYED. THIS is no temporary breakdown of public institutions, such as occurred in Uganda in the dying days of the Tito Okello regime before Yoweri Museveni's National Liberation Movement took power in January 1986. It is not a collapse of public order, such as that from which the former Belgian Congo had to be rescued by a United Nations (UN) intervention shortly after independence in June 1960. Somalia cannot even properly be characterized as a "failed state": there is simply no state that could be said to have failed. The nonexistence of the state goes well beyond the absence of anything that could be described as a government, since Mohamed Siad Barre fled from Mogadishu in his last operational tank in January 1991. The elements out of which a state must be constructed are equally nonexistent. The shells of the burnt-out ministry buildings of what used to constitute the Somali government contain no bureaucrats, nor is there any cadre of qualified people, waiting in the wings, who could be organized into any new machinery of government. There is no tax collection system. There is no army or police force. Such government-like functions that continue to be performed are accomplished outside any hierarchical structure of order, and are organized through local-level clan structures, through the networks of Somali Islam, or by businessmen operating outside either the constraints or the protection that the state provides. The mobile telephone system, catering to an essential need of one of the world's most garrulous peoples, works far more efficiently without a state than in almost any other part of the world where it works with one.

The condition of statelessness poses challenges at many levels. For the people who manage the international system, it poses an affront to what that system ought to be: it is taken for granted that this system is composed of states, which form the essential building blocks of global public order, and an area of inhabited territory that lacks such a structure is not just anomalous but permits the existence of "pirates" or "terrorists" who operate outside the bounds of acceptable behavior. For Somali people, though the state's absence (given some of its activities when it did exist) is not an entirely unmixed curse, the lack of public order leads to massive numbers of deaths (not only directly through conflict, but indirectly through the absence of effective distribution networks, medical facilities, and other services), imposes restrictions on movement, and prevents any form of "development" that might eventually provide the foundation for a better life.

For the purposes of this volume, the absence of a state in Somalia poses a particularly stark challenge to the idea of "peacebuilding," and to the processes through which peace might plausibly be built. Peacebuilding, as Devon Curtis makes clear in the Introduction of this volume, involves setting priorities and "establishing legitimate institutional hierarchies at the level of the state." Throughout the literature, it is broadly assumed that peacebuilding is about forming a state in which the conflicting parties have a share, and which in turn can then furnish the essential infrastructural basis for continued peace, notably in terms of order and development. Even much of the literature on Somalia, indeed, starts from the premise that the first step on the road back to peace must be to reestablish the Somali state—in a form characterized by all the desiderata of the "good governance" agenda beloved of aid agencies—because there is simply no conception of how "peace" can exist without one.[1] If, as is all too clearly the case, this premise cannot be met, then the desired outcome that the state is intended to achieve cannot be provided either.

What happens, therefore, when there *is* no state, and precious little chance of forming one? This chapter starts by examining the tangled relations between Somalis and the states that have been imposed on them, which provide the essential background to the sources of statelessness and the problems of peacebuilding through statebuilding. It then looks at some of the attempts that have been made to build peace in Somalia: the bringing together of different factions and the negotiation of some settlement in which they could all share—an enterprise that has invariably collapsed, not least because it assumed the existence of a state or the possibility of creating one. The chapter next examines two further kinds of peacebuilding, on the one hand in Somaliland (and to some degree Puntland) by building a partial state on the basis of local institutions, on the other hand through the Union of Islamic Courts (UIC), which briefly attained power in Mogadishu and beyond in the second half of 2006. Much of this, inevitably, is a distinctively Somali story, and given the peculiarities—breakdown not only of the Somali state but much more basically of Somali society as a whole—it cannot be assumed that there are "lessons" from Somalia that may be applied to the rest of Africa and beyond. The Somali case does nonetheless have resonances that may be of broader interest.

Somalis and the State

Over very large areas of Africa, the "state" was a colonial invention, imposed on peoples who had survived for countless generations without one. Rarely, however, was the mismatch between indigenous cultures and colonial statehood so blatant as in the Somali case. This mismatch was made all the more stark by the very homogeneity of the Somali people.[2] External observers have often been surprised that a territory having the apparent advantages that most of its colonially created equivalents lack—common nationhood, language, religion, culture, and lifestyle—should prove quite unable to sustain a common structure of government. A paradox this may be, but not a contradiction. The very fact that Somalis had so much in common meant that there was no need for the colonial state, as there often was elsewhere, to bring together and mediate between the disparate peoples encompassed within the newly created boundaries. Somalis had their own mechanisms for managing the often fractious relationships between themselves, to which the colonial state was generally an irrelevance, and at worst positively damaging. These mechanisms, moreover, were profoundly antithetical to the hierarchies of statehood. Nineteenth-century traveler Richard Burton's famed comment on the Somalis—"each man his own sultan"[3]—perfectly expressed the rejection of this obligation to obey that underlies the institutions of governance. Where individuals did gain authority, this was derived from their wisdom, piety, or ability to articulate some project of broad appeal, and was personal to themselves. What passed for the colonial state in British-ruled Somaliland involved little more than the supervision, with the lightest of touches, of existing conflict-management mechanisms, while in Italian Somalia, colonial statehood remained almost entirely alien to the indigenous population.

The First Republic, which derived from the independence of the former British and Italian Somalilands and their union on July 1, 1960, and was overthrown by the military coup of October 1969, perfectly illustrated this mismatch. Democratic to the point of anarchy, it rested on chaotic coalitions of clan factions for which the principal nationalist party, the Somali Youth League, provided a forum for squabbles over patronage, rather than an ideology or an organization. The one element that could be used to foment a sense of national unity, the claim for the "reunification" with Somalia of Somalis who had been incorporated by colonialism into the neighboring territories of Kenya, Ethiopia, and the French Somali Coast (Djibouti), ensured bad relations with its neighbors and with other African states for which the colonial borders were sacrosanct. It also led to the decision to form, with Soviet assistance, an army that might be used to reclaim these territories, but that actually posed the greatest danger to those who had created it.

The 1969 coup, ushering in the regime of Mohamed Siad Barre, which was to rule Somalia for the next twenty-two years, tested the idea of Somali statehood to destruction, by seeking to impose a level of central control that Somali society was entirely unable to sustain. In essence, Siad sought to create a hierarchical structure, backed by the Soviet Union in exchange for key military facilities in a strategically sensitive area. He sought to legitimize these structures through the project of Somali unification. The formal abolition of the clan system and the establishment of a Marxist-Leninist vanguard party were never more than window-dressing: in practice, the government was run, as everyone recognized, by an alliance of the three clans—Marehan, Ogaden, and Dulbahante—with which Siad was most closely associated. The raison d'être of this entire enterprise collapsed as early as 1977–78, when Somali forces overran the Somali-inhabited area of southeastern Ethiopia, the Soviet Union switched sides to the Ethiopians, and the Somali army was driven out by an Ethiopian and Cuban force, with heavy Soviet backing.[4] The next thirteen years witnessed the long drawn-out death throes of the Somali state, as Siad sought to hang on by means of opportunistic international and domestic clan alliances, in the course of which any coherent Somali army gave way to the clan militias that paved the way for subsequent "warlords." A particularly vicious incident in this descent into anarchy, the systematic bombing of the northern capital of Hargeisa in mid-1988, which resulted in an estimated 40,000 deaths, destroyed whatever legitimacy the state may still have possessed in the northern part of the country. When Siad eventually fled in January 1991, this led not to the takeover of government by an organized guerrilla force (as happened in Uganda in 1986, and in Ethiopia in May 1991), but rather to the destruction of government and the partition of the national territory, Mogadishu included, between the fiefdoms of different factions. Although at one level a well-organized opposition was not needed to overthrow the collapsing Siad regime (in sharp contrast, notably, to the herculean effort required to oust the Derg in Ethiopia), more fundamentally both government and guerrillas were victims of the fissiparous nature of Somali society.

Statebuilding and Peacebuilding

The first and most familiar external involvement in Somalia, Operation Restore Hope, launched by the United States with UN backing and participation late in 1988, was not a statebuilding or peacebuilding exercise at all. A disastrous attempt at post–Cold War "humanitarian intervention," it sought to guarantee the safe delivery of humanitarian relief, but without tackling the underlying conditions that had created the need for the relief in the first place.[5] The entire operation lacked a plausible political agenda, and the US and UN forces found themselves sucked into domestic political conflicts between those Somali factions that benefited from their presence and those that lost out. Whether a properly resourced, long-term intervention, with an agenda explicitly geared to rebuilding the Somali state, could have succeeded therefore remains an open question, though I remain extremely skeptical. A very high level of political skill, and a deep familiarity with Somali norms and practices, would have been needed in order to prevent the statebuilders and peacebuilders from becoming embroiled in the conflicts of a deeply factionalized society, and there is nothing in the experience of external intervention in other failed or fractured states to suggest that it could have worked in Somalia. There is a very high likelihood that "statebuilding" would merely have taken the form of a one-size-fits-all model derived from Western norms, and would rapidly have degenerated into a personal autocracy sustained by external military and financial patronage, replicating the characteristics of Somali states that had failed in the past.

Even that, however, could scarcely have been worse than the outcome that actually ensued, when faction leaders (often described as "warlords") were able to garner the prestige derived from having seen off the United States and its allies, together with considerable quantities of cash and weapons, and entrench themselves far more effectively than before.

It is scarcely necessary to recount the long and dismal history of attempts at externally brokered Somali "peace settlements" from the time of the UN withdrawal in early 1995 onward, since these all shared essentially the same structural difficulties, which in turn fatally undermined the objectives that they were intended to achieve. Three such difficulties were particularly damaging. First, there was the question of whom to negotiate *with*. The attempt to re-create a Somali state, in a situation in which the imposition of a framework of public order by prolonged and expensive external military force was not a viable option, entailed brokering some kind of deal with existing faction leaders, since they alone controlled the force that would be needed to make the deal stick, or that could conversely be used to destroy it. This strengthened faction leaders as a whole, since they thus became the recognized interlocutors between Somali society and the outside world, even when they enjoyed little legitimacy within the sections of Somali society that they claimed to represent. At the same time, it led to further factionalism, since the way for subordinates to gain external recognition was to present themselves as independent operators, who would thus need to be bought off by the external brokers. One result of this was to destroy whatever leverage might otherwise have been possessed by local mediators, commonly described as "elders," through whom the endless squabbles between different clans and factions had previously been patched up. In much of Somalia, and especially in the towns and their immediate hinterlands, "elders" in this sense no longer exist, their authority having been fatally undermined by lawless and heavily armed young men with varying allegiances to different faction bosses.

Second, there was the question of what to negotiate *about*. Since there was no state, there was no prize, control of which would have provided a tempting inducement to faction leaders to agree among themselves, and moderate their behavior in order to help maintain an instrument of governance that they could all use. There was no scenario equivalent to the negotiations between the National Party government and the African National Congress in South Africa between 1990 and 1994, or between outgoing colonial regimes and their would-be nationalist successors during African decolonization. There were no ministries, no buildings and staff and organizational structures that would confer some kind of power on the politicians who controlled them. There were only the empty shells of destroyed former government buildings, and the empty titles of minister of this or that which could be bandied about in the negotiation process. Nor was there any shared "idea of the state": any set of common attitudes and beliefs about how a Somali state would work, or what it would do, that might create an ideology of statehood sufficient to temper the divisions or moderate the demands of the politicians who would have to form it. The only inducement on offer was therefore external payoffs of one kind or another that would provide specific incentives to individual politicians to participate in particular settlements, but that could not be used to develop a common agenda for a workable structure of government. Signatures on dotted lines, in the comfortable hotels in other countries of the region in which the negotiations took place, could not be made to stick in the form of real political settlements on the ground in shattered Somalia.[6] Many inducements were in any event zero-sum: plums that were offered to one faction leader could not go to another, and an adverse allocation would be accepted only until a shift in bargaining power enabled a leader to challenge it. Outbreaks of vicious fighting on the ground were often orchestrated to strengthen one faction against another at critical points in the negotiations: the "peacebuilding" process itself fomented conflict.

Third, there were problems deriving from Somalia's place in a fractured region—and, especially after the events of September 11, 2001, in a fractured world. Central to the regional dilemma was Ethiopia. As the dominant state in the region, with a large Somali population in its own territory and a long and indefensible border with Somalia, Ethiopia had a legitimate interest in any settlement, and an incentive to moderate conflicts that would inevitably spill over its own frontier. At the same time, the antipathy between highland Ethiopians and Somalis runs long and deep: between highlander and lowlander, agriculturalist and pastoralist, Christian and Muslim, hierarchical statist society and egalitarian stateless society. Any Ethiopian involvement thus stirred more than the usual Somali resentment at external intervention. Correspondingly, any settlement that excluded Ethiopian interests, or those Somali factions best disposed toward accommodation with Addis Ababa, would arouse Ethiopian efforts at destabilization, for which the means of manipulation through clan factions were always available, while any settlement that broadly met with Ethiopian approval would likewise seem illegitimate in the eyes of many Somalis. Beginning in 1998, these problems were compounded by the war between Ethiopia and Eritrea; and especially after Eritrea's defeat in 2000, the regime in Asmara sought to encourage a "second front" in southeastern Ethiopia, to relieve the pressure in the north. This activity was entirely opportunistic: state power in Eritrea, as in Ethiopia, lies with Christian highlanders, and the threat posed by militant Islam to the regime in Asmara was more intense than that for its southern neighbor, all the more so since inept Eritrean diplomacy aroused the hostility also of Muslim regional states. And if this was not enough, the global "war on terror" revived US interest in Somalia, as a threatening ungoverned space in which Islamist militants could thrive, and from which indeed attacks on the US embassies in Nairobi and Dar-es-Salaam, and on the USS *Cole* in Aden, appeared to derive. Like Ethiopia, which rapidly signed up as a US regional ally and enforcer, the United States had an interest in "stability" in Somalia, and in the creation of an effective Somali state; but in practice, as the result of a general suspicion of Islam as a basis for governance, and a particular concern to liquidate Al-Qaida militants using Somali territory, its impact was almost entirely counterproductive.[7] In short, external engagement in Somalia not only completely failed to create the state-based structures of public order that outsiders viewed as the essential precondition for "peace," but also—by introducing new prizes for faction leaders and tying internal divisions to external agendas—intensified the existing levels of conflict.

Alternative Approaches

At this point it is helpful to look at two very different approaches that have been used to create structures of order on a largely indigenous basis, in different parts of Somalia, and that—in dramatically different ways—provide some insight into alternative ways of managing Somali conflicts.

The Somaliland Experiment

The first of these is the establishment in 1991 of the breakaway Republic of Somaliland, encompassing the formerly British-ruled area of the united Somali Republic formed in 1960. Somaliland has now maintained an effective but unrecognized independence for two decades, and has (for all its problems) achieved a level of peace, order, and participatory government markedly greater than in former Italian

Somalia to the south. The formal basis for the Somaliland regime lies straightforwardly in the model of postcolonial statehood. Its boundaries are those of the former British colony; its legal claim to separate statehood lies in the five-day existence of an independent Somaliland in June 1960, and the assertion that the union with Somalia then voluntarily entered into can likewise be voluntarily rescinded; and whenever opportunity offers, the regime emphasizes its "Britishness," in order to advertise its difference from its ex-Italian counterpart.[8] In practice, however, this is no standard postcolonial state. The institutional legacy of British colonialism has been virtually obliterated, and nothing remains of the forms of rule—administration, military, taxation system—that elsewhere ensured continuity between colonial and independent statehood.

Instead, the Somaliland state rests on complex processes of interclan bargaining. Central to its creation is the fact that one group of clans, the Isaaq, accounts for a dominant share of its population; it is also centrally placed within Somaliland, and very few Isaaq live in the other Somali-inhabited territories. Somaliland was thus of necessity an Isaaq-dominated state. The Isaaq had been particularly opposed to the Siad Barre regime, in which they had little part, and from which—most obviously in the bombing of Hargeisa—they had badly suffered. Despite divisions both between and within the different Isaaq clans, in respect of which the Isaaq differ little from other Somalis, and the need to reach some accommodation with non-Isaaq clans within the territory (notably the Issa and Gadabursi from the Dir clan family in the west of the territory, and the Dulbahante and Warsangeli from the Darod in the east), Somaliland thus possessed a core population with a commitment to its "own" state, and a history of alienation from the former Somalia. It was also able to draw on some political continuity through the Somali National Movement, the dominant political party of the 1950s and 1960s, which provided a framework through which to facilitate the process of political reconciliation. Its aged leader, Mohamed Haji Ibrahim Egal, became the first president of newly independent Somaliland.[9]

A second key factor was the process by which the new state was established, as the culmination in May 1991 of the "Grand Conference of the Northern Peoples," or in local terms a *Guurti*, at which representatives of all the northern clans met and argued over the course of several weeks about the best way forward for the peoples of the region following the collapse of the government in Mogadishu. This provided a legitimate basis for the historic decision to assert the region's independence, founded in indigenous custom and allowing for deals to be made and compromises to be reached that would ensure some place in the new state for all of its constituent peoples. Again, this should not obscure the levels of factionalism, breaking out on occasion into violence, that have continued to affect Somaliland politics. The Dulbahante and Warsangeli, in particular, have clan territories that overlap across the former colonial frontier into the area of ex-Italian Somalia that comes under the sway of the quasi-autonomous "Puntland" administration. Prominent individuals in each of these clans may classify themselves as Puntlanders at one moment, and Somalilanders at another, as the power of the rival regimes in the border areas, and the inducements on offer from each side, shift one way or the other. In the west, the Issa especially are heavily involved in the government of Djibouti, and have a substantial population in the Somali region of Ethiopia, again allowing them to play off different options. Even within the "core" Isaaq constituency, clan and subclan rivalries remain, and the Habr Yunis clan in particular have often been at odds with the government in Hargeisa. This, however, is part of the normal cut-and-thrust of Somali politics, which is *never* "stable," in the sense of the regular processes of authoritative management associated with "government" in statist systems of rule. "Authority" in Somali society is inherently volatile; any settlement is necessarily temporary, and may be disowned or need to be negotiated as the situation changes; violence is never far beneath the surface, and is indeed a normal accompaniment to the process of bargaining; the elders' task of managing conflict is never done. However troubling to outsiders, this is how the Somali system works, and any process of "peacebuilding" can never plausibly do more than provide for the mechanisms through which inherent conflicts can in some way be mediated.

A third and paradoxical element in the comparative success of the Somaliland experiment is the ambiguous engagement of the international community. The avowed aim of the Somaliland government is to achieve full recognition as a sovereign state, with a place in the United Nations and the African Union, that can engage with other international actors, not least with potential investors and aid donors, on the same basis as other states throughout the world. It is indeed bizarre that Somalia continues to be recognized globally as a state, even though it has not for two decades had a government capable of exercising even minimal control over most of its notional territory, whereas Somaliland is formally recognized by not a single other state or international institution, even though it has managed for a similar period to govern most of its own territory with at least a modicum of peace and participation. The unfulfilled quest for recognition places the Somaliland authorities under constraints analogous to those facing southeastern European states seeking admission to the European Union: they are obliged—subject to other pressures that they also must take into account—to behave in a way that is in line with their overall goal. Whether Somaliland would retain a broadly consensual political structure should this quest be achieved, and should the greatly increased aid funds generated by recognition become available to its government, must remain very much open to question.

The Islamist Experience

The second and more distinctive experiment in building peace by creating new structures of authority is the regime established in Mogadishu by the Union of Islamic Courts in early 2006, and rapidly extended to much of the rest of Somalia in the latter part of that year, before its collapse in the face of Ethiopian invasion (supported by the United States) in late December. Despite this collapse, the Islamist forces have since regrouped, and present a significant and increasing threat to the transitional federal government, which is formally recognized by most of the international community but which has been quite unable to impose its authority over much of the national territory, and particularly Mogadishu. Any plausible future structure of governance, at least in southern Somalia, is far more likely to derive from the Islamists than from any other source.

There can be little doubt that the Union of Islamic Courts was, at base, a genuine indigenous initiative, seeking to harness the unifying values of Islam in order to bring peace to people who had suffered badly from the lack of it. During the long period after 1991 when no state existed, institutions based in Islam had spontaneously formed in order to meet the critical needs of the population. The most prominent among these were the courts, created for the most part within the territories of particular clans or subclans, and meting out justice with popular consent on the basis of *sharia*. To these were added schools and medical services, as well as other social services, that could draw on the charitable precepts of Islam and provide some substitute for the collapsed institutions of the state. Another and particularly important way in which Islam substituted for state failure was the provision of banking and money transfer systems, notably Al-Barakaat, through which funds from the diaspora could be channeled, with remarkable speed and efficiency, to needy recipients inside the country.

From early 2006 these initiatives coalesced into a single organization, the UIC, which drove out the principal "warlords" struggling to control Mogadishu and almost instantly created a level of peace within the shattered city that had not been seen for over fifteen years. Checkpoints between the territories of different subclans (or just armed gangs) were dismantled, and public order was restored. People were able to travel peaceably around the city and beyond, in a way that had previously been impossible. There was, to be sure, a price to be paid: Islamic justice was swift and often brutal, and the edicts of the new rulers rested on a purist and intolerant form of Islam that was at odds with the easygoing faith of most Somali Muslims; attempts were even made to prohibit watching the 2006 football World Cup on satellite television—an odd move, since both Iran and Saudi Arabia were playing. The benefits of the UIC were nonetheless enormous, and the area under its control rapidly expanded as the factional militias that had previously carved up Somalia between them melted away before it. It became possible—in the most optimistic scenario—to envisage a united and peaceful Somalia, under strict but broadly consensual Islamist control.

This vision was most obviously aborted by Ethiopian intervention, launched by a disciplined and well-equipped army to which the large but ragtag forces assembled by the UIC could offer no effective resistance. Behind this, of course, lay the challenge that an Islamist government in Somalia posed to both regional and global hegemons. The regime in Addis Ababa had watched with growing alarm as the Islamist bandwagon rolled, apparently unstoppably, toward its own frontier, reviving along the way the irredentist project of uniting all Somalis under a common flag. The Somaliland regime was even more directly threatened. Militarily, the best option open to the Ethiopians was to seek to stop the UIC within Somalia, before it crossed the frontier and created further mayhem within Ethiopian territory. Although the initiative undoubtedly lay with the Ethiopian government, it was able to gain the support, both military (notably through satellite intelligence) and diplomatic, of the United States, to which an overtly Islamist regime in a strategically sensitive part of the post-9/11 world was unthinkable. In the event, the task proved much easier than either the Ethiopians or the Americans could have expected. The UIC forces melted away; the

Ethiopian army went on to occupy Mogadishu; and fleeing Islamists were pursued through the mangrove swamps of southwestern Somalia. The old warlords were back, now under obvious and much resented Ethiopian protection, and peacebuilding returned to square one.

Behind this debacle, however, lay deeper problems in peacebuilding through Islam in Somalia that need to be more fully explored. To start, the contradictions of external engagement with Somali peacebuilding on the part of broadly Western-oriented agencies were precisely replicated on the Islamist side. The engagement of the UIC with the global movement for Islamic renewal, and notably with Wahhabi elements based in Saudi Arabia, affected the balance of power within the UIC, and strengthened those factions associated with a more "purist" or "fundamentalist" conception of Islam, which was at odds with the popular Islam of most Somalis.[10] This weakened the union's legitimacy with its popular base—a weakening that could only have intensified as its initial allure wore off and normal factional politics resumed—increased divisions within the union itself, and led to the articulation of agendas that could only ring alarm bells, both regionally and globally. It led to an incursion of foreign Islamists, for whom Somalia became the latest frontline in a global project, in a way that also reduced indigenous legitimacy and increased external distrust. The UIC even received a contingent of Eritrean military advisers, with whose bewilderment one can only sympathize: nothing could be further from the ruthlessly disciplined Eritrean People's Liberation Front than the chaos they encountered in Somalia.

The UIC likewise exemplifies a recurring pattern in Somalia politics, illustrated by the jihad of Sayyid Mohamed Abdalla Hassan in the early twentieth century, or the Somali Youth League in the 1950s. In each case, a single leader or small group, drawn from a particular clan base, generates a charismatic project with an appeal extending well beyond the original core. As further supporters join in, the movement develops a momentum of its own, normal clan divisions are suspended, and even skeptics are obliged to take part, lest they be left high and dry by the defection of their own followers. As its scope increases, however, so the movement's coherence diminishes, until a sharp check to its ambitions leads it to fall apart into its constituent sections, and "normal" politics resumes. The core of the UIC lay in the Ayr subclan of the Habr Gidir clan, and even if it had not been abruptly stopped by Ethiopian armed forces, it is virtually inevitable that its limitations would have been revealed in some other way.

Is There a Future for Somali Peacebuilding?

In a volume on peacebuilding in Africa, Somalia lies at the bottom of the pile. In all of the other cases considered, there is at least some framework within which a settlement of conflicts can be attempted, and in several of them the essential elements of a postconflict settlement are in place, and the challenge lies in tackling issues such as demobilization, security sector reform, economic reconstruction, and institution building, in order to prevent a backslide into war. Somalia, in contrast, remains mired in ongoing conflict. The fractious nature of Somali society itself, the chronic instability of the regional environment, and the insertion of the region into global conflict agendas conspire to prevent the emergence of any plausible framework for peace. The engagement of external actors, even those seeking to stabilize Somalia and the Horn of Africa as a whole, has almost invariably intensified conflict rather than moderated it.

There are nonetheless two pointers to how a measure of peace might be promoted in Somalia, no matter how difficult these may be to implement in practice. The first is that peacebuilding has to precede statebuilding, not the other way round. A viable state can only be the *outcome* of a successful process of reconciliation: it can never be the means by which public order is restored. The resistance to hierarchy inherent in Somali society as a whole, the lack of effective instruments of control at the disposal of a revived Somali state, and the inevitable collapse of such a state into a squabble for benefits among its constituent factions all underline the futility of the "peacebuilding through statebuilding" approach that is often the key to success elsewhere.

The second pointer is that, precisely because of its stateless, fractious, and often violent nature, Somali society has over time developed its own mechanisms for conflict management that—no matter how time-consuming, uncertain, and often exasperating (to outsiders) these may be—nonetheless provide the only plausible way forward. The key to the success of such mechanisms is their insulation from external engagement, the effect of which is to destabilize the delicate and ever-changing relationships between domestic actors. In a globalized world, in which Somalis themselves are among the most globalized of peoples, this is an extremely difficult task. It must involve at the minimum the forcible suppression of means by which Somalis—with piracy as the most obvious example—destabilize the rest of the world, and a recognition that the pursuit of agendas such as radical Islam can have only highly adverse consequences for domestic well-being. Paradoxically, these two ways in which the Somali imbroglio is seen to threaten external interests may well be at odds with one another: the most effective way to suppress piracy would be through the imposition of an Islamic state capable of imposing domestic order, at the cost of arousing international hostility. But within the limits that the outside world can tolerate, the only practicable solution is to let Somalis build their own peace, in their own way, themselves.

Notes

1. For a discussion of the often divergent implications of governance and statebuilding, see Menkhaus, "Somalia."

2. See Lewis, *Understanding Somalia and Somaliland,* the most recent updating of this classic introduction to Somalia.

3. Cited from Drake-Brockman, *British Somaliland,* 102.

4. For an appraisal of the Siad Barre regime, see Samatar, *Socialist Somalia.*

5. See Lyons and Samatar, *Somalia;* Clarke and Herbst, eds., *Learning from Somalia.*

6. See Menkhaus, "Crisis in Somalia."

7. Ibid.

8. See Höhne, "Political Identity, Emerging State Structures, and Conflict in Northern Somalia." The placards that greeted a group of visiting British parliamentarians in 2004, bearing a picture of Queen Elizabeth II and the headline "The Queen, Our Mother," are particularly touching.

9. Europa Publications, *Africa South of the Sahara 1997,* 871.

10. See Menkhaus, "Crisis in Somalia."

Bibliography

Abi-Saab, Georges. *The United Nations Operation in the Congo, 1960–1964*. Oxford: Oxford University Press, 1978.

ActionAid, CAFOD, and CARE International. *Consolidating the Peace?: Views from Sierra Leone and Burundi on the United Nations Peacebuilding Commission*. June 2007.

Adaka Boro Centre. "Boro: Secret file of Niger Delta's Famous Godfather." http://www .adakaboro.org/resources/articles/37-articles/79-borogodfather.

Addison, Tony. "Conflict and Peace-Building: Interactions Between Politics and Economics." *Round Table* 94, no. 381 (2005): 405–11.

Addison, Tony, and Mark McGillivray. "Aid to Conflict-Affected Countries: Lessons for Donors." *Conflict, Security, and Development* 4, no. 3 (2004): 347–67.Rafeeuddin

Adebajo, Adekeye. "Ending Global Apartheid: Africa and the United Nations," In *From Global Apartheid to Global Village: Africa and the United Nations*, edited by Adekeye Adebajo, 3–50. Scottsville: University of KwaZulu-Natal Press, 2009.

———. "Liberia: A Warlord's Peace." In *Ending Civil Wars: The Implementation of Peace Agreements*, edited by Stephen Stedman, Donald Rothchild, and Elizabeth Cousens, 599–630. Boulder: Rienner, 2002.

———. *Liberia's Civil War: Nigeria, ECOMOG, and Regional Security in West Africa*. Boulder: Rienner, 2002.

———. "The Security Council and Three Wars in West Africa." In *The United Nations Security Council and War: The Evolution of Thought and Practice Since 1945*, edited by Vaughan Lowe, Adam Roberts, Jennifer Welsh, and Dominik Zaum, 466–493. Oxford: Oxford University Press, 2008.

Afako, Barney. "Negotiating in the Shadow of Justice: The Juba Talks." *Accord*, update to issue 11: *Initiatives to End the Violence in Northern Uganda 2002–09 and the Juba Peace Process* (2010): 21–23. Available online at Conciliation Resources, www.c-r.org /accord/juba.

African Development Bank (AfDB). *AfDB/Burundi: Launch of Infrastructure Action Plan for Sustainable Development and Regional Integration*. Tunis, April 2010.

———. *African Development Report, 2008–2009: Focus on Conflict Resolution, Peace, and Reconstruction in Africa*. Tunis, May 2009.

———. *Strategy for Enhanced Engagement in Fragile States*. Tunis, January 2008.

African Development Bank (AfDB) and World Bank. *Sierra Leone: Information Note on African Development Bank and World Bank Joint Assistance Strategy, 2009–2012*. Tunis, 2009.

African Rights. *Death, Despair, and Defiance*. London: African Rights, 1994.

African Security Dialogue and Research (ASDR). "Feasibility and Needs Assessment of ECOWAS Parliaments." Accra: ASDR, 2008.

African Union. *Policy Framework on Post-Conflict Reconstruction and Development in Africa*. AU Commission, Conflict Management Division, Addis Ababa, July 2006.

African Union and NEPAD. *AU/NEPAD African Action Plan: Updated Final Draft Version*, 10th African Partnership Forum (APF), Tokyo, April 7–8, 2008.

———. *The AU/NEPAD African Action Plan, 2010–2015: Advancing Regional and Continental Integration in Africa*. Midrand: NEPAD Secretariat, Governance, Peace, and Security Programme, June 2009.

Agoagye, Festus. "The African Mission in Burundi: Lessons from the First African Peacekeeping Operation." *Conflict Trends* 2 (2004): 9–15.

Ake, Claude. *Democracy and Development in Africa.* Washington, DC: Brookings Institution, 1996.

Akokpari, John, Angela Ndinga-Muvumba, and Tim Murithi, eds. *The African Union and Its Institutions.* Johannesburg: Jacana, 2008.

Albert, Isaac O. "Understanding Peace in Africa." In *Peace and Conflict in Africa,* edited by David Francis, 31–45. London: Zed Books, 2008.

Ali, Taisier, and Robert O. Matthews, eds. *Durable Peace: Challenges for Peacebuilding in Africa.* Toronto: University of Toronto Press, 2004.

———. Introduction to *Durable Peace: Challenges for Peacebuilding in Africa,* edited by Taisier Ali and Robert O. Matthews, 3–15. Toronto: University of Toronto Press, 2004.

Allen, Chris. "Understanding African Politics." *Review of African Political Economy* 22, no. 65 (1995): 301–20.

Allen, Tim. "The International Criminal Court and the Invention of Traditional Justice in Northern Uganda." *Politique Africaine* 107 (2007): 147–166.

———. *Trial Justice: The International Criminal Court and the Lord's Resistance Army.* London: Zed, 2006.

Amin, Samir. *Imperialism and Unequal Development.* New York: Monthly Review Press, 1977.

Amnesty International. "Uganda: First Steps to Investigate Crimes Must Be Part of Comprehensive Plan to End Impunity." January 30, 2004.

Ampiah, Kweku, and Sanusha Naidu, eds. *Crouching Tiger, Hidden Dragon?: Africa and China.* Scottsville: University of KwaZulu-Natal Press, 2008.

Anderlini, Sanam Naraghi. *Women Building Peace: What They Do, Why It Matters.* Boulder: Rienner, 2007.

Andersen, Regine. "How Multilateral Development Assistance Triggered the Conflict in Rwanda." *Third World Quarterly* 21, no. 3 (2000): 441–56.

Andreas, Peter. "Criminalized Legacies of War: The Clandestine Political Economy of the Western Balkans." *Problems of Post-Communism* 51, no. 3 (2004): 3–9.

Anstee, Margaret. *Orphan of the Cold War: The Inside Story of the Collapse of the Angolan Peace Process.* London: Macmillan, 1996.

Armon, Jeremy, and Andy Carl, eds. *Accord,* no. 1: *The Liberian Peace Process, 1990–1996.* London: Conciliation Resources, 1996.

Atkinson, Philippa, and Nicholas Leader. "The 'Joint Policy of Operation' and the 'Principles and Protocols of Humanitarian Operation' in Liberia," HPG Report 3. London: Overseas Development Institute, March 2000.

Atwood, David, and Fred Tanner. "The UN Peacebuilding Commission and International Geneva." *Disarmament Forum,* Special issue on the Peacebuilding Commission, UNIDIR no. 2 (2007): 27–36.

Aukerman, Miriam. J. "Extraordinary Evil, Ordinary Crime: A Framework for Understanding Transitional Justice." *Harvard Human Rights Journal* 15 (Spring 2002): 39–98.

Autesserre, Séverine. "DR Congo: Explaining Peace Building Failures, 2003–2006." *Review of African Political Economy* no. 113 (September 2007): 423–41.

———. "Penser les conflits locaux: L'échec de l'intervention international au Congo." In *L'Afrique des Grands Lacs, annuaire 2007–2008,* 179–97. Paris: L'Harmattan, 2009.

———. "The Trouble with the Congo." *Foreign Affairs* 87, no. 3 (2008): 94–110.

Ayoob, Mohammed. "State Making, State Breaking, and State Failure." In *Managing Global Chaos,* edited by Chester Crocker, Fen Osler Hampson and Pamela Aall, 37–51. Washington, DC: US Institute of Peace, 1996.

Baden, Sally. *Post-Conflict Mozambique: Women's Special Situation, Population Issues, and Gender Perspectives to Be Integrated into Skills Training and Employment Promotion.* Geneva: International Labour Office, 1997.

Baker, Bruce, and Roy May. "Reconstructing Sierra Leone." *Commonwealth and Comparative Politics* 42, no. 1 (2004): 35–60.

Ball, Nicole. "The Challenge of Rebuilding War-Torn Societies." In *Managing Global Chaos,* edited by Chester Crocker, Fred Osler Hampson, and Pamela Aall, 607–22. Washington, DC: US Institute of Peace, 1996.

Baptista-Lundin, Irae, Martinho Chachiua, Antonio Gaspar, Habiba Guebuza, and Guilherme Mbilana. "'Reducing Costs through an Expensive Exercise': The Impact of Demobilization in Mozambique." In *Demobilization in Sub-Saharan Africa: The Development and Security Impacts,* edited by Kees Kingma, 173–212. New York: St. Martin's, 2000.

Barker, Rodney. *Political Legitimacy and the State.* Oxford: Oxford University Press, 1990.

Barnett, Michael, Hunjoon Kim, Madalene O'Donnell, and Laura Sitea. "Peacebuilding: What Is in a Name?" *Global Governance* 13, no. 1 (2007): 35–58.

Barth, Elise Fredrikke. *Peace as Disappointment: The Reintegration of Female Soldiers in Post-Conflict Societies: A Comparative Study from Africa.* Oslo: International Peace Research Institute [PRIO], 2002.

Bass, Gary. "Jus Post Bellum." *Philosophy and Public Affairs* 32, no. 4 (2004): 384–412.

Bayart, Jean-François. "Africa in the World: A History of Extraversion." *African Affairs* 99, no. 395 (2000): 217–267.

Bayreuth University and the Instituto Nacional de Estudos e Pesquisa (INEP) in Guinea-Bissau. "Local Strategies of Conflict Management in Guinea-Bissau."

Beetham, David. *The Legitimation of Power.* Basingstoke: Palgrave Macmillan, 1991.

Belasco, Amy. "The Cost of Iraq, Afghanistan, and Other Global War on Terror Operations since 9/11." *Congressional Report Service,* June 2009.

Bellamy, Alex. "The Institutionalisation of Peacebuilding: What Role for the UN Peacebuilding Commission." In *Palgrave Advances in Peacebuilding: Critical Developments and Approaches,* edited by Oliver P. Richmond, 193–212. London: Palgrave Macmillan, 2010.

———. *Kosovo and International Society.* Basingstoke: Palgrave, 2002.

Berdal, Mats. *Building Peace after War.* Adelphi Paper. London: Routledge, 2009.

———. *Disarmament and Demobilization After Civil Wars.* Adelphi Paper 303. London: International Institute for Strategic Studies, 1996.

Biersteker, Thomas J. "Prospects for the UN Peacebuilding Commission." *Disarmament Forum,* Special issue on the Peacebuilding Commission, UNIDIR no. 2 (2007): 37–44.

Biesheuvel, Piet, Tom Hamilton-Baillie, and Peter Wilson. *Sierra Leone Security Sector Reform Programme: Output to Purpose Review.* London: Security Sector Development Advisory Team [SSDAT], 2007.

Bilgin, Pinar, and Adam D. Morton. "From 'Rogue' to 'Failed' States? The Fallacy of Short-Termism." *Politics* 24, no. 3 (2004): 169–80.

Blumenson, Eric. "The Challenge of a Global Standard of Justice: Peace, Pluralism, and Punishment at the International Criminal Court." *Columbia Journal of Transnational Law* 33, no. 3 (2005–6): 801–74.

Bojicic-Dzelilovic, Vesan. "World Bank, NGOs, and the Private Sector in Post-War Reconstruction." *International Peacekeeping* 9, no. 2 (2002): 81–98.

Boothby, Neil, Jennifer Crawford, and Jason Halperin. "Mozambique Child Soldier Life Outcome Study: Lessons Learned in Rehabilitation and Reintegration Efforts." *Global Public Health,* February 2006.

Boulden, Jane. "Rules of Engagement, Force Structure, and Composition in UN Disarmament Operations." In *Disarmament and Conflict Resolution Project: Managing Arms in Peace Processes: The Issues,* edited by UN Institute for Disarmament Research (UNIDIR), 135–68. Geneva, 1996.

Boutros-Ghali, Boutros. *An Agenda for Development,* Report of the Secretary-General, UN Doc. A/48/935, May 6, 1994.

———. *An Agenda for Peace: Preventive Diplomacy, Peacemaking, and Peacekeeping.* New York: United Nations, UN Doc. A/47/277-S/24111, June 17, 1992.

Branch, Adam. "International Justice, Local Injustice." *Dissent* 53, no. 3 (2004): 22–26.

———. "Uganda's Civil War and the Politics of ICC Intervention." *Ethics and International Affairs* 21, no. 2 (2007): 179–98.

Brown, Michael E. ed. *The International Dimensions of Internal Conflict.* Cambridge: MIT Press, 1996.

Brown, Taylor, Richard Fanthorpe, Janet Gardener, Lansana Gberie, and Mohammed Gibril Sesay. "Sierra Leone: Drivers of Change." IDL Group, March 2005.

Bryden, Alan, Boubacar N'Diaye, and 'Funmi Olonisakin, eds. *Challenges of Security Sector Governance in West Africa.* Geneva: Democratic Control of Armed Forces [DCAF], 2008.

Bryden, Alan, and 'Funmi Olonisakin. *Security Transformation in Africa.* Geneva: Centre for Democratic Control of Armed Forces [DCAF]) 2010.

Bunwaree, Sheila. "NEPAD and Its Discontents." In *The African Union and Its Institutions,* edited by John Akokpari, Angela Ndinga-Muvumba, and Tim Murithi, 227–40. Johannesburg: Jacana, 2008.

Burke-White, William W. "Proactive Complementarity: The International Criminal Court and National Courts in the Rome System of Justice." *Harvard International Law Journal* 49, no. 1 (2008): 53–108.

Bush, Kenneth. *A Measure of Peace: Peace and Conflict Impact Assessment (PCIA) of Development Projects in Conflict Zones,* Working Paper no. 1. Ottawa: International Development Research Centre, Peacebuilding and Reconstruction Programme, 1998.

Bush, Kenneth, and Robert J. Opp. "Peace and Conflict Impact Assessment." In *Cultivating Peace: Conflict and Collaboration in Natural Resource Management,* edited by Daniel Buckles, 185–204. Ottawa: International Development Research Institute, 1999, http://www.idrc.ca/en/ev-27981-201-1-DO_topic.html.

Byman, Daniel L. "Friends Like These: Counterinsurgency and the War on Terrorism," *International Security* 31, no. 2 (2006): 79–115.

Call, Charles T. "Building States to Build Peace? A Critical Analysis." *Journal of Peacebuilding and Development* 4, no. 2 (2008): 60–74.

———, ed. *Constructing Justice and Security after War.* Washington, DC: United States Institute of Peace, 2007.

Call, Charles, and Susan Cook. "On Democratization and Peacebuilding" *Global Governance* 9, no. 2 (2003): 233–46.

Call, Charles, with Vanessa Wyeth, eds. *Building States to Build Peace.* Boulder: Rienner, 2008.

Callaghy, Thomas, Ronald Kassimir, and Robert Latham, eds. *Intervention and Transnationalism in Africa: Global-Local Networks of Power.* Cambridge: Cambridge University Press, 2001.

Carnahan, Michael, and Clare Lockhart. "Peacebuilding and Public Finance." In *Building States to Build Peace*, edited by Charles Call with Vanessa Wyeth, 73–102. Boulder: Rienner, 2008.

Cassidy, Robert M. "The Long Small War: Indigenous Forces for Counterinsurgency," *Parameters* 36, no. 2 (2006): 47–62.

Castaneda, Carla. "How Liberal Peacebuilding May Be Failing Sierra Leone." *Review of African Political Economy* 36, no. 120 (2009): 235–51.

Center for International Cooperation and International Peace Institute. "Taking Stock and Looking Forward: A Strategic Review of the Peacebuilding Commission." New York, April 2008.

Centre for Humanitarian Dialogue. *Charting the Roads to Peace: Facts, Figures, and Trends in Conflict Resolution.* Mediation Data Trends Report. Geneva: Centre for Humanitarian Dialogue, 2007.

Chandler, David. *Empire in Denial: The Politics of Statebuilding.* London: Pluto, 2006.

Chayes, Sarah. "Dangerous Liaisons." *Guardian*, July 7, 2003.

Chazan, Naomi, Robert Mortimer, John Ravenhill, and Donald Rothchild. *Politics and Society in Contemporary Africa.* Boulder: Rienner, 1993.

Cheng, Christine, and Dominik Zaum, eds. *Corruption and Post-Conflict Peacebuilding: Selling the Peace?* Abingdon: Routledge, 2011.

Cheo, Martha. "Women and Peacebuilding in Sierra Leone: Initiatives and Limitations." Unpublished presentation, University of Cambridge, March 2009.

Chopra, Jarat. "Building State Failure in East Timor." *Development and Change* 33, no. 5 (2002): 979–1000.

———. "The UN's Kingdom in East Timor." *Survival* 42, no. 3 (2000): 27–40.

Clark, Kimberly Mahling. "The Demobilization and Reintegration of Soldiers: Perspectives from USAID." *Africa Today* (1st and 2nd Quarters 1995): 49–60.

Clarke, Walter, and Jeffrey Herbst, eds. *Learning from Somalia: The Lessons of Armed Humanitarian Intervention.* Boulder: Westview, 1997.

Cliffe, Sarah, and Nick Manning. "Practical Approaches to Building State Institutions," In *Building States to Build Peace*, edited by Charles Call with Vanessa Wyeth, 163–84. Boulder: Rienner, 2008.

Coalition for International Justice. *Soil and Oil: Dirty Business in Sudan.* Washington, DC: US Institute of Peace, 2006.

Coghlan, Benjamin, et al., "Mortality in the Democratic Republic of the Congo: A Nationwide Survey." *Lancet* (January 7–13, 2006): 44–61.

Cohn, Carol, Felicity Hill, and Sara Ruddick. "The Relevance of Gender for Eliminating Weapons of Mass Destruction." *Disarmament Diplomacy* 80 (Autumn 2005). http://www.acronym.org.uk/dd/dd80/80ccfhsr.htm.

Colletta, Nat J., et al. *Interim Stabilization: Balancing Security and Development in Post-Conflict Peacebuilding.* Sweden: Sthlm Policy Group, 2008.

Colletta, Nat J., Markus Kostner, and Ingo Wiederhofer. *Case Studies in War-to-Peace Transition: The Demobilization and Reintegration of Ex-Combatants in Ethiopia, Namibia, and Uganda.* World Bank Discussion Paper no. 331 (June 1996).

———. *The Transition from War to Peace in Sub-Saharan Africa.* Washington, DC: World Bank, 1996.

Collier, Paul. *War, Guns, and Votes: Democracy in Dangerous Places.* London: Bodley Head, 2009.

Collier, Paul, Anke Hoeffler, and Dominic Rohner. "Beyond Greed and Grievance: Feasibility and Civil War." *Oxford Economic Papers* 61, no. 1 (2009): 1–27.

Commission on Global Governance. *Our Global Neighbourhood.* New York: Oxford University Press, 1995.

Cramer, Christopher. *Civil War Is Not a Stupid Thing: Accounting for Violence in Developing Countries.* London: Hurst, 2006.

Crocker, Chester A., Fen Osler Hampson, and Pamela R. Aall, eds. *Leashing the Dogs of War: Conflict Management in a Divided World.* Washington, DC: US Institute of Peace Press, 2007.

Curran, David, and Tom Woodhouse. "Cosmopolitan Peacekeeping and Peacebuilding in Sierra Leone: What Can Africa Contribute?" *International Affairs* 83, no. 6 (2007): 1055–1070.

Curtis, Devon. "The South African Approach to Peacebuilding in the Great Lakes Region of Africa." In *Constitutionalism and Democratic Transitions: Lessons from South Africa,* edited by Veronica Federico and Carlo Fusaro, 153–76. Florence: Firenze University Press, 2006.

Dahrendorf, Nicola. "MONUC and the Relevance of Coherent Mandates: The Case of the DRC." In *Security Sector Reform and UN Integrated Missions: Experience from Burundi, the DRC, Haiti, and Kosovo,* edited by Heiner Hänggi and Vincenza Scherrer, 67–112. Vienna: Lit Verlag, 2008.

Daley, Patricia. *Gender and Genocide in Burundi: The Search for Spaces of Peace in the Great Lakes Region.* Oxford: Currey, 2007.

Darby, John, and Roger Mac Ginty, eds. *Contemporary Peacemaking: Conflict, Peace Processes, and Post-War Reconstruction.* 2nd ed. Basingstoke: Palgrave Macmillan, 2008.

———. *The Management of Peace Processes,* Ethnic and Intercommunity Conflict Series. Basingstoke: Macmillan, 2000.

Das Gupta, Monica, Helene Grandvoinnet, and Mattia Romani, *Fostering Community-Driven Development: What Role for the State?* Policy Research Working Paper no. 2969. Washington, DC: World Bank, January 2003.

Dayal, Rajeshwar. *Mission for Hammarskjöld.* Princeton: Princeton University Press, 1976.

Deen, Thald, "UN Credibility at Stake over Iraq, Warn Diplomats." *Inter Press Service,* October 20, 2002.

Del Castillo, Graciana. *Rebuilding War-Torn States: The Challenge of Post-Conflict Economic Reconstruction.* Oxford: Oxford University Press, 2008.

Deng, Francis et al. *Sovereignty as Responsibility: Conflict Management in Africa.* Washington, DC: Brookings Institution, 1996.

Department for International Development (DFID). *Building the State and Securing the Peace.* London, 2009.

———. *Providing Budget Support to Developing Countries.* London, 2008.

———. *Why We Need to Work More Effectively in Fragile States.* London, 2005.

de Waal, Alex. "Darfur, the Court, and Khartoum: The Politics of State Non-Cooperation," In *Courting Conflict? Justice, Peace, and the ICC in Africa,* edited by Nicholas Waddell and Phil Clark, 29–36. London: Royal African Society, 2008.

———. "Mission without End? Peacekeeping in the African Political Marketplace," *International Affairs* 85, no. 1 (2009): 99–113.

de Zeeuw, Jeroen. "Projects Do Not Create Institutions: The Record of Democracy Assistance in Post-Conflict Societies." *Democratization* 12, no. 4 (2005): 481–504.

Dobbins, James, et al. *The UN's Role in Nation-Building: From the Congo to Iraq.* Santa Monica, CA: Rand Corporation, 2005.

Dolan, Chris. "Collapsing Masculinities and Weak States: A Case Study of Northern Uganda." In *Masculinity Matters: Men, Masculinities, and Gender Relations in Development,* edited by Frances Cleaver, 57–63. Zed Books: London, 2003.

———. *Social Torture: The Case of Northern Uganda, 1986–2006.* New York: Berghahn, 2009.

Dolan, Chris, and Jessica Schafer. *The Reintegration of Ex-Combatants in Mozambique: Manica and Zambezia Provinces.* Oxford: Refugee Studies Programme, 1997.

Doyle, Michael W., and Nicholas Sambanis. *Making War and Building Peace: United Nations Peace Operations.* Princeton: Princeton University Press, 2006.

Drake-Brockman, R. E. *British Somaliland.* London: Hurst and Brackett, 1912.

Duffield, Mark. *Development, Security and Unending War.* Cambridge: Polity Press, 2007.

———. *Global Governance and the New Wars: The Merging of Development and Security.* London: Zed, 2001.

———. "The Political Economy of Internal War: Asset Transfer, Complex Polticial Emergencies, and International Aid." In *War and Hunger: Rethinking International Responses to Political Emergencies* edited by J. Macrae and A. Zwi, 11–28. London: Zed, 1996.

———. "Social Reconstruction and the Radicalization of Development Aid as a Relation of Global Liberal Governance." *Development and Change* 33, no. 5 (2002): 1049–1071.

Dulic, Dragana. "Peace Building and Human Security: The Kosovo Case." Brussels, Human Security Working Paper Series, 2008, http://www.etcgraz.at/cms/fileadmin/user_upload/humsec/Workin_Paper_Series/WP_Dulic.pdf.

Du Pisani, Andre. *Rumours of Rain: Namibia's Post-Independence Experience.* Johannesburg: South African Institute of International Affairs, 1991.

Dzinesa, Gwinyayi A. "A Comparative Perspective of UN Peacekeeping in Angola and Namibia." *International Peacekeeping* 11, no. 4 (2004): 644–63.

———. "A Participatory Approach to DDR: Empowering Local Institutions and Abilities." *Conflict Trends,* no. 3 (2006): 39–43.

———. "Postconflict Disarmament, Demobilization, and Reintegration of Former Combatants in Southern Africa." *International Studies Perspectives* 8, no. 1 (2007): 75–98.

———. *Swords into Ploughshares: Post-Conflict Disarmament, Demobilisation, and Reintegration in Zimbabwe, Namibia, and South Africa.* Occasional Paper no. 120. Pretoria: Institute for Security Studies, 2006.

Dzinesa, Gwinyayi A., and Martin Rupiya. "Promoting National Reconciliation and Regional Integration: The Namibian Defence Forces from 1990 to 2005." In *Evolutions and Revolutions: A Contemporary History of Militaries in Southern Africa,* edited by Martin Rupiya, 199–234. Pretoria: Institute for Security Studies, 2005.

Economic Community of West African States. "ECOWAS Conflict Prevention Framework." MSC/REG 1/01/08, January 2008.

———. "ECOWAS Protocol on Democracy and Good Governance." 2001.

Ellis, Stephen. "How to Rebuild Africa." *Foreign Affairs* 84, no. 5 (2005): 135–48.

Englebert, Pierre. *State Legitimacy and Development in Africa.* Boulder: Rienner, 2002.

Englebert, Pierre, and Denis Tull. "Post-Conflict Reconstruction in Africa: Flawed Ideas about Failed States." *International Security* 32, no. 4 (2008): 106–39.

Ero, Comfort. "UN Peacekeeping in West Africa: Liberia, Sierra Leone, and Côte d'Ivoire." In *From Global Apartheid to Global Village: Africa and the Nations,* edited by Adekeye Adebajo, 283–304. Scottsville: University of KwaZulu-Natal Press, 2009.

Europa Publications. *Africa South of the Sahara 1997.* London: Europa, 1997.

Evans, Gareth. *The Responsibility to Protect: Ending Mass Atrocity Crimes Once and For All.* Washington DC: Brookings Institution Press, 2008.

Evans, Glynne. *Responding to Crises in the African Great Lakes.* Adelphi Paper no. 311. London: International Institute of Strategic Studies, 1997.

Falola, Toyin. "The Past in the Yoruba Present." In *Ethnicity and Democracy in Africa,* edited by Bruce Berman, Dickson Eyoh, and Will Kymlicka, 148–65. Athens: Ohio University Press, 2004.

Farr, Vanessa. "A Gendered Analysis of International Agreements on Small Arms and Light Weapons." In *Gender Perspectives on Small Arms and Light Weapons: Regional and International Concerns,* edited by Vanessa A. Farr and Kiflemariam Gebre-Wold, 14–24. Bonn: Bonn International Center for Conversion, Brief 24, July 2002.

———. *Gendering Demilitarization as a Peacebuilding Tool.* Bonn: Bonn International Center for Conversion, 2000.

Fine, Ben. "The Developmental State Is Dead: Long Live Social Capital?" *Development and Change* 30, no. 1 (1999): 1–19.

Fitzsimmons, Tracy. "Engendering Justice and Security after War." In *Constructing Justice and Security After War,* edited by Charles T. Call, 351–74. Washington, DC: US Institute of Peace, 2007.

Fortna, Virginia Page. *Peace Time: Cease-Fire Agreements and the Durability of Peace.* Princeton: Princeton University Press, 2004.

———. "Scraps of Paper? Agreements and the Durability of Peace." *International Organization* 57, no. 2 (2003): 337–72.

Francis, David. Introduction to *Peace and Conflict in Africa,* edited by David Francis, 3–15. London: Zed Books, 2008.

———, ed. *Peace and Conflict in Africa.* London: Zed Books, 2008.

Francis, Diana. *People, Peace, and Power: Conflict Transformation in Action.* London: Pluto Press, 2002.

François, Monika, and Inder Sud. "Promoting Stability and Development in Fragile and Failed States." *Development Policy Review* 24, no. 2 (2006): 141–60.

French, Howard. *A Continent for the Taking: The Tragedy and Hope of Africa.* New York: Knopf, 2004.

Frynas, Jedrzej G. *Oil in Nigeria: Conflict and Litigation Between Oil Companies and Village Communities.* Hamburg: Lit Verlag, 2000.

Fukuyama, Francis. *State-Building: Governance and World Order in the 21st Century.* Ithaca, NY: Cornell University Press, 2004.

———. "Stateness First." *Journal of Democracy* 16, no. 1 (January 2005): 84–88.

Galtung, Johan. *Peace by Peaceful Means: Peace and Conflict, Development and Civilization.* London: Sage, 1996.

———. *Transcend and Transform: An Introduction to Conflict Work.* London: Pluto, 2004.

———. "Violence, Peace, and Peace Research." *Journal of Peace Research* 6, no. 3 (1969): 167–91.

Gamba, Virginia. *Small Arms in Southern Africa: Reflections on the Extent of the Problem and Its Management Potential.* Monograph no. 42. Pretoria: Institute for Security Studies, 1999.

Gberie, Lansana. "Rescuing a Fragile State: The Case of Sierra Leone." In *Rescuing a Fragile State: Sierra Leone 2002–2008,* edited by Lansana Gberie. Waterloo, Ontario: Wilfred Laurier University Press, 2009.

Ghani, Ashraf, and Clare Lockhart. *Fixing Failed States: A Framework for Fixing a Fractured World.* Oxford: Oxford University Press, 2008.

Giustozzi, Antonio. *Respectable Warlords? The Politics of State-Building in Post-Taliban Afghanistan.* Working Paper no. 33. London: LSE Crisis States Research Centre, 2003.

Gompert, David, Olga Oliker, Brooke Stearns Lawson, Keith Crane, and K. Jack Riley. *Making Liberia Safe: Transformation of the National Security Sector.* Santa Monica, CA: RAND, 2006.

Goodhand, Jonathan, and David Hulme. "From Wars to Complex Political Emergencies: Understanding Conflict and Peace-Building in the New World Order." *Third World Quarterly* 20, no. 1(1999): 13–26.

Gould, David, ed. *The New Conditionality: The Politics of PRSPs.* London: Zed, 2005.

Government of South Africa, Department of Public Service and Administration (DPSA). "South Africa's E-Government Experience: Towards the Next Steps." Presentation to MinExco, Reserve Bank, Tshwane-Pretoria, April 14–18, 2008.

Government of Uganda. *Peace, Recovery and Development Plan for Northern Uganda.* Kampala, 2007.

———. *Referral of the Situation concerning the Lord's Resistance Army Submitted by the Republic of Uganda.* December 16, 2003.

Grävingholt, Siehe J., Stefan Gänzle, and Sebastian Ziaja. "Policy Brief: Concepts of Peace-Building and State Building—How Compatible Are They?" Berlin: German Development Institute, 1990.

Greenhill, Kelly, and Solomon Major. "The Perils of Profiling: Civil War Spoilers and the Collapse of Intrastate Peace Accords." *International Security* 31, no. 3 (2006): 7–40.

Hagman, Lotta. *Lessons Learned: Peace-Building in Haiti.* New York: International Peace Academy, 2002.

Hague Convention IV and Regulation (1907); Geneva Convention III (1949).

Hänggi, Heiner. "Security Sector Reform." In *Post-Conflict Peacebuilding: A Lexicon,* edited by Vincent Chetail, 337–49. Oxford: Oxford University Press, 2009.

Hänggi, Heiner, and Vincenza Scherrer. *Towards a Common UN Approach to Security Sector Reform: Lessons Learned from Integrated Missions.* Policy Paper no. 25. Geneva: DCAF, 2007.

Hanlon, Joseph. "Bringing It All Together: A Case Study of Mozambique." In *Post-Conflict Development: Meeting New Challenges,* edited by Gerd Junne and Willemijn Verkoren, 273–87. Boulder: Rienner, 2005.

———. *Peace without Profit: How the IMF Blocks Rebuilding in Mozambique.* Oxford: Currey, 1996.

Hanson-Alp, Rosalind. "Civil Society's Role in Sierra Leone's Reform Process: Experiences from Conciliation Resources' West Africa Programme." In *Security System Transformation in Sierra Leone, 1997–2007,* Working Paper no. 7, edited by Paul Jackson and Peter Albrecht. Birmingham, UK GFN-SSR and International Alert, 2009.

Hara, Fabienne. "Burundi: A Case of Parallel Diplomacy." In *Herding Cats: Multiparty Mediation in a Complex World,* edited by Chester A. Crocker, Fen Osler Hampson, and Pamela Aall, 135–158. Washington, DC: US Institute of Peace, 1999.

Harbeson, John W. "Military Rulers in African Politics." In *The Military in African Politics,* edited by John W. Harbeson, 1–20. New York: Praeger and Johns Hopkins University Press, 1987.

Harris, Ian M., Larry J. Fisk, and Carol Rank. "A Portrait of University Peace Studies in North America and Western Europe at the End of the Millennium." *International Journal of Peace Studies* 3 no. 1 (1998): 91–112.

Harrison, Graham. *The World Bank and Africa: The Construction of Governance States.* London: Routledge, 2004.

———. "The World Bank and Theories of Political Action in Africa." *British Journal of Politics and International Relations* 7, no. 2 (2004): 215–40.

Hartzell, Caroline, and Matthew Hoddie. *Crafting Peace: Power-Sharing Institutions and the Negotiated Settlement of Civil Wars.* University Park: Pennsylvania State University Press, 2007.

Heathershaw, John. "Seeing Like the International Community: How Peacebuilding Failed (and Survived) in Tajikistan." *Journal of Intervention and Statebuilding* 2, no. 3 (2008): 329–51.

———. "Unpacking the Liberal Peace: The Dividing and Merging of Peacebuilding Discourses." *Millennium: Journal of International Studies* 36, no. 3 (2008): 597–621.

Heathershaw, John, and Daniel Lambach. "Introduction: Post-Conflict Spaces and Approaches to Statebuilding." *Journal of Intervention and Statebuilding* 2, no. 3 (2008): 269–89.

Hennop, Ettiene. *Operations Rachel 1995–2001* Occasional Paper no. 53 (Pretoria: Institute for Security Studies, 2001).

Herbst, Jeffrey. "Responding to State Failure in Africa." *International Security* 21, no. 3 (1996–97): 120–44.

Hermele, Kenneth. "Guerra e estabilização: Uma análise a médio prazo do Programa de Recuperação Económica de Moçambique (PRE)." *Revista Internacional de Estudos Africanos* nos. 8–9 (1988): 339–49.

———. *Mozambican Crossroads: Economic and Politics in the Era of Structural Adjustment.* Report no. 3. Bergen: Chr. Michelsen Institute, 1990.

Hewlett-Bolton, Anthony C. "Aiming at Holistic Approaches to Justice Sector Development." In *Security System Transformation in Sierra Leone, 1997–2007*, Working Paper no. 7, edited by Paul Jackson and Peter Albrecht. Birmingham, UK GFN-SSR and International Alert, 2009.

Heywood, Andrew. *Key Concepts in Politics.* Palgrave Key Concepts. Basingstoke: Palgrave, 2000.

Hill, Richard, Jon Temin, and Lisa Pacholek. "Building Security Where There Is No Security." *Journal of Peacebuilding and Development* 3, no. 2 (2007): 38–52.

Hoffman, Bruce. "The Pragmatist." *Atlantic Monthly*, July–August 2004.

Hoffman, Mark. "What Is Left of the Liberal Peace?" *LSE Connect* 21, no. 2 (2009): 10–11.

Hoge, Warren. "UN Gives Suspect List to Prosecutor." *International Herald Tribune*, April 7, 2005.

Höhne, Markus V. "Political Identity, Emerging State Structures, and Conflict in Northern Somalia." *Journal of Modern African Studies* 44, no. 3 (2006), 397–414.

Holsti, Kalevi. *The State, War, and the State of War.* Cambridge: Cambridge University Press, 1996.

Holtzman, Steven. *Rethinking "Relief" and "Development" in Transitions from Conflict*, Occasional Paper. Washington, DC: Brookings Institution, January 1999.

Honwana, Alcinda. "Children of War: Understanding War and War Cleansing in Mozambique and Angola." In *Civilians in War*, edited by Simon Chesterman, 123–42. Boulder: Rienner, 2001.

Howard, Lise Morjé. "UN Peace Implementation in Namibia: The Causes of Success." *International Peacekeeping* 9, no. 1 (2002): 99–132.

Human Rights Watch (HRW). *Killings in Kiwanja: The UN's Inability to Protect Civilians.* Washington, DC, December 2008.

———. *Nigeria: Crackdown in the Niger Delta.* May 1, 1999.

———. *Nigeria, the Niger Delta: No Democratic Dividend.* New York, 2002.

———. *The Price of Oil: Corporate Responsibility and Human Rights Violations in Nigeria's Oil Producing Communities.* January 1999.

———. *Rivers and Blood: Guns, Oil and Power in Nigeria's Rivers State.* February 2005.

———. *Selling Justice Short: Why Accountability Matters for Peace.* July 7, 2009.

———. *Sudan: Stop Abyei Abuses, Hold Forces Accountable.* May 26, 2011.

Human Security Centre. *Human Security Brief 2006.* Vancouver: Liu Institute for Global Issues, University of British Columbia, 2006.

———. *Human Security Brief 2007.* Vancouver: Liu Institute for Global Issues, University of British Columbia, 2008.

———. *Human Security Report 2005: War and Peace in the 21st Century.* Oxford: Oxford University Press, 2005.

Human Security Report 2009/2010. *The Causes of Peace and the Shrinking Costs of War.* Vancouver: Simon Fraser University, 2011.

Hume, Cameron. *Ending Mozambique's War: The Role of Mediation and Good Offices.* Washington, DC: United States Institute of Peace Press, 1994.

Huyse, Luc. "Justice after Transition: On the Choices Successor Elites Make in Dealing with the Past." *Law and Social Inquiry* 20, no. 1 (1995): 51–78.

Ifejika, Ezidinma N. "Namibia: The UNTAG Experience." Paper presented at the conference "Restructuring the Security Forces for a New South Africa," Harare, Zimbabwe, January 26–28, 1994. Also in *The Southern African Peacekeeping and Peacemaking Project.* New York: Institute of International Education, 1994.

Ihonvbere, Julius. "Critical Evaluation of the Failed 1990 Coup in Nigeria." *Journal of Modern African Studies* 29, no. 4 (1991): 601–26.

Ikelegbe, Augustine. "Engendering Civil Society: Oil, Women Groups, and Resource Conflicts in the Niger Delta Region of Nigeria." *Journal of Modern African Studies* 43, no. 2 (2005): 241–70.

International Commission on Intervention and State Sovereignty (ICISS). *The Responsibility to Protect: Report of the International Commission on Intervention and State Sovereignty.* Ottawa: International Development Research Centre, 2001.

International Criminal Court. *Ninth Report of the Prosecutor of the International Criminal Court to the UN Security Council Pursuant to UNSCR 1593 (2005).* June 2009.

———. "Statement of the Prosecutor of the International Criminal Court to the United Nations Security Council on the Situation in Darfur, the Sudan, pursuant to UNSCR 1593 (2005)." June 5, 2009.

International Criminal Court–Office of the Prosecutor (ICC-OTP). "Paper on Some Policy Issues before the Office of the Prosecutor." September 2003.

———. "Policy Paper on the Interests of Justice." 2007.

International Crisis Group (ICG). *Burundi: Democracy and Peace at Risk,* Africa Report no. 120. Nairobi, November 30, 2006.

———. *Darfur Rising: Sudan's New Crisis,* Africa Report no. 76. Nairobi/Brussels, March 25, 2004.

———. *Fuelling the Niger Delta Crisis.* Africa Report no. 118. Brussels, September 28, 2006.

———. *The Khartoum-SPLA Agreement: Sudan's Uncertain Peace,* Africa Report no. 96. Nairobi/Brussels, July 25, 2005.

———. *Liberia: Uneven Progress in Security Sector Reform,* Africa Report no. 148. Brussels, January 12, 2009.

———. *Liberia and Sierra Leone: Rebuilding Failed States,* Africa Report no. 87. Dakar/Brussels, December 8, 2004.

———. *Security Sector Reform in the Congo,* Africa Report no. 104. Nairobi/ Brussels, February 13, 2006.

———. *Sierra Leone after Elections: Politics as Usual,* Africa Report, no. 49. Freetown and Brussels, July 15, 2002.

International Development Association. "IDA 14: Aid Delivery to Conflict Affected IDA Countries—The Role of the World Bank." Athens: November 2004.

International Monetary Fund. *Rebuilding Fiscal Institutions in Post-Conflict Countries.* Washington, DC: IMF, Fiscal Affairs Department, 2004.

International Peace Academy. *The Infrastructure of Peace in Africa: Assessing the Peacebuilding Capacity of African Institutions.* New York, 2002.

Isima, Jeffrey. "Cash Payments in Disarmament, Demobilisation, and Reintegration Programmes in Africa." *Journal of Security Sector Management* 2, no. 3 (2004).

Jackson, Paul. "Chiefs, Money, and Politicians: Rebuilding Local Government in Post-War Sierra Leone." *Public Administration and Development* 25, no. 1 (2005): 49–58.

Jahn, Beate. "The Tragedy of Liberal Diplomacy: Democratization, Intervention, Statebuilding (Part 1)." *Journal of Intervention and Statebuilding* 1, no. 1 (2007): 87–106.

———. "The Tragedy of Liberal Diplomacy: Democratization, Intervention, Statebuilding (Part 2)." *Journal of Intervention and Statebuilding* 1, no. 2 (2007): 211–29.

Jarstad, Anna, and Timothy D. Sisk. *From War to Democracy: Dilemmas of Peacebuilding.* Cambridge: Cambridge University Press, 2008.

Jaye, Thomas. "An Assessment Report on Security Sector Reform in Liberia." Monrovia: Governance Reform Commission, September 22, 2006.

———. "Expert Networks and Security Sector Transformation." In *Security Sector Transformation in Africa,* edited by Alan Bryden and 'Funmi Olonisakin. Geneva: Geneva Centre for the Democratic Control of Armed Forces, 2010.

———. "Liberia: Parliamentary Oversight and Lessons Learned from Internationalized Security Sector Reform." New York: Centre on International Cooperation, 2009.

Jaye, Thomas, and Osman Gbla. "Parliamentary Needs Assessment." Parliamentary Oversight Committee on Defense, Internal, and Presidential Affairs of the Republic of Sierra Leone, 2008.

Jenkins, Rob. "Organizational Change and Institutional Survival: The Case of the UN Peacebuilding Commission." *Seton Hall Law Review* 38 (2008): 1327–64.

Jennings, Kathleen M. "The Struggle to Satisfy: DDR Through the Eyes of Ex-Combatants in Liberia." *International Peacekeeping* 14, no. 2 (2007): 1–15.

———. "Unclear Ends, Unclear Means: Reintegration in Postwar Societies—The Case of Liberia." *Global Governance* 14, no. 3 (2008): 327–45.

Jeong, Ho-Won. *Peacebuilding in Postconflict Societies: Strategy and Processes.* Boulder: Rienner, 2005.

Johnson, Douglas. *The Root Causes of Sudan's Civil Wars.* Oxford: Currey, 2003.

Johnson, Isabelle. *Redefining the Concept Good Governance.* Ottawa: Canadian International Development Agency, July 2007.

Jonah, James O. C. "The Security Council, the General Assembly, the Economic and Social Council, and the Secretariat." In *From Global Apartheid to Global Village: Africa and the United Nations,* edited by Adekeye Adebajo, 65–86. Scottsville: University of KwaZulu-Natal Press, 2009.

Junne, Gerd, and Willemijn Verkoren eds. *Post-Conflict Development: Meeting New Challenges.* Boulder: Rienner, 2005.

Kahler, Miles. "Aid and State Building." Paper delivered at the annual meeting of the American Political Science Association, Chicago, August 30–September 2, 2007.

Kahn, Clea, and Elena Lucchi. "Are Humanitarians Fuelling Conflicts? Evidence from Eastern Chad and Darfur." *Humanitarian Exchange Magazine,* no. 43, June 2009.

Kalyvas, Stathis N. *The Logic of Violence in Civil War.* Cambridge: Cambridge University Press, 2006.

Kandeh, Jimmy. "Rogue Incumbents, Donor Assistance, and Sierra Leone's Second Post-Conflict Elections of 2007." *Journal of Modern African Studies* 46, no. 4 (2008): 603–35.

Kasereka, Roger. "Dynamiques locales et pressions extérieures dans la conflictualité armée au Nord-Kivu: Cas des territoires de Beni-Lubero." PhD diss., University of Ghent, 2010.

Keen, David. *The Benefits of Famine: A Political Economy of Famine and Relief in Southwestern Sudan, 1983–89.* Oxford: Currey, 2008.

———. *Complex Emergencies.* Cambridge: Polity, 2008.

———. *Conflict and Collusion in Sierra Leone.* London: Palgrave Macmillan, 2005.

———. "Liberalization and Conflict." *International Political Science Review* 26 no. 1 (2005): 73–89.

———. "War and Peace: What's the Difference?" In *International Peacekeeping,* special issue, "Managing Armed Conflicts in the 21st Century," 7, no. 4 (2001): 1–22.

Keen, David, and Vivian Lee. "Civilian Status and the New Security Agendas." In *Realising Protection: The Uncertain Benefits of Civilian, Refugee, and IDP Status,* by Sarah Collinson, James Darcy, Nicholas Waddell, and Anna Schmidt. HPG Report no. 29. London: Overseas Development Institute, 2009.

Kennedy, David. *The Dark Sides of Virtue: Reassessing International Humanitarianism.* Princeton: Princeton University Press, 2004.

Kievelitz, Uwe, Thomas Schaef, Manuela Leonhardt, Herwig Hahn, and Sonja Vorweck. *Practical Guide to Multilateral Needs Assessments in Post-Conflict Situations.* Social Development Paper no. 15. New York: United Nations Development Group, 2004.

King, Charles. *Ending Civil Wars.* Adelphi Paper no. 308. London: Oxford University Press, 1997.

Kingma, Kees. "Demobilisation, Reintegration, and Peace-Building." In *Demilitarisation and Peace-Building in Southern Africa: Concepts and Processes,* vol. 1, edited by Peter Batchelor and Kees Kingma, 133–62. Aldershot: Ashgate, 2004.

———. "Demobilization, Reintegration, and Peacebuilding in Africa." *International Peacekeeping* 9, no. 2 (2002): 181–201.

Kirsch, Philippe. "Address to the United Nations General Assembly," November 1, 2007.

———. "Introductory Remarks." In *The International Criminal Court and National Jurisdictions,* edited by Mauro Politi and Federica Gioia, 1–6. Aldershot: Ashgate, 2008.

Knight, Mark, and Alpaslan Ozerdem. "Guns, Camps, and Cash: Disarmament, Demobilization, and Reinsertion of Former Combatants in Transitions from War to Peace." *Journal of Peace Research* 41, no. 4 (2004): 499–516.

Knight, W. Andy. "Disarmament, Demobilization, and Reintegration and Post-Conflict Peacebuilding in Africa: An Overview." *African Security* 1, no. 1 (2008): 24–52.

Kotze, Dirk. "Democratisation and Development: A Difficult Relationship." In *Palgrave Advances in Peacebuilding: Critical Developments and Approaches,* edited by Oliver P. Richmond, 213–34. Basingstoke: Palgrave Macmillan, 2010.

Kreimer, Alcira, John Eriksson, Robert Muscat, Margaret Arnold, and Colin Scott. *The World Bank's Experience with Post-Conflict Reconstruction.* Washington, DC: World Bank, Operations Evaluation Department, 1988.

Kritz, Neil J. "Coming to Terms with Atrocities: A Review of Accountability Mechanisms for Mass Violations of Human Rights." *Law and Contemporary Problems* 59, no. 4 (1996): 127–52.

Landsberg, Chris. "The Birth and Evolution of NEPAD." In *The African Union and Its Institutions,* edited by John Akokpari, Angela Ndinga-Muvumba, and Tim Murithi, 207–26. Johannesburg: Jacana, 2008.

Landsman, Stephan. "Alternative Responses to Serious Human Rights Abuses: Of Prosecution and Truth Commissions." *Law and Contemporary Problems* 59, no. 4 (1996): 81–92.

Le Billon, Philippe. "The Political Ecology of Transition in Cambodia, 1989–1999: War, Peace and Forest Exploitation." *Development and Change* 31 (September 2000), 785–805.

Le Billon, Philippe, and Estelle Levin. "Building Peace with Conflict Diamonds? Merging Security and Development in Sierra Leone." *Development and Change* 40, no. 4 (2009): 693–715.

Lebor, Adam. *Complicity with Evil: The United Nations in the Age of Modern Genocide.* New Haven: Yale University Press, 2006.

Lecoutere, Els, Koen Vlassenroot, and Timothy Raeymaekers. "Conflict, Institutional Changes, and Food Insecurity in Eastern DR Congo." *Afrika Focus* 22, no. 3 (2009): 41–63.

Lederach, John Paul. *Building Peace: Sustainable Reconciliation in Divided Societies.* Washington, DC: US Institute of Peace Press, 1997.

———. *The Moral Imagination: The Art and Soul of Building Peace.* Oxford: Oxford University Press, 2005.

Lemarchand, René. "Burundi 1972: Genocide Denied, Revised, and Remembered." In *Forgotten Genocides: Oblivion, Denial, and Memory,* edited by René Lemarchand, 37–50. Philadelphia: University of Pennsylvania Press, 2011.

———. *Dynamics of Violence in Central Africa.* Philadelphia: University of Pennsylvania Press, 2009.

———. "Genocide in the Great Lakes: Which Genocide? Whose Genocide?" In *Dynamics of Violence in Central Africa,* edited by René Lemarchand, 69–78. Philadelphia: University of Pennsylvania Press, 2009.

———. "The 1994 Rwanda Genocide." In *Century of Genocide: Critical Essays and Eyewitness Accounts,* edited by Samuel Totten and William Parsons, 395–414. New York: Routledge, 2009.

———. "Reflections on the Crisis in Eastern Congo." *Brown Journal of World Affairs* 16, no. 1 (2009): 119–32.

Le Roux, Len. "The Governance of Defence in South Africa: Eleven Years into Democracy." Unpublished paper written for the African Security Sector Network project on Governing Security Establishments, 2005.

Le Sage, Andre. "Engaging the Political Economy of Conflict: Towards a Radical Humanitarianism." *Civil Wars* 1, no. 4 (1998): 27–55.

Lewis, Ioan M. *Understanding Somalia and Somaliland: Culture, History, and Society.* London: Hurst, 2008.

Lidén, Kristoffer, Roger Mac Ginty, and Oliver Richmond, eds. "Liberal Peacebuilding Reconstructed." *International Peacekeeping Special Issue* 16, no. 5 (November 2009).

Lord's Resistance Army. "LRA Position Paper on Accountability Truth and Reconciliation in the Context of Alternative Justice System for Resolving the Northern/ Eastern Ugandan and Southern Sudan Conflicts." Juba, August 19, 2006.

Luckham, Robin. *The Politics of Institutional Design: A Concept Paper on Strengthening Democratic Governance in Conflict-Torn Societies.* Working paper. Sussex: Institute of Development Studies, 2000.

Lunn, John. *The African Great Lakes Region: An End to Conflict?* Working Paper no. 06/51. London: House of Commons, International Affairs and Defense Section, October 2006.

Luttwak, Edward. "Give War a Chance." *Foreign Affairs* 78, no. 1 (1999): 36–44.

Lyons, Terrence, and Ahmed Samatar. *Somalia: State Collapse, Multilateral Intervention, and Strategies of Political Reconstruction.* Washington, DC: Brookings Institution, 1995.

Mac Ginty, Roger. *No War, No Peace: The Rejuvenation of Stalled Peace Processes and Peace Accords*. Baskingstoke: Palgrave Macmillan, 2006.

———. "Reconstructing Post-War Lebanon: A Challenge to the Liberal Peace?" *Conflict, Security, and Governance* 7, no. 3 (2007): 457–82.

MacQueen, Norrie. "Peacekeeping by Attrition: The United Nations in Angola." *Journal of Modern African Studies* 36, no. 3 (1998): 399–422.

Malik, Nesrine. "Sudan Election Didn't Need Fraud." *Guardian,* April 24, 2010. http://www.guardian.co.uk/commentisfree.

Malone, David M., and Heiko Nitzschke. "Economic Agendas in Civil Wars: What We Know, What We Need to Know." Discussion Paper no. 2005/07, WIDER, United Nations University, 2005.

Mamdani, Mahmood. *Citizen and Subject: Contemporary Africa and the Legacy of Late Colonialism*. Princeton: Princeton University Press, 1996.

———. "From Justice to Reconciliation: Making Sense of the African Experience." In *Crisis and Reconstruction,* edited by Colin Leys and Mahmood Mamdani, 17–25. Uppsala: Nordisk Afrikainstitutet, 1997.

———. "The Politics of Naming: Genocide, Civil War, Insurgency." *London Review of Books,* March 8, 2007.

Mani, Rama. *Beyond Retribution: Seeking Justice in the Shadows of War*. Cambridge: Polity, 2002.

Mansfield, Edward, and Jack Snyder. *Electing to Fight: Why Emerging Democracies Go to War*. Boston: MIT Press, 2005.

Marshall, Judith. *War, Debt, and Structural Adjustment in Mozambique: The Social Impact*. Ottawa: North-South Institute, 1992.

Martin, Harriet. *Kings of Peace, Pawns of War: The Untold Story of Peace-Making*. London: Continuum, 2006.

Marysse, Stefaan, and Sara Geenen. "Les contrats chinois en RDC: L'impérialisme rouge en marche?" In *L'Afrique des Grands Lacs, annuaire 2007–2008,* 287–313. Paris: L'Harmattan, 2009.

Matloff, Judith. "Crisis in the Heart of Africa." *Christian Science Monitor,* October 30, 1996.

Maundi, Mohammed Omar, et al. *Getting In: Mediators' Entry into the Settlement of African Conflicts*. Washington, DC: US Institute of Peace Press, 2006.

Máusse, Miguel A. "The Social Reintegration of the Child Involved in Armed Conflict in Mozambique." *South Africa: Institute for Security Studies,* Monograph 37, April 1999.

Mbembe, Achille, and Sarah Nuttall. "Writing the World from an African Metropolis." *Public Culture* 16, no. 3 (2004): 347–72.

McAskie, Carolyn. "The International Peacebuilding Challenge: Can New Players and New Approaches Bring New Results?" Lloyd Shaw Lecture in Public Affairs, Dalhousie University, Halifax, Nova Scotia, November 22, 2007.

McGovern, Mike. *Making War in Côte d'Ivoire*. London: Hurst, 2011.

McMullin, Jaremey. "Reintegration of Combatants: Were the Right Lessons Learned in Mozambique?" *International Peacekeeping* 11, no. 4 (2004): 625–43.

Menkhaus, Ken. "The Crisis in Somalia: Tragedy in Five Acts." *African Affairs* 106, no. 424 (2007): 357–90.

———. "Governance without Government in Somalia: Spoilers, State Building, and the Politics of Coping." *International Security* 31, no. 3 (2006–7): 74–106.

———. *Impact Assessment in Post Conflict Peace Building: Challenges and Future Directions*. London: Interpeace, International Peace Building Alliance, July 2004.

————. "Somalia: Governance vs. Statebuilding." In *Building States to Build Peace,* edited by Charles T. Call, 187–215. Boulder: Rienner, 2008.

Menkhaus, Ken, and John Prendergast. *Political Economy of Post-Intervention Somalia.* Somalia Task Force Issue Paper no. 3 (April 1995), http://www.netnomad.com/menkhaus.html.

Metsola, Lalli, and Henning Melber. "Namibia's Pariah Heroes: SWAPO Ex-Combatants Between Liberation Gospel and Security Interests." In *The Security-Development Nexus: Expressions of Sovereignty and Securitization in Southern Africa,* edited by Lars Buur, Steffen Jensen, and Finn Stepputat, 85–105. Uppsala: NordiskaAfrikainstitutet, 2007.

Mhone, Guy C. Z. "Developmentalism and the Role of the State." Paper prepared for workshop on Growth and Development for the Premier's Policy Development Unit, KwaZulu Natal Provincial Government, February 2003.

Michailof, Serge, Markus Kostner, and Xavier Devictor. *Post-Conflict Recovery in Africa: An Agenda for the Africa Region.* Africa Regional Working Paper no. 30. Washington, DC: World Bank, 2001.

Milliken, Jennifer, and Keith Krause. "State Failure, State Collapse, and State Reconstruction: Concepts, Lessons, and Strategies." *Development and Change* 33, no. 5 (2002): 753–74.

Mkandawire, Thandika. "Thinking about Development States in Africa." *Cambridge Journal of Economics* 25, no. 3 (2001): 289–314.

Moller, Bjorn. *Africa's Sub-Regional Organizations: Seamless Web or Patchwork?* Regional and Global Axes of Conflict, Working Paper no. 56. Copenhagen: Danish Institute of International Affairs, August 2009.

Moore, David. "Levelling the Playing Fields and Embedding Illusions: 'Post-Conflict' Discourse and Neo-Liberal 'Development' in War-Torn Africa." *Review of African Political Economy* 27, no. 83 (2000): 11–28.

Moreno-Ocampo, Luis. "Building a Future on Peace and Justice." Presentation at the eponymous conference in Nuremberg, June 25, 2007, 2.

————. "The International Criminal Court: Seeking Global Justice." *Case Western Reserve University Journal of International Law* 40, nos. 1–2 (2008): 215–25.

————. "Remarks by the Prosecutor of the International Criminal Court." Chicago, April 9, 2008.

————. "Statement at the Eleventh Diplomatic Briefing of the International Criminal Court." ICC-DB11-ST-LMO-ENG, The Hague, October 10, 2007.

————. "Statement on the Uganda Arrest Warrants." The Hague, October 14, 2005.

Moro, Leben. "Oil, Conflict, and Displacement in Sudan." D.Phil. thesis, Oxford University, 2008.

Muggah, Robert. "No Magic Bullet: A Critical Perspective on Disarmament, Demobilization, and Reintegration (DDR) and Weapons Reduction in Post-Conflict Contexts." *Round Table* 94, no. 379 (April 2005): 239–52.

Mugumya, Geoffrey. *Exchanging Weapons for Development in Mali: Weapons Collection Programmes Assessed by Local People.* Geneva: UNIDIR, 2004.

Murithi, Tim. "African Indigenous and Endogenous Approaches to Peace and Conflict Resolution." In *Peace and Conflict in Africa,* edited by David Francis, 16–30. London: Zed Books, 2008.

————. "The UN Peacebuilding Commission," In *From Global Apartheid to Global Village: Africa and the United Nations,* edited by Adekeye Adebajo, 351–72. Scottsville: University of KwaZulu-Natal Press, 2009.

————. "Towards a Symbiotic Partnership: The UN Peace Building Commission and the Evolving AU/NEPAD Post-Conflict Reconstruction Framework." In *A*

Dialogue of the Deaf: Essays on Africa and the United Nations, edited by Adekeye Adebajo and Helen Scanlon, 243–60, Durban: University of KwaZulu-Natal Press, 2006.

Mwanasali, Musifiky. "The View from Below." In *Greed and Grievance: Economic Agendas in Civil Wars,* edited by Mats Berdal and David M. Malone, 137–53. Boulder: Rienner, 2000.

Myrttinen, Henri. "Disarming Masculinities." *Disarmament Forum* 4 (2003): 37–46.

Nakaya, Sumie. *Aid in Post Conflict (Non) State Building: A Synthesis.* New York: City University of New York, Program on States and Security, http://www.statesandsecurity.org/_pdfs/Nakaya.pdf.

Nathan, Laurie. *No Ownership, No Commitment: A Guide to Local Ownership of Security Sector Reform.* Birmingham: University of Birmingham, 2007.

New Partnership for Africa's Development (NEPAD). *African Post-Conflict Reconstruction Policy Framework.* Midrand: NEPAD Secretariat, Governance, Peace, and Security Programme, July 2005.

———. "Declaration on Democracy: Political, Economic, and Corporate Governance." AHG/235 (XXXVIII) Annex 1, June 18, 2002.

———. "Governance in Africa's Development: Progress, Prospects, and Challenges." Ninth Africa Partnership Forum, Governance and Development, Algiers, November 12–13, 2007.

———. "G8-Africa Action Plan," G8 Kananaskis Summit, Canada, 2002.

Newbury, David. *The Land Beyond the Mists: Essays on Identity and Authority in Precolonial Congo and Rwanda.* Athens: Ohio University Press, 2009.

Nielsen, Barbara. "Sudan Experience Project: Interview #7, 1 June 2006." In *Sudan Experience Project,* edited by US Institute of Peace and Association for Diplomatic Studies and Training, 1–20. Washington: US Institute of Peace Press, 2006.

Nilsson, Anders. *Reintegrating Ex-Combatants in Post-Conflict Societies.* Stockholm: Swedish International Development Cooperation Agency [SIDA], 2005.

Nouwen, Sarah. "Complementarity in Uganda: Domestic Diversity or International Imposition?" In *The International Criminal Court and Complementarity: From Theory to Practice,* edited by Carsten Stahn and Mohamed El Zeidy. Cambridge: Cambridge University Press, 2011.

———. "Justifying Justice." In *The Cambridge Companion to International Law,* edited by James Crawford and Martti Koskenniemi, 327–51. Cambridge: Cambridge University Press, 2012.

Nouwen, Sarah, and Wouter Werner. "Doing Justice to the Political: The International Criminal Court in Uganda and Sudan." *European Journal of International Law* 21, no. 4 (2010): 941–65.

Nzongola-Ntalaja, Georges. *The Congo from Leopold to Kabila: A People's History.* London: Zed Books, 2002.

Ohlson, Thomas, and Stephen John Stedman. *The New Is Not Yet Born: Conflict Resolution in Southern Africa.* Washington, DC: Brookings Institution, 1994.

Okumu, Wafula. "The African Union: Pitfalls and Prospects for Uniting Africa." *Journal of International Affairs* 62, no. 2 (2009): 93–111.

Olonisakin, 'Funmi. *Peacekeeping in Sierra Leone: The Story of UNAMSIL.* Boulder: Rienner, 2008.

Open Society Justice Initiative. *Between Law and Society: Paralegals and Primary Justice Services in Sierra Leone.* New York, 2006.

Orend, Brian. "Justice after War." *Ethics and International Affairs* 16, no. 1 (2002): 43–56.

Orentlicher, Diane F. "Settling Accounts: The Duty to Prosecute Human Rights Violations of a Prior Regime." *Yale Law Journal* 100, no. 8 (1991): 2537–2615.

Organisation for Economic Cooperation and Development (OECD). *Concepts and Dilemmas of Statebuilding in Fragile Situations: From Fragility to Resilience.* Paris: OECD, Development Assistance Committee, 2008.

———. *Participatory Development and Good Governance.* Paris, 1995.

———. *Supporting Statebuilding in Situations of Conflict and Fragility, Policy Guidance.* Paris: OECD, Development Assistance Committee, 2011.

Otobo, Eloho. "A UN Architecture to Build Peace in Post-Conflict Situations." *Development Outreach: Fragility and Conflict* 11, no. 2 (October 2009): 46–49.

Owen, Taylor. "Human Security: Conflict, Critique, and Consensus." *Security Dialogue* 35, no. 3 (2004): 373–87.

Oyefusi, Aderoju. "Oil-Dependence and Civil Conflict in Nigeria." Centre for the Study Of African Economies, University of Oxford, CSAE WP 2007-09, Oxford: CSAE.

———. "Oil-Dependence and Civil Conflict in Nigeria." PhD diss., University of Benin, 2007.

———. "Trust and the Breakdown of Civil Order in Nigeria's Delta Region: Evidence from Historical Conflict Episodes." *Round Table* 98, no. 403 (2009): 483–92.

Ozerdem, Alpaslan. "Disarmament, Demobilization, and Reintegration of Former Combatants in Afghanistan: Lessons Learned from Cross-Cultural Perspective." *Third World Quarterly* 23, no. 5 (2002): 961–75.

Paes, Wolf-Christian. "Eyewitness: The Challenges of Disarmament, Demobilisation, and Reintegration in Liberia." *International Peacekeeping* 12, no. 2 (Summer 2005): 253–61.

Pan-African Ministers Conference for Public and Civil Service. "A Framework for Pan-African Public Administration Involvement in Post-Conflict Reconstruction and Development (PCRD)." Concept paper. Bujumbura, Burundi, April 8–9, 2008.

———. Report on the Launch Conference of the African Management Development Institutes Network. Johannesburg, August 25–26, 2005.

———. Report of the Second Ministerial Bureau Meeting. Addis Ababa, December 10, 2006.

———. Report of the Third Ministerial Bureau Meeting. Johannesburg, March 31, 2007.

———. "Stellenbosch Declaration," Stellenbosch, May 4–7, 2003.

Pantuliano, Sara. "Comprehensive Peace? An Analysis of the Evolving Tension in Eastern Sudan." *Review of African Political Economy* 33, no. 110 (September 2006): 709–20.

Papagianni, Katia. "Participation and State Legitimation." In *Building States to Build Peace,* edited by Charles Call with Vanessa Wyeth, 49–72. Boulder: Rienner, 2008.

Paris, Roland. *At War's End: Building Peace After Civil Conflict.* Cambridge: Cambridge University Press, 2004.

———. "Human Security: Paradigm Shift or Hot Air?" *International Security* 26, no. 2 (2001): 87–102.

Paris, Roland, and Timothy D. Sisk, "Conclusion: Confronting the Contradictions." In *The Dilemmas of Statebuilding: Confronting the Contradictions of Postwar Peace Operations,* edited by Roland Paris and Timothy D. Sisk, 304–15. London: Routledge, 2009.

———. "Introduction: Understanding the Contradictions of Postwar Statebuilding." In *The Dilemmas of Statebuilding: Confronting the Contradictions of Postwar Peace Operations,* edited by Roland Paris and Timothy Sisk, 1–20. London: Routledge, 2009.

————. *Managing Contradictions: The Inherent Dilemmas of Post-War Statebuilding.* New York: International Peace Institute, 2007.

Patel, Ana Cutter, Pablo De Greiff, and Lars Waldorf, eds. *Disarming the Past: Transitional Justice and Ex-combatants.* New York: Social Science Research Council, International Center for Transnational Justice, 2009.

Patrick, Stewart, and Kaysie Brown. *Greater Than the Sum of Its Parts? Assessing "Whole of Government" Approaches to Fragile States.* Boulder: Rienner, 2007.

Pincus, John. "State Simplification and Institution Building in a World Bank Financed Development Project." In *Reinventing the World Bank,* edited by John Pincus and John Winters, 76–101. New York: Cornell University Press, 2002.

Ping, Jean. "Take a Stand for Africa's Peace." *Sunday Independent* (South Africa), July 18, 2010.

Plank, David. "Aid, Debt, and the End of Sovereignty: Mozambique and Its Donors." *Journal of Modern African Studies* 31, no. 3 (1993): 407–30.

Polman, Linda. *The Crisis Caravan: What's Wrong with Humanitarian Aid?* New York: Metropolitan Books, 2010.

————. *We Did Nothing: Why the Truth Doesn't Always Come Out When the UN Goes In.* London: Viking, 1997.

Ponzio, Richard. "United Nations Peacebuilding Commission: Origins and Initial Practice." *Disarmament Forum,* Special issue on the Peacebuilding Commission, UNIDIR no. 2 (2007): 5–15.

Potgieter, Jakkie. "The Price of War and Peace: A Critical Assessment of the Disarmament Component of United Nations Operations in Southern Africa." September 1997, http://www.iss.co.za/pubs/Books/SocietyUnderSiege1/Potgieter.pdf.

Pouligny, Béatrice. "Civil Society and Post-Conflict Peacebuilding: Ambiguities of International Programmes Aimed at Building New Societies." *Security Dialogue* .36, no. 4 (2005): 495–510.

————. "Local Ownership." In *Post-Conflict Peacebuilding: A Lexicon,* edited by Vincent Chetail, 174–87. Oxford: Oxford University Press, 2009.

Powell, Kristiana. *Security Sector Reform and Protection of Civilians in Burundi: Accomplishments, Dilemmas, and Ideas for International Engagement.* CENAP/NSI Paper, July 2007.

Power, Samantha. *Chasing the Flame: One Man's Flight to Save the World.* New York: Penguin, 2008.

Prendergast, John, and Colin Thomas Jensen. "Sudan: A State on the Brink?" *Current History* 108, no. 718 (2009): 208–13.

Preston, Rosemary. "Integrating Fighters after War: Reflections on the Namibian Experience, 1989–1993." *Journal of Southern African Studies* 23, no. 3 (1997): 453–72.

Prunier, Gérard. *Africa's World War: Congo, the Rwandan Genocide, and the Making of a Continental Catastrophe.* Oxford: Oxford University Press, 2009.

————. "Rebel Movements and Proxy Warfare: Uganda, Sudan, and the Congo." *African Affairs* 103, no. 412 (2004): 359–83.

Pugh, Michael. "The Political Economy of Peacebuilding: A Critical Theory Perspective." Submission to the United Nations Commission on Human Rights, 62nd Session, High-Level Task Force on Implementation of the Right to Development, Geneva, November 14–18, 2005. http://www2.ohchr.org/english/issues/development/docs/acuns_rtd_pugh.doc.

Pugh, Michael, Neil Cooper, and Mandy Turner, eds. *Whose Peace? Critical Perspectives on the Political Economy of Peacebuilding.* Basingstoke: Palgrave Macmillan, 2008.

Pupavac, Vanessa. "Refugee Advocacy, Traumatic Representations, and Political Disenchantment." *Government and Opposition* 43, no. 2 (2008): 270–92.

———. "Therapeutic Governance: Psycho-Social Intervention and Trauma Risk Management." *Disasters* 25, no. 4 (2001): 358–72.

Putnam, Tonya L. "Human Rights and Sustainable Peace." In *Ending Civil Wars: The Implementation of Peace Agreements,* edited by Stephen John Stedman, Donald Rothchild, and Elizabeth Cousens, 237–71. Boulder: Rienner, 2002.

Raeymaekers, Timothy. "Sharing the Spoils: The Reinvigoration of Congo's Political System." *Politorbis* 42, no. 1 (2007): 23–29.

Rafeeuddin, Ahmed, Kulessa Manfred, and Malik Khalid M., eds. *The Role of the UNDP in Reintegration and Reconstruction Programmes: Lessons Learnt in Post-Conflict Situations.* New York: United Nations Development Programme, 2002.

Ramsbotham, Oliver, Tom Woodhouse, and Hugh Miall. *Contemporary Conflict Resolution.* 2nd ed. Cambridge: Polity, 2005.

Rashid, Ahmed. "Letter from Afghanistan: Are the Taliban Winning?" *Current History* 106, no. 696 (2007): 17–20.

Rees, Edward. *Security Sector Reform (SSR) and Peace Operations: "Improvisation and Confusion" from the Field.* New York: United Nations, Department of Peacekeeping Operations, March 2006.

Rehn, Elizabeth, and Ellen Johnson Sirleaf. *Women, War, and Peace: The Independent Experts' Assessment on the Impact of Armed Conflict on Women's Role in Peacebuilding.* New York: UNIFEM, 2002.

Reno, William. "Bottom-Up Statebuilding?" In *Building States to Build Peace,* edited by Charles Call with Vanessa Wyeth, 143–62. Boulder: Rienner, 2008.

———. *Warlord Politics and African States.* Boulder: Rienner, 1998.

Reyntjens, Filip. *The Great African War: Congo and Regional Geopolitics, 1996–2006.* Cambridge: Cambridge University Press, 2009.

Reyntjens, Filip, and René Lemarchand. "Mass Murder in Eastern Congo 1996–1997." In *Forgotten Genocides: Essays in Memory, Oblivion, and Denial,* edited by René Lemarchand, 20–36. Philadelphia: University of Pennsylvania Press, 2011.

Richmond, Oliver P. "Becoming Liberal, Unbecoming Liberalism: Liberal-Local Hybridity via the Everyday As a Response to the Paradoxes of Liberal Peacebuilding." *Journal of Intervention and Statebuilding* 3, no. 3 (2009): 324–44.

———, ed. *Palgrave Advances in Peacebuilding.* Basingstoke: Palgrave Macmillan, 2010.

Rigby, Andrew. "Civil Society, Reconciliation, and Conflict Transformation in Post-War Africa." In *Ending Africa's Wars,* edited by Oliver Furley and Roy May, 47–63. Aldershot: Ashgate, 2006.

Rome Statute of the International Criminal Court, July 17, 1998, 2187, United Nations Treaty Series 90.

Rotberg, Robert, ed. *When States Fail: Causes and Consequences.* Princeton: Princeton University Press, 2004.

Rothchild, Donald S. *Managing Ethnic Conflict in Africa: Pressures and Incentives for Cooperation.* Washington, DC: Brookings Institution Press, 1997.

Rugumamu, Severine M. *Does the UN Peacebuilding Commission Change the Mode of Peacebuilding in Africa?* Dialogue on Globalisation Briefing Paper. New York: Friedrich-Ebert-Stiftung, 2009.

Russell, Peter. "The Exclusion of Kosovo from the Dayton Negotiations." *Journal of Genocide Research* 11, no. 4 (2009): 487–511.

Rustad, Siri Aas. "Between War and Peace: 50 Years of Power-Sharing in Nigeria." *CSCW Policy Brief.* Oslo: International Peace Research Institute (PRIO), 6, 2008.

Ruzibiza, Abdul Joshua. *Rwanda: L'histoire secrète.* Paris: Editions du Panama, 2005.

Sadomba, Frederick, and Gwinyayi Albert Dzinesa. "Identity and Exclusion in the Post-War Era: Zimbabwe's Women Former Freedom Fighters." *Journal of Peacebuilding and Development* 2, no. 1 (2004): 51–63.

Samatar, Ahmed. *Socialist Somalia: Rhetoric and Reality.* London: Zed, 1988.

Samuels, Kirsti. "Post-Conflict Peacebuilding and Constitution-Making." *Chicago Journal of International Law* 6, no. 2 (2006): 1–20.

———. "Sustainability and Peace-Building: A Key Challenge." *Development in Practice* 15, no. 6 (2005): 728–36.

Saunders, Chris. "UN Peacekeeping in Southern Africa: Namibia, Angola, and Mozambique." In *From Global Apartheid to Global Village: Africa and the United Nations,* edited by Adekeye Adebajo, 269–82. Scottsville: University of KwaZulu-Natal Press, 2009.

Sayigh, Yezid. *Confronting the 1990s: Security in the Developing Countries.* Adelphi Paper no. 251. London: International Institute for Strategic Studies, 1990.

Schabas, William A. "Prosecutorial Discretion v. Judicial Activism at the International Criminal Court." *Journal of International Criminal Justice* 6, no. 4 (2008): 731–61.

Scharpf, Fritz. *Governing Europe: Effective and Democratic?* Oxford: Oxford University Press, 1999.

Schellhaas, Constanze, and Annette Seegers. "Peacebuilding: Imperialism's New Disguise?" *African Security Review* 18, no. 2 (2009): 2–15.

Scheye, Eric. *Pragmatic Realism in Justice and Security Development: Supporting Improvement in the Performance of Non-State/Local Justice and Security Networks.* The Hague: Clingendael, July 2009.

Schnabel, Albrecht. "Post-Conflict Peace-Building and Second Generation Preventive Action." *International Peacekeeping* 9, no. 2 (2002): 7–30.

Schoeman, Maxi. "South Africa." In *Security and Democracy in Southern Africa,* Wits P&DM Governance Series, edited by Gavin Cawthra, Andre du Pisani, and Abillah Omari, 155–71. Johannesburg: Wits University Press, 2007.

Scott, James. *Seeing Like a State: How Certain Schemes to Improve the Human Condition Have Failed.* New Haven: Yale University Press, 1999.

Serwer, Daniel, and Patricia Thomson. "A Framework for Success: International Intervention in Societies Emerging from Conflict." In *Leashing the Dogs of War,* edited by Chester Crocker, Fen Hampson, and Pamela Aall, 369–87. Washington, DC: US Institute of Peace, 2007.

Shikola, Teckla. "We Left Our Shoes Behind." In *What Women Do in Wartime: Gender and Conflict in Africa,* edited by Meredith Turshen and Clotilde Twagiramariya, 138–49. London: Zed, 1998.

Sibanda, Philip. "Lessons from UN Peacekeeping in Africa: From UNAVEM to MONUA." In *From Peacekeeping to Complex Emergencies: Peace Support Missions in Africa,* edited by Jakkie Cilliers and Greg Mills, 119–27. Johannesburg: South African Institute of International Affairs, 1999.

Sisk, Timothy D. *International Mediation in Civil Wars.* Studies in Security and Conflict Management. London: Routledge, 2008.

Slim, Hugo. *Killing Civilians: Method, Madness, and Morality in War.* London: Hurst, 2007.

Snodgrass, Donald. "Restoring Economic Functioning in Failed States." In *When States Fail: Causes and Consequences,* edited by Robert Rotberg, 256–68. Princeton: Princeton University Press, 2004.

Spear, Joanna. "Disarmament and Demobilisation." In *Ending Civil Wars: The Implementation of Peace Agreements,* edited by Stephen John Stedman, Donald Rothchild, and Elizabeth M. Cousens, 141–82. Boulder: Rienner, 2002.

———. "Disarmament, Demobilisation, Reinsertion, and Reintegration in Africa." In *Ending Africa's Wars: Progressing to Peace,* edited by Oliver Furley and Roy May, 63–80. Aldershot: Ashgate, 2006.

Stearns, Jason. "Laurent Nkunda and the National Congress for the Defence of the People (CNDP)." In *L'Afrique des Grands Lacs, annuaire 2007–2008,* 245–67. Paris: L'Harmattan, 2009.

Stedman, Stephen J. "Negotiation and Mediation in Internal Conflicts." In *The International Dimensions of Internal Conflict,* edited by Michael E. Brown, 341–76. Cambridge: MIT Press, 1996.

———. "Spoiler Problems in Peace Processes." *International Security* 22, no. 2 (1997): 5–53.

Stedman, Stephen J., Donald S. Rothchild, and Elizabeth M. Cousens, eds. *Ending Civil Wars: The Implementation of Peace Agreements.* Boulder: Lynne Rienner, 2002.

Stepanova, Ekaterina. *Anti-Terrorism and Peace-Building during and after Conflict.* Stockholm: SIPRI, June 2003.

Storey, Andy. "Structural Adjustment, State Power, and Genocide: The World Bank and Rwanda." *Review of African Political Economy* 28, no. 89 (2001): 365–85.

Street, Annie, Jennifer Smith, and Howard Mollet. "Experiences of the United Nations Peacebuilding Commission in Sierra Leone and Burundi." *Journal of Peacebuilding and Development* 4, no. 2 (2008): 33–46.

Suchman, Mark. "Managing Legitimacy: Strategic and Institutional Approaches." *Academy of Management Review* 20, no. 3 (1995): 571–610.

Takasu, Yukio. "Note for Effective Joint Endeavours for Peacebuilding." Chairperson of the Peacebuilding Commission. New York, June 23, 2008, http://www.un.emb-japan.go.jp.

Thakur, Ramesh. "Developing Countries and the Intervention-Sovereignty Debate." In *The United Nations and Global Security,* edited by Richard Price and Mark Zacher, 193–208. New York: Palgrave, 2004.

Thomson, Brian. "Sierra Leone: Reform or Relapse? Conflict and Governance Reform." London: Chatham House Report, June 2007.

Thomson, Janice. *Mercenaries, Pirates, and Sovereigns: State-Building and Extra-Territorial Violence in Early Modern Europe.* Princeton: Princeton University Press, 1994.

Thorne, Kristina. "Rule of Law through Imperfect Bodies? The Informal Justice Systems of Burundi and Somalia." *Humanitarian Dialogue* (November 2005): 1–8.

Torjesen, Stina, and Neil MacFarlane. "R before D: The Case of Post Conflict Reintegration in Tajikistan." *Conflict, Security, and Development* 7, no. 2 (2007): 311–32.

Trivedy, Roy. "Conflict Prevention, Resolution, and Management: Improving Coordination for More Effective Action." *IDS Bulletin* 32, no. 2 (2001): 79–89.

Tull, Denis M. "Congo Facing a Third War?" *SWP Comments.* Hamburg: German Institute for International and Security Affairs, September 2004.

Tull, Denis M., and Andreas Mehler. "The Hidden Costs of Power-Sharing: Reproducing Insurgent Violence in Africa." *African Affairs* 104, no. 416 (2005): 375–98.

Turshen, Meredeth, and Clotilde Twagiramariya, eds. *What Women Do in Wartime: Gender and Conflict in Africa.* London: Zed, 1998.

Ukeje, Charles. "From Aba to Ugborodo: Gender Identity and Alternative Discourse of Social Protest among Women in the Oil Delta of Nigeria." *Oxford Development Studies* 32, no. 4 (2004): 605–17.

United Nations. "African Perspectives on Security Sector Reform, Final Report. "New York: May 14, 2010.

————. *The Blue Helmets: A Review of United Nations Peacekeeping.* New York, 1996.

————. *Charter of the United Nations,* June 6, 1945, art. 39.

————. "First Session of the Organisational Committee of the UN Peacebuilding Commission." May 18, 2007.

————. *Implementing the Responsibility to Protect.* Report of the Secretary-General, UN Doc. A/63/677, January 12, 2009.

————. *In Larger Freedom: Towards Development, Security, and Human Rights for All.* Report of the Secretary-General, UN General Assembly, 59th Session, March 21, 2005.

————. *Integrated Disarmament, Demobilization, and Reintegration Standards (IDDRS).* New York, 2006.

————. *A More Secure World: Our Shared Responsibility,* Report of the UN High-Level Panel on Threats, Challenges, and Change. New York, 2004.

————. *No Exit without Strategy: Security Council Decision-Making and the Closure or Transition of United Nations Peacekeeping Operations.* Report of the Secretary-General, UN Doc. S/2001/391, April 20, 2001, 2.

————. *Peace Accords for Angola,* UN Doc. S/22609, May 17, 1991.

————. "The Peacebuilding Commission." Resolution 60/180, adopted by the General Assembly, 60th Session, on December 30, 2005.

————. "Peacebuilding Commission Guidelines for the Participation of Civil Society in the Meetings of the Peacebuilding Commission." Submitted by the Chairman on the Basis of Informal Consultations, June 2007.

————. *Report of the Ad Hoc Committee on the Establishment of an International Criminal Court.* UN Doc. A/50/22, 1995.

————. *Report of the Panel of Experts on Violations of Security Council Sanctions Against UNITA.* UN Doc. S/2000/203 March 10, 2000.

————. *Report of the Panel on United Nations Peace Operations (Brahimi Report).* A/55/305-S/2000/809, 2000.

————. *Report of the Secretary-General on Peacebuilding in the Immediate Aftermath of Conflict.* UN Doc. A/63/881-S/2009/304, June 11, 2009.

————. *Review of the United Nations Peacebuilding Architecture.* A/64/868-S/2010/393. July 21, 2010.

————. "Revised Draft Outcome Document of the High-Level Plenary Meeting of the General Assembly of September 2005, Submitted to the Secretary General." August 5, 2005.

————. *The Role of the United Nations Peacekeeping in Disarmament, Demobilization, and Reintegration.* Report of the Secretary General, UN Doc. S/2000/101, February 11, 2000.

————. *Seventh Progress Report of the Secretary-General on the United Nations Mission in Liberia.* UN Doc. S/2005/391, June 16, 2005.

————. "Strengthening Governance and Public Administration Capacities for Development." ECOSOC Committee of Experts on Public Administration, New York, April 14–18, 2008.

————. "What Is DDR?" New York: UN Disarmament, Demobilization, and Reintegration Resource Centre, 2009.

United Nations Department of Peacekeeping Operations (DPKO). *Disarmament, Demobilization, and Reintegration of Ex-Combatants in a Peacekeeping Environment: Principles and Guidelines.* New York: DPKO Lessons Learned Unit, 1999.

United Nations Development Programme (UNDP). *Governance for Sustainable Human Development.* New York, 1997.

———. *Human Development Report 1994.* New York, 1994.

———. *Niger Delta Human Development Report.* Abuja, 2006.

———. "Practice Note: Disarmament, Demobilisation, and Reintegration of Ex-Combatants." New York, 2005.

United Nations Institute for Disarmament Research (UNIDIR). *Applying Participatory Monitoring and Evaluation (PM&E) Approaches to Weapons Collection and Weapons for Development Programmes.* Geneva, 2002.

United Nations Office of the Special Adviser on Africa. *Overview: DDR Processes in Africa,* June 14, 2007. http://www.un.org/africa/osaa/speeches/overview.pdf.

United Nations Peacebuilding Fund. "Key Figures as of 28 February 2010." http://www.unpbf.org/index.shtml.

———. "The Peacebuilding Fund Brochure." 2009, http://www.unpbf.org/docs/PBF_Brochure.pdf.

United Nations Peacebuilding Support Office. "Chair's Summary on Peacebuilding Commission Working Group on Lessons Learned: Lessons Learnt on Sustainable Reintegration in Postconflict Situations." April 2, 2009.

United Nations Security Council. *Final Report of the Group of Experts on the Democratic Republic of the Congo Re-established Pursuant to Resolution 1857.* 2009.

United States. National Security Presidential Directive/ NSPD-44, on the Management of Interagency Efforts Concerning Reconstruction and Stabilization. Washington, December 7, 2005.

———. Reconstruction and Stabilization Civilian Management Act, Title XVI of the Duncan Hunter National Defense Authorization Act for Fiscal Year 2009, S. 3001, P.L. 110–417, signed into law October 14, 2008.

———. State Department Quadrennial Diplomacy and Development Review. "Leading through Power: The First Quadrennial Diplomacy and Development Review." US Department of State and USAID, 2010.

University Teachers for Human Rights-Jaffna (UTHR-J). *Let Them Speak: Truth about Sri Lanka's Victims of War.* Special Report no. 34. Jaffna: UTHR-J, December 13, 2009.

Urquhart, Brian. *Hammarskjold.* New York: Knopf, 1972.

Uvin, Peter. *Aiding Violence: The Development Enterprise in Rwanda.* West Hartford, CT: Kumarian, 1998.

van der Spuys, Elrena. "The Changing Fortunes of Police Accountability: Observations from South Africa." Cape Town: University of Cape Town, Institute of Criminology, 2008.

Van Houten, Pieter. "The World Bank's (Post-)Conflict Agenda: The Challenge of Integrating Development and Security." *Cambridge Review of International Affairs* 20, no. 4 (2007): 639–57.

Vieira de Mello, Sergio. "How Not to Run a Country: Lessons for the UN from Kosovo and East Timor." Unpublished review of his experience as Special Representative of the Secretary-General (SRSG) in Kosovo and East Timor.

Vines, Alex. "Disarmament in Mozambique." *Journal of Southern African Studies* 24, no. 1 (1998): 191–205.

Vircoulon, Thierry. *Réformer le "peace making" en République Démocratique du Congo.* Note de l'Ifri, Programme Afrique Sub-Saharienne, February 2009.

Vircoulon, Thierry, and Florence Liégeois. *Violences en brousse: Le "peacebuilding" international face aux conflits fonciers.* Note de l'Ifri, Programme Afrique Saharienne, February 2010.

Vlassenroot, Koen, and Timothy Raeymaekers. "Kivu's Intractable Security Conundrum." *African Affairs* 108, no. 432 (2009): 475–84.

———. "The Politics of Rebellion and Intervention in Ituri: The Emergence of a New Political Complex?" *African Affairs* 103, no. 412 (2004): 385–412.

Von Gienanth, Tobias, et al. "Elections in Post-Conflict Countries: Lessons Learned from Liberia, Sierra Leone, DRC, and Kosovo." Seminar Report. Accra, June 12–14, 2008.

Wallensteen, Peter. *Understanding Conflict Resolution: War, Peace, and the Global System.* 2nd ed. London: Sage, 2007.

Walter, Barbara F. *Committing to Peace: The Successful Settlement of Civil Wars.* Princeton: Princeton University Press, 2001.

Watts, Michael. "Petro-Insurgency or Criminal Syndicate? Conflict and Violence in the Niger Delta." *Review of Africa Political Economy* 34, no. 114 (2007): 637–60.

Wierda, Marieke, and Michael Otim. "Justice at Juba: International Obligations and Local Demands in Northern Uganda." In *Courting Conflict? Justice, Peace, and the ICC in Africa,* edited by Nicholas Waddell and Phil Clark, 21–28. London: Royal African Society, 2008.

Willame, Jean-Claude. "De l'ONUC à la MONUC: La communauté internationale au chevet du Congo," In *Congo 1960: Echec d'une decolonisation,* edited by Colette Braeckman et al., 145–56. Brussels: GRIP, 2010.

Willett, Susan. "Demilitarisation, Disarmament, and Development in Southern Africa." *Review of the African Political Economy* 25, no. 77 (1998): 409–30.

———. "Introduction: Security Council Resolution 1325: Assessing the Impact on Women, Peace, and Security." *International Peacekeeping* 17, no. 2 (2010): 142–58.

Willibald, Sigrid. "Does Money Work? Cash Transfers to Ex-Combatants in Disarmament, Demobilisation, and Reintegration Processes." *Disasters* 30, no. 3 (2006): 316–39.

Women Peace and Security Network (WIPSEN) and UNDP. "Gender Assessment of Security Sector Institutions in West Africa: The Case of Côte d'Ivoire." Unpublished report, 2010.

Woodward, Susan. "Economic Priorities for Successful Peace Implementation," In *Ending Civil Wars: The Implementation of Peace Agreement,* edited by Stephen J. Stedman, Donald Rothchild, and Elizabeth M. Cousens, 183–214. Boulder: Rienner, 2002.

World Bank. *Breaking the Conflict Trap: Civil War and Development Policy.* New York: Oxford University Press, 2003.

———. "Country Policy and Institutional Assessments: 2008 Assessment Questionnaire." Washington, DC: Operations Policy and Country Services, September 5, 2008.

———. *Establishment of a State and Peacebuilding Fund.* Washington, DC: Operations Policy and Country Services, 2008.

———. *A Framework for World Bank Involvement in Post-Conflict Reconstruction.* Washington, DC, April 25, 1997.

———. *Governance: The World Bank's Experience.* Washington, DC, 1994.

———. *Greater Great Lakes Regional Strategy for Demobilisation and Reintegration.* Washington, DC, 2002.

———. *Post-Conflict Reconstruction: The Role of the World Bank.* Washington, DC, 1998.

———. *The Role of the World Bank in Conflict and Development: An Evolving Agenda.* Washington: World Bank Conflict Prevention and Reconstruction Unit, 2004.

World Bank, State and Peacebuilding Fund. *Progress Report.* Washington, DC, 2009.

World Federalist Movement—Institute for Global Policy, "Press Briefing by the PBC Organisational Committee Chair, Ambassador Peter Wittig and the Peacebuilding Support Office Deputy Head, Mr. Eloho Otobo." April 13, 2010.

Yannis, Alexandros. "Kosovo: The Political Economy of Conflict and Peacebuilding." In *The Political Economy of Armed Conflict: Beyond Greed and Grievance*, edited by Karen Ballentine and Jake Sherman, 167–96. Boulder: Rienner 2003.

Zartman, I. William. *Negotiation and Conflict Management*. London: Routledge, 2008.

Zaum, Dominik. "The Norms and Politics of Exit: Ending Postconflict Transitional Administrations." *Ethics and International Affairs* 23, no. 2 (2009): 189–208.

———. *The Sovereignty Paradox: the Norms and Politics of International Statebuilding*. Oxford: Oxford University Press, 2007.

Contributors

CHRISTOPHER CLAPHAM is an associate of the Centre of African Studies at the University of Cambridge and editor of the *Journal of Modern African Studies*. His books include *Africa and the International System: The Politics of State Survival* (1996) and *African Guerillas* (1998).

DEVON CURTIS is a lecturer in the Department of Politics and International Studies at the University of Cambridge, and a fellow of Emmanuel College. Her main research interests and publications deal with power-sharing and governance arrangements following conflict, African rebel movements, and critical perspectives on conflict, peace, and development. She is currently writing a book about peacebuilding in Burundi.

GWINYAYI A. DZINESA was a senior researcher at the Centre for Conflict Resolution in Cape Town, South Africa. Previously, he was a lecturer in the Department of International Relations at the University of the Witwatersrand, a visiting scholar at the International Peace Research Institute, Oslo, and a research and publications officer at the Centre for Defence Studies at the University of Zimbabwe. He has coedited *Region-Building in Southern Africa: Progress, Problems and Prospects* (2012), and has published widely on peace, security, and development issues in Africa.

COMFORT ERO is the Africa program director at the International Crisis Group. Prior to ICG, she was deputy director of the Africa program at the International Center for Transitional Justice and the political affairs officer and policy adviser to the special representative of the secretary-general at the United Nations Mission in Liberia. She holds a PhD in international relations from the London School of Economics.

GRAHAM HARRISON is a professor of politics at the University of Sheffield, and an editor of *Review of African Political Economy* and *New Political Economy*. He has published four books on aspects of African politics, including *Neoliberal Africa: The Impact of Global Social Engineering* (2010) and *The World Bank and Africa: The Construction of Governance States* (2004).

EBOE HUTCHFUL is a professor of Africana studies at Wayne State University, Michigan, and chair of the African Security Sector Network, a network spanning African think tanks, civil society organizations, security practitioners, and parliamentarians active in security sector governance and transformation. He also heads African Security Dialogue and Research, a nongovernmental organization based in Accra, Ghana. He is the author of *Ghana's Adjustment Experience: The Paradox of Reform* (2002); coauthor of *Military and Militarism in Africa* (1998); and coeditor of *Budgeting for the Military Sector in Africa: The Processes and Mechanisms of Control* (2006).

EKA IKPE is a research associate with the Conflict Security and Development Group, King's College London, University of London. She holds a PhD in economics from the School of Oriental and African Studies, University of London. She has researched and published on a range of issues in the fields of development economics and security and development. Most recently she is coeditor of *Women, Peace and Security: Translating Policy into Practice* (2011).

DAVID KEEN is a professor of conflict studies at the London School of Economics. His recent books include *The Benefits of Famine: A Political Economy of Famine and Relief in Southwest Sudan 1983–9* (2008), *Complex Emergencies* (2007), *Endless War? Hidden Functions of the "War on Terror"* (2006), and *Conflict and Collusion in Sierra Leone* (2005).

GILBERT M. KHADIAGALA is the Jan Smuts Professor of International Relations and head of the department at the University of Witwatersrand, Johannesburg, South Africa. He is the author of *Meddlers or Mediators? African Interveners in Civil Conflicts in Eastern Africa* (2007), coauthor of *Sudan: The Elusive Quest for Peace* (2007), editor of *Security Dynamics in Africa's Great Lakes Region* (2006), and coeditor of *Conflict Management and African Politics: Ripeness, Bargaining, and Mediation* (2008).

CHRIS LANDSBERG is a professor of politics and head of the department at the University of Johannesburg. He is the author of *The Diplomacy of Transformation: South Africa Foreign Policy and Statecraft* (2010) and *The Quiet Diplomacy of Liberation: International Politics and South Africa's Transition* (2004); he is coeditor of *South Africa in Africa: The Post-Apartheid Era* (2007), *Government and Politics in the New South Africa* (2006), and *From Cape to Congo: Southern Africa's Evolving Security Challenges* (2003).

RENÉ LEMARCHAND is a professor emeritus of political science at the University of Florida. He has written extensively on the Great Lakes region, including *The Dynamics of Violence in Central Africa* (2009). His latest book is an edited volume, *Forgotten Genocides: Oblivion, Denial, and Memory* (2011), which, in addition to chapters on Namibia, Burundi, and eastern Democratic Republic of the Congo includes discussions of mass killings and genocide in Europe, Asia, and the Middle East. He served as regional adviser on governance and democracy with USAID in Abidjan (1992–96) and Accra (1996–98).

SARAH NOUWEN is a lecturer in law at the University of Cambridge and a fellow of the Lauterpacht Centre for International Law and Pembroke College, where she teaches and researches international law and transitional justice. She holds a PhD (Cantab) and LLM (Utrecht) in international law and an MPhil in international relations (Cantab). She was a visiting professional at the International Criminal Court and worked as a consultant for foreign ministries, Ugandan and Senegalese NGOs, and the African Union High Level Implementation Panel for Sudan.

'FUNMI OLONISAKIN is the director of the Conflict, Security and Development Group at the International Policy Institute, King's College, London. She previously worked in the United Nations Office of the Special Representative of the Secretary-General for Children and Armed Conflict. She has held teaching and research positions at the University of Lagos, Nigeria, and at the Institute of Strategic Studies and the University of Pretoria in South Africa. Most recently, she is author of *Peacekeeping in Sierra Leone: The Story of UNAMSIL* (2007) and coeditor of *Women, Peace and Security: Translating Policy into Practice* (2011).

PAUL OMACH is a senior lecturer in the Department of Political Science and Public Administration at Makerere University. His research interests include conflict, security, the state, and international relations in Africa. His most recent publications include *Politics, Conflict and Peacebuilding in Uganda: The Domestic–International Nexus* (2010) and "Political Violence in Uganda: the Role of Vigilantes and Militias" (*Journal of Social, Political and Economic Studies* 35, no. 4 [2010]).

ADEROJU OYEFUSI is a senior lecturer at the University of Benin, Nigeria. He was a visiting research fellow at the Centre of African Studies, University of Cambridge in 2008–9. He has published widely on civil unrest, youth, conflict prevention, natural resources, and wealth-sharing in the Niger Delta, including "Trust and the Breakdown of Civil Order in Nigeria's Delta Region: Evidence from Historical Conflict Episodes" (*The Round Table* 98, no. 403 [2009]).

SHARATH SRINIVASAN is the director of the Centre of Governance and Human Rights at the University of Cambridge, where he is also David and Elaine Potter Foundation lecturer in governance and human rights in the Department of Politics and International Studies, and a fellow of King's College. He has researched on Sudan for the past six years, where he also previously worked.

DOMINIK ZAUM is a reader in international relations at the University of Reading, and a senior research fellow at the Department for International Development (DFID). His most recent publications include *Corruption and Post-Conflict Peacebuilding: Selling the Peace* (2011), with Christine Cheng; and *The United Nations Security Council and War: The Evolution of Thought and Practice since 1945* (2008), with Vaughan Lowe, Adam Roberts, and Jennifer Welsh.

Index

www.ingramcontent.com/pod-product-compliance
Lightning Source LLC
Chambersburg PA
CBHW021846020426

42334CB00013B/213